MW01529331

MISSION CRITICAL
SMALLER DEMOCRACIES' ROLE IN GLOBAL STABILITY OPERATIONS

EDITED BY
CHRISTIAN LEUPRECHT, JODOK TROY, DAVID LAST

CENTRE POUR LE
MAINTIEN DE LA PAIX
PEARSON
1994 **15** 2009 PEACEKEEPING CENTRE

QCIR
QUEEN'S CENTRE FOR INTERNATIONAL RELATIONS

McGill-Queen's University Press
Montreal & Kingston • London • Ithaca

SCHOOL OF
Policy Studies
Queen's
UNIVERSITY

Publications Unit
Robert Sutherland Hall
138 Union Street
Kingston, ON, Canada
K7L 3N6
www.queensu.ca/sps/

The preferred citation for this book is:
Leuprecht, C., J. Troy, and D. Last, eds. 2010. *Mission Critical: Smaller Democracies' Role in Global Stability Operations.* Montreal and Kingston: Queen's Policy Studies Series, McGill-Queen's University Press.

Library and Archives Canada Cataloguing in Publication

Mission critical : smaller democracies' role in global stability operations / edited by Christian Leuprecht, Jodok Troy, David Last.

Co-published by the Pearson Peacekeeping Centre, the Swedish National Defence College and the Queen's Centre for International Relations.
Includes bibliographical references.
ISBN 978-1-55339-244-6 (pbk.)

1. Peacekeeping forces. 2. Armed Forces—Operations other than war. 3. Nation-building. 4. Security, International. 5. States, Small. I. Leuprecht, Christian, 1973- II. Troy, Jodok III. Last, David M IV. Queen's University (Kingston, Ont.). Centre for International Relations V. Försvarshögskolan Sweden) VI. Pearson Peacekeeping Centre

JZ6374.M58 2010   355.4
C2010-903390-6

CONTENTS

ACKNOWLEDGEMENTS

This book is the result of emerging and growing research collaboration in the social sciences among the service academies and military universities of smaller democracies on the one hand, and researchers who have given thought to the tasks these countries and their armed forces might take on, on the other hand. In part, the book is born out of frustration that so much of the research agenda on international security takes its cue from the United States. At the same time, it acknowledges the importance of the American perspective. But there is also a sense that the body of knowledge on global stability operations stands to benefit from greater pluralism, findings that many US observers will be quick to affirm. This, however, is easier said than done. While many smaller democracies have rather limited military and financial resources to bring to bear, they have even less research capacity. While some have long-standing traditions of research as well as higher education for their officer corps, others are venturing into virgin territory. The paucity of resources can also be a cause of parochialism among academies who, until quite recently, may have had a rather narrow domestic focus and scholars whose primary objective was as instructors and whose limited institutional resources made it difficult to connect with counterparts abroad.

This book is part of a larger project to bolster the research capacity both on and within smaller democracies on matters of international security, especially in the empirical, but also in the normative, realm. It brings together some well-established scholars in the field with emerging ones and others who have thus far not had much opportunity to have had their work showcased beyond the borders of their home country. Ergo, the book seeks to disseminate and transfer knowledge on global security from sources, on topics, and using approaches that are both new and innovative.

The book started as a collaborative project among Swedish, Canadian, and Austrian scholars in an effort initiated by Professor Franz Kernic, Institute for Leadership and Management at the Swedish National

Defence Academy (SNDC). Since Swedes and Canadians have quite similar interests, values, and objectives, reaching out to its Canadian equivalent, the Royal Military College of Canada, seemed like an obvious way to bolster the long-standing Swedish-Canadian partnership in the area of global stability. The initial foray came in the form of a Swedish invitation to a workshop held in Stockholm in June 2009 that brought together Swedish and Canadian researchers. The workshop's costs were also underwritten by the Austrian Institute for European and Security Policy. A follow-up workshop was held jointly by the Royal Military College of Canada and the Queen's Centre for International Relations in Kingston, Ontario, Canada in October 2009. The chapters in this book largely consist of revised versions of papers originally presented at these two workshops. To complement the book, the editors also reached out to some scholars conducting timely work in the field.

Aside from Swedish and Canadian contributors, the volume is rounded out with work by Austrian, Dutch, German and Brazilian authors. The result is a multidisciplinary book whose contributors come from political science, sociology, anthropology, and the pedagogical sciences. Several contributions by senior scholars notwithstanding, over half of the volume showcases the work of younger scholars. Of particular significance is the balance of gender, with half the authors being women. Since fields of global stability, military sociology, and civil-military relations tend to be overwhelmingly dominated by male researchers, a volume that is fairly gender-balanced is no small feat. Moreover, almost half the authors live and work outside the country of their birth. The book, then, really amounts to an international effort that tries to break out of the common mould that habitually defines collections on global stability operations.

Still, the final product would not have been possible without the help of several key institutional and individual players. Financially, the book would not have been viable without subventions from the Swedish National Defence College and the Pearson Peacekeeping Centre (PPC). Aside from Dr. Franz Kernic at the Swedish National Defence College, special thanks goes to BGen (ret'd) Bo Wranker, administrative head at the Institute for Leadership and Management for his support. At the PPC, we are especially grateful to Dr. Ann Livingstone, vice president, research and education, for her vision and long-standing support of research concerning global stability operations and to Kathryn Robicheau who looked after administrative matters for the PPC.

Once again the Queen's Centre for International Relations, a Centre of Excellence funded by the Canadian Department of National Defence's Security and Defence Forum, provided unparalleled support in bringing this project to fruition. At the QCIR, Maureen Bartram once again handled this project and related administrative and financial concerns with utmost competency and efficiency. Mark Howes designed the cover, Valerie Jarus handled the layout, and Anne Holley-Hime copy-edited the chapters with proficiency in record time. Finally, Inge van Osch made available the photograph which graces this book's cover. She took it on the grounds of the Dutch embassy in Kinshasa, capital of the Democratic Republic of Congo, while conducting fieldwork for the chapter that she co-authored for this volume.

Flowers growing along a razor wire offer an apt metaphor for this book: Smaller democracies bridge divides by means of a special ability to infuse with colour and life a global-security backdrop whose canvas is marred by tall fences. In their contributions to global stability operations, smaller democracies are the wallflowers of international security. The sweet-smelling perennial flowers of *Cheiranthus cheiri* came to be called wallflowers because they are hardy in that they often grow along walls, rocks, and quarries. But a wallflower also describes a person who stands at the sidelines of a social activity because of shyness or unpopularity. Although easily overlooked, wallflowers, like smaller democracies, provide an indispensable complement to an otherwise inhospitable landscape.

Christian Leuprecht   Jodok Troy   David Last
New Haven, May 2010   Vienna, May 2010   Kingston, May 2010

TAKING ALLIES SERIOUSLY: MODEST RESPONSES BY MODEST COUNTRIES?

Jodok Troy and Christian Leuprecht

When John Hillen (1997) wrote: "Superpowers Don't Do Windows," he was advocating more than describing; regular American army officers wanted to "fight and win the nation's wars decisively," not get mired in protracted and messy policing operations. The matter of how countries *are* contributing to global stability operations is one thing, how they *ought* to contribute quite another. Distinguishing between facts and values is important: How countries *ought* to contribute to global stability does not follow from what they *are* contributing. So, there are two separate questions here: What are different countries contributing to global stability; and what should they be contributing?

Smaller democracies face a conundrum. They are not tempted to embark on expeditionary operations by themselves, and they seldom have a direct interest in the missions to which they contribute, but they do share a common interest in global stability. They benefit disproportionately from safe international trade routes and a stable international system with predictable rules. Since they are small, they are also disproportionately vulnerable to disruptions of both. They also have an interest in forestalling certain externalities associated with disrupted trade routes and political instability abroad, such as economic and conflict refugees. Their contribution can be a quid pro quo for the protection they enjoy under Pax Americana's security umbrella, with the costs of maintaining armed forces and contributing to global stability still far lower than they

Mission Critical: Smaller Democracies' Role in Global Stability Operations, ed. C. Leuprecht, J. Troy, and D. Last. Montreal and Kingston: Queen's Policy Studies Series, McGill-Queen's University Press. © 2010 Queen's Centre for International Relations, Queen's University at Kingston. All rights reserved.

would have to incur if they did not enjoy the dividend that flows from American protection. Since they are maintaining armed forces anyway, they are motivated to justify their utility by sending them on expeditionary missions—a justification supported by the military profession. Not only do armed forces understand this logic, they much prefer the "away game" over the apparently mundane routine of the "home game" with the attendant risk of sliding down to the status of heavily armed gendarmes. In expeditionary operations, senior officers gain valuable experience by taking on leadership roles not available at home.

Motivations to contribute to global stability missions vary, but are often indirect rather than direct. Neack (1995) makes the case for enlightened self-interest. Political or financial credit with a major power may be important for small players (e.g., Sokolsky 2004). Participation may confer legitimacy: poorer states, with lower state legitimacy but also less political repression, contribute more frequently to African regional peacekeeping (Victor 2010). The top 10 contributors to UN missions— Pakistan, Bangladesh, India, Nigeria, Ghana, Nepal, Jordan, Uruguay, Ethiopia and Kenya—as well as numerous others from Fiji to Morocco, have hard currency as their primary motivation (Monnakgotla 1996). Other countries, such as Mongolia, are in it for a different sort of "whole of government" operation: defence abroad in a conflict zone, development at home, and diplomacy in allied capitals (Mendee and Last 2008). Mongolia is in Sierra Leone and Iraq for political credit with the US, and financial credit that helps pay for an army in a poor country (i.e., 115/182 on the UN development index with a GDP per capita of US$2,700). For poor countries, development activities abroad are not a priority, and Mongolia's diplomatic targets are in Washington, New York and Brussels.

Still, the away game can be a difficult sell, as the electorates of contributing democracies oscillate between ambivalence and opposition. Democratic politics is premised on politicians having to repeat job interviews at regular intervals, euphemistically known as elections, so they find themselves torn: there are some rewards for good global citizenship on the one hand, but, on the other hand, expeditionary missions yield little domestic payoff. There are two reasons for this.

First, democratic electorates have an aversion to seeing their soldiers return in body bags. Dying for your country when its territorial integrity is threatened is one thing, dying for "global stability" quite another. Judging by arms advertisements—and we assume the industry knows what it is doing—casualty aversion in western democracies has increased since the end of the Cold War (Schörnig and Lembcke 2006).

Second, expeditionary missions are expensive. In addition to the costs associated with the actual mission, countries usually make long-term commitments of development aid, and they have to keep up and equip standing forces to stand at the ready for international deployment. This is not a new observation. When asked what it takes to win a war, Philip II of Spain's aide-de-camp is famously said to have replied: "Three things: Money, money, and more money." However, the last two decades have seen a considerable shift with respect to transparency. In the past, we knew these missions were expensive but actual costs were pretty opaque. As democracies have become more fiscally transparent, so has the cost of their contribution to global stability. With democratic governments curtailing expenditures, benefits and services, and raising taxes to rein in their over-stretched coffers, expenses associated with global stability are subject to growing popular scrutiny. In democracies, the three biggest budget items tend to be national defence, health care, and education. As national debts escalate, choosing among the three increasingly becomes a zero-sum game. In public opinion surveys across smaller democracies, respondents consistently prioritize health care and education over defence, a phenomenon Samuel Huntington (1957) excoriated as "antimilitaristic liberalism." When health care costs grow by 6 percent annually but economic growth is flat, the balance has to come from somewhere. And given the sheer size of defence departments and budgets, it is virtually impossible to control public spending without affecting defence expenditures.

The costs of expeditionary stability operations result in a paradox: The costs of not participating outweigh the benefits of participating, while the costs of a full-fledged commitment outweigh the benefits of a more limited engagement. Ergo, the sub-optimal outcomes of global stability operations should come as no surprise; small states will generally make small commitments. Urlacher (2008) has developed a general theory for major contributions to UN peacekeeping, reflecting incentives and capacity. Poor states (most of the top ten contributors to UN peacekeeping) have largely economic incentives, but wealthy states (small democracies) are less likely to make major contributions unless they have colonial ties (ibid.). These sub-optimal outcomes are likely exacerbated by endogenous effects (group norms): The average behaviour among the group further influences the behaviour of others in that group. There are few incentives to lever, if any, that might change the behaviour of states in regard to global stability operations.

The Cold War paradigm for peacekeeping called for contributions from competent, impartial middle powers that were not embroiled in colonial or superpower machinations (cf. von Horn 1966). Each of the countries represented in the collection can be described in this way. Still, there has been a significant change since the end of the Cold War. Before 1989, the overarching international-security objective was to avoid Armageddon, but small democracies contributed behind the skirts of the superpowers: Peacekeeping amounted to "cold war by other means" (Maloney 2003). The "War on Terror" aside, the hope behind global stability missions since 1989 is that small democracies' collective indirect interest will add up to more than piecemeal gains of a little diplomatic credit here and a little financial credit there. That is unlikely to materialize unless participating countries put the pieces together more effectively. This volume is, therefore, not just about describing global stability missions as they are, but also as they might be. They might be the beginning of the "system maintenance force" (Barnett 2004), but manifest not in the US Marine Corps as described by Barnett (in what amounts to a quasi-imperial police force, cf. Lyons 1999; Anderson and Killingray 1991; Marenin 1982), but an international middle class of states goaded by self-interested altruism. This is how community policing began in the English-speaking world: the middle class funded police forces that kept the cities safe for property and business (Taylor 1998; Uchida 2010). Stability operations by (relatively) impartial middle-powers can still evolve as international community policing, coexisting with the heavier-handed imperial policing of coalition and unilateral missions by major powers or big neighbours, just as the Royal Irish Constabulary and Metropolitan police models coexisted in the early 20th century (Hawkins 1991).

In the larger scheme of things though, there is reason for optimism: Results are actually better than one might expect. Historically, there has probably never been a longer period of sustained relative international peace and, as a result, affluence. The generations of democratic citizens born after the end of World War II are among the first in modern history to have been spared major international war but, consequently, do not share the pacifism that memories of war tend to induce. While the drivers of this significant aberration along the international-security timeline need not detain us here, never have smaller democracies had as big a stake in maintaining global stability and, arguably, never have they committed more troops and funds to more far-flung places to further this end. Ostensibly, then, both the proximate and distal role smaller democracies play in global stability operations is not to be underestimated.

Yet, their role has also been poorly understood, in part because this phenomenon has received comparatively little scholarly attention (when contrasted with research on actual peacekeeping missions or the US role in global stability, for instance). Smaller democracies "do windows" in many cases, as Hillen (1997) intimates, they may actually be much more proficient at it than their allied superpower(s). A curious egalitarianism pervades the international system whereby it is implicitly assumed that most countries perform most tasks equally well—or, at the very least, superpower(s) necessarily do everything better than anyone else because they can harness economies of scale. Measured in terms of outcomes, however, it turns out that this claim does not actually obtain. Smaller democracies have a comparative, perhaps absolute, advantage over their larger allies in stabilization efforts (Last 2001). The purpose of this book is to explore what they are good at, why they are good at it, and the implications that follow for the purpose of optimizing global stability operations. To this end, the book is divided into four thematic parts: the challenges of collaboration in the changing global security environment; coordinating disarmament, development and reconstruction at the international margins; necessary and sufficient competencies for collaboration; and a final section that combines positive and normative insights into the provision of security as a common good.

In Part I, three chapters address the changing environment of global missions. Christian Leuprecht's (*Royal Military College of Canada*) structural approach details the challenge of looming demographic and fiscal changes: More "heavy lifting" will be needed to safeguard global stability while fewer countries will be able to do such heavy lifting. Soft power, closer collaboration among allies, and the need to solicit help from new participants thus become indispensable to meet demand: "Opportunities and challenges for national and international security in an aging world are substantial" and "proactive policies that are designed both to take full advantage of the opportunities created by global aging while mitigating the costs created by this phenomenon will enhance international security through the twenty-first century." In the pursuit of global stability, there are different ways of doing business.

Sarah Meharg and Kristine St-Pierre (*Pearson Peacekeeping Centre*) provide a conceptual survey of modus operandi of peace operations and crisis management and offer an overview of specific approaches that have emerged to manage complexity and make interventions more effective. Only "by understanding the nature of the security environment and how this environment shapes and influences operations" can we manage the complexity of peace operations effectively.

Drawing on qualitative evidence gathered in the field in the Democratic Republic of Congo, Ingrid van Osch and Joseph Soeters (*Royal Dutch Military College*) use the United Nations Organization Mission DR Congo (MONUC) to show unequivocally just how difficult global stability work really is. Analyzing the mission using a pragmatist approach, they offer critical insights into shortcomings in legitimacy and reputation that pervade global stability operations. Ultimately, what matters is that the "host nationals desire to see the efforts of MONUC, not only symbolically, but effectively." The authors also point out the "importance of reflection and controlled experimentation in a constantly changing environment and that lessons learned need to be stored in the institutional memory of the mission." The significance of these observations lies in the fact that, rather than philosophizing, the authors draw on evidence to arrive at these conclusions inductively.

Part II deals with (re)building communities of states to facilitate the participation of smaller democracies in global stability operations. The development of the European Union's Common Foreign, Security and Defence Policy (CFSP and ESDP) illustrates that there are places where states have come to expect peace, where they are working to foster such expectations, and where peace is hoped for rather than expected. Franco

Algieri and Arnold Kammel (*Austrian Institute for European and Security Policy*) examine the institutional and political framework of civilian and military operations and missions in the context of the European Union (EU) and assess how well the emerging division of labour works using Austria's participation in global stability operations as a critical case study. "Differentiation," the authors find, "might become the tool for avoiding a marginalized role of the EU in comparison to the major powers of the 21st century." For relatively small states such as Austria, participation in global stability operations is of disproportionate significance precisely because "Austria's security is indivisibly bound up with the security of the European Union." In practical terms, Austria's security policy today "continues along the lines of pragmatic neutrality by participating in EU Petersberg and NATO [partnership for peace] tasks." Therefore, although they may transcend small democracies' immediate range of geopolitical interests, countries such as Austria "will continue to take an active part in crisis management operations and missions of the European Union, be they of a civilian, military or civil-military nature."

Kai Michael Kenkel (*Catholic University of Rio de Janeiro*) shows how Brazil is emerging as an integral partner in global stability, demonstrating the comparative advantage that a rising democracy and economic power can bring to global stability operations. Southern hemispheric states, such as Brazil, are among global stability's most important troop and police contributors. The emergence of Brazil as a global power broker, however, challenges long-held orthodoxies: "The gap between the normative foundations for such missions—a modern conception of sovereignty and a concern for human rights—and more traditional motivations, such as international influence and military prestige, must be addressed." Brazil's peacebuilding approaches can serve as a new model and as a "source of fruitful insights for the established northern peacekeeping powers. Openness to the responses developed by states such as Brazil to the difficulties of new missions is an important key to meeting the challenges these interventions will bring in the future."

David Last (*Royal Military College of Canada*) argues that professional research and education can help to form transnational global stability professionals not just from the armed forces but also from the rest of government, from NGOs and from the private sector. Contrary to Huntington's functional description of armed forces, the fundamental purpose of most of today's defence forces is "not to defeat military enemies, but to combine the political, economic, and social policies of diverse small states, each with modest expeditionary forces, in order to support stabilization and development." Research and education are the means by which the necessary synergies are achieved. Drawing on examples from medicine, social policy, and military technical cooperation, the author illustrates alternative models of governing scientific and technical cooperation amongst independent contributors. Last finds "that defence universities in small countries may be well placed to build research and education networks that will improve transnational cooperation in operations if they behave more like universities."

Part III of the book examines in greater detail two competencies that emerge as critical to mission success: leadership and private military contractors. How do we train effective leaders and what ought to be the nature of that training? Given the differentiation of leadership tasks, the key insight of Bo Talerud (*Swedish National Defence Academy*) is that different sorts of leadership might be required—leadership that is sensitive both to collaboration and to learning. The shoemaker knows how to make a shoe, but he does not know where it pinches; so, learning collaboratively and fostering collaborative learning are important leadership roles. Leadership, especially transformational leadership, is ubiquitous in military research and practice; but less work has been done on followers, workers and the way they react to different types of leadership. If the military leaders are fostered in a leader-oriented authoritarian culture, then is it really all that surprising when they have trouble cooperating with different players, such as civil and foreign organizations? Mission success demands a more collaborative leader, with the ability to transfer knowledge, exchange ideas, and effect changes in behaviour.

The sort of leader Talerud describes is important in work with the growing number of private security and military companies (PSMCs). Gerhard Kümmel (*Bundeswehr Institute of Social Sciences, Germany*) prods us to rethink the basic idea behind privatization. Rather than assuming that PSMCs are a natural and inevitable component of global stability operations, scholars following the tradition of Morris Janowitz (1960) raise concerns about the civilianization of missions. It turns out, for instance, that PSMCs, while quite effective at some levels, are more costly for core functions. The evidence suggests that now, more than ever, public must be weighed carefully against private interests, and economic motivations ought not trump policy objectives outright. More than ever, future research on PSMCs needs to build a stronger evidence base: "Access contractors and access soldiers through qualitative or quantitative research; look at the diversity of contractors and at the diversity within the military to determine where and why military-contractor relations and cooperation are easier to achieve; and identify best practices with regard to contract oversight."

Finally, Part IV of the volume explores how to operationalize the collaboration, competencies, and cooperation of the earlier chapters in a way that shares the burden among great, middle, and small powers while optimizing outcomes. Ironically, while trust is one of the means to this end, trust is inherently more problematic in hostile areas than in stable ones. How, then, can we tell whether trust is fragile or robust? What sorts of governance structures foster or undermine trust? Megan Thompson and Ritu Gill (*Defence Research and Development Canada, Toronto*) review key results from the trust literature to identify the formal and organizational reinforcement that is required to build robust trust among countries, allies, and locals. They observe that the increased complexity of today's peace operations "is reflected in the focus on whole of government (WoG) responses that seek to integrate various government agencies within a single mission space and mandate." The authors vividly illustrate that "optimal effectiveness and efficiency is best facilitated by relationships that are based upon the notion of trust."

Donna Winslow (*US Army Logistics University*) examines one of the thornier subjects in these new missions: the social scientists and especially the anthropologist's contribution to human terrain systems. "Do no harm to the subject being studied" is the prevailing academic mantra. But scholars do not know how the data they provide will be used. Without civilian oversight and review, the military has no way of knowing the reliability of the information that is being provided. Winslow's chapter details the shift from potentially coercive social science—or its potentially nefarious application—to a more collaborative social science that is less prone to abuse and more likely to serve the common good. Ethnographic knowledge, "is not something to be collected like sea shells and placed in a classificatory grid; it emerges in the ethnographic occasion, which is the encounter between the ethnographer and the persons with whom the ethnographer produces the knowledge." Winslow makes a strong case for civilian social scientists to continue "studying military and intelligence organizations from the inside and educating the military about its own organizational culture and about other cultures and societies so that the military can carry out its own cultural intelligence operations."

In the concluding chapter David Last (*Royal Military College of Canada*) encapsulates this shift from coercive to collaborative operations by focusing on the rule of law, its purpose, the need to be consistent, and the dangers of hypocrisy and contradiction in building rule-of-law societies abroad: The "rule of law at home and democratic oversight of security services is linked to respect for internal debates abroad, including debates about social mores and market reforms." Comparing the examples of four transnational missions under the United Nations in terms of the involvement of small powers, the author infers: "Collaborative and consensual stabilization involving many small and supportive democracies is more likely to be associated with stable outcomes." The reason, Last surmizes, is that smaller democracies are more inclined to "a strategy of community building in which state policies are sensitive to the imposition of rules on others, including secession and incorporation of territory."

Smaller democracies can make an important contribution to global stability. In the emerging security environment, they can develop new competencies, build communities at the margins, and work collaboratively with other small states. Their strategic partnership is a function of the comparative advantages they enjoy in building institutions, working at the transnational level, with international and local communities and in multinational operations. From the perspective of "modest" democracies, the challenge of global stability operations in the 21ˢᵗ century is to bring together small democratic powers to project stabilization missions globally in support of a consensus that will survive a changing world order. The objective, therefore, is to reject the technological "fantasy" of high-tech war (e.g., Singer 2009) and instead understand the challenges that new missions face in terms of their social context of violence.

REFERENCES

Anderson, D.M., and D. Killingray, eds. 1991. *Policing the Empire: Government, Authority, and Control, 1830–1940.* Manchester: Manchester University Press.

Barnett, T.P.M. 2004. *The Pentagon's New Map: War and Peace in the 21ˢᵗ Century.* New York: Putnam.

Hawkins, R. 1991. The "Irish Model" and the Empire: A Case for Reassessment. In *Policing the Empire: Government, Authority, and Control, 1830–1940,* ed. D.M. Anderson and D. Killingray, 18-32. Manchester: Manchester University Press.

Hillen, J. 1997. Superpowers Don't Do Windows. *Orbis* 41 (2):241-257.

von Horn, C. 1966. *Soldiering for Peace.* London: Cassell.

Huntington, S. 1957. *The Soldier and the State: The Theory and Politics of Civil-Military Relations.* Cambridge, MA: Harvard University Press.

Janowitz, M. 1960. *The Professional Soldier: A Social and Political Portrait.* Glencoe, IL: Free Press.

Last, D. 2001. Picking Up Peaces: Comparative Advantage in Post-Conflict Reconstruction. In *Over Here and Over There: Canada–US Defence Cooperation in an Era of Interoperability,* ed. D.G. Haglund, 145-167. Kingston: Queen's Quarterly for the Queen's Centre for International Relations.

Lyons, W. 1999. *The Politics of Community Policing: Rearranging the Power to Punish.* Ann Arbor: University of Michigan Press.

Maloney, S.M. 2003. *Canada and U.N. Peacekeeping: Cold War by other means.* St. Catharines: Vanwell Publishing.

Marenin, O. 1982. Parking Tickets and Class Repression: The Concept of Policing in Critical Theories of Criminal Justice. *Contemporary Crises* 6:241-266.

Mendee, J., and D. Last, 2008. Whole of Government Responses in Mongolia: From Domestic Response to International Implications. Pearson Papers, 11:2.

Monnakgotla, K. 1996. The Naked Face of UN Peacekeeping: Noble Crusade or National Self-Interest. *African Security Review* 5 (5):53-61.

Neack, L. 1995. UN Peace-Keeping: In the Interest of Community or Self? *Journal of Peace Research* 32 (2):181-196.

Schörnig, N., and A.C. Lembcke. 2006. The Vision of War without Casualties: On the Use of Casualty Aversion in Armament Advertisements. *Journal of Conflict Resolution* 50 (2):204-227.

Singer, P.W. 2009. *Wired for War: The Robotics Revolution and Conflict in the Twenty-First Century.* New York: Penguin Books.

Sokolsky, J.J. 2004. *The "Away Game": Canada-United States Security Relations Outside North America*, IRRP Working Papers No. 2004-091.

Taylor, D. 1998. *Crime, Policing, and Punishment: 1750–1914*. London: Palgrave Macmillan.

Uchida, C.D. 2010. The Development of American Police: An Historical Overview. In *Critical Issues in Policing: Contemporary Readings*, ed. R.G. Dunham and G.P. Alpert, chap. 2. Long Grove, IL: Waveland Press.

Urlacher, B. 2008. Contributions to UN Peacekeeping Operations: Who and Why? Paper presented at the annual meeting of the ISA's 49th Annual Convention, Bridging Multiple Divides, Hilton, San Francisco, CA, USA. At http://www.allacademic.com/meta/p252244_index.html (accessed 19 May 2010).

Victor, J. 2010. African Peacekeeping in Africa: Warlord Politics, Defense Economics, and State Legitimacy. *Journal of Peace Research* 47 (2):217-229.

PART 1: THE CHANGING ENVIRONMENT OF NEW MISSIONS

AT THE DEMOGRAPHIC CROSSROADS: INTERNATIONAL SECURITY STRATEGY FOR THE 21ST CENTURY

CHRISTIAN LEUPRECHT

Much of the recent literature that takes a strategic view of demography paints a rather dismal picture of the future: over-aging, immigration, rising dependency ratios, along with the ability to service entitlement programs and public debt, are posited as harbingers of decline. Yet this article contends that the future is not actually all that bleak. The future security environment, and the West's ability to act on it, is a matter of understanding the strategic realm for action now to maximize leverage in the future. Demographic trends provide a good indication of both the location and type of conflict for which to prepare. A scan of the demographic horizon suggests that there will be more heavy lifting to do in international security with fewer countries and resources to do the lifting. Rather than painting the devil on the wall, demographic projections reduce the uncertainty with respect to the future security environment, thus helping us grasp how best to position ourselves strategically today so as to continue to asset our interests in the future.

To be successful, Grand Strategy requires objectives, concepts, and resources to be balanced appropriately with a view to defeating one's enemy. Trouble is, of course, that generals are always well prepared to fight the last war. That is because, in the words of Yogi Berra, predictions are always difficult, especially when they involve the future. Yet, grand

Mission Critical: Smaller Democracies' Role in Global Stability Operations, ed. C. Leuprecht, J. Troy, and D. Last. Montreal and Kingston: Queen's Policy Studies Series, McGill-Queen's University Press. © 2010 Queen's Centre for International Relations, Queen's University at Kingston. All rights reserved.

strategy is all about the future. But how is one to strategize about a future that is inherently difficult to predict? One way out of this conundrum is to rely on independent variables that can be projected into the future with reasonable accuracy. Aside from environmental indicators, the most consistent of those is demography, specifically demographic change and difference. It turns out that the demographic approach leads to strategic conclusions about the integration of military, political, and economic means in pursuit of states' ultimate objectives in the international system that offer an alternative to what is currently on offer. The importance of this alternative is not to be underestimated: As this chapter shows, owing to unprecedented demographic developments, any margin of error with respect to grand strategy is quickly disappearing.

Waxing and waning neo-Malthusian "end-of-the-world-as-we-know-it" gestations notwithstanding (e.g., Ehrlich 1968), demography had long been relegated to the epiphenomenal margins of grand strategy. However, starting with Paul Kennedy's *Preparing for the Twenty-First Century* (1994), a wave of recent hawkish neo-conservative mongering about the perils of over-aging (Weigel 2005; Jackson and Howe 2008) and immigration (Huntington 2004; Ferguson 2004; Steyn 2006) culminating in the US National Intelligence Council's *Global Trends 2025* (2008), fertility, mortality, and migration have been maturing in grand strategy as independent variables in their own right. Still, much of that literature feels a lot like neo-Nebuchadnezzarian harbingers of the devil's writing on the wall. Yet, the purpose of grand strategy is not to posit demography as destiny. The future is not necessarily all that bleak. Provided that the strategic implications of demography are both understood and acted upon, we can fashion our world in accordance with demographic change instead of having demographic change fashion our world for us.

The world is at a demographic crossroads. Throughout all of history, high birth rates had ensured predominantly young populations with few older people. War and epidemics, such as the plague, would intervene to depress population growth (Anderson 1996; Livi-Bacci 2007). By contrast, depressed population growth today is a function of a historically unprecedented decline in birth rates (Easterlin and Crimmins 1985). That is, women are consistently having fewer or no children than at any previous time in history (for reasons that are beyond the scope of this chapter). Demographically, the world is entering virgin territory. On the one hand, demographic trends suggest that there will be more "heavy lifting" to do with respect to international security. On the other hand, some countries are far better positioned to weather the impending demographic storm than others. Ergo, fewer countries will end up having to do more of the heavy lifting on security, and with fewer resources.

The bad news is that demand for armed forces will grow as demographic determinants of domestic instability rise over the next 20 years. The good news is (1) that the demographic determinants of international war are on the decline and (2) that demographic projection allows us to pinpoint the likely hotspots. In other words, analysis of the demographic evidence in this chapter suggests that armed forces should prepare for international interventions rather than international war. If the dictum that the generals are always well prepared to fight the last war holds, then prevailing military strategy runs a real danger of having armed forces bet on the wrong horse. Owing to two competing trends, they will find it increasingly difficult to cope with growing demand for their services. Maintaining the armed forces' functional imperative in a tightening labour market means substituting capital for labour. Increased strain on demographic and fiscal resources means smaller but more capable, effective, and professional armed forces. But with soldiers' median age on the rise, and defence spending atrophying under competing political priorities in democratic countries with aging populations, the inclination will be to shift armed forces' dwindling fiscal resources from capital to labour. Due to nuanced demographic trends and political structures, the crowding out will be more rapid and severe in some countries than in others. The downside of this trend is that fewer countries will need to bring a greater proportion of armed and fiscal resources to bear on a less secure world. The upside, however, is that demographic trends are also opening up opportunities to look for new friends as partners in international security. These developments place a premium on soft power (cf. Nye 2004), which include being intentionally strategic about international security regimes and institutions, and international collaboration among armed forces of traditional allies and demographically emerging powers.

The first section of the chapter examines the impact of population growth and decline (of 50 percent in the developing world from 5.3 billion in 2005 to over 8 billion by 2050) as well as migration on international war and domestic demographic instability. Four substantive implications follow: First, demographic developments suggest that the high-tech fantasy of the "big war" with countries such as China and Russia that the hawks are fretting about is a strategic folly whose pursuit ties increasingly scarce demographic and financial resources to a wrong-headed vision. Second, time is on "our" side: Maturing population structures will make some "rogue states," such as Iran, North Korea, and Venezuela, more politically stable. Third, youth bulges will emerge as a growing driver of political instability in select African, Middle Eastern, and Asian countries. Fourth, demographic convergence is providing a welcome opportunity to make new friends in the pursuit of global stability, especially in the Americas. Some of these claims have been advanced elsewhere. But the analytical implications for the strategic pursuit of soft power and new friends relative to the demographic context of political instability is novel.

The second new contribution of this chapter is to analyze shifts in overall global economic activity as well as the relative position of public finances in developed countries to make the case that the relationship between population growth/decline and public finances is becoming increasingly consequential in terms of countries' capacity to bring scarce demographic and financial resources to bear on international security. Rapid population expansion in the developing world compounded by rapid gains in per capita income translates into the bulk of economic growth shifting to developing countries. As the world's global GDP (estimated using PPP-adjusted gross national income/capita in current US dollars) produced by developed countries (with the richest billion people on the planet) grows by only one-fifth between 2005 and 2050, its share is effectively cut in half, from 60 percent to about 23 percent—less than it was as late as 1820! The emerging reality is that fewer countries will be doing more but with fewer resources. The conclusion expounds these findings and draws inferences concerning strategies to mitigate their impact.

DEMOGRAPHIC CONSTRAINTS ON INTERNATIONAL ARMED CONFLICT

Rarely can analysts of politics claim to be documenting new phenomena. Population aging, however, is one of these revolutionary variables. Never before has humanity witnessed such dramatic, widespread aging among the world's most industrialized and powerful democracies. Two long-term demographic trends coincided to produce population aging: decreasing fertility rates and increasing life expectancy. Fertility rates refer to the average number of children born per woman in a given country. For a state to sustain its population (assuming zero net immigration), fertility levels must exceed about 2.1 children per woman.

Today the United States is the sole liberal democracy that comes close to meeting this requirement. Most are well below this average and have been for decades. As Figure 1 shows, the proportion of the world's population that resides in advanced industrialized democracies will continue to decline: from 24 percent in 1980, to 18 percent today, and 16 percent by 2025. This is a remarkable reversal: Between 1700 and 1900, Europe's population and its overseas offshoots had doubled its proportion of the world's total population from 20 percent to 40 percent (Maddison 2007, 378). As late as 1950, Europe, Japan, and North America together comprised roughly one-third of the world's population, compared to one-fifth today and under one-seventh by 2050. By 2030, that translates into an expected total increase of less than 40 million people by 2030 (primarily concentrated in North America as Europe's overall population starts to shrink) as opposed to 1.5 billion people in the rest of the world.

In absolute terms India's population will grow the most (by 240 million to 1.45 billion people followed by an increase of 100 million in China for a total population of 1.3 billion). Growth will also be strong throughout Africa, Latin America, and the Caribbean. Much of Eastern and Central Europe, Russia, Italy, and Japan, by contrast, will see their populations

FIGURE 1
Developed World Population as a Percentage of World Total

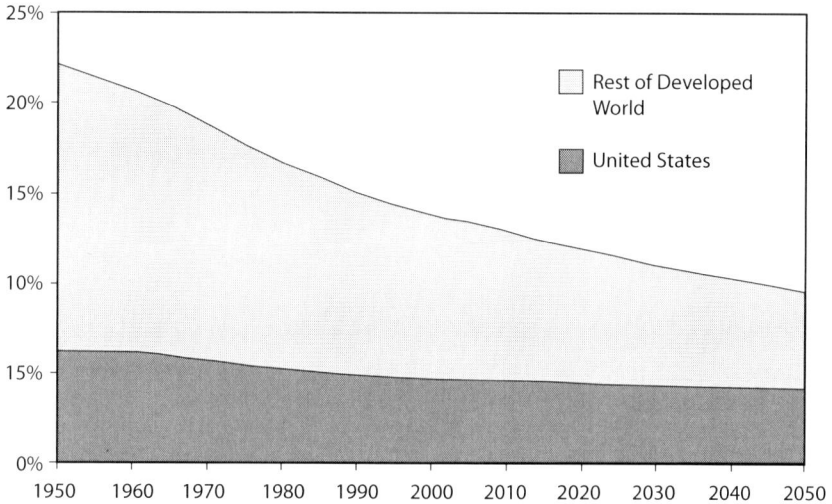

Source: United Nations 2008; for demographic scenarios see Jackson and Howe 2008, 190, Figure 5-3. Reproduced with permission from Jackson and Howe 2008.

decline by as much as 10 percent. Bucking the trend are the traditional Anglo-Saxon settler countries, the United States, Canada, Australia, and New Zealand, where population growth is projected to exceed 10 percent. Its current growth rate of 1.4 percent notwithstanding, China's population, by contrast, is projected to start declining by 2025 (when it will officially be overtaken by India as the world's most populist country although many demographers already believe India to be more populous than China). Russia's population, by contrast, is projected to fall from 141 to 130 million by 2025 while its population ages rapidly (Eberstadt 2009). While these developments have but a moderate effect on the pecking order among the world's three most populous countries, Table 1 shows that the impact on "the rise and fall" of other "great powers" (measured by population size) is marked.

By 2025, for instance, the number of women of child-bearing age will be barely half of what it is today. The drag on Russian productivity is expected to be considerable (although it will be offset in the short-term by rising rents from Russia's vast wealth in natural resources). In fact, Vladimir Putin has referred to the precipitous decline of Orthodox Slavs as the country's greatest security threat: "The most acute problem facing Russia today is demography," he told the Kremlin in his 2006 State of the Union Address. This is a function not only large swaths of land that are already under-populated but also of a combination of higher fertility rates

TABLE 1
Largest Countries Ranked by Population Size, 1950, 2005, and 2050

Ranking	1950	2005	2050
1	China	China	India
2	India	India	China
3	United States	United States	United States
4	Russian Federation	Indonesia	Indonesia
5	Japan	Brazil	Pakistan
6	Indonesia	Pakistan	Nigeria
7	Germany	Bangladesh	Bangladesh
8	Brazil	Russian Federation	Brazil
9	UK	Nigeria	Ethiopia
10	Italy	Japan	DR Congo
11	Bangladesh	Mexico	Philippines
12	France	Vietnam	Mexico
		(14) Germany	(18) Japan
		(20) France	(26) Germany
		(21) UK	(27) France
		(23) Italy	(32) UK
			(39) Italy

Source: Adapted from Jackson and Howe 2008; future rankings for select developed countries which are projected to fall below 12th place are indicated in parentheses.

and migration by ethnic minorities that are poised to eclipse Orthodox Slavs (Hahn 2007).

Due to steep declines in fertility rates over the past century and substantial increases in longevity, allied countries are aging at unprecedented rates and to an unprecedented extent. The scope of the aging process is remarkable. By 2050, at least 20 percent of the population in allied countries, but also of China and Russia, will be over 65. In Japan it will be as high as one-third of the population. By 2050 China alone will have more than 330 million people over 65. Population aging, as Table 2 shows, is accompanied by a diffusion of absolute population decline. Russia's population is already decreasing by 500,000–700,000 people per year.

These projections are highly unlikely to be wrong. Moreover, the trends are largely irreversible. The reason for this certainty is simple: the elderly of the future are already born. Anyone over the age of 40 in 2050 has already been born! Except for some global natural disaster, disease pandemic, or other worldwide calamity, the number of people in the world who are over 65 will grow exponentially over the coming decades. Even in democracies with comparatively good demographic prospects, the proportion of that cohort is projected to double by 2040. Only major increases in immigration rates or fertility levels will prevent this inevitable rise in the number of elderly from resulting in significant increases in states' median ages (Eberstadt 2001). Either outcome is

TABLE 2
Countries Projected to Have Declining Populations, by Period of the Onset of Decline, 1981–2045

Already Declining	Onset of Decline: 2009–2029	Onset of Decline: 2030–2050
Hungary (1981)	Italy (2010)	Azerbaijan (2030)
Bulgaria (1986)	Slovakia (2011)	Denmark (2031)
Estonia (1990)	Bosnia and Herzegovina (2011)	Belgium (2031)
Georgia (1990)	Greece (2014)	Thailand (2033)
Latvia (1990)	Serbia (2014)	North Korea (2035)
Armenia (1991)	Portugal (2016)	Singapore (2035)
Romania (1991)	Cuba (2018)	Netherlands (2037)
Lithuania (1992)	Macedonia (2018)	Switzerland (2040)
Ukraine (1992)	Spain (2019)	UK (2044)
Moldova (1993)	Taiwan (2019)	Puerto Rico (2044)
Belarus (1994)	South Korea (2020)	Kazakhstan (2045)
Russian Federation (1994)	Austria (2024)	
Czech Republic (1995)	Finland (2027)	
Poland (1997)	China (2029)	
Germany (2006)		
Japan (2008)		
Croatia (2008)		
Slovenia (2008)		

Source: Adapted from Jackson and Howe 2008; excludes countries with fewer than 1 million people.

unlikely, however. Immigration to Europe, for instance, would have to be four orders of magnitude higher (at 1 percent which is equivalent to four million migrants annually) than historical levels to forestall population aging.[1] Across Western Europe, for instance, rates of immigration would have to be at least double what they are today (assuming no outmigration, a problem to be discussed below). Yet, electorates seem reticent about current levels of immigration, let alone increasing those rates. States such as Russian and Japan have actually moved to restrict immigration. Far from encouraging more immigration, population aging may actually be a catalyst of rising xenophobic anti-immigrant sentiment. It appears that as states' dominant ethnic groups begin to recede in both political power and numbers, they often grow more hostile towards immigrants (Teitelbaum and Winter 1998). Social aging may thus counteract the implementation of at least one strategy to cancel out the negative effects of population aging: immigration.

In fact, industrialized countries, such as Germany, already register net negative migration. In Europe the net migration rate has been hovering around 0.28 percent whereas in North America, Australia, and New Zealand they register around 0.4 percent. Moreover, by the third generation, the fertility patterns of immigrants (who account for 85 percent of

Europe's total population growth among the EU-25 as opposed to only 40 percent in the United States; cf. European Commission 2004, 25) tend to approximate the national norm (which, of course, is below or at replacement across industrialized democracies). Productivity gains that flow from immigration are largely cancelled out by subsequent family reunions: The education and health costs associated with immigrants, their children, and the eventual family reunion with their parents actually have a negative net fiscal impact in the short term. So, the benefits of immigration for social aging are less obvious than they appear.

Significant increases in fertility are equally unlikely. While American and French exceptionalism of above-replacement fertility rates persist[2] and jurisdictions such as Sweden, Norway, Germany, and Quebec have managed to raise their fertility rates through targeted pro-natalist policies, these fertility spikes appear temporary and difficult to sustain over the long term.[3] Moreover, pro-natalist policies are costly. They actually increase governments' fiscal burden, at least in the short run. The most effective pro-natalist policy is to pay women not to work but the fiscal cost-benefit tradeoffs aside, there are also important productivity tradeoffs in that countries with low fertility are also facing acute shortages of skilled labour. With more women now in post-secondary education than men, and women, on average, faring better in their educational outcomes, investing heavily in their education only to pay them to stay at home does not seem to make a whole lot of sense.

In short, neither immigration nor fertility are likely to cancel out social aging. Population aging thus becomes a virtual inevitability. Ergo, countries will need to learn to live with their demographic trends and strategize accordingly.

DOMESTIC DEMOGRAPHIC INSTABILITY: MIGRATION AND URBANIZATION

The combination of significant (1) aging, (2) diversification of populations, and (3) a reversal of the urban-rural split (from 30–70 in 1950 to 70–30 by 2050 cf. UN Secretariat 2008) is without historical precedent. Since urban populations are both younger and more diverse than rural ones, one might also add a growing urban-rural divide and territorial differentiation as subsidiary challenges. For the first time in history, more people now live in cities than in the countryside. As urban growth outpaces national population growth by a factor of 1.5, the proportion of urban dwellers across the world is expected to rise to 57 percent by 2025. In the less-developed world, where population growth is greatest, however, three billion more people will be living in cities (in addition to the 2.3 billion urban dwellers in 2005), a 50 percent increase from 42.7 percent in 2005 to 67 percent by 2050. In sub-Saharan Africa, the growth will be three-fold, from 3,000 today to 1 billion by mid-century. While much attention has been focused on the growth of mega-cities, most of the urban growth is expected to transpire in secondary centres along migratory crossroads. Owing to pressures on education, sanitation, energy supply, transportation, food storage and distribution, let alone interethnic relations, these developments raise the spectre of systemic disorder (Evans 2009; Nichiporuk 2000; Taw and Hoffmann 1994, chap. 2), just as youthful populations, rapid development, and urbanization did during the first half of the nineteenth century when confronted with undemocratic governance. Indeed, a recent intelligence forecast cautioned that "lagging economies, ethnic affiliations, intense religious convictions, and youth bulges will align to create a 'perfect storm' for internal conflict" in the near future (NIC 2005, 97).

As mega-cities are likely to continue to receive the bulk of attention, they are likely to become hubs of volatility with the population influx vastly exceeding employment prospects on overtaxed services (Goldstone 2010). In fact, where the annual rate of urban population growth exceeds 4 percent, the probability of civil conflict has been found to be 40 percent; where the rate of growth is between 1 and 4 percent, it is half that at 20 percent, and where it is less than 1 percent it is 19 percent. In other words, disproportionately high rates of urbanization are associated with a disproportionately high probability of civil conflict.

These migratory trends are also likely to cause growing disequilibria among ethnic populations, as the "sons of the soil" have to contend with an influx of other ethnic groups. Prominent examples where population differentials are already a source of conflict include Israel, Lebanon and Nigeria as well as native populations across the Americas and Oceania which register some of the highest fertility (and migratory) rates in the world.

Migration and age structure have several connections, one of which is that the most mobile populations also tend to be youthful. That is, migrants are overwhelmingly between 15 and 35 years old. There are a number of reasons for this, but perhaps most importantly, these age groups stand to reap the greatest long-term payoff from migrating and they have the least to lose from being uprooted. While Europe will continue to attract the bulk of migrants, as some of the aforementioned countries harness the working-population benefits that flow from the demographic transition (i.e., the gradual closing of the gap in excess fertility over mortality) and as others continue to develop, including India and China, they are likely to start seeing immigration as well. As migratory flows within Europe, within Asia but also within Africa, are likely to pick up, flows in North America are likely to abate as Central and South America's populations age and economic development continues apace.

Countries further along the demographic transition in Latin America and Asia, such as India, China, Brazil, and Mexico, will start to benefit from international migration's human-capital and technology-transfer effect as educated and affluent expatriates return to their countries of origin. In China, however, that benefit may be offset as the comparative advantage associated with a large working-age population relative to a small proportion of children and elderly starts to wane around 2015, a problem that is further exacerbated by a growing excess of men over women among China's population (cf. Howe and Jackson 2004). The ratio of working-age adults to elderly is projected to shrink from just under 10 in 2000 to 2.6 by 2050 when China's median age is projected to be just over 45 years of age. That median age will make China one of oldest populations in the world—older than Japan, the country with the oldest population today—and is projected to have a median age of 43 by then.[4] Owing to continued migratory flows and lower levels of development in many of the migrants' native countries, the challenge migration poses for Europe is more immediate than for North America.

DOMESTIC DEMOGRAPHIC INSTABILITY: YOUTH

Global population is expected to grow by 1.2 billion by 2025, an increase of not quite 20 percent from the current 6.8 billion. However, that is well below the rate of increase between 1980 and 2009 when the globe's population grew by 2.4 billion. While the rate of growth may be slowing, the impact of the absolute growth is still staggering. The populations of 50 countries are projected to grow by a third, in some cases by two thirds, by 2025 (which, of course, places additional stress on natural resources, services, and infrastructure). These are predominantly large, Islamic countries of 60 million people or more that are located primarily in sub-Saharan Africa as well as the Middle East and South Asia. With the demographic transition progressing more rapidly in the Middle East and South Asia (Figure 2), the challenges associated with population growth, such as youth bulges, will be greatest in sub-Saharan Africa.

Countries with so-called "youth bulges"[5] (the proportion of the adult population aged 15–29) are depicted in Figure 3; they have been shown to be at a greater risk for civil conflict (Urdal 2006, 2007; Leahy et al. 2007; Kahl 2006; Goldstone 2002; Homer-Dixon 1999) due to strains on systems of schooling and socialization as well as un- or under-employment, concomitant propensity for deviance, and countries in which more than 60 percent of the population is under 30, have been shown to be four times as prone to civil war than countries with mature populations (Leahy et al. 2007).

Another way to make the case for the correlation between fecundity, youth bulges, and the propensity for conflict is to examine the association between a country's position along the demographic transition and the outbreak of civil war (as shown in Figure 4): The further along a country's population is in the demographic transition, the lower the probability of civil war.

FIGURE 2
The Global Population Structure, 1970–2025

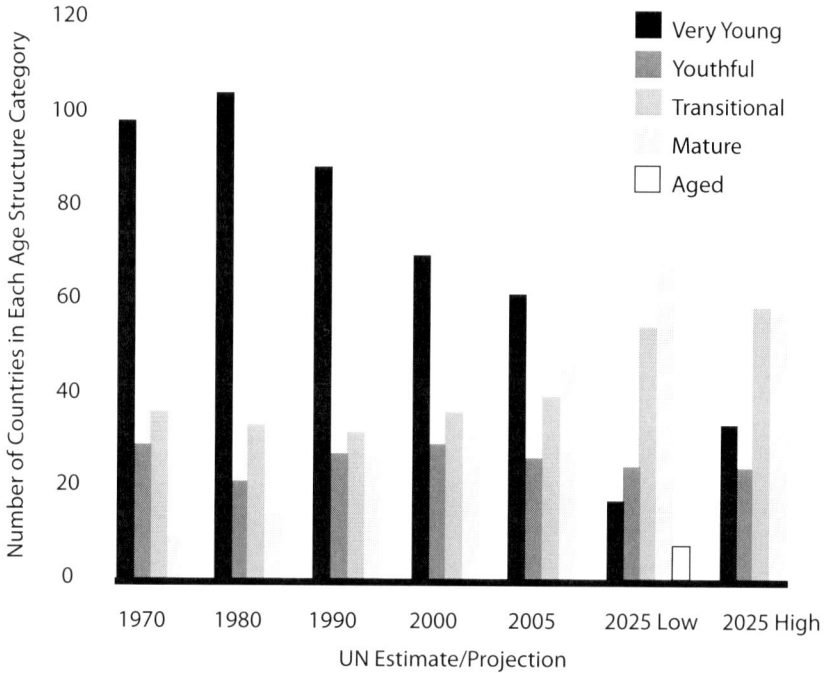

Source: Reproduced with permission from Leahy et al. 2007, 19.

FIGURE 3
Geographic Distribution of the Youth Bulge, 2005

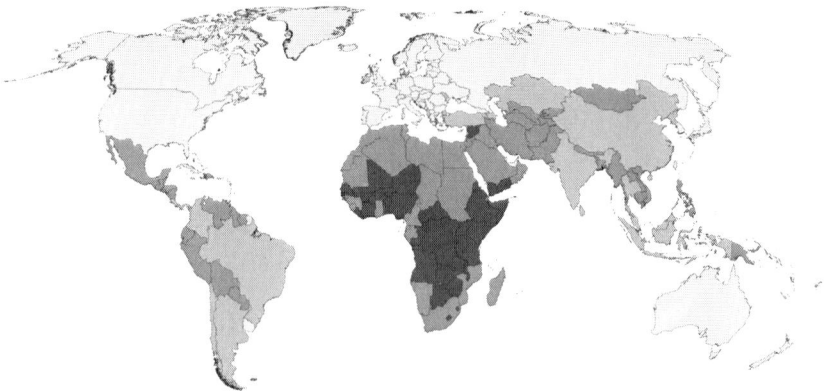

Demographic Stress Categories (youth bulge—young adults aged 15–29 years—as a proportion of all adults aged 15 and older): darkest areas are extreme (50 percent); lighest areas are low (less than 30 percent).

Source: Reproduced with permission from Cincotta, Engelman and Anastasion 2003, 43.

FIGURE 4
Demographic Transition and Outbreak of Civil War

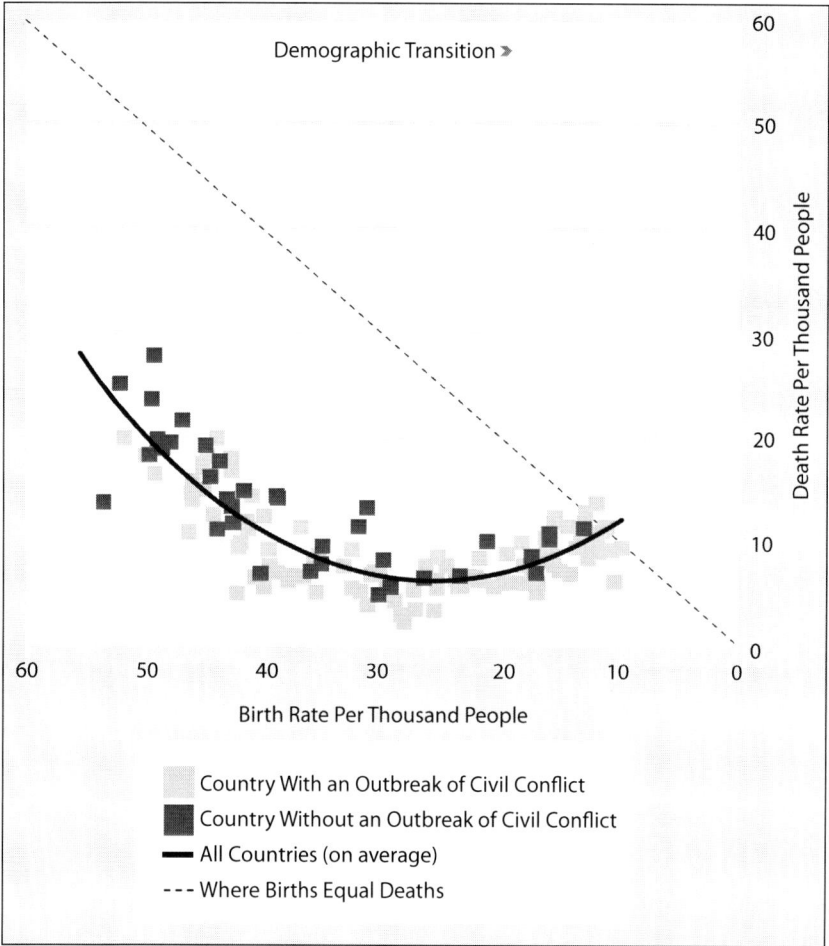

Source: Reproduced with permission from Cincotta, Engelman and Anastasion 2003, 28.

Although youth bulges are on the wane in the Middle East and Southeast Asia, by 2025 three-quarters of the countries with persistent youth bulges will be in sub-Saharan Africa. A key driver of this development is HIV/AIDS which delays the entry of populations with high incidence rates of infection through the demographic transition by compromising the elderly proportion of the population. So, the bulk of conflict and political instability will continue to be scattered across the Middle East, Asia, and some Pacific islands but is likely to be concentrated in sub-Saharan Africa. Since conflict is the single greatest "push factor" of migration, immigration pressures from sub-Saharan Africa to Europe (but also to places such as South Africa, as Lindy Heinecken's 2001 micro-study on the subject has demonstrated) are expected to continue unabated and may accelerate as climate change makes life even less viable in that part of the world.

However, as youth bulges transition into bulges in the working-age population, some Asian, Latin American, and North African countries have the potential to harness not only the economic returns of the demographic transition (Bloom, Canning and Sevilla 2003) but also "democratic returns" (see Figure 5). They include Turkey, Lebanon, Iran, Morocco, Algeria, Tunisia, Colombia, Costa Rica, Chile, Vietnam, Indonesia, Malaysia, and Thailand. For instance, as Iran's population matures over

FIGURE 5
Age Structure and Governance

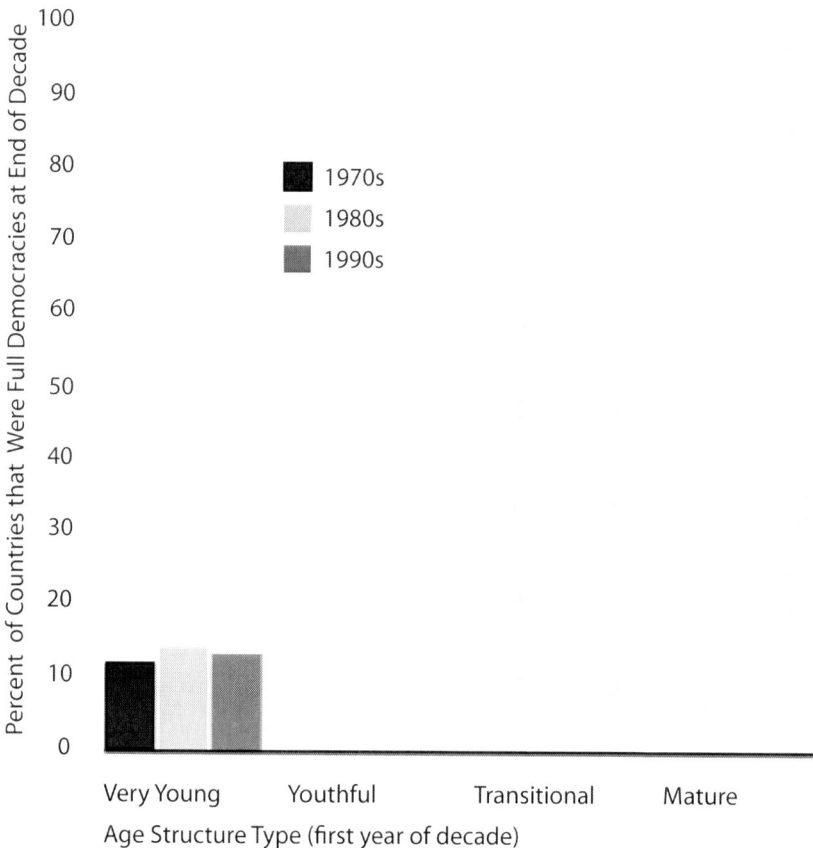

Source: Reproduced with permission from Leahy et al. 2007, 25.

the coming decade (and approximates China's current age structure with a large working-age population but relatively few children and elderly), prospects for improved education and higher standards of living are likely to become an impetus for political moderation. Since Iran's population structure will be more mature than that of its neighbours, demographically, the risk of it initiating international war is on the wane.

Over the same period, by contrast, populations in the West Bank/ Gaza strip, its arch-nemesis Iraq, and neighbouring Saudi Arabia will continue to grow and remain comparatively youthful which means we can expect continued political instability and outmigration among those countries. Still, the youth bulge will be greatest in Afghanistan, Pakistan, the Democratic Republic of Congo, Ethiopia, Nigeria, Guatemala, Iraq, Ethiopia, Angola, Chad and Yemen, producing population growth rates of over 2 percent annually (see Table 3) with populations in those countries doubling every 30–35 years.

TABLE 3
Fastest Growing Countries 2005–2010 (at least 1 million people)

Country*	Annual Growth Rate %
Liberia	4.1
Niger	3.9
Afghanistan, Burkina Faso	3.4
Syria, Timor L'este, Uganda	3.3
Benin, **Palestine (occupied)**	3.2
Eritrea	3.1
Jordan	3.0
Burundi, **Tanzania, Yemen**	2.9
Chad, Congo (DR), **Gambia,** Malawi, **UAE**	2.8
Angola, Rwanda, Madagascar, **Sierra Leone**	2.7
Ethiopia, Kenya, **Senegal**	2.6
Guatemala, Togo	2.5
Kuwait, Mali, Mauritania, PNG, Zambia	2.4
Cameroon, Côte d'Ivoire, **Guinea**, Mozambique, **Nigeria, Somalia**	2.3
Guinea-Bissau, Iraq, Pakistan, Sudan	2.2
Ghana, **Oman, Saudi Arabia**	2.1
Honduras, **Libya**	2.0
Cen.Afr.Rep., Congo, Namibia, Nepal	1.9
Bolivia, **Egypt**, Gabon, Ireland, Laos, Paraguay, Philippines	1.8
Israel, **Malaysia**, Venezuela	1.7
Cambodia, Haiti, Panama, **Tajikistan**	1.6
Algeria, Colombia	1.5

*Countries with 50 percent or more Muslim population in **Bold**.
Source: United Nations 2008.

Even if fertility rates in Nigeria or Afghanistan were to decline, they are currently so high that, at best, each country might barely transition from a young to a youthful age structure by 2025.

FISCAL IMPLICATIONS OF DEMOGRAPHIC CHANGE: KNOWING ON WHICH HORSE TO BET

Global population aging is thought to prolong US power dominance in the twenty-first century (Haas 2010), which, in turn, has significant implications for international security. First, the massive costs created by aging populations, especially in combination with probable slow-downs in economic growth—with a drag of 1 percent on GDP due to slowing employment growth in Europe, for instance—will preclude other major powers from increasing military expenditures to match US defence spending. Rather, demographic factors are likely to curtail military expenditures further. Regardless, demographic developments are bound to crowd out spending on defence. In short, defence spending is unlikely to escalate which should, overall, portend well for international peace. Second, aging populations and shrinking workforces will cause other great powers to spend more of their defence budgets on personnel costs and military pensions at the expense of researching, developing, and purchasing technologically sophisticated weaponry. The more states spend on military personnel and pensions as opposed to weapons, the greater the gap between US (and allied) military capacity and that of possible challengers. As the cost of engaging the US in an international conflict grows, the probability of a major international war engaging the US declines. Third, although the US population is aging, it is doing so to a lesser extent and less quickly than those of possible challengers. As a result, the pressures of elderly care over military spending is favourable, and the increased substitution of labour for capital in defence budgets will be smaller for the United States than among its competitors. The remainder of this sub-section will elaborate why the fiscal implications of demographic change militate against paradigm shifts away from the status quo of international security.

An unprecedented 70 percent of people in the developed world are between 15 and 64 years of age. Yet, as Figure 6 shows, the United States and some other Anglo-Saxon countries are aging less rapidly than other countries, owing largely to higher fertility rates and immigration.

Never before has that proportion been so high—and it is only expected to decline henceforth. This has important implications for consumption, productivity, tax revenue, and fiscal expenditures. Over the next two decades the proportion of seniors to the working age population will climb from fewer than 1 in 4 to 1 in 2 in countries such as Japan. In many countries the aging effect is exacerbated by a contracting working-age cohort although that effect is less pronounced in countries with higher

FIGURE 6
Elderly Population by Country (as a proportion of the total population)

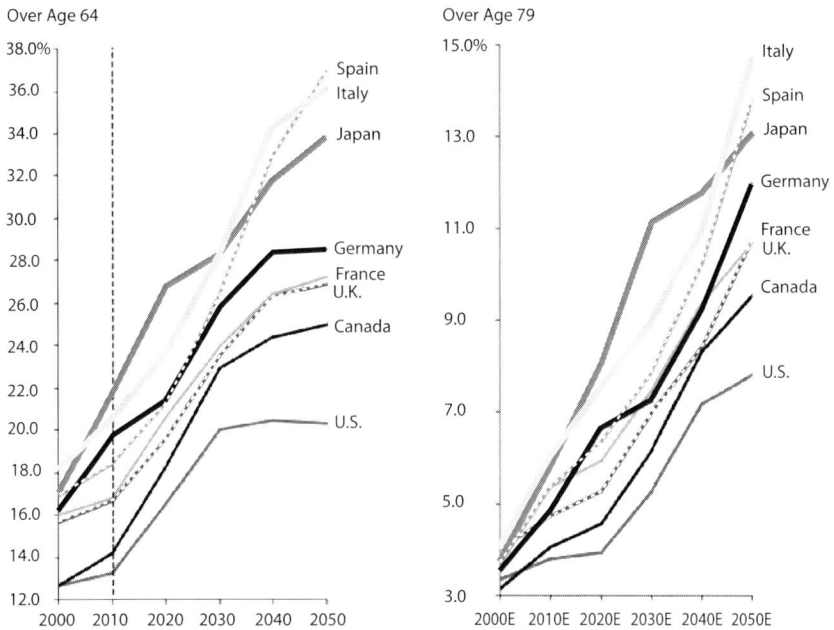

Source: US Census Bureau, as cited in Culhane 2001, 7.

immigration and/or effective pro-natalist policies including the UK, France, Belgium, the Netherlands, and Scandinavia. At constant per capita expenditures, by 2040 Germany will have to increase its annual spending on elderly care more than seven-fold relative to its current spending on defence. France would have to spend more than five times as much, and Japan more than 15 times as much (Haas 2007, 120-121).

Given the magnitude of the costs created by the NATO allies' and great powers' aging populations, substantial increases in these states' expenditures for economic development and defence are unlikely. Among NATO allies at least, the massive costs of aging are likely to create so austere a financial climate that there will be little room for politicians to begin substantial new spending in areas not related to the care of seniors. We may already be witnessing this trend. Despite concerns about growing Chinese power and North Korea's missile and nuclear programs, Japan reduced its defence budget every year from 2003 to 2008. The cuts were linked explicitly to mushrooming costs generated by its aging population. The Japanese government is on record as stating that general expenditures will have to be cut 25–30 percent to cope with expenses associated with population aging.

Similar pressure for cuts in defence spending to finance elder-care costs are building in France and Germany. In February 2006, the EU Commission warned Germany that it had to cut discretionary spending across the board "to cope with the costs of an aging population." Speaking on behalf of the government, Germany's Minister of Finance, Peer Steinbrück, agreed with this analysis and promised to put the commission's recommendations into practice. This decision is a continuation of a policy that Germany has followed over the past decade of "letting defence spending languish … while investing in social welfare instead." Even in the post-September 11 world, "cutting social programs or raising taxes to buy weapons is considered [in Germany] politically impossible."

Also in 2006, the French president created the Public Finance Guidance Council, lead by the prime ministers and the ministers of the economy, finance, and industry, whose primary purpose is to reduce France's national debt. It has grown significantly in recent years in no small measure due to increasing costs for elderly care. The council's primary policy mandate is to reduce to a substantial degree expenditures "of all public players," including the military.

Population aging is likely to crowd out military spending—but not just in the democratic world. China, for instance, is projected to become the first country to grow old before becoming an advanced industrial state. Even if its economy were to continue growing rapidly, by 2035 its median age will reach that of France, Germany, and Japan today, but at levels of per capita GDP that are significantly lower, and with massive unfunded pension liabilities of state-owned enterprises (Haas 2007, 124). With its economic and fiscal constraints approaching those of most Western European countries (Eberstadt 2006) but with far greater shortfalls between the government's obligations to the elderly versus saved assets (England 2005, 87, 89, 91; Longman 2004, 55-56; Jingyuan 2002, 183), China's ability to invest in defence and security will be crowded out as its leaders, by about 2020, will be faced with a dilemma: tolerate growing levels of poverty among a mushrooming elderly population, or curtail other spending to provide the requisite resources to safeguard internal stability by alleviating these circumstances.

No country will be able to challenge NATO's and especially the US's military dominance without the ability to wage highly technologically sophisticated warfare (Posen 2003). Social aging, however, will cause militaries to spend more on personnel and less on capital, such as weapons development and procurement. This trend is already evident in NATO member countries today, especially when escalating pension and health-care liabilities are factored in. Since 1995, both France and Germany have dedicated nearly 60 percent of their military budgets to personnel. Canada spends about half its budget on personnel. Germany spends almost four times more on personnel than on weapons procurement. France, Japan, and Russia spend nearly 2.5 times more. By contrast, the United States dedicates less than 1.3 times more money to personnel than to weapons purchases (Haas 2007, 140-141).

There are two reasons why population aging causes military-personnel costs to rise. First, as demographic growth slows but economies continue to grow, the labour market tightens. Concomitantly, the nature of modern military organizations—as Morris Janowicz (1960) observed four decades ago—is less and less "an organization set apart" for a uniquely specific purpose (as Huntington in 1957 purported), but is instead increasingly approximating any other private- or public-sector organization. As a result, it competes for the same highly skilled and educated labour. The combination of a tightening labour market and growing competition of a small pool of highly qualified labour causes salaries to grow exponentially.[6] In 2008 the Russian government announced plans to raise military salaries to 25 percent above the average wage by 2020 and to improve housing and pension benefits for military personnel. China, its conscripted force notwithstanding, had to raise officers' wages by 85 percent and soldiers' wages by 92 percent between 1992 and 2002. In fact, the Chinese government—which is usually coy and conservative in revealing its defence expenditures—is on record as identifying growing personnel expenses as the greatest driver in the growth of China's defence budget over those 10 years (People's Republic of China 2004).

Second, pension liabilities (which are often un- or under-funded) are escalating. Russia, for instance, has been spending more on retired military personnel than on either weapons procurement or military research and development (International Institute for Strategic Studies 2010). Similarly, rising pension costs are the second most important reason for increases in Chinese military spending over the past decade (after the aforementioned pay raises for active personnel; *idem*). Pensions, of course, are a liability in that they are ongoing and growing obligations that add little value to defence capabilities. In countries such as Germany, which pays its pension obligations out of general revenue (i.e., current contributions, instead of being invested to grow, pay for current liabilities—a system commonly known as "pay as you go"), every Euro spent on retirement benefits is one Euro less to spend on other services, let alone weapons, research, or personnel. The United States, the United Kingdom, and Canada, by contrast, use funded pensions to augment social security. Pay-as-you-go systems redistribute revenue from the working-age population to pensioners through taxes. When the benefits paid replace a high proportion of average earnings, they also create a disincentive to save and work past the normal retirement age, both of which depress GDP growth (an issue to which we shall return below). In light of population aging, pay-as-you-go systems are fiscally unsustainable because they have to be paid for either through tax increases by the working-age population or through issuance of government debt (thus crowding out defence spending). Yet, as Figure 7 shows, many pay-as-you-go countries already register some

FIGURE 7
Gross Earning of Average Production Worker, 1998
(thousands of dollars of equal purchasing power)

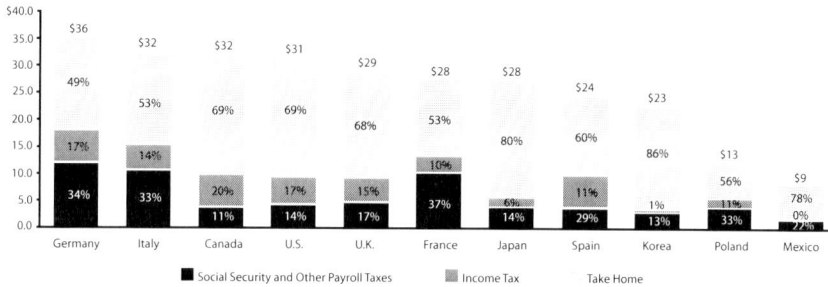

Note: Excludes VAT.
Source: OECD 2000a, as cited in Culhane 2001, 16.

of the highest marginal tax rates in the world. This is problematic insofar as high payroll taxes are a drag on a workforce's competitiveness. Pay-as-you-go is a vicious circle: As countries raise taxes to pay for pay-as-you-go, their workers become increasingly uncompetitive, thus further undermining the ability to pay for the pay-as-you-go system.

In 1998, the average German worker was four times as expensive ($35,900) as his Mexican counterpart ($8,700) with 51 percent of his pay going to taxes, excluding VAT. Social security and payroll taxes made up 34 percent of a German worker's taxes—but covered only 76 percent of social-security expenditures! As the dependency ratio of the working-age population to elderly in Germany is halved by 2050 (Figure 8), considerable increases in payroll taxes are to be expected.

As Europe, Japan, and South Korea lose one quarter to one-third of their prime labour force by 2050, the dependency gap widens. Notable in Table 4 is stagnating or declining populations of prime working age due to aging outpacing growth even in countries with high rates of immigration, such as France, Spain, and Switzerland. While their labour force faces an unprecedented decline, the proportion of their population over 60 years of age will rise by 50 percent on average. However, in countries whose labour force continues to grow, such as the United States, Canada, and Spain, the proportion of the population over 60 will actually double over the same period, to 16–17 percent in the US and 28–30 percent in Canada, for example. Similar trends, albeit time-delayed, obtain for South Korea, China, and Ireland. As Table 4 details, by 2050, the population over 60 years of age will reach 35 to 40 percent in many of these countries. Europe's working-age population, for instance, has been on the wane since its apex of 480 million in 2005 and, by 2050, is expected to revert to its 1950s level of 330 million.

FIGURE 8
Elderly Support Ratio: Actual Workers/Population Aged Over 64

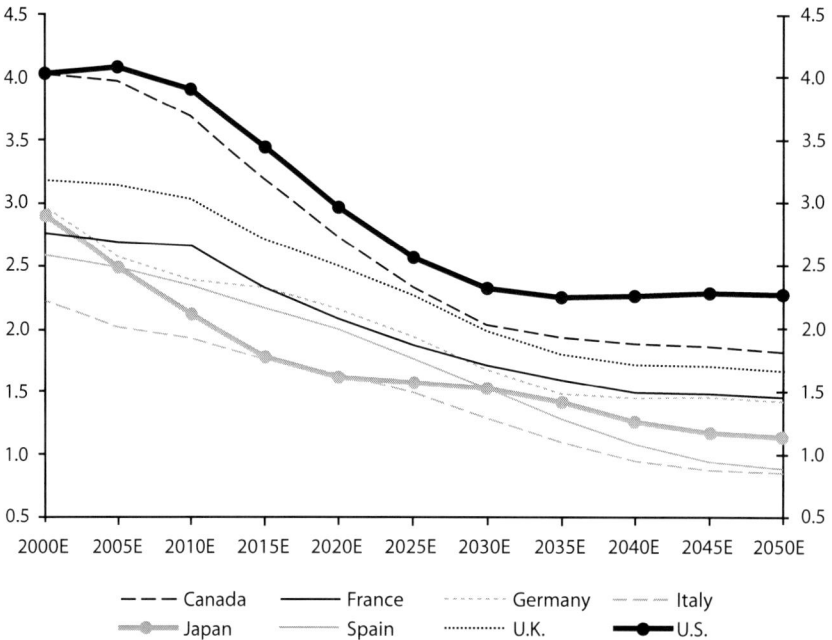

Source: US Census Bureau, as cited in Culhane 2001, 10.

A growing dependency ratio aggravates the situation further by depressing GDP growth as people work less, exercise their exit option in favour of lower-tax jurisdictions, migrate to the underground economy, opt not to work at all, and, squeezed by high taxes, opt for fewer children. Modest retirement promises and funded public and private pension plans have direct and indirect benign effects on demographic growth by encouraging fecundity and immigration along with stronger economic-growth prospects (Table 5), thus positioning countries that operate in this vein demographically and fiscally more robustly with respect to their international-security capacities.

As populations age and the dependency ratio between the old and the young becomes increasingly strained, pension systems turn out to be integral to the capacity to contribute to international security. Funded pension systems redistribute income through the purchase of assets by workers and the sale of assets by retirees. As they encourage workers to save, they increase capital and thereby productivity and GDP growth. The United States and Canada have fairly well-funded pension systems (especially compared to China, France, Germany, and Russia).[7] The implications for public finances in terms of total government outlays and public

TABLE 4
Aging and Labour Force Change in Major European and Other Countries, 2009–2050

	% Change in:		
	Total Population	Population 15–60	Population 60+
Bulgaria	−29	−46	13
Belarus	−24	−42	46
Ukraine	−23	−40	21
Japan	−20	−37	19
Romania	−19	−38	50
Poland	−16	−38	70
Russia	−18	−36	47
Germany	−14	−32	32
Hungary	−11	−26	33
S. Korea	−9	−36	146
Portugal	−6	−26	54
EUROPE	−6	−24	47
Italy	−5	−24	41
Greece	−2	−23	54
Czech Republic	−1	−23	57
Denmark	1	−6	29
Austria	2	−18	59
Finland	2	−10	36
China	5	−17	175
Netherlands	5	−9	53
Belgium	8	−7	52
France	9	−6	56
Switzerland	13	−4	56
Spain	14	−13	93
Sweden	14	4	40
United Kingdom	18	7	51
United States	28	15	97
Canada	32	9	116
Ireland	39	17	164

Source: OECD 2009a.

old-age cash payments are dramatic. As Table 6 shows, at the turn of the millennium government outlays (excluding health-care costs) ranged from almost 50 percent in France to 29 percent in the United States. In 1997, cash benefits ranged from 4.4 percent in Canada to 13.2 percent in Italy.

Owing to low social-security promises, the United States, the United Kingdom, and Canada are less affected by social aging. As borne out in the political culture of those countries, polling data show that Americans have the highest prediction of when they would retire (67.2) and (by far) the lowest expectations regarding governmental support of their retirement.[8] As seen in Figure 9, while Canada and some other countries compare favourably in terms of public health-care expenditures as a proportion of GDP, Germany and France (but also the United States) fare poorly.

TABLE 5
Fertility and Longevity Expectations

	Fertility Rate				Life Expectancy at Birth			
	1960	2000E	2020E	2050E	1960	2000E	2020E	2050E
United States	3.31	2.06	2.18	2.22	70.0	77.1	79.9	83.9
Canada	3.61	1.60	1.64	1.70	71.4	79.4	81.7	83.7
Japan	2.02	1.41	1.52	1.70	69.0	80.7	80.7	84.1
United Kingdom	2.81	1.73	1.72	1.70	70.8	77.7	77.7	83.1
Germany	2.49	1.38	1.51	1.70	70.3	77.4	80.4	83.0
France	2.85	1.75	1.73	1.70	71.0	78.8	81.3	83.5
Italy	2.55	1.18	1.25	1.70	69.9	79.0	81.4	83.5
Spain	2.89	1.15	1.31	1.70	70.2	79.6	81.3	83.5
Netherlands	3.13	1.64	1.67	1.70	73.4	78.3	81.0	83.3
Switzerland	2.51	1.47	1.56	1.70	71.7	79.6	80.6	83.7
Denmark	2.59	1.73	1.72	1.70	72.3	76.5	79.8	82.8
Finland	2.58	1.70	1.70	1.70	68.9	77.4	80.4	83.0
Norway	2.90	1.81	1.77	1.70	73.4	78.7	81.2	83.4
Sweden	2.34	1.53	1.60	1.70	73.5	79.6	81.8	83.7
China	5.72	1.82	1.81	1.80	49.5	71.4	76.7	80.9
India	5.81	3.11	2.26	2.02	45.5	62.5	69.4	77.0

Source: US Census Bureau 2010.

TABLE 6
Retirement Spending as a Percentage of GDP, 2000–2050

Country	Total Government Outlays	Cash Public Old Age Benefits	Basic Old Age Pensions (Roseveare)			European Commission November 2000	
	2000E %	(1997) %	2000E %	2010E %	2050E %	2000E %	2050 %
Canada	37.8	4.4	5.0	5.3	8.7	NA	NA
France	51.2	10.7	9.8	9.7	14.4	12.1	15.8
Germany	43.0	10.5	11.5	11.8	17.5	10.3	14.6
Italy	46.7	13.2	12.6	13.2	20.3	14.2	13.9
Japan	38.2	5.5	7.5	9.6	16.5	NA	NA
Spain	38.5	8.6	9.8	10.0	19.1	9.4	17.7
UK	38.4	6.4	4.5	5.2	4.1	5.1	3.9
US	29.3	5.6	4.2	4.5	7.0	4.2	6.8

Source: OECD 2000b and 2000c; Roseveare et al. 1996; Commission of the European Communities 2000; as cited in Culhane 2001, 15.

FIGURE 9
Health-Care Expenditures as a Percentage of GDP (2006)

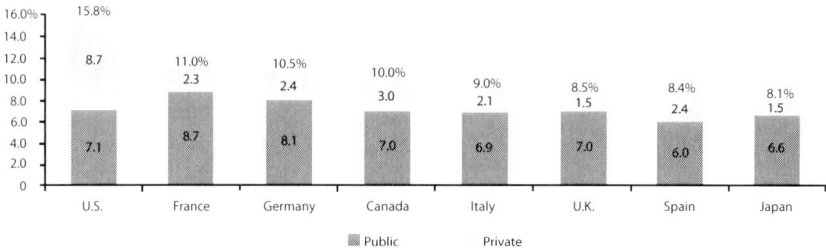

Source: OECD 2009b.

What is more, countries which are already facing the greatest expenditure burden for its old population aggravate matters further: As evidenced in Table 7, instead of liberalizing working conditions, they ease their unemployment burden by encouraging early retirement, thus enlarging the pool of unused potentially productive labour. That aggravates social conflicts over issues such as pensions, migration, and labour/employer relations (Friedman 2005) and presents opportunities for countries to invest instead in technology to spur gains in productivity.

TABLE 7
Labour Capacity

Country	Unused Labour Capacity 55–65 %	Men Out of the Labour Force, Age 59 %	Early Retirement Age	Replacement Rate at Early Retirement Age %	Implicit Tax on Earnings in Next Year %
France	60	53	60	91	80
Italy	59	53	55	75	81
Netherlands	58	47	60	91	141
United Kingdom	55	38	60	48	75
Germany	48	34	60	62	35
Spain	47	36	60	63	–23
Canada	45	37	60	20	8
United States	37	26	62	41	–1
Sweden	35	26	60	54	28
Japan	22	13	60	54	47

Source: Gruber and Wise 1999, 29.

Although the United States' population, too, is aging, Table 8 documents that due to above-replacement fertility and persistent immigration, America has the youngest population among G8 countries. The combination of fertility and immigration (along with comparatively low welfare-state and state-pension obligations, with most of the latter liabilities funded) will strengthen America's relative demographic position vis-à-vis the other G8 countries. According to 2008 estimates published by the UN, between 2010 and 2050 the United States will remain the largest net receiver of international migrants. Half of those migrating to the developed world choose the United States which results in an annual rate of migration five times greater than that of the second-place country in this category: Canada (1.1 million people vs. 214,000). However, as a proportion of its total population, Canada will continue to have the highest immigration rate in the industrialized democratic world. The compound effect of migration to these two allies means that North America's global leadership role is likely to prevail—and the Canada is likely to become an increasingly important defence partner because of its relatively rosy demographic and, as of late, fiscal outlook.

TABLE 8
Median Age by Country, 1950–2050

Country	Year 1950	Year 2000	Year 2050
United States	30.0	35.1	41.7
United Kingdom	34.6	37.7	42.5
Russia	25.0	36.5	44.0
France	34.5	37.7	44.8
China	23.9	29.6	45.2
Germany	35.4	40.0	51.7
Japan	22.3	41.4	55.1

Source: United Nations 2008.

By contrast, Table 9 lists the countries whose median age is expected to be 50 or higher by 2050. European countries figure prominently but with key notable exceptions throughout Western Europe in what neoconservative theologian George Weigel piously fantasizes about as "Europe committing demographic suicide, systematically depopulating itself." Europe is about to witness "the greatest sustained reduction in population since the Black Death in the fourteenth century" (Ferguson 2004).[9]

China's median age will surpass the United States' by 2025. In China, France, Germany, Japan, and Russia, the working-age population is also projected to decline by 2050 or increase modestly (the UK). Figure 10 contrasts those trends with the United States where the working-age cohort is expected to grow by 23 percent.

TABLE 9
Countries Whose Median Age is Projected to be 50 or Over by 2050

Taiwan	56.3	Hong Kong, SAR	54.0	Armenia	52.3
Japan	56.2	Ukraine	54.0	Croatia	52.1
Bulgaria	55.9	Romania	53.9	Cuba	52.0
South Korea	55.5	Slovakia	53.9	Germany	51.8
Slovenia	55.3	Latvia	53.8	Belarus	51.7
Czech Republic	55.0	Italy	53.5	Hungary	51.2
Poland	54.4	Greece	53.3	Portugal	51.1
Singapore	54.3	Lithuania	52.8	Austria	50.9
Spain	54.2	Bosnia and Herzegovina	52.7	Georgia	50.2

Excludes countries with populations of less than 1 million.

Source: United Nations 2007; and *Population Projections for Taiwan Areas: 2008–2056*, Council for Economic Planning and Development, Taiwan, http://www.cepd.gov.tw/encontent/m1.aspx?sNo=0001457. For demographic scenario, see Jackson and Howe 2008, 190.

FIGURE 10
Working Age Population (aged 20–60) by Country, 2000–2050
(index 2000=100)

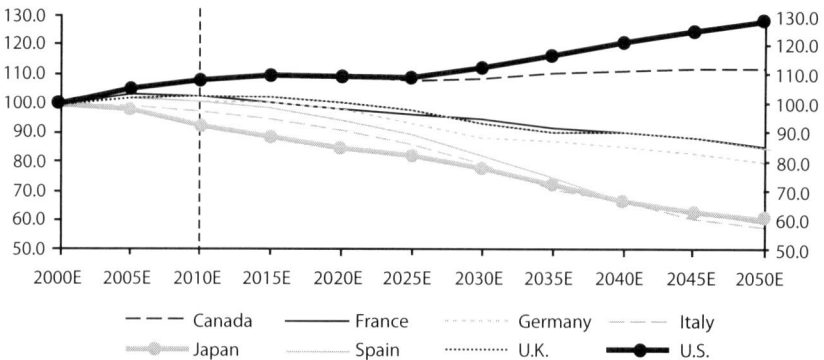

Source: US Census Bureau, as cited in Culhane 2001, 8.

(North) America's youth demographics will help offset some of the challenges of social aging. Over the coming decades (North) America's growing labour force will enhance economic growth and innovation thereby providing the government with additional revenue without having to raise taxes, borrow, or cut spending (see Table 10).

As a rule of thumb, countries with slower demographic growth tend to have slower GDP growth. Yet, the differences are significant: Whereas GDP is expected to rise by only 30 percent in Japan, Spain, and Italy as a result of an aging population, it is projected to rise some 300 percent in the United States. That is, demographic differentials (largely owing to higher fertility) account for a difference in economic growth by a magnitude of 10!

TABLE 10
Real GDP Annual Compound Growth Rate (labour hours and productivity), 1981–1999.

	1981–1989	1990–1995	1996–1999
US			
GDP	3.64	2.52	4.84
Labour hours	2.06	1.04	2.30
Labour productivity	1.31	1.02	2.30
Italy			
GDP	2.36	1.59	1.38
Labour hours	0.04	(1.09)	0.71
Labour productivity	2.33	2.72	0.67
Canada			
GDP	3.25	1.51	3.53
Labour hours	1.81	0.17	2.59
Labour productivity	1.42	1.34	0.92
France			
GDP	2.40	1.30	2.53
Labour hours	(0.95)	(0.94)	0.91
Labour productivity	3.41	2.26	1.61
Germany			
GDP	n.a	1.62	1.72
Labour hours	n.a.	(0.62)	(0.41)
Labour productivity	n.a.	2.26	2.14
Japan			
GDP	4.09	2.15	1.31
Labour hours	0.95	(0.73)	(0.76)
Labour productivity	3.12	2.89	2.07
Spain			
GDP	2.70	1.67	3.69
Labour hours	(1.70)	(0.86)	3.34
Labour productivity	3.89	2.58	0.34
U.K.			
GDP	3.54	2.37	2.78
Labour hours	0.22	0.60	1.29
Labour productivity	3.37	1.78	1.47

Source: Gust and Marquez 2000, 669.

The OECD's 1999 data on labour-force participation in Figure 11 make clear, for persons aged 15–64 (an expanded definition of working age used by most demographers, whereas economists usually look at the population 2060), that there was high employment in the United Kingdom, Canada, and the United States (economists usually consider 77 percent full employment), moderate employment in Japan (due to low female participation rates) and Germany, and low employment in France, Italy and Spain. In other words, North America enjoys not only a comparative demographic advantage but also harnesses that advantage more effectively.

FIGURE 11
Labour Force Participation Rates, 1999 (ages 15–64)

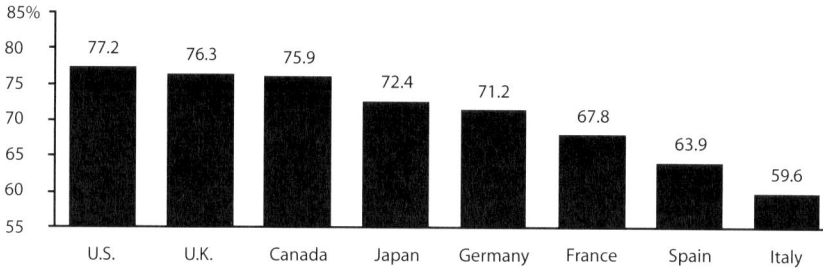

Source: OECD 2000a, 216.

Whereas labour-force participation further mitigates the impact of social aging in Anglo-Saxon countries (and has potentially positive implications for recruiting prospects), it exacerbates it in much of continental Europe.

INTERNATIONAL SECURITY STRATEGY IN THE AGE OF POPULATION AGING

Some countries are better positioned vis-à-vis demographic change than others and some will even have security benefits accrue to them, especially as a result of the continental multiplier effect in North America that is generated by virtue of the demographic advantage and concomitant economic growth enjoyed by the United States. In the context of slowing economic growth, increased costs of labour, and defence spending that is being crowded out, no state or combination of states appears likely to overtake the United States' position of economic and military dominance. Haas (2010) argues that global aging is likely to extend US hegemony (because the other major powers will lack the resources necessary to overtake the United States' economic and military power lead) and deepen it as these other states are likely to fall even farther behind the United States. The demographic developments suggest that there is no other country on the horizon that is able to muster the American's combination of innovation, economic growth, and low ratio of spending on capital versus personnel (which is key to military dominance on the high-tech battlefield of fourth generation warfare). Global population aging is thus likely to generate considerable security benefits for North America.

Yet, population aging will also transform the security environment in challenging ways. As more countries, and especially NATO allies, face growing fiscal constraints, fewer allies will end up having to pay a growing share of the common international security interests. But even for those countries, which are relatively well positioned, that will become increasingly difficult as they face their own fiscal challenges growing out of population aging. There will be a need to do more with less. In effect, the economic impact of population aging will challenge allied countries that lack the fiscal room necessary to maintain the extent of its global position and involvement, let alone adopt major new initiatives.

Compounding the problem is the fact that global aging may help make the twenty-first century a particularly dangerous time for US international interests. Population aging will beset much of the world at some point this century. In fact, the aging problem in many developing states is likely to be as acute as for industrialized countries, but the former have the added disadvantage of growing old before growing rich, thus greatly handicapping their ability to pay for elder-care costs (cf. Qiao 2006). If the strain on governments' resources caused by the cost of aging populations becomes sufficiently great, it has the potential to exacerbate systematically both the number of fragile states and the extent and depth of that fragility. As fragile states are prospective havens for organized crime and terrorism, the prospect of having to contend with a proliferation of fragile states with significantly fewer resources at the allies' disposal could prove the single greatest security challenge of this century (Jackson and Howe 2008, chap. 4–5). This is complemented by an already reduced capacity to realize other key international objectives, including preventing the proliferation of weapons of mass destruction (WMD), funding nation-building, engaging in military humanitarian interventions, and various other costly strategies of international conflict resolution and prevention.

Several important implications follow for defence and the armed forces. First, bilateral defence relationships will become even more important as the United State's proportion of the developed world's population and GDP continues to rise (Figure 12). Among its allies, America will be shouldering a growing fiscal burden of expenditures on international security. It needs a mitigation strategy which will be outlined below.

Population aging will hamper the ability of a number of allies to "step up to the plate." Afghanistan may already provide some preliminary empirical evidence to this effect. Following the logic of relative population aging, the Anglo-Saxon allies, that is, not only the United States but to a lesser extent Canada, the UK and Australia, are becoming relatively more important allies.

Second, as populations throughout the Americas mature and their economies develop, their strategic significance grows. As some traditional allies across Europe struggle in their ability to contribute financial and military prowess to international missions, Central and Latin American countries will be in a position to fill some of that void. Preliminary evidence to this end is evidenced by Mexican financial contributions to the reconstruction effort in Haiti as well as Brazil's military leadership in Haiti. Together, these countries will become cognizant that stable countries right across the continent are in their best interest as "pull" factors increase

FIGURE 12
US Population and GDP (in 2005 PPP dollars), as a Percentage of Developed-World Totals (1950–2050)

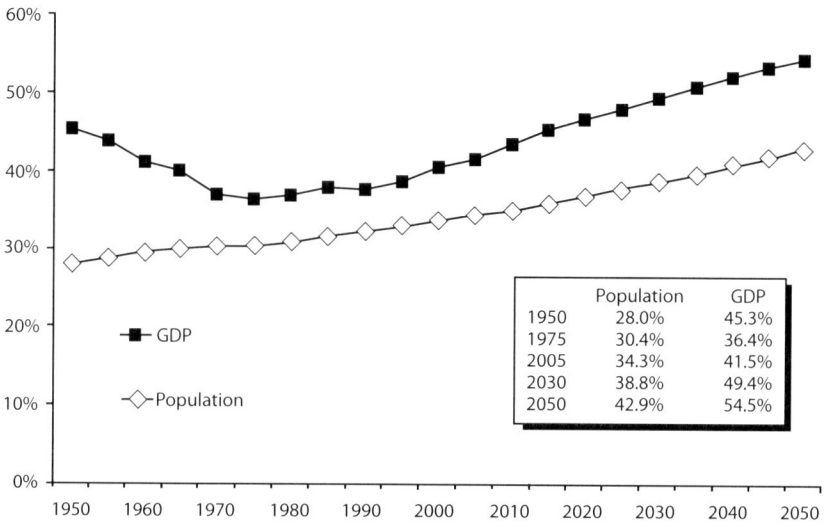

	Population	GDP
1950	28.0%	45.3%
1975	30.4%	36.4%
2005	34.3%	41.5%
2030	38.8%	49.4%
2050	42.9%	54.5%

Source: Cited in Jackson and Howe 2008, 192, Figure 5-5. Reproduced with permission from Jackson and Howe 2008.

with improved economic conditions, and "push" factors such as political instability in Haiti, persist. So, collaboration across the Americas is likely to grow. Yet many countries in the Americas harbour suspicions about US interests and, for political reasons, do not want to be seen as too cozy with the United States. This should provide an interesting opportunity for "middle-power" allies, such as Canada and Australia, to expand their traditional role of honest broker and take on a continental leadership role that should allow it to punch well above its weight.

Third, due to demographic aging, the probability of a major international war continues to diminish. Specifically, the demographic challenges faced by China and Russia make an international military conflict between one of them and North America increasingly unlikely. Haas (2007) refers to this as "a geriatric peace." For the same reason, it is highly improbable that any disputes over the Arctic would ever escalate to the point of a war. Global aging also increases the likelihood of continued peaceful relations between the United States and other great powers. Copeland (2000) and Gilpin (1981) have shown that the probability of international conflict grows when either the dominant country anticipates a power transition in favour of a rising state or states, or when such a transition actually occurs. By adding substantial support to the continuation of US hegemony, global aging counteracts either outcome. Haas (2010) surmises that an aging world thus decreases the probability that either hot or cold wars will develop between the United States and other great powers. Given its geopolitical location, this portends well, especially for Canada.

Fourth, due to youth bulges and echo booms in the arc of sub-Sahara through the Middle East and Asia, the world is likely to become more dangerous and unstable. When troops and reconstruction/development funds are deployed in the service of international security and stability, it will, in all likelihood, be in that part of the world. Where expeditionary, civil-affairs, and psychological-operations capabilities are concerned, allied armed forces ought to start preparing accordingly. Many of the West's immigrants originate in countries from this arc of instability. Given the likelihood of future involvement in the provision of security in this part of the world, diasporas will become increasingly important to mission success (and legitimacy).

Fifth, as apprehensive as countries may be about contributing troops, as situations arise where they deem intervention is in its interest, fewer allies will be in a position to contribute and those countries with more favourable demographic trends such as Canada, Australia, and New Zealand but also the UK, France, the Netherlands, and the Scandinavian countries, should prepare themselves (both at the level of mass psychology and operationally) to take on a greater share of the burden. This is not a normative observation but a sociological one: Among many of the traditional allies, the fiscal and defence capabilities are likely to erode further. So, if a country deems a given situation is in need of intervention, it will have to put its money (and troops) where its mouth is. At the same time, it may be able to mitigate some of that growing burden by providing assistance and collaborating more closely with the rest of the Americas.

Sixth, defence budgets will continue to be strained. Although the strain will be less than that experienced by some of its allies, population aging is bound to marginalize defence spending. So, allied armed forces should not be expecting significant increases in its budget or personnel. As funds become even scarcer than they already are, careful strategic planning will be imperative. For example, given the way international security will be developing, the potential need to deploy tanks is diminishing precipitously. With resources at a premium and the personnel-to-capital expense ratio on the rise, the armed forces cannot afford procurement "errors." For example, at its current 4-to-1 ratio on personnel vis-à-vis capital, the last thing the Canadian Forces will want to do is expand its troop strength. On the contrary, the CF will want to work on diminishing its troop levels to free up money for development and procurement. This will be especially difficult in a tight labour market that will cause the costs for highly qualified personnel to rise significantly. The only way out of this predicament is to curtail the size of the force, focus on education to impart requisite skills, and develop an aggressive plan to substitute capital for labour (or, at an absolute minimum, ensure that personnel costs do not end up consuming even more of the defence budget than they already do).

Seventh, allies will have to minimize sub-optimal outcomes arising from collective action problems. That holds at the international level where, in light of these rising constraints, it will be in their interest to play a major role in international institutions and to make them work as best as it possibly can. That is, the allies must work actively to preserve and enhance soft power. Since the ability for NATO and it member countries to assert themselves on the ground will face mounting financial, personnel, and *matériel* constraints, the allies will have to maximize their returns from international institutions. Similarly, having to make do with less at home means allies will have to harness synergies among domestic institutions and government departments. The "whole-of-government" comprehensive approach *is* the future.

In sum, the opportunities and challenges for national and international security in an aging world are substantial. The aging crisis is less acute in some countries than in others. Where it is less acute, countries have better prospects to shape international security according to their national interests. Still, the magnitude of the costs will be unprecedented (due to the compound effect of diminished overall contributions and expanded demand), as will the constraints they will impose on defence spending.

The more countries sustain their comparative demographic advantage and relatively superior ability to pay for the costs of their elderly population, the more we are likely to see a middle-power renaissance among those allied countries that continue to enjoy fairly favourable demographic developments. It is in the allies' strategic and defence interests to rein in the costs of old-age security and health care as much as possible, minimize the gap between elder-care obligations and resources set aside for them, raise the retirement age, and maintain as open an immigration policy as possible to keep their median age relatively low. Proactive policies that are designed both to take full advantage of the opportunities created by global aging while mitigating the costs created by this phenomenon will enhance international security through the twenty-first century.

NOTES

1. To keep dependency rates of working-age adults to senior citizens at 1995 levels until 2050, for example, France would have to average 1.7 million immigrants per annum, Russia 4.7 million, Germany 3.4 million, and Japan 10 million. These figures vastly exceed historical norms (United Nations 2000, 24, 26).
2. For one possible explanation see Longman (2006).
3. In fact, its pro-natalist policies notwithstanding, Italy's fertility rate is among the lowest in the world at 1.28.

4. The effects of China's one-child policy on median age notwithstanding, in 2008 the Chinese government significantly increased the fines for wealthy couples who violated the law and had more than one child.
5. Demographers are not particularly fond of this term because technically they are not bulges, only a large proportion of the population that is youthful.
6. A 2006 report by the European Defence Agency (2006) makes precisely this point.
7. In 1999, the United States' funded pension assets totaled 84 percent of GDP which is among the highest percentages in the world. Canada's were 55 percent funded. Germany's funded pension assets totaled 7 percent of GDP, and France's 5 percent (Culhane 2001, 14).
8. Only 27 percent of Americans believe that the national government should bear most of their retirement costs; this percentage ranged from 45 (France) to 72 (Spain) in European countries (AgeWave and HarrisInteractive 2009).
9. For the most comprehensive review of the subject with respect to Europe of which I am aware see Grant et al. (2004).

REFERENCES

Anderson, M., ed. 1996. *British Population History: From the Black Death to the Present Day*. Cambridge: Cambridge University Press.

AgeWave and HarrisInteractive. 2009. *Retirement at the Tipping Point: The Year that Changed Everything. A National Study Exploring How Four Generations Think About Retirement*. At http://www.agewave.com/RetirementTippingPoint.pdf (accessed 31 March 2010).

Bloom, D., D. Canning, and J. Sevilla. 2003. *The Demographic Dividend: A New Perspective on the Economic Consequences of Population Change*. Santa Monica, CA: RAND.

Cincotta, R.P., R. Engelman, and D. Anastasion. 2003. *The Security Demographic: Population and Civil Conflict After the Cold War*. Washington, DC: Population Action International.

Commission of the European Communities. 2000. *The Future Evolution of Social Protection from a Long-Term Point of View: Safe and Sustainable Pensions*. A Communication from the Commission to the Council, to the European Parliament and to the Economic and Social Committee, November, Brussels.

Copeland, D.C. 2000. *The Origins of Major War*. Ithaca, NY: Cornell University Press.

Culhane, M.M. 2001. *Global Aging: Capital Market Implications*. New York: Goldman Sachs Strategic Relationship Management Group.

Easterlin, R.A., and E.M. Crimmins. 1985. *The Fertility Revolution: A Supply-Demand Analysis*. Chicago: University of Chicago Press.

Eberstadt, N. 2001. The Population Implosion: Can America Be Saved? *Foreign Policy* 123 (March/April):42-53.

— 2006. Growing Old the Hard Way: China, Russia, India. *Policy Review* 136 (April/May).

— 2009. Drunken Nation: Russia's Depopulation Bomb. *World Affairs* 171 (4):51-62.

Ehrlich, P. 1968. *The Population Bomb*. New York: Ballantine Books.

England, R.S. 2005. *Aging China: The Demographic Challenge to China's Economic Prospects*. Westport, CT: Praeger.

European Commission. 2004. *The Social Situation in the European Union: Overview.* At http://europa.eu.int/comm/employment_social/social_situation/docs/ssr2004_brief_en.pdf (accessed 31 March 2010).

European Defence Agency. 2006. *An Initial Long-Term Vision for European Defence Capability and Capacity Needs.* Brussels: EDA.

Evans, M. 2009. Lethal Genes: The Urban Military Imperative and Western Strategy in the Early Twenty-First Century. *Journal of Strategic Studies* 32 (4):515-552.

Ferguson, N. 2004. The Way We Live Now: 4-4-04; Eurabia? *The New York Times Magazine,* 4 April, p. 13.

Friedman, B. 2005. *The Moral Consequences of Economic Growth.* New York: Alfred Knopf.

Gilpin, R. 1981. *War and Change in World Politics.* Cambridge: Cambridge University Press.

Goldstone, J.A. 2002. Population and Security: How Demographic Change can Lead to Violent Conflict. *Columbia Journal of International Affairs* 56:245-263.

— 2010. The New Population Bomb: The Four Mega-Trends that Will Change the World. *Foreign Affairs* 89 (1):31-43.

Grant, J., S. Hoorens, S. Sivadasan, M. van het Loo, J. DaVanzo, L. Hale, S. Gibson, and W. Butz. 2004. *Low Fertility and Population Aging: Causes, Consequences, and Policy Options.* Santa Monica, CA: Rand Europe for the European Commission.

Gruber, J., and D.A. Wise, eds. 1999. *Social Security and Retirement around the World.* Chicago: National Bureau of Economic Research, The University of Chicago Press.

Gust, C., and J. Marquez. 2000. Productivity Developments Abroad. *Federal Reserve Bulletin* (83). Washington, DC: Federal Reserve System. At http://www.federalreserve.gov/pubs/bulletin/2000/1000lead.pdf (accessed 28 July 2010).

Haas, M.L. 2007. A Geriatric Peace? The Future of US Power in a World of Aging Populations. *International Security* 32 (1):112-147.

— 2010. America's Golden Years? US Security in an Aging World. In *Political Demography: Interests, Conflict, and Institutions,* ed. M. Duffy Toft, J. Goldstone, and E. Kaufmann. New York: Palgrave Macmillan.

Hahn, G.M. 2007. *Russia's Islamic Threat.* New Haven, CT: Yale University Press.

Heinecken, L. 2001. Strategic Implications of HIV/AIDS in South Africa, Conflict, Security and Development. *Conflict, Security, Development* 1 (1):109-115.

Homer-Dixon, T. 1999. *Environment, Scarcity, and Violence.* Princeton, NJ: Princeton University Press.

Howe, N., and R. Jackson. 2004. *The Graying of the Middle Kingdom.* Washington, DC: Centre for Strategic and International Studies.

Huntington, S. 1957. *The Soldier and the State: The Theory and Politics of Civil–Military Relations.* Boston: Belknap Press.

— 2004. *The Challenges to America's National Identity.* New York: Simon and Schuster.

International Institute for Strategic Studies. 2010. *The Military Balance 2010.* London: IISS.

Jackson, R., and N. Howe. 2008. *The Graying of the Great Powers: Demography and Geopolitics in the 21st Century.* Washington, DC: Center for Strategic and International Studies.

Janowitz, M. 1960. *The Professional Soldier: A Social and Political Portrait.* Glencoe, IL: Free Press.

Jingyuan, K. 2002. Implicit Pension Debt and Its Repayment. In *Restructuring China's Social Security System,* ed. M. Wang. Beijing: Foreign Languages Press.

Kahl, C.C. 2006. *States, Scarcity, and Civil Strife in the Developing World.* Princeton, NJ: Princeton University Press.

Kennedy, P. 1994. *Preparing for the Twenty-first Century.* New York: Vintage Books.

Leahy, E., with R. Engelman, C. Gibb Vogel, S. Haddock, and T. Preston. 2007. *The Shape of Things to Come—Why Age Structure Matters To A Safer, More Equitable World.* Washington, DC: Population Action International.

Livi-Bacci, M. 2007. *A Concise History of World Population,* 4th edition. Oxford: Blackwell.

Longman, P. 2004. *The Empty Cradle: How Falling Birthrates Threaten World Prosperity and What to do about it.* New York: Basic Books.

— 2006. The Return of Patriarchy. *Foreign Policy* 153 (March/April):56-65.

Maddison, A. 2007. *Contours of the World Economy 1-2030 AD: Essays in Macro-Economic History.* Oxford: Oxford University Press.

National Intelligence Council (NIC). 2005. *Mapping the Global Future.* Washington, DC.

— 2008. The Demographic Discord. In *Global Trends 2025: A Transformed World,* chapter 2, 18-26. Washington, DC: National Intelligence Council.

Nichiporuk, B. 2000. *The Security Dynamics of Demographic Factors.* Document MR-1088-WFHF/RF/DLPF/A. Santa Monica, CA: RAND Corporation.

Nye, J.S. Jr. 2004. *Soft Power: The Means to Success in World Politics.* Online: Public Affairs.

Organisation for Economic Co-operation and Development (OECD). 1999. *Health Data 1999, A Comparative Analysis of 29 Countries.* Paris: OECD.

— 2000a. *OECD Economic Outlook, No. 67* (June). Paris: OECD.

— 2000b. *OECD Economic Outlook, No. 68* (December). Paris: OECD.

— 2000c. *Social Expenditure Database.* Paris: OECD.

— 2009a. *Demographic and Labour Force Database, Society at a Glance: OECD Social Indicators 2009.* Paris: OECD.

— 2009b. *OECD Health Data 2009.* At http://stats.oecd.org/Index.aspx?DataSetCode=HEALTH (accessed 29 July 2010).

People's Republic of China. 2004. Chapter IV: Defense Expenditure and Defense Assets. *White Paper on National Defense.* At http://www.fas.org/nuke/guide/china/doctrine/natdef2004.html (accessed 31 March 2010).

Posen, B.R. 2003. Command of the Commons: The Military Foundation of U.S. Hegemony. *International Security* 28 (1):5-46.

Qiao, H. 2006. *Will China Grow Old Before Getting Rich?* Global Economic Paper No. 138. New York: Goldman Sachs Economic Research Group.

Roseveare, D., W. Leibfritz, D. Fore, and E. Wurzel. 1996. *Ageing Populations, Pension Systems and Government Budgets: Simulations for 20 OECD Countries.* Working Paper No. 168. Paris: OECD Economics Department.

Steyn, M. 2006. *America Alone: The End of the World as We Know It.* Washington, DC: Regnery Publishing.

Taw, J.M., and B. Hoffman. 1994. *The Urbanization of Insurgency: The Potential Challenge for U.S. Army Operations.* Rand Monograph Report-398-A, chapter 2, 7-15. Santa Monica, CA: RAND.

Teitelbaum, M.S., and J. Winter. 1998. *A Question of Numbers: High Migration, Low Fertility, and the Politics of National Identity.* New York: Hill and Wang.

United Nations. 2000. *Replacement Migration: Is it a Solution to Declining and Ageing Populations?* Population Division, 20 March.

— 2007. *2007 Population Prospects*. Department of Economic and Social Affairs, Population Division. At http://www.un.org/esa/population/ (accessed 28 July 2010).

— 2008. *World Population Prospects: The 2008 Revision Population Database*.

United Nations Secretariat. Population Division. 2008. *World Urbanization Prospects: The 2007 Revision Population Database.* At http://esa.un.org/unup (accessed 31 March 2010).

US Census Bureau (USCB). 2010. International Data Base. At http://www.census.gov/ipc/www/idb/ (accessed 14 July 2010).

Urdal, H. 2006. A Clash of Generations? Youth Bulges and Political Violence. *International Studies Quarterly* 50 (3):607-630.

— 2007. The Demographics of Political Violence: Youth Bulges, Insecurity and Conflict. In *Too Poor for Peace? Global Poverty, Conflict and Security in the 21st Century*, ed. L. Brainard and D. Chollet, 90-100. Washington, DC: Brookings Institution Press.

Weigel, G. 2005. *The Cube and the Cathedral: Europe, America, and Politics without God.* New York: Basic Books.

ACCOMMODATING COMPLEXITY IN NEW OPERATIONS

SARAH JANE MEHARG AND KRISTINE ST-PIERRE

The evolution of peace operations—and the environment in which they occur—is neither straightforward nor linear. Systems are interconnected in ways that were previously unfamiliar causing actors to rethink the ways in which they intervene, as well as the environment in which they are intervening. New security threats require a corresponding shift in approaches that reflect the complexity of the reality on the ground. While there is evidence that complexity is being accommodated into policy and guidance at both the strategic and operational level, approaches vary both in the way they manage complexity and in their ability to do so.

This chapter explores the complex environment of peace operations and offers a typology of specific approaches that have emerged to better manage complexity and increase the effectiveness of interventions. The chapter discusses the commonalities among approaches and concludes with a set of recommendations for working more effectively with complexity.

INTRODUCTION

Peace operations are constantly evolving and adapting to the challenges of new security environments. This ongoing evolution, however, is neither straightforward nor linear (Bellamy, Williams and Griffin 2004). Since the first "blue helmets" were deployed in 1956, the concept of peacekeeping has changed dramatically. Originally, it referred to the interposition of a neutral force between parties in conflict to stop or contain hostilities, support a ceasefire, or supervise the implementation of a peace agreement

Mission Critical: Smaller Democracies' Role in Global Stability Operations, ed. C. Leuprecht, J. Troy, and D. Last. Montreal and Kingston: Queen's Policy Studies Series, McGill-Queen's University Press. © 2010 Queen's Centre for International Relations, Queen's University at Kingston. All rights reserved.

(UN 1992). While traditional peacekeeping is far from obsolete, the concept is constantly evolving as a result of changes within the peace and security environment.

Since the conflicts of the 1990s in places such as Bosnia-Herzegovina, Sierra Leone and Rwanda, mechanisms of peace operations have been compelled to change and adapt to new environments at an unprecedented rate. These "new" operations—referred to in the literature as "peace operations," "complex peace operations," and "contemporary peace operations"[1]—are defined as the range of operations conducted by the international community and encompass all types of operations short of counterinsurgencies and war, including traditional peacekeeping, peace enforcement, reconstruction and stabilization operations. They are multidimensional, multifaceted, and multifunctional involving a range of actors and covering multiple sectors (St-Pierre 2008). They are also understood as more comprehensive and more reflective of the context in which operations are being undertaken.

Peace operations are not an end in itself; they are a strategic tool for achieving an identified goal (Gowan and Johnstone 2007, 3; and Jones 2006, ix). Peace operations should be viewed in the context of a continuum of crisis management, extending from prevention of conflicts through conflict management and sustainable peace. As part of this continuum, peace operations should be dynamic and flexible; they should be able to adapt to changing and/or unforeseen circumstances and should allow for the optimal response for a specific situation. At the same time, peace operations should also demonstrate a degree of coherence in their planning and management, as well as clearly defined guidelines. Striking a balance between these challenges remains daunting.

In this chapter, the notion of complexity is applied to the *context* of operations, rather than the *nature* of the operations themselves.[2] The complexity of the environment in which peace operations are conducted has motivated the international community to be more flexible and to come up with innovative approaches that reflect the multiple interconnected elements that make up different conflict environments.[3] There is no agreed upon model of peace operations that can be universally applied in any context, yet, to avoid ad hoc planning and management of operations, there are universal tenets that inform all international operations. These tenets are the consent of the parties involved, impartiality, and non-use of force except in self-defence and defence of the mandate (UN DPKO/DFS 2008). To further contribute to the effectiveness of operations, multilateral interventions are now influenced by the principles of contemporary interventions that include legitimacy, credibility, and national and local ownership (ibid.). These add an additional layer of standardization to peacekeeping and illustrate an interest in the *quality* of interventions, which can further improve effectiveness. In practical terms, therefore, it becomes critical that stakeholders understand the environment in which they operate to both ensure that they adhere to these principles and that they advance the effectiveness of operations.

This chapter begins by exploring complex systems and the environment of peace operations. The chapter then presents a typology of specific approaches that have emerged to manage complexity and increase the effectiveness of interventions. The chapter goes on to discuss the commonalities among approaches and conditions under which specific aspects of complexity are ignored. The conclusion presents a set of recommendations for working more effectively with complexity.

UNDERSTANDING COMPLEX SYSTEMS

> From time immemorial, man has tried to make sense of the enormous complexity and frequent unpredictability of human behaviour. A multitude of systems have been constructed to try to make that which is incomprehensible comprehensible. To "make sense" has ordinarily meant to be definable in terms that are linear—logical and rational. But the process, and therefore the experience, of life itself, is organic—that is to say, nonlinear by definition. This is the source of man's inescapable intellectual frustration. (Hawkins 2002, 53)

Peace operations constitute a major mechanism of the international community and their evolution can be understood as a response to the complex environment into which they are deployed.

According to Robert Jervis, a system is a set of units or elements that are interconnected in a way that changes in one part of the system produce non-linear changes in other parts of the system (1997; and Snyder and Jervis 1993).[4] In other words, changes or disruptions cannot occur without affecting other parts of the system (Cilliers 1998; and Aoi, de Coning and Thakur 2007). In addition, the properties and behaviour of the system as a whole are different than those of its parts. Therefore, in order to understand the system in its entirety, it is imperative that we study not only the individual parts, but the relationships and interconnections among them.

Many analogies have been devised to describe this environment. Perhaps the most useful is Joseph Nye's "three dimensional chessboard" in which the bottom board—representative of transnational power—is influenced by a myriad of factors that cannot be easily influenced or controlled in the aftermath of violent contemporary armed conflicts (2009). These factors include continued hostilities, corrupt opportunism, political upheaval, ethnic divisions, insurgencies, transnational terrorism, intelligence community agendas, mass exploitation, pandemics, climate change, drug and human trafficking, etc. Nye is suggesting that complex systems cannot be calculated simply when we aim to mitigate violence and instability through interventions. In such environments, measuring merely offers stakeholders the illusion of control over their actions and impacts (Meharg 2009, 260).

As peace operations are intended to manage change within a specific environment, they are not neutral in their effects, causing both "intended" and "unintended" consequences (Aoi, de Coning and Thakur 2007). Unintended consequences in peace operations are outcome(s), both negative and/or positive, that were not anticipated during the mission planning process. While it is impossible to fully understand all the inter-actions and behaviours of complex systems (Jervis 1997), the international community through a process of trial and error is beginning to identify and understand the impact of unintended consequences (both positive and negative) of peace operations. Similarly, the international community is moving beyond linear relationships—where a cause is directly related to an effect—towards non-linear, more complex, approaches that better reflect the reality on the ground.

Peace operations have been under intense scrutiny since the early 1990s. Collectively, our awareness of the complexity of the environment into which peace operations are deployed has greatly increased. In earlier days of peacekeeping, the environment was thought to be quite simple, even easy to navigate. Many mechanisms and tools tend to oversimplify complex human conditions thereby promoting a false sense of overconfi-dence in the efficacy of international interventions (Meharg 2009, 124). In such an environment of change and complexity, mechanisms that worked well with yesterday's reality may not be as relevant and useful in today's environments (ibid., 13). It is only understandable that as our awareness grows, we adapt our interventions in order to be able to better manage the complex environment.

Accommodating complexity in new operations

While all operations face the fundamental challenge of establishing a secure and safe environment, operations will differ in the way security is sought and achieved (St-Pierre 2008). As a response to the increasingly complex environment in which missions are deployed and to the lack of confidence in UN peacekeeping missions, numerous approaches to establishing security and to rebuilding states affected by conflict have emerged over the years. These approaches also reflect the pressing need to better integrate communications, coordination and cooperation within operational environments, and to ensure utmost sophistication in plan-ning and management in order to achieve positive results.

The literature identifies 10 approaches, which have been practiced by various actors at the strategic level and operationalized in the field. They are:

1. 3D
2. Whole-of-Government
3. Joined-up

4.   Interagency
5.   Comprehensive
6.   Integrated Missions
7.   Hybrid/Joint Operations
8.   Provincial Reconstruction Teams
9.   Clusters
10. One UN

The following section examines each approach on the basis of their level of integration and objectives (see Table 1). For clarity, the approaches are divided into two categories: (i) Strategic-level approaches; and (ii) Operational-level approaches. It is important to note that variations exist within each approach. Each approach is also examined in terms of its strengths and weaknesses and the opportunities and/or risks it presents. This typology allows for a preliminary analysis of the way in which approaches have, to date, succeeded or failed in coping with complexity, and of the environment in which the approaches could be most adequate or useful. As societies and post-conflict environments differ tremendously, it seems perhaps futile to attempt to identify patterns that can be replicable or applied elsewhere. However, by understanding these approaches and their method, we can better prepare policy-makers and mission planners to anticipate possible outcomes and to develop adequate policies and mission structures.

Strategic-level approaches

3D

The 3D approach[5] brings together the three dominant departments of government: defence, diplomacy, and development, in recognition of the interdependency between each dimension. Security enables development, effective governance enhances security, and development creates opportunities and multiplies the reward of improved security and good governance (Jorgensen 2008). The approach aims to improve the synchronization of efforts in the field by providing countries with a mechanism through which departments can share information and resources (Independent Panel 2008).

First introduced by Canada, the descriptor "3D" is often used interchangeably to describe an integrated, whole-of-government and/or comprehensive approach. While these approaches all seek to improve collective efficiencies and effectiveness, they should not be confounded, as each present distinct characteristics from one another. In many ways, the 3D approach is seen as the precursor to more encompassing and integrated approaches.

TABLE 1
Levels of Integration and Objectives of Current Approaches

	Approaches	Level of Integration	Main Objective(s)
Strategic-level approaches	3D	• National governmental department level (strategic) as well as field-level (tactical); • Collocation and sharing of information between defence, diplomacy and development.	• Synchronization of specific national governmental policy efforts in an international intervention, such as Afghanistan or Haiti.
	Whole-of-Government (WoG)	• National governmental department level (strategic) as well as field-level (tactical); • Collocation and sharing of information among a broad spectrum of governmental stakeholders, including Justice, Police, and Health.	• A total government effort, in which staff, resources and material are coordinated towards achieving a national objective in an international intervention.
	Joined-up	• National governmental department level (strategic, operational, tactical); • Specific to the UK government (Foreign and Commonwealth Office [FCO], Department for International Development [DFID], the Ministry of Defence [MOD], and periodically, the Home Office); across the safety and justice sector in the country receiving assistance; and across donor and development agencies.	• To manage international intervention activities in complex environments; and • a shared and overarching vision and goals inform interlinked, objective-based sector strategies within the government.
	Interagency	• National governmental department level (strategic); • Specific to the United States government (The Department of Defense [DoD], Central Intelligence Agency [CIA], Department of State [DoS], Federal Bureau of Investigation [FBI], the Department of Homeland Security [DHS], and others).	• Untangle lines of authority; • de-conflict overlapping roles and responsibilities; and • improve strategic coordination in a timely and efficient manner.
	Comprehensive	• UN • Regional organizations (NATO) • National level	• Planned application and coordination of specialized capacities of stakeholders; and • enhance coherence, efficiency, sustainability and legitimacy of operations and their outcomes.

TABLE 1
(Continued)

	Approaches	Level of Integration	Main Objective(s)
Operational-level approaches	Integrated Missions	• Integrate overall UN mission planning structures and functions (military, political/developmental and humanitarian)	• Enhance efficiency of UN response; and • ensure smooth transition from peacekeeping to peacebuilding.
	Hybrid/ Joint Operations	• Between UN and other stake-holders (including regional organizations, multinational forces, and individual states)	• Enhance efficiency of overall response; • rely on comparative advantage of actors; and • burden-sharing.
	Provincial Reconstruction Teams (PRTs)	• Between military and civilian elements of an intervention	• Enhance efficiency of reconstruction efforts; • ensure coherent responses to problems; and • rely on relative strengths of military and civilian elements.
	Clusters	• United Nations, Red Cross Movement and other NGOs, country level	• Improve leadership, accountability, predictability, timeliness, and effectiveness of humanitarian response; • strengthen "collaborative responses" through predictable and accountable leadership; and • enhance partnerships and complementarity.
	One UN	• United Nations agencies, country level	• Enhance coherence through one leader, one program, one budget, and where appropriate, one office; • cut costs and focus the delivery of programs; and • enhance cooperation among UN agencies.

Source: Authors' compilation.

The 3D approach is sometimes viewed as being "too narrow in its logic and mode of application" (Cooper 2005, vii). For one, the approach is viewed as limiting as it only includes a handful of the many departments and agencies that often contribute to an intervention. Despite contributing very real and practical assistance to international interventions, non-governmental agencies, non-state actors, and the private sector are also excluded from this framework. The approach also requires a high degree of collaboration among departments, which is often restricted by the departments' different mandates, operating procedures and bureau-cratic cultures (ibid.). Departments often portray different perspectives as to their roles with regards to international policies.

Another concern stems from the uneven representation between the actors in the field; the defence "D" tends to dominate all other agendas (Olson and Gregorian 2007). The emphasis on defence has further com-plicated the dialogue concerning the politicization and militarization of humanitarian aid and assistance, traditionally the remit of humanitarian agencies acting within the humanitarian space. More specifically, some accuse military forces of employing their aid and assistance resources to ensure their own security amidst a potentially hostile population and achieve their own security agenda. The main complaint among the humanitarian sector is that the military and defence sector is unaware of the principles governing humanitarian space and pays no heed to the unintended negative consequences of their presence and activities (Meharg 2007).

The evidence surrounding the failures of 3D efforts in Afghanistan often point to what is seen as a "weak and ineffectual" development "D" and the unwillingness of humanitarian agencies to cooperate with defence actors (Cornish 2008). However, the failure of these efforts may in fact lie in the model itself; the focus on the integration of defence, diplomacy and development functions—rather than on keeping them separate—is proving to be counterproductive for the development gains required to secure stability (CCIC 2007, 4; and Meharg 2007).

Whole-of-government

A whole-of-government (WoG) approach implies an all-inclusive govern-ment effort, in which staff, resources and material are coordinated towards achieving a national objective in an international intervention (DFAIT 2010; and Jorgensen 2008). The WoG goes beyond the 3D approach by being inclusive of all governmental departments and agencies fulfilling national interests in complex interventions primarily through focusing all available tools and resources of intervention in its defined geograph-ical area of responsibility. This approach is being used by Canada and Australia, with more recent applications by Sweden, the Netherlands, and Norway (de Coning and Friis 2008).

While most of the literature on whole-of-government includes only the three major areas of defence, diplomacy, and development, the term implies the recognition of the need to include other governmental sectors such as police, justice (courts), corrections (penitentiaries), health, edu-cation, and public safety, among others. Each embodies intervention at different scales and levels, nationally and internationally (Meharg 2009).

Among governments who employ the WoG approach, there is a gen-eral understanding that it is more effective than the more isolationist silo approach to operations when dealing with post-conflict states (Roberts 2008; and Jorgensen 2008). Although the WoG approach emphasizes horizontal assessment, planning, implementation and evaluation, recent experiences in Afghanistan demonstrate that while the WoG approach is highly practical at the tactical level—field realities ensure that synchronization of efforts is more practical than not—it is not as easily managed at the strategic level within various national departments. Government departments contributing to the same international intervention project have very different objectives to meet, and this can impact the ways in which approaches are formalized (Higginbotham in Meharg 2009, 223).[6] Although partners in the whole-of-government approach, each seeks to get something different out of each project they are collectively involved in. Time and effort must be invested in order for different government agencies to harmonize their policies and actions.

As with the 3D approach, critics also point to the WoG's focus on defence at the expense of other government departments and warn against the increasing militarization of humanitarian and development assistance, especially in Afghanistan (CCIC 2007). In addition, some practitioners have questioned the approach's ability or willingness to take into account the needs and requirements of the host country (Friis and Jamyr 2008).

Joined-up

Recognizing that a fragmented or isolationist approach is not sustainable over the long run for the host nation involved, the United Kingdom (UK) has adopted a *joined-up* approach for managing international intervention activities in complex environments. Such "joining up" is intended to take place at three levels: across UK government departments (Foreign and Commonwealth Office [FCO], Department for International Development [DFID], the Ministry of Defence [MOD], and periodically, the Home Office); across the safety and justice sectors in the country receiving assistance; and across donor and development agencies (FCO 2009).[7]

The UK has pioneered an inter-ministerial pooling approach—also known as "joined-up government"—in the field of conflict management, which essentially puts the government in a position to exercise authority across multiple institutions (Klotzle 2006; and UK 2003). The central achievement of this approach is the establishment of the *Global Conflict Prevention Pool* and the *Africa Conflict Prevention Pool* in 2001. These *Conflict Prevention Pools* integrate the expertise of the DFID, the MOD, and the FCO and provide pooled funding for joint initiatives to promote security, development, and good governance in states threatened or affected by violent conflict (Klotzle 2006). Nevertheless, departments' conflicting mandates and cultures has led to a lack of consensus on common priorities and on ways of achieving them (de Coning et al. 2009).

Interagency

The *interagency approach* is a US term describing the process through which the Department of Defense (DoD), Central Intelligence Agency (CIA), Department of State (DoS), Federal Bureau of Investigation (FBI), the Department of Homeland Security (DHS), and others, work to untangle lines of authority, de-conflict overlapping roles and responsibilities, and improve coordination in a timely and efficient manner (Krawchuk 2005). The interagency approach encourages departments and agencies to reach across bureaucratic territorial schisms and share resources, and to organize themselves for maximum efficiency and information sharing with the ability to function quickly under new operational definitions. The US interagency approach to intervention requires new systems, procedures and programs that underpin coordination among departments and which facilitate and institutionalize interagency roles and responsibilities.

There has been more resistance against the interagency approach in the United States government than with the whole-of-government or joined-up approaches in Australia, the UK, and Canada. The US departments and agencies are much more rigidly entrenched in their traditional roles and responsibilities (and territorial claims) than their other national counterparts; moreover, their departments and agencies are more fully resourced than Australian, British or Canadian equivalents. In these other nations, teaming up has become more of a necessity due to limited resources and more focused goals in areas of operation.

Comprehensive

According to Karsten Friis and Pia Jamyr, researchers at the Norwegian Institute of International Affairs (NUPI), "the comprehensive approach concept should be understood in the context of an increasingly complex and interdependent international conflict management system" (Friis and Jamyr 2008, 2). NATO, the EU, the US and Canada understand *comprehensive* as distinct from 3D, whole-of-government, joined-up, and interagency approaches to operations.[8] The comprehensive approach is the planned application and coordination of specialized capacities of stakeholders—in various autonomous, yet hinged, sectors—to a complex environment through a coherent, efficient, sustainable and legitimate agenda of activities, outcomes and intended impacts to underpin long-term peace and security (Meharg 2009, 229). In plain terms, because crisis environments are so complex, it takes a spectrum of efforts, a concert of actors, and diverse capacities to achieve international peace and security goals.

The comprehensive approach is underpinned by a complete understanding of who is doing what, when, how, to what ends, with what means, and to what effects, outcomes, or impacts. This approach permits the mapping of the entire spectrum of sectors, stakeholders and activities in a certain operational area. The rationale underpinning the comprehensive approach is that by understanding who and what is occurring in an operational space, duplication of efforts are decreased and competencies are enhanced. The comprehensive approach can be applied through a purely national governmental lens (i.e., mapping out only Canada's activities and actors in an operational environment) as well as through an international lens (i.e., mapping out all activities and actors in an operational environment).

The fact that coordination occurs at the strategic level not only allows for greater flexibility, but also enables greater freedom of action on the part of actors (Friis and Jamyr 2008). This independence allows for coordination to occur with more actors. In fact, humanitarian and non-governmental stakeholders support the comprehensive approach because it allows for increased freedom of action and independence, which is representative of their intervention world views. The approach, however, runs the risk of un-coordination in the field, as actors will engage according to their own principles, mandates and resources (ibid.). As coordination occurs only at the strategic level, the approach is unlikely to generate the level of coherence witnessed as part of an integration approach.

Many in the NGO community also reject civil-military integration as combining incompatible goals and rejects its "ultimate ends" logic, with the long term benefits of peace and protection arrived at by sacrificing the emergency protection and assistance needs of large segments of the population (Olson and Gregorian 2007).

Operational-level approaches

Integrated missions

In seeking greater coherence in its approach to mission planning, the UN developed the concept of integrated missions with an Integrated Mission Planning Process (IMPP), which defines the steps towards ensuring integration at all levels of mission planning. Commissioned by the UN Executive Committee for Humanitarian Affairs, the *Report on Integrated Missions: Practical Perspectives and Recommendations* defines "integrated mission" as:

> an instrument with which the UN seeks to help countries in the transition from war to lasting peace, or to address a similarly complex situation that requires a system-wide UN response, through subsuming actors and approaches within an overall political-strategic crisis management framework. (Eide et al. 2005, 3)

The objective of integrated missions is "to bring the UN's resources and activities closer together and ensure that they are applied in a coherent way across the political, military, developmental and humanitarian sectors" and it is based, in part, on the recognition that more coherent approaches to conflict resolution are needed to manage the transition from war to peace (ibid.). It is also based on the assumption that the integration of mission planning and management processes will enhance efficiency (Gordon 2006, 50). As integration can take many forms and can occur at many levels, the concept continues to evolve. Table 2 identifies levels of integration in current UN peace operations and their respective characteristics. Four levels of integration can be identified: full integration, partial integration, limited integration and no integration.

TABLE 2
Levels of Integration of Current UN Peace Operations

Level of Integration	Characteristics	Examples[a]
Full Integration	• Post-conflict situation • No large-scale humanitarian emergency • Political missions • No separate OCHA office	• UNAMA (Afghanistan) • BINUB (Burundi) • MINUSTAH (Haiti) • UNAMI (Iraq) • UNMIL (Liberia)
Partial Integration	• UN Humanitarian Coordinator (HC) located within mission • HC acts as DSRSG and reports directly to SRSG • Separate OCHA office outside of mission	• UNOCI (Côte d'Ivoire) • MONUC (DRC) • UNIOSIL (Sierra Leone) • UNMIS (Sudan) • UNMIT (Timor Leste)
Limited Integration	• HC is separate from mission	• MINURCAT (Chad-CAR) • UNAMID (Darfur) • UNMIK (Kosovo)
No Integration[b]	• Chapter VI mandate • Limited civilian component • Limited humanitarian component • Separate and independent humanitarian component	• UNFICYP (Cyprus) • UNMEE (Ethiopia-Eritrea) • UNOMIG (Georgia) • UNDOF (Golan Heights) • UNMOGIP (India-Pakistan) • UNIFIL (Lebanon)[c] • UNTSO (Middle East) • UNRWA (Middle East)[d] • MINURSO (Western Sahara)

[a] Examples include all UN peacekeeping and political missions administered under the DPKO in addition to the UN political mission in Iraq (UNAMI) and the UN Relief and Works Agency for Palestine Refugees in the Near East (UNRWA).
[b] All non-integrated missions, except the mission in Lebanon, were created before the IMPP was developed.
[c] The mission in Lebanon is an exception, as it has a Chapter VII mandate, but the peacekeeping and humanitarian components as well as the military and civilian components remain separate.
[d] UNRWA, created on 8 December 1949 by UN General Assembly resolution 302 (IV), is not a UN peacekeeping mission per se, but it was created to protect and assist Palestinian refugees after the 1948 Arab-Israeli war.

Source: Reproduced with permission from St-Pierre 2008, 15. Based on Eide et al. 2005; ODI 2007; and Weir 2006.

An integrated mission approach means that the UN Humanitarian Coordinator (of the UN Office for Coordination of Humanitarian Affairs), which has traditionally remained outside of peacekeeping mission structures, is fully integrated within the mission structure (often taking on the role of a Deputy Special Representative of the Secretary General (SRSG)) and reports directly to the SRSG (ibid.). In such cases, the SRSG thus oversees the political, military, and humanitarian strategies. While this model appears to be preferred by practitioners in the field, it is not always feasible (ODI 2007). In a partial integrated mission approach, UN Office for the Coordination of Humanitarian Affairs (OCHA) retains its separate identity and as a result, the focus of integration concentrates more on coordination and information sharing. United Nations missions that are not considered to be integrated are missions that, in most cases, operate under a Chapter VI mandate and comprise a limited civilian component.

While the approach has the potential to generate cohesive and concerted action by the UN, there is a risk that the level of effort required for internal coordination can result in less attention being spent on coordination with local actors (Friis and Jamyr 2008). It is thus important to recognize that integration may not always be *feasible* or even *desirable*, and that not all elements of a mission need to be integrated at all times; the need for integration should derive from the goals that are to be achieved and from the inherent benefits of integration in the specific case being considered (ISS Today 2007). At the same time, however, analysis suggests that integration is most successful when implemented in the planning stage of a mission rather than after a mission has begun. This is particularly relevant in missions where there is both a major military and major humanitarian component operating side-by-side.

Hybrid/joint operations

Hybrid operations distinguish how the UN as an organization functions with other organizations. Hybrid operations are those in which UN and non-UN forces share—following different frameworks—peacekeeping or peace enforcement responsibilities (Jones and Cherif 2004; and St-Pierre 2007).[9] In a 2004 report prepared for the United Nations Department of Peacekeeping Operations Best Practices Unit, Jones and Cherif identified four types of hybrid frameworks: integrated, coordinated, parallel and sequential. Each type exhibits a different level of integration between the UN and non-UN components. Further differentiation can be made by looking at the nature of the non-UN component, i.e., whether it is a regional organization, multinational force or individual state (ibid.). Table 3 provides an overview of the four hybrid frameworks with examples of specific deployments.

TABLE 3
Hybrid Operations: Characteristics and Examples

Types of Hybrid Frameworks	Characteristics	Examples
Integrated	UN and non-UN actors operate with single or joined chain of command	• Darfur (UN and AU, NATO, EU)
Coordinated	UN and non-UN actors are coordinated but operate under different chains of command	• Kosovo (UN, NATO, EU) • Chad (UN, EU)
Parallel	UN deploys alongside other organizations; no formal coordination	• Afghanistan (UN, NATO, EU) • DRC (UN, EU) • Iraq (UN, NATO, EU)
Sequential	UN precedes or follows other forces	• Côte d'Ivoire (UN, France/EU) • DRC (UN, EU) • Haiti (UN, Coalition) • Sierra Leone (UN, UK)

In a more recent article, Jones further categorizes hybrid operations based on the formal relationship between organizations: short-term military support; civilian-military division of labour; linked peacekeeping-observer operations; handover operations; and integrated operations. He warns, however, that such categorization "obscures more than it reveals" (Jones 2007, 6-7).

Source: Reproduced with permission from St-Pierre 2008, 17. Based on Jones and Cherif 2004; and St-Pierre 2007, 4.

Hybrid operations constitute attractive options for the future as they combine UN legitimacy with regional capability (CIC 2006; and Gowan and Johnstone 2007). Hybrid and joint operations portray a number of strengths. For one, they can allow for a rapid and effective response by encouraging partnerships and helping to facilitate the mobilization of resources (Guéhenno 2008). Regional actors in hybrid operations can also ease UN responsibilities by taking on some, or all, peacekeeping and peace enforcement tasks, reinforce a UN mission at short notice, for example, during elections or if violence breaks out, and provide the UN with more time to prepare for a mission by deploying in advance of the UN force (Durch and Berckman 2006; Jones and Cherif 2004; CIC 2006).

Given the increasing pressure for better-developed inter-institutional arrangements, the UN has undertaken new institutional agreements with both the European Union and African Union (Andrews and Holt 2007). These developments demonstrate the UN's adaptability to the substantive changes in complex conflicts and point to the growing flexibility with which the UN and the international community can respond to crises, due in part to the growing number of actors that the UN can rely on (St-Pierre 2007). Nevertheless, while the approach seeks to build on the comparative advantage of each partner, different perspectives and criteria for taking action must often be reconciled.

Hybrid operations can face the same major impediments to their success as other types of operations including a lack of resources and adequate infrastructure, inadequate security conditions to allow deployment, and, perhaps most importantly, lack of political will by member states (GA 2009). True hybrid operations, such as UNAMID, also face the added challenge of command and control, where communication and coordination becomes crucial components of the successful functioning of an operation. The combination of lack of processes and procedures with a lack of political will and resources can thoroughly undermine effective and rapid action.

Provincial reconstruction teams

The Provincial Reconstruction Team (PRT) concept is a relatively new approach to peace operations. Broadly understood, a PRT is a joint civilian and military structure that was first introduced in 2002 as part of the US plan for transitioning from war-fighting to "stabilization and reconstruction" operations (Gordon 2006). The US Department of State defines the PRT concept as "a civilian-military inter-agency effort that is the primary interface between US and Coalition partners and provincial and local governments" (US Department of State 2007). More specifically, PRTs are seen as "an important tool in achieving [US] counterinsurgency strategy by bolstering moderates, promoting reconciliation, fostering economic development and building provincial capacity." Examples include projects that help the local population rebuild damaged transportation routes, infrastructure, and wells (US Department of State 2006).

Increasingly, PRTs are seen as the practical application of the intervening actor's national strategy for undertaking international interventions. For example, Canada's PRT in Afghanistan is viewed as the operationalization in the field of its whole-of-government strategy at home.

In general, PRTs have a standard core structure comprised of a headquarters, civil-military (CIMIC) sections, logistics, military observers, civilian reconstruction personnel, and support capabilities such as security, logistic engineers and interpreters (Gordon 2006, 46). Given their joint civilian and military structure, PRTs are multi-agency, benefiting from the combined presence of experts from various departments and agencies (de Coning et al. 2009). PRTs are also multi-national, combining a mix of national and international personnel. Their overall aim can be divided into three core functions: (i) improve governance; (ii) administer reconstruction projects; and (iii) enhance security. Table 4 identifies PRT core functions and objectives, and provides a list of strategies that are used in achieving these objectives.

TABLE 4
PRT Core Functions, Objectives and Strategies

Core Functions	Objectives	Strategies
Governance	• Extend authority of central government at local and provincial levels	• Maintain close links with central government • Build leadership and institutional capacity at local and provincial levels • Provide technical and organizational support
Reconstruction	• Undertake development projects (economic and health infrastructures)	• Deliver reconstruction and humanitarian assistance in remote and/or insecure areas • Coordinate with UN political mission and agencies, international associations, and NGOs
Security	• Enhance security through force protection	• Support security sector • Quick-impact projects (QIPs) (to win "hearts and minds") • Effects-Based Operations • Active patrolling • CIMIC community-level activities • Information-sharing

Source: Reproduced with permission from St-Pierre 2008, 19. See also Gordon 2006; Drolet 2006; Perito 2007; and Office of the Coordinator for Reconstruction and Stabilization (S/CRS) et al. 2006.

PRTs also operate in a variety of environments with specific security challenges, and as a result, they are often tailored to the area in which they operate. PRTs vary based on the different approaches, perspectives, and *modus operandi* of the nations involved in the PRT. Personality and nationality of commanders also play a role, as do policy priorities and national security and reconstruction agendas of contributing countries. PRTs also diverge in size and composition, in the impact of force protection measures, and in the balance between protection and reconstruction efforts in the relative autonomy of the civilian components of the PRT (Gordon 2006, 46). The division between the military and civilian component of a PRT also differs. While PRTs are defined as a mix of military and civilian units, they are for the most part commanded by military officers and the military component is often much larger (Stephenson 2007). Still, the ratio of military to civilian changes with each PRT, and civilian units are, on the whole, increasing (Buchann 2007).

The emergence of PRTs not only complicates the discourse on humanitarian space, but also adds to the debates regarding the role and function of military personnel, humanitarians, development objectives and diplomatic/political initiatives. The situation in Iraq, as in Afghanistan, is one in which peacebuilding and reconstruction efforts are pitted against counter-insurgency and stabilization operations. While PRTs have the ability to operate in insecure areas and deliver critical reconstruction and humanitarian assistance where non-governmental organizations cannot, the simultaneous support to combat operations and provision of assistance effectively blurs the distinction between humanitarian and politico-military responses (Gordon 2006). Many practitioners, including humanitarian non-governmental organizations (NGOs), have criticized the application of the PRT concept on the basis that it militarizes humanitarian assistance, effectively jeopardizing both the short- and long-term goals of assistance (Shevlin 2007, 12; and Wheeler and Harmer 2006). There is also much concern with aid being used for military objectives and the increased targeting of both PRTs and humanitarians (CCIC 2007). As Brandsma explains, "[t]here is a possibility of PRTs eclipsing the achievements of NGOs in winning the hearts and minds of the people, as a result of blurring the lines between aid and military" (2007, 13). However, because there have been very few objective evaluations of the performance of PRTs and their impact on humanitarian operations, the effectiveness of this approach remains a matter of debate (Gordon 2006).

There has been much debate in recent years about the performance of PRTs and the feasibility and practicality of "exporting" the PRT concept to post-conflict environments, other than Afghanistan. One important lesson arising from Canada's PRT experience in Kandahar is the need for each PRT to be designed based upon local circumstances in terms of mandate, composition, command and control relationships, resources, and activities (DND 2007, 27). Another lesson is the need for integrated training prior to deployment of the PRT team, to ensure greater cohesion and more coordinated responses in the field (ibid.).

Clusters

The 2005 Secretary-General's report *Strengthening of the coordination of emergency humanitarian assistance of the United Nations* and subsequent resolution in the Economic and Social Council called for the establishment of more routine and formal approaches to sector coordination among UN agencies and partners (UN ECOSOC 2005). The report identified significant gaps in sectors such as water and sanitation, shelter and camp management, and protection, as well as the need to reinvest in systemic capacity for humanitarian response. The idea behind these reforms was to map the response capacities of national, regional, and international actors; strengthen these response capacities; apply benchmarks to measure UN performance; improve coordination among actors; and fill the identified gaps in UN response.

Following this, the *Humanitarian Response Review* (HRR) recommended assigning responsibilities by sector to lead organizations and developing *clusters* of relevant partners to develop preparedness and response capacities. In September 2005 the Principals of the Inter-Agency

Standing Committee (IASC) agreed to establish cluster leads in nine key areas: logistics, emergency telecommunications, emergency shelter, health, nutrition, water/sanitation, early recovery, camp coordination and management, and protection (IASC 2006). Table 5 presents the nine areas and their cluster leads.

TABLE 5
Humanitarian Cluster Approach

Sector or Area of Activity	Global Cluster Lead(s)
Nutrition	UNICEF
Health	WHO
Water/Sanitation	UNICEF
Emergency Shelter	UNHCR[a]
	IFRC[b]
Camp Coordination/ Management	UNHCR[a]
	IOM[b]
Protection	UNHCR[a]
	UNHCR/OHCHR/UNICEF[c]
Early Recovery	UNDP
Logistics	WFP
Emergency Telecommunications	OCHA/UNICEF/WFP

[a] Cluster lead(s) in situations of significant population displacement due to conflict.
[b] Cluster lead(s) in disaster situations.
[c] Cluster leads in disaster situations or in complex emergencies without significant displacement.
Source: IASC 2006.

The cluster approach aims to improve leadership, accountability, predictability, timeliness, and effectiveness of humanitarian responses, and pave the way for recovery in complex environments affected by conflict as well as natural disasters. In essence, the cluster approach represents a substantial strengthening of the "collaborative response" with the additional benefits of predictable and accountable leadership—which in turn could enhance partnerships and complementarity among the UN, Red Cross Movement, and NGOs.

Since 2005, the cluster approach has been applied in 25 of the 27 countries with Humanitarian Coordinators, and has been used in eight humanitarian emergencies or disaster situations requiring a multi-sectoral response involving a wide range of international humanitarian actors

(Humanitarian Reform). A preliminary evaluation, commissioned by the IASC and carried out by the Overseas Development Institute (ODI), found that despite some initial drawbacks—including increased work loads and leadership conflicts—there was evidence of systemic improvement in coordinated humanitarian response (Stoddard et al. 2007). The progress, however, has been uneven across countries with some clusters faring better than others. The proliferation of sub-clusters has also complicated existing platforms for information sharing (Stobbaerts, Martin and Derderian 2010). Médecins Sans Frontières also cautions against making humanitarian action subordinate to political objectives (ibid.).[10]

In July 2009, the Global Public Policy Institute, in cooperation with Group URD, began a second phase of the cluster approach evaluation, focusing on the results and effects of the cluster approach at the country level. The evaluation will focus on six country case studies (Uganda, Myanmar, Haiti, Chad, Gaza, DRC), providing country-specific recommendations, as well as overall conclusions and lessons learned (GPPI).

One UN

The *One UN* approach is a reform concept presented in the Secretary General's *Report of the High-Level Panel on System-wide Coherence, Delivering as One*, based on a legacy of fragmentation and divergent implementation of strategy and achievement of goals in the field (UN 2006). It describes a specific internal approach employed only by the UN.

In February 2006, the Secretary-General announced the formation of a High-level Panel to explore how the United Nations system could work more coherently and effectively across the world in the areas of development, humanitarian assistance, and the environment. It suggested that conflicting UN agencies needed to become a coherent entity in the field to offer a more holistic approach to UN programming (ibid.).

This approach is implemented at the country level, with one leader, one program, one budget, and where appropriate, one office; moreover, the approach is intended to cut costs and focus the delivery of much needed programs (ibid.). The approach aims at creating a stronger commitment for UN agencies to work together on the implementation of one strategy and in the pursuit of one set of goals.

The concept of the *One UN* approach is being tested in eight countries—Albania, Cape Verde, Mozambique, Pakistan, Rwanda, Tanzania, Uruguay and Viet Nam—to identify how the greater UN family can ensure efficient and more effective development operations, while aiming to speed up activities to help achieve the Millennium Development Goals by 2015 (UNDGa). The pilot projects work towards consolidating the UN presence, allowing various UN agencies to play to their strengths, while also building on the strengths of other members of the UN family. While a formal evaluation of the eight pilot countries will be conducted by the

UN Evaluation Group, in the meantime the UN Development Group (UNDG) undertook an informal stocktaking exercise to gather emerging issues, lessons learned and recommendations (UNDGb; UNFPA 2008; and UNIFEM 2008).[11] In general, UN agencies agreed that the "Delivering as One" approach provided a positive and promising way forward. Despite having unique challenges that were complex and time-consuming, the initiative has increased communication among agencies as well as enhanced their understanding of each other's mandate and ability to work holistically.

DISCUSSION

The above approaches suggest that there is a strong connection between coherence at the national level and coherence in the field. Therefore, lack of coherence at home is likely to result in inadequate coordination on the ground (de Coning et al. 2009). This is especially true for the strategic-level approaches whereby the level and effectiveness of internal coordination will directly affect the effectiveness of an external intervention. There are, however, exceptions as field responses also suggest that necessity often breeds opportunity: operating environments will force actors to work together in the field even if little communication can be observed at the strategic level (Fraser 2008; and Jorgensen 2008).[12] Indeed, concepts are often superseded by what is happening on the ground, or "learning by doing."[13]

The approaches also highlight the tension between the need to "master the specificity of conflict situations" at the same time as taking adequate and timely action (Malone 2010). On the one hand, there is a need for a stronger appreciation of the context in which we operate, as each society has complex historical and cultural structures (Cooper 2005; Berdal 2010; Friis and Jamyr 2008). The typology suggests that when complexity is ignored, and linear, traditional models are employed, the outcomes are less desirable, undermining long-term peace and security. Approaches should not be based on inflexible templates or blueprints, but on an understanding of the environment, the underlying causes of the conflict, and the actors involved.

On the other hand, there is also a need to keep track of the evolving nature of interventions and learn from good and bad experiences to ensure that future interventions are well-planned and executed in the most effective way. While it may be impossible to identify exactly what types of approaches are suitable for dealing with what type of complexity, the typology does allow for a preliminary assessment of the conditions under which specific aspects of complexity are ignored. Indeed, some approaches may in fact be more suitable for dealing with certain types of complexity. For example, some approaches are better at internal coordination than external coordination. Some are more flexible in allowing for more actors to be involved. Other approaches are more in sync, allowing for greater mobilization of resources and more cohesive action.

These differences point to the need to improve the instruments, better understand what we want to do with these instruments and the effects and impacts they have on the ground. It also points to the need for stakeholders to have a clear understanding of what are effective and successful peace operations, something which currently does not exist (Meharg 2009, 248). Nevertheless, from the typology, we are able to identify a number of requirements that appear to be crucial for working with, and managing, complexity. An approach, therefore, should, among other things:

- keep civilian and military functions separate;
- have a core set of actors in charge of joint planning and assessments;
- have a process for sharing information across horizontal and vertical lines, and should be in place;
- allow for organizational flexibility;
- demonstrate appropriate leadership;
- have a good understanding of political and cultural context;
- make use of local knowledge; and
- allow for external objective evaluations of their performance and impact on humanitarian and security outcomes.

Finally, it is important to remember that approaches are a means to an end. They are a way of achieving a secure and stable environment, not an end in themselves (Friis and Jamyr 2008, 21).

CONCLUSION AND RECOMMENDATIONS

Intervention into post-conflict environments is high on the international community's political agenda, and will likely remain so in the years to come. Current trends suggest that the demand for peace operations will continue to rise, with the UN taking the lead and managing regional security organizations in interventions. Continuing commitments on the part of member states, through the support to the UN and other regional organizations, is a key to ensuring peace operations are legitimate, effective and yield positive results, both for the interveners and the recipient populations in conflict-affected places around the world.

As demonstrated by the above typology, approaches to coordinating and managing complexity will differ. Understanding which tool is right for the job in a complex environment can mean the difference between failure and success (UN DPKO/DFS 2008, 31). Certain contexts may be more conducive to a known approach, while others may require innovative thinking and greater flexibility in the way we work. The reality is that relying solely on what we know about existing approaches limits our ability to be creative and discover new ways of working with such complexity.

Five recommendations for improving the accommodation of complexity in contemporary peace operations are offered.

1. **Striking a balance**

    a. **Balance between policy and practice**: Although guidelines, doctrine and policy can accommodate complexity at the strategic and operational levels, it becomes critical that field-level practice also be able to accommodate complexity. There must be a balance between policy and the realities of field practice in order to maintain flexibility, while attempting to harness—not merely *politically* accommodate—complexity for the best outcomes of a peace operation.

    b. **Balance between flexibility and coherence**: It is essential to continue to emphasize flexibility in peace operations and provide space for improvisation based on specific circumstance and contexts. Operations, however, could avoid relying too heavily on ad hoc structures and could seek coherence in planning and management to move beyond mere accommodation.

2. **Improve best practices based on emerging trends**: It is important to further study the modalities of operations to further define best practices and improve the conduct of peace operations. Although all operations are unique, best practices remain crucial as they can contribute to the refinement of future operations. In particular, how different approaches play out in the field, and the better practices that come out of their application, can dictate and define their utility and applicability in the future.

3. **Better frameworks for cooperation**: Given the complexity and robustness of contemporary peace operations, actors will likely continue to rely more and more on partnerships when conducting peace operations (UN DPKO/DFS 2009). It is necessary to continue developing systematic frameworks to strengthen cooperation and partnerships among all actors operating in the field. The growing importance of multinational forces in peace operations requires that concrete steps be taken to ensure a more seamless transition between such forces and UN missions, which in turn implies better inter-institutional arrangements.

4. **Improved integration throughout the operational planning cycle:** While integration in peace operations may not always be feasible, integration will be most successful when it is implemented and supported throughout the conflict management cycle, from the initial planning stage of a mission, to its deployment and to the planning and carrying out of its exit strategy. Integration at the forefront will

increase the possibility for coherence among all actors and will help define the meaning of shared responsibility in a specific context.

5. **Training and education about complex systems**: Although the reality of the complex environment has become mainstreamed within some international community circles, this is not yet the case in the training and education community. Training and education required for peace operations must reflect the realities of the environment. Courses could accommodate critical thinking regarding complex systems by mainstreaming complexity exercises through their existing curricula. With increased training and education, fewer will be overwhelmed by the environment, and more will be able to employ a systems theory perspective to harness complexity to the advantage of interventions.

Managing complexity in peace operations is a difficult task. Only by understanding the nature of the security environment and how this environment shapes and influences operations can the international community better understand the interconnections and multi-variances of the tasks at hand. It is with this understanding that the international community will be able to fully harness the positive aspects of complexity and use it to the advantage of its operations.

NOTES

1. Some analysts and practitioners drop the "peace" and refer to the spectrum of operations as "complex operations."
2. The terms *complex* and *complicated* both refer to something that is composed of numerous interconnected parts. While *complicated* also refers to something that is difficult to analyze, understand and explain, from complexity theory, the term *complex* refers to both the known and unknown variables (i.e., intended and unintended consequences of an action). By using the term *complex*, we also acknowledge that the properties and behaviours of peace operations as a whole are different from those of its parts. Therefore, to understand a peace operation in its entirety, one cannot simply look at the sum of its parts; one must look at the relationship and interconnections among the parts.
3. The international community is understood as the combination of global and regional security organizations such as the UN and NATO, aligned and non-aligned states, international organizations such as the ICRC, non-governmental organizations like CARE and Oxfam, host nations to peace operations and other types of humanitarian interventions, non-state actors and recipient populations in these host nations, the security and defence sectors, and private sector transnational corporations such as Haliburton and Bechtel involved in the development and post-conflict projects.
4. Systems theory is an interdisciplinary field of science that studies the nature of complex systems. More specifically, systems theory offers a framework by

which one can analyze and/or describe any group of objects that work in concert to produce some result.

5. It is also described internationally as *boots, suits, sandals, and badges*. The term badges is representative of civilian police, which has become a dominant sector in international interventions, and will continue to increase in the future.

6. In Canada the Department of National Defence is involved in Afghanistan to win hearts and minds and gain consent, which comes directly from counter-insurgency theory. The Canadian International Development Agency is mandated to improve the quality of the lives of Afghans, while the Department of Foreign Affairs and International Trade is involved in governance and promoting democratic values.

7. The British FCO (Foreign and Commonwealth Office) focuses on the following key roles: supporting British nationals overseas; helping keep Britain safe; funding programs; building strong relationships; documents and legal services; and honours. "Helping keep Britain safe" includes counter-terrorism, weapons proliferation, preventing and resolving conflict, promoting a low-carbon/high-growth global economy; and developing effective international institutions.

8. Although the North Atlantic Treaty Organization (NATO) has developed a formalized Comprehensive Approach strategy for its operations, this section focuses on the so-called "small c" comprehensive approach as a mechanism for undertaking operations in complex environments.

9. It should be noted that an operation authorized by the UN Security Council, but conducted by a regional organization, refers to a Chapter VIII mission and is not considered a hybrid operation.

10. MSF decided not to participate in the Cluster Approach at the global level to safeguard their independence and neutrality. However, they have been taking part in the clusters at the field level, recognizing the need for information sharing.

11. See also progress reports by UNEP, UNIFEM, WHO, UNCTAD, UNESCO, and UNIDO.

12. For example, Brigadier-General David Fraser argues that the contemporary operating environment in Afghanistan has forced the host government, non-governmental organizations (NGOs), the United Nations (UN), coalition forces, and many other organizations and agencies to work together and bring their different strengths and capabilities to bear collectively.

13. Comments provided to author during the conference *Stability Operations and International Conflict Management—Lessons Learned from recent Canadian, Austrian, Swedish and German operations*, Queen's University, Kingston, 30 October 2009.

REFERENCES

Andrews, K., and V. Holt. 2007. *United Nations-Africa Union Coordination on Peace and Security in Africa.* A Better Partnership for African Peace Operations Issue Brief. Washington, DC: Henry L. Stimson Center.

Aoi, C., C. de Coning, and R. Thakur, eds. 2007. *Unintended Consequences of Peacekeeping Operations*. Hong Kong: United Nations University Press.

Bellamy, A.J., P. Williams, and S. Griffin. 2004. *Understanding Peacekeeping*. Cambridge: Polity.

Berdal, M. 2010. Presentation at the International Development and Research Centre (IDRC), Ottawa. 16 February.

Brandsma, T. 2007. The Benefits of the Military in Humanitarian Roles. *Journal of International Peace Operations* 3 (1):13.

Buchann, G. 2007. Presentation at the Pearson Peacekeeping Centre, Ottawa. 18 December.

Canadian Council for International Co-operation (CCIC). 2007. Briefing Paper—Submission to the Independent Panel on Afghanistan. Ottawa, Canada: CCIC.

Center on International Cooperation (CIC). 2006. *Annual Review of Global Peace Operations 2006*. Boulder: Lynne Rienner Publishers.

Cilliers, P. 1998. *Complexity and Postmodernism: Understanding Complex Systems*. London and New York: Routledge.

Cooper, A.F. 2005. Adding 3Ns to the 3Ds: Lessons from the 1996 Zaire Mission for Humanitarian Interventions. Working Paper No. 4. Waterloo, Ontario: Centre for International Governance Innovation.

Cornish, S. 2008. Rethinking Deeper Integration: The Case for Safeguarding Independent Humanitarian Action in Afghanistan and Beyond. *The Pearson Papers* 11 (1):71-86.

de Coning, C., and K. Friis. 2008. Introduction: How to Conceptualise "Comprehensive approach"? In *Comprehensive Approach: Challenges and Opportunities in Complex Crisis Management*, ed. K. Friis and P. Jarmyr, 2-9. Oslo: NUPI.

de Coning, C., H. Lurås, N.N. Schia, and S. Ulriksen. 2009. *Norway's Whole-of-Government Approach and its Engagement with Afghanistan*. Oslo, Norway: NUPI.

Department of National Defence (DND). 2007. *Evaluation of CF/DND Participation in the Kandahar Provincial Reconstruction Team*. Ottawa: DND. At www.crs-csex.forces.gc.ca/reports-rapports/2007/pdf/138P077-eng.pdf (accessed 14 August 2009).

Department of Foreign Affairs and International Trade (DFAIT). 2010. START-Stabilization and Reconstruction Task Force. At http://www.international.gc.ca/start-gtsr/index.aspx (accessed 25 January 2010).

Drolet, J.D. 2006. Provincial Reconstruction Teams: Afghanistan vs. Iraq—Should We Have a Standard Model? US Army War College Strategy Research Project. Carlisle: USAWC.

Durch, W., and T.C. Berckman. 2006. *Who Should Keep The Peace?* Washington, DC: The Henri L. Stimson Center.

Eide, E.B., A.T. Kaspersen, R. Kent, and K. von Hippel. 2005. *Report on Integrated Missions: Practical Perspectives and Recommendations*. New York: UN ECHA.

Foreign and Commonwealth Office (FCO). 2009. At http://www.fco.gov.uk/en/fco-in-action/strategy (accessed 14 August 2009).

Fraser, D. Personal communication, 2008.

Friis, K., and P. Jamyr, eds. 2008. *Comprehensive Approach: Challenges and Opportunities in Complex Crisis Management*. Oslo: NUPI.

General Assembly (GA) Special Committee on Peacekeeping Operations. 2009. *2009 Will Be "Critical Year" for Peacekeeping, with Capacity Overstretched More*. GA/PK/199, 23 February. At www.un.org/News/Press/docs/2009/gapk199.doc.htm (accessed 13 August 2009).

Global Public Policy Institute (GPPI). *Cluster Approach Evaluation Phase II, July 2009-March 2010*. At www.gppi.net/consulting/cluster_approach/ (accessed 10 February 2010).

Gordon, S. 2006. The Changing Role of the Military in Assistance Strategies. In *Resettling the Rules of Engagement—Trends and Issues in Military-Humanitarian Relations*, ed. V. Wheeler and A. Harmer, 39-52. Humanitarian Policy Group Research Report 21. London, UK: Overseas Development Institute.

Gowan, R., and I. Johnstone. 2007. New Challenges for Peacekeeping: Protection, Peacebuilding and the "War on Terror." Coping with Crisis Working Paper Series. New York, NY: International Peace Academy.

Guéhenno, J.-M. 2008. *Remarks of the Under-Secretary for Peacekeeping Operations to the Special Committee on Peacekeeping Operations*, 10 March. At http://www.un.org/en/peacekeeping/articles/article100308.htm (accessed 15 August 2009).

Hawkins, D.R. 2002. *Power vs. Force: The Hidden Determinants of Human Behavior*. New York: Hay House.

Humanitarian Reform. *Cluster Approach*. At http://www.humanitarianreform.org/Default.aspx?tabid=310 (accessed 15 August 2009).

Independent Panel on Canada's Future Role in Afghanistan. 2008. *Report of the Independent Panel on Canada's Future Role in Afghanistan*. Ottawa: Public Works and Government Services. At http://dsp-psd.tpsgc.gc.ca/collection_2008/dfait-maeci/FR5-20-1-2008E.pdf (accessed 14 August 2009).

Inter-Agency Standing Committee (IASC). 2006. *Guidance Note on Using the Cluster Approach to Strengthen Humanitarian Response*, 24 November. At http://www.humanitarianreform.org/humanitarianreform/Portals/1/cluster%20approach%20page/Introduction/IASCGUIDANCENOTECLUSTERAP-PROACH.pdf (accessed 12 August 2009).

ISS Today. 2007. *Peacekeeping Reform: Democratisation, Devolution Or Multilateralism?*, 15 June. At www.issafrica.org (accessed 3 February 2008).

Jervis, R. 1997. *System Effects*. Princeton: Princeton University Press.

Jones, B.D. 2006. Preface. In *Annual Review of Global Peace Operations 2007*. New York: Center on International Cooperation.

— 2007. Looking to the Future: Peace Operations in 2015. Background paper commissioned for the *International Forum for the Challenges of Peace Operations*. New York: Center on International Cooperation.

Jones, B.D., and F. Cherif. 2004. Evolving Models of Peacekeeping, Policy Implications and Responses. Report prepared for the United Nations Department of Peacekeeping Operations' Peacekeeping Best Practices Unit. New York: New York University Center on International Cooperation.

Jorgensen, Colonel M.P. 2008. *A Strategy for Effective Peace-Building: Canada's Whole-of-Government Approach in Afghanistan*. Canada: Canadian Forces College. At http://www.cfc.forces.gc.ca/papers/nssc/nssc10/jorgensen.pdf (accessed 25 January 2010).

Klotzle, K. 2006. International Strategies in Fragile States: Expanding the Toolbox? *Bertelsmann Group for Policy Research Policy Analysis No. 1*. Munich: Center for Applied Policy Research at the University of Munich.

Krawchuk, F.T. 2005. Combating Terrorism: A Joint Interagency Approach. *Land-power Essay series No. 05-1*. Arlington: Institute of Land Warfare. At http://www.comw.org/tct/fulltext/0501krawchuk.pdf (accessed 21 August 2009).

Malone, D. 2010. Commentary at the International Development and Research Centre (IDRC), Ottawa, 16 February.

Meharg, S. 2007. *Helping Hands, Loaded Arms*. Ottawa: Canadian Peacekeeping Press.

— 2009. *Measuring What Matters in Peace Operations and Crisis Management*. Kingston: McGill-Queen's University Press.

Nye, J.S. 2009. Commentary: Hard Times, Soft Power. *Globe and Mail*, 18 February.

Office of the Coordinator for Reconstruction and Stabilization (S/CRS) at Department of State, Joint Center for Operational Analysis/United States Joint Forces Command, and Bureau of Policy and Program Coordination, United States Agency for International Development. 2006. *Provincial Reconstruction Teams in Afghanistan: An Interagency Assessment*, 5 April. Washington, DC: US Government.

Olson, L., and H. Gregorian, eds. 2007. Civil-Military Coordination: Challenges and Opportunities in Afghanistan and Beyond. *Journal of Military and Strategic Studies* 10 (1).

Overseas Development Institute (ODI). 2007. Protection in Practice—UN Integrated Missions. Report from the 9 February meeting *Protection in Practice: Concepts, Strategies, and Dilemmas*. Washington, DC: ODI.

Perito, R.M. 2007. The US Experience with Provincial Reconstruction Teams in Iraq and Afghanistan. *Testimony before the House Armed Services Committee, Subcommittee on Oversight and Investigations*, 17 October.

Roberts, C. 2008. Africa-Stan: Afghanistan's Lessons for a Whole-of-Canada Africa Strategy. *Vanguard*. At www.vanguardcanada.com/Africa-stanRoberts (accessed 8 August 2009).

Shevlin, J. 2007. Ethical Considerations for PRTs in Afghanistan. *Journal of International Peace Operations* 3 (1):12.

Snyder, J., and R. Jervis. 1993. *Coping with Complexity in the International System*. Boulder: Westview Press.

Stephenson, J. "Spike." 2007. Sharing the Humanitarian Space. *Journal of International Peace Operations* 3 (2):15.

Stobbaerts, E., S. Martin, and K. Derderian. 2010. Integration and UN Humanitarian Reforms. In *Humanitarian Reform: Fulfilling its Promise?*, 18-20, Forced Migration Review 29, University of Oxford. UK: Refugee Studies Centre. At www.fmreview.org/FMRpdfs/FMR29/18-20.pdf (accessed 9 February 2010).

Stoddard, A., A. Harmer, K. Haver, D. Salomons, and V. Wheeler. 2007. *Cluster Approach Evaluation*. UK: Overseas Development Institute. At www.odi.org.uk/hpg/papers/hpgcommissioned-ocha-clusterapproach.pdf (accessed 15 August 2009).

St-Pierre, K. 2007. Hybridizing UN Peace Operations: The Role of the European Union and Canada. *Review of European and Russian Affairs* 3 (2):1-18.

— 2008. *Then and Now: Understanding the Spectrum of Complex Peace Operations*. Ottawa: Pearson Peacekeeping Centre.

United Kingdom (UK). 2003. *Stabilization Unit*, 2003. At http://www.stabilisationunit.gov.uk/ (accessed 15 August 2009).

United Nations (UN). 1992. *An Agenda for Peace*, A/47/277-S/24111. At www.un.org/Docs/SG/agpeace.html (accessed 15 August 2009).

— 2006. *Delivering as One: Report of the Secretary General's High-Level Panel*. New York: UN.

United Nations Department of Peacekeeping Operations and Department of Field Support (UN DPKO/DFS). 2008. *United Nations Peacekeeping Operations Principles and Guidelines*. New York: UN.

— 2009. A New Partnership Agenda: Charting A New Horizon For UN Peacekeeping. DPKO/DFS non-paper. New York: UN.

United Nations Development Group (UNDGa). *UN Reform and Coherence: Delivering as One*. At www.undg.org/index.cfm?fuseaction=Print&P=7# (accessed 3 February 2010).

United Nations Development Group (UNDGb). *Stocktaking*. At www.undg.org/index.cfm?P=568 (accessed 3 February 2010).

UN ECOSOC. 2005. *Resolution on Strengthening of the Coordination of Emergency Humanitarian Assistance of the United Nations*, A/60/87-E/2005/78. At http://www.un.org/docs/ecosoc/documents/2005/resolutions/Resolution%20 2005-4.pdf (accessed 14 August 2009).

UNFPA. 2008. *Stocktaking of the Implementation of the UN "Delivering as One" Initiative*. At www.undg.org/docs/8804/UNFPA+stocktaking+of+pilotsds-Rev+24+03l.doc (accessed 3 February 2010).

UNIFEM. 2008. *Progress Report: UNIFEM Experience in the "Delivering As One" Pilot Countries*. At www.undg.org/docs/8516/UNIFEM-Progress-Report_One-UN. doc (accessed 3 February 2010).

US Department of State. 2006. Operation Enduring Freedom. *Fact Sheet*. Washington, DC: Office of the Spokesman. At www.state.gov/r/pa/prs/ps/2006/60083.htm (accessed 9 February 2010).

— 2007. Provincial Reconstruction Teams (PRTs). *Fact Sheet*. Baghdad, Iraq: US Embassy Baghdad. At www.state.gov/p/nea/rls/91433.htm (accessed 9 February 2010).

Weir, E. 2006. Conflict and Compromise: UN Integrated Missions and the Humanitarian Imperative. *KAIPTC Monograph* No. 4. Guana: KAIPTC.

Wheeler, V., and A. Harmer, eds. 2006. *Resettling the Rules of Engagement—Trends and Issues in Military-Humanitarian Relations*. Humanitarian Policy Group Research Report 21. London, UK: ODI.

FRAGILE SUPPORT: MONUC'S REPUTATION AND LEGITIMACY IN THE DEMOCRATIC REPUBLIC OF CONGO

INGRID VAN OSCH AND JOSEPH SOETERS

Despite MONUC's efforts and achievements, the relationship between MONUC and the population of the Democratic Republic of Congo (DRC) appears to be strained. We intend to provide insight as to why this relationship is strained and how it can be improved. MONUC's presence in the DRC needs to be considered with respect to the historical background, MONUC's difficulty in dealing with dissimilar views about the implementation of the paradoxical mandate, disinformation in Kinshasa and unequal expectations in the eastern provinces. This context proves the importance of legitimacy and reputation. Four Ps of classical pragmatism—practical, pluralistic, participatory and provisional—enable us to locate the sore spots of MONUC's reputation and legitimacy and help us to find ways to relax the strained relationship with the host-nation's population in favor of the effectiveness of the mission.

Atako bute ewumeli, ntongo ekotana kaka.

However long the night, the sun always comes up in the morning.

Congolese proverb (in Lingala)[1]

Mission Critical: Smaller Democracies' Role in Global Stability Operations, ed. C. Leuprecht, J. Troy, and D. Last. Montreal and Kingston: Queen's Policy Studies Series, McGill-Queen's University Press. © 2010 Queen's Centre for International Relations, Queen's University at Kingston. All rights reserved.

"White is a dangerous color for vehicles … "[2] The foreign director of a major company in the Democratic Republic of Congo (DRC) tells us that the cars of his firm can have any colour of the rainbow except for white. It is not exceptional for people in the streets of Kinshasa to throw rocks at the white UN vehicles belonging to the *Mission de l'Organisation des Nations Unies en République Démocratique du Congo* (MONUC). Even pushing the vehicles on their sides or putting burning towels in the fuel tanks is a possibility that needs to be taken seriously. In November 2009, at the time of our research visit to the DRC, demonstrators were considered to be one of the major potential threats in Kinshasa, DRC's capital city. That was the same week in which the Congolese government voiced serious criticism regarding the UN mission in their country, which was broadcast nationwide on television. Incidents against MONUC have also occurred in the east of the country, although to a much lesser extent. Here, the main potential threats are rebels from the major armed groups, *les Forces Démocratiques de Libération du Rwanda* (FDLR), ex-combatants of *le Congrès National pour la Défense du Peuple* (CNDP, which is in the process of being almost entirely integrated in the Congolese national army) and local Mayi-Mayi militia. Still, eyes are kept open for possible demonstrations against MONUC as well. While driving through Congolese villages in white vehicles with "UN" written on them in clear black characters, we have seen local faces that are hard to read. They show a mixture of sadness, frustration, aggression and hope. People wave at the vehicles. Are they waving joyfully or expressing their unease with MONUC? The cautiousness for local demonstrators indicates that the mission is teetering on the brink of political and societal support in the host nation.

Despite the fact that MONUC was set up in 1999, in over a decade it has not managed to establish itself positively. This must be frustrating for the people involved. Within the mission there are so many people who put their ideals into practice and risk their lives to advance the situation in the DRC. More generally, the international community has put in so much effort and resources—with the best intentions—that a lack of host nation support for the mission is remarkable, to say the least. The interstate relations between the DRC and its neighbouring countries have opened up opportunities, a growing number of combatants is surrendering and the majority of people we interviewed within the mission feel the security situation is improving and think that the DRC would be worse off without MONUC. *How then, is it possible that the relationship between MONUC and the host-nation population and authorities is so strained?*

Legitimacy—i.e., conformity to political and social expectations—and reputation—i.e., achievement and self-presentation—seem to be important concepts to understand the position of UN missions in general (van Doorn and Mans 1968), and of MONUC's position in the DRC in particular. Therefore we answer the above question within a framework based on institutional theory from administrative and organizational studies

(Deephouse and Suchman 2008). According to this theory legitimacy and reputation are key factors in the process of becoming and being accepted by the general public and elites in society. Legitimacy and reputation refer to the acceptance and support by the general public and relevant elites of an organization's right to exist and to conduct its affairs in its chosen manner. An organization's legitimacy is known more readily when it is absent, rather than when it is present. When there is a lot of press coverage, chances are high that the organization's actions are not considered appropriate, proper or desirable (ibid.).

Institutional theory tells us that organizations can contribute to a development of gaining stability and acceptance by improving their legitimacy and reputation. There are at least four ways that are conducive to such a development (Lawrence, Winn and Devereaux Jennings 2001): influencing (particularly with respect to [non-]decision-making), disciplining (including surveillance and normalization), forcing (using, among others, physical violence) and dominating (through material superiority and rule-related practices). Obviously, of these four mechanisms, influencing is the most important in terms of UN peacekeeping, although in the context of robust mandates, disciplining and forcing are relevant, too. As to influencing, one mechanism is particularly relevant, which is the formation of coalitions with external stakeholders and/or the co-optation of support from outside the organization (Rodrigues and Child 2008).

These are useful, yet rather general concepts. While formulating an answer to our question, we found that the four Ps of classical pragmatism in relation to public administration, introduced by political scientist Patricia Shields (2008), provide a more specific dowsing rod for identifying MONUC's problems and possible solutions. The four Ps—i.e., Practical, Pluralistic, Participatory and Provisional—enable us to locate the sore spots of MONUC's reputation and legitimacy. This perspective is based on the work of the philosopher and psychiatrist David H. Brendel (2006), who introduced four Ps to classify the major tenets of classical pragmatism. Patricia Shields refers to them in order to "more fully understand the terrain of classical pragmatism in relation to contemporary public administration" (Shields 2008, 205). By framing MONUC by the four Ps, the theoretical value of this case becomes visible. Therefore, this case also contributes to our understanding of the relation between UN missions and the host nationals in general, which is an issue in need of attention (Polman 2003; Pouligny 2006). This way, this chapter does not only provide a case study of MONUC, but it also exemplifies how the four Ps of classical pragmatism form a theoretical tool for analyzing peacekeeping missions.

Before applying the four Ps of classical pragmatism, the first part of this chapter elaborates on the case of MONUC. We need to consider the historical and cultural context in which MONUC entered the stage. MONUC deployed to a country with a traumatic history of suppression, conflict and mistrust in foreign intervention. It is therefore not surprising that the mission goes through a continued search for the best imple-mentation of the mandate, which is not beneficial to MONUC's struggle for reputation and legitimacy. Our findings from the DRC confirm this struggle by illustrating, beside the optimistic approaches of many people within the mission, a strong sense of opposition against MONUC and lack of support by the host nationals.

After elaborating on the case of MONUC, the second part applies the four Ps of classical pragmatism. It gives in-depth insight into the problems MONUC deals with and offers a way MONUC could handle these prob-lems. This section is also exemplary for analyzing peacekeeping missions in general. By directing us to the answer for why the relationship between MONUC and the host nationals is strained, and additionally providing us with possible solutions, the application of the four Ps could not only offer an analytical tool, but also a way forward.

A THEATRE RAVAGED BY A TRAUMATIC HISTORY

The DRC is one of the largest countries in Africa, covering an area roughly equivalent to the USA east of the Mississippi. Around 66 million people live in the DRC, most of them concentrated in the major cities. A large part of the country is covered in rainforest. Hardly any passable roads connect the east to the west. Especially during the rainy season the roads are more pools of mud than anything else. Therefore the western part of the country, including the capital, Kinshasa, is geographically discon-nected from the east. Travelling within the country is mostly done by air with unreliable local aviation companies. The country contains lucrative reserves of minerals such as diamonds, gold, copper, zinc, cobalt and coltan (a mineral used to produce tantalum). These riches did not benefit the country.

To give a small impression of the DRC's traumatic political and so-cial memory, a short account of its history will be sketched below. This history includes the suppressive reign of the Belgian King Leopold II between 1885 and 1908 (Hochschild 2006). After this period the DRC was a formal Belgian colony until 30 June 1960. Tumultuous years followed the DRC's independence with Patrice Lumumba as first minister and Joseph Kasavubu as president. Between these two rivals serious tensions existed particularly about the future administrative status of this giant country. Should the newly formed independent state of the Congo be based on national unity or become a federalist state? Soon after independ-ence, disorder broke out. Belgium sent its troops to the DRC, without the agreement of the Congolese government, for the declared purpose of restoring law and order and protecting Belgian nationals. On 12 July 1960, the Congolese government asked the United Nations for military assistance in order to protect the national territory of the DRC against external aggression. At this point, the UN started operation ONUC in order to assist the new government in maintaining law and order and to provide technical assistance. While the UN was present in the country, there was an attempt of secession by the mineral-rich province of Katanga. Lumumba was murdered under unclear circumstances, while Kasavubu remained president. He slowly disappeared from the stage, while chief of the army Joseph-Désiré Mobutu gained more power. In 1964, the UN terminated operation ONUC. The following year Mobutu named himself the new head of the state. He renamed the country Zaire. The situation in Zaire became relatively stable under his dictatorship.

However, the government was accused of human rights violations and corruption. In 1994, the situation worsened dramatically because, among other reasons, refugees from Rwanda and Burundi entered the DRC. Among the refugees were members of the *interahamwe*, militia groups who took part in the genocide in Rwanda. In the refugee camps they managed to regroup and continue fighting from there. These refugees later became part of the FDLR. The country now finds itself at the centre of what is sometimes called "Africa's World War" (BBC 2010) as several African countries got involved in the conflict (Prunier 2009). This conflict had political, economical and ethnical elements. All parties took advantage of the chaos in order to plunder the rich natural resources of the country. In 1997 Rwanda invaded Zaire to clear extremist Hutu militias. Anti-Mobutu rebels took advantage of this. They captured Kinshasa and installed Laurent Désiré Kabila as president. The country was renamed the Democratic Republic of Congo. This did not rid the DRC from its battleground. Rebel groups, supported by different countries, clashed in order to gain power in the mineral-rich East, victimizing the local population. In 1998 this situation led to a peace enforcement operation by troops from the Southern African Development Community, mainly consisting of units from Angola and Zimbawe (Coleman 2007). When in January 2001 Laurent Désiré Kabila was murdered, his son, Joseph Kabila, took over (Prunier 2009).

As said, the above historic description of the DRC is a sketched impression. The DRC's collective memory is tremendously complex. Moreover, as Kevin Dunn makes clear in his argument about the DRC's identity, Westerners will find the political dynamics of the civil war incomprehensible, because these dynamics "are seemingly outside the logic of established state-centric approaches to international relations" (Dunn 2003, 4). Dunn argues that the DRC is used in the Western discourse as a marker of the "exotic, the unknown, and the unknowable" (ibid., 180). Referring to European colonial powers, cold war superpowers and regional forces, Dunn states that "intervention in the Congo has been intimately tied to the Congo's identity, particularly in external actors' attempts to control the definition of the Congo and its sovereignty" (ibid., 9). Mistrust in foreign intervention is therefore understandable, although the Congolese interpretation of post-colonial history is not merely anti-Western (Rubbers 2009). It is in this context of suppression, conflict and foreign intervention that we should consider MONUC's entrance on the stage.

One and a half years before Joseph Kabila's appointment as new president, the UN started MONUC. The way the mission developed since its inception in 1999 is evidence of its struggle with the changing environment and evolving interpretations of its main tasks. MONUC originated in response to the Lusaka Cease-Fire Agreement, signed by the warring African states and the government of the DRC on 10 July 1999 and a few weeks later by the Congolese rebel groups. In the Lusaka Agreement, the UN was requested to implement the peace agreement and to "track down all armed groups in the DRC" (Lusaka Agreement 1999). However, the UN's past incapability to resolve conflict during and after the Rwandan genocide in 1994, the UN Security Council's lack of strategic interest in the DRC, and the absence of the UN in designing the Lusaka Ceasefire, made the Security Council cautious about initiating support, which was "translated into the authorization of a peacekeeping force with a far too modest observation mandate, inadequate resources, a halting deployment, and little diplomatic follow-up or leverage in support of implementation" (Roessler and Prendergast 2006, 230). It was indeed a small observation mission, mandated with far too little resources to protect civilians all over the country. The Lusaka signatories continuously violated the agreement, making use of the "benefits of war," meaning the exploitation of the country's natural resources (Prunier 2009). With young Kabila as the new president, new hope arose, especially when he indicated he wanted to reinforce the Lusaka Agreement. Now, ten years further, the country is internally still in conflict predominantly due to endless local disputes (Autessere 2008).

MONUC constantly faces new challenges. Its mandate has been adjusted several times due to changing influences and external criticism. The number of troops and financial resources has been raised several times over the past decade. The implementation of the mandate has been a major point of discussion during MONUC's presence in the DRC. Although its main official objective has always been the protection of civilians, Holt and Berkman argue that the interpretation hereof and the extent of force allowed has not always been clear, especially as the mission deals with many different nationalities and includes both military and civilians. It took years of struggling before MONUC had begun to develop a "coherent strategic framework for civilian protection and for how much force the mission should exercise" (Holt and Berkman 2006, 157). Especially during the Ituri crisis in 2003 and the crisis in Bukavu of 2003/2004, the situation on the ground asked for continuous reconsideration of the mandate's implementation. In 2005, the newly appointed Eastern Division Commander and Deputy Force Commander Major General Patrick Cammaert introduced a new, more aggressive tactic. Finally, there was a transition from a static observation mission towards a more robust implementation of the mandate. This is more fitting to a mandate based on Chapter VII of the UN Charter, which allows peace enforcement.

By December 2009 a total of 20,509 uniformed MONUC employees are active in the DRC, comprising 18,646 troops, 705 military observers and 1,158 police. Additionally, 1,005 international civilian personnel, 2,613 local civilian staff and 648 United Nations volunteers are employed (*MONUC Facts and Figures* 2010). Nearly 60 nations have contingents. The two major troop-contributing countries are India and Pakistan, with India providing the majority of the North Kivu Brigade and Pakistan the majority of the South Kivu Brigade. MONUC has an approved budget of US$1.35 million. Gradually, MONUC has turned into the largest and most robust UN mission on the planet. That seems highly necessary in a region of the world where over the past ten years about four million people have lost their lives due to man-made violence; clearly a tragedy beyond description (Prunier 2009).

THE CONTESTED MANDATE

The robustness of the mission was endorsed on 22 December 2008 when the Security Council declared and reaffirmed with Resolution 1856 that the mandate has four main points of focus. All these points are designed to support the Government of the DRC and therefore have to be worked out in close cooperation with the local authorities (UN Security Council Resolution 1856, 2008).

The protection of civilians is the most important point, implying that the focus is military, although MONUC is an integrated mission. This means that MONUC contains a peacekeeping force but also a civilian staff working within the mission on issues such as human rights and political affairs and, since the beginning of 2005, officially even includes all humanitarian UN agencies. Officers from the substantive component, meaning the civil humanitarian units, "act as conduits between military and humanitarian actors on the ground, and […] promote cooperation towards the overarching goal of 'protection'" (Holt and Berkman 2006, 173).

The second point of focus concerns the Congolese national army, the FARDC. MONUC is not entitled to directly fight against the armed groups itself, but it is tasked to coordinate operations with the FARDC and support the FARDC during these operations if necessary, by means of logistic support or indirect fire support. Next to that, MONUC is concerned with the disarmament, demobilization, repatriation, resettlement and reintegration of foreign, armed groups (DDRRR) and the disarmament, demobilization and reintegration of Congolese combatants (DDR). This means that MONUC tries to persuade the armed groups to put down their weapons and make a choice: they can choose to reintegrate into society and build up a life as a civilian—in the case of the foreign combatants, in their home countries such as Rwanda or Uganda—or they can choose to integrate into the FARDC. Other cases have proven that in general the reintegration of ex-fighters is a major issue in solving (post-) conflict situations (Tessema and Soeters 2006).

The FARDC has hardly had any training so far. Combined with the integration of ex-combatants as a result of the DDR/DDRRR process, the Congolese national army needs to develop and improve its performance as a professional army and raise its professional standards in terms of conduct and discipline. That is why the third point of focus in the mandate is the training and mentoring of the FARDC in support of the security sector reform (SSR).

The final point of focus is the territorial security of the DRC, which mainly consists of the observing and monitoring of the government, the FARDC and the armed groups. One of MONUC's tasks is to restore trust in the local government. After years of exploitation and suppression, durable stability in the DRC is only possible if the government is able to legitimately use its authority. That is why MONUC cannot and will not take over the Congolese government, but will work towards stability by supporting an independent host-nation government.

As the earlier mentioned history of MONUC connotes, the mission had to go through some major struggles and it still is. One of the main challenges is how MONUC is supposed to deal with dissimilar views about the implementation of the mandate. The Brahimi Report of 2000 confirms this challenge of UN missions when it recommended "clear, credible, and achievable mandates" (Brahimi Report 2000). Considering MONUC, the rough road towards effectiveness shows that "for the UN to play an effective role in the coordination of sensitive security sector re-forms, there must first be a unanimous view within the mission regarding its mandate and strategy" (Onana and Taylor 2008, 513).

An example of dissimilar views is the extent of force used. Although the use of force is obviously not unique to MONUC, it is an issue that has led to many discussions. Using too little force can lead to loss of control of the situation and incapability to protect civilians. Using too much force can lead to militias' retaliation towards local civilians because of MONUC's actions. It can also lead humanitarian agencies to distance themselves from the mission because of their fear of "losing access to vul-nerable populations and endanger the safety of their unarmed workers" (Holt and Berkman 2006, 175). Finally, it can influence troop contributing countries' willingness to deliver to the mission. After all, the political leaders of such countries do not want to lose the support of their voters by sending their men and women away to a country where the chances are high they will not survive.

In order to strongly position itself in the host country, it is import-ant that on such important issues all contributing parties walk in the same direction. The varying views within MONUC concerning the implementation of the mandate make it hard to operate with one voice, which can negatively impact the mission. Coherence "will maximize influence and effectiveness, while encouraging national ownership of the reform process and avoiding a piecemeal approach to planning and assistance" (Onana and Taylor 2008, 514). If MONUC is indecisive about major issues such as the use of force, this shows a lack of coherence. This is not a unique problem, though. Differences in national operational styles leading to divergent views on how to conduct the operations are very common in multinational military missions (Soeters and Manigart 2008).

Another important struggle is the paradox in the mandate. The main focus is the protection of civilians, immediately followed by the support of the FARDC. However, the FARDC is accused of significant human rights violations, a situation that has even become worse since the integration of former armed groups. Most ex-combatants do not know any other life than an armed life and when they are offered a reasonable salary to join the FARDC (which is, in the end, often not paid due to corrupt FARDC commanders and the lack of administration) they see the best career opportunities in the FARDC. One can imagine that the standards of professionalism and discipline are low in a national army that consists of hardly trained and hardly paid military, united with ex-combatants. The Security Council Resolution 1906 of 23 December 2009 therefore reiterated that MONUC is authorized to use all necessary means to carry out the tasks of its mandate. This also means that it can use force against *any* party that puts civilians under imminent threat of physical violence, thus including the FARDC. In order to distance MONUC from the misbehaviour of the FARDC, the Security Council stressed that the support is "strictly conditioned on FARDC's compliance with international humanitarian, human rights and refugee law and on an effective joint planning of these operations" and it called upon MONUC to "intercede with the FARDC command if elements of a FARDC unit receiving MONUC's support are suspected of having committed grave violations of such laws." In the worst case, when negotiation is not an option anymore and the situation persists, MONUC has to "withdraw support from these FARDC units" (UN Security Council Resolution 1906, 2009).

These two examples are important challenges, which are directly concerned with MONUC's struggle for legitimacy and reputation. The lack of coherence within the mission makes it hard to strongly position the mission in the DRC. The paradox in the mandate can damage the host nationals' trust in the mission. If we combine these challenges with the DRC's traumatic history, colored by suppression and mistrust in foreign intervention, we can understand that it is of major importance that MONUC is able to institutionalize itself as a body that is there to help. Our findings from our fieldwork in the DRC are to be considered in this context.

FINDINGS FROM THE DRC

The people we have interviewed during our two-week research period in November 2009 have given us a mixed impression of the situation the mission finds itself in. The most noticeable responses were the negative critiques about the mission. These critiques came from both within the mission as well as from outside. From outsiders, we have heard comments such as "If MONUC will quit, nothing will happen" (Interview 2), and from a Flemish-Congolese respondent we have heard "MONUC is indifferent to me. The Chinese at least fill the potholes" (Interview 3). These are troubling remarks as they are an indication of the lack of support for the mission. It signals MONUC's fragile reputation. A report on the perception of the population in 2005 prepared by *Bureau d'Etudes, de Recherches et de Consulting International* (BERCI) already showed that the public perception of MONUC is not very positive:

> The population of the western provinces of the country, where there is a smaller presence of MONUC, and which suffered little or no violent combat at the time of the rebellion, views MONUC in a far less positive light as compared to the eastern provinces, where MONUC has a significant presence, and there is considerable violent combat. (BERCI 2005)

Our respondents in 2009 still confirm this perception. For example, one of the UN-respondents does not dare walk alone on the streets of Kinshasa because of possible rebellions against MONUC. Another respondent in Kinshasa puts it this way: "The population only sees the HQ, but they don't see the production. There is a whole bunch of white vehicles with UN written on [them] going back and forth. So the security situation in Kinshasa fluctuates. You have things like rock throwing" (Interview 9).

So the problem in Kinshasa derives from the fact that there is no immediate physical conflict, while the standard of living of the local population is very low. The host nationals expect MONUC to improve their poor living conditions (Interview 9). MONUC HQ is located in Kinshasa because of the availability of facilities and, more importantly, political contact with the DRC government. But the host nationals in the city do not understand what MONUC does for them. On the contrary, the mission can have unintended negative consequences for the host nationals. For example, with the arrival of comparatively affluent UN troops, the basic commodity prices may rise, which makes goods even less affordable for the locals (Aoi, de Coning, and Thakur 2007). One of the respondents is aware of MONUC's position in this:

> Some of these people are so poor, you can't even imagine how poor they are, and they see people who are rich. Would you feel like protesting? Why are people begging on the streets? Because they have nothing. And they see you;

you have everything. So they like to have part of it; it is human nature. Is it tiresome? Yes. Is it stressful? Yes. But you still have to look from their eyes and you have to be sensitive to this. (Interview 9)

To give the impression that MONUC does something directly for the host nationals, it organizes activities, such as patrols through the city in order to create an atmosphere of safety. However, these are "more symbolic than anything else" (Interview 23). The host nationals cannot grasp MONUC's intentions. One respondent recounted an incident when two UN employees in a UN vehicle were stopped by a local. When they asked why they were stopped, the local answered: "We are paying for your fuel and you should not be idling here" (Interview 9). Thinking that MONUC is paid by the DRC government is an example that the host nationals have a wrong idea about the mission. The BERCI report of 2005 already pointed this out: "It would seem that the 'negative' perception of MONUC in the west of the country has been caused more by a campaign of disinformation and / or rumors than by any real knowledge of the UN's mission" (BERCI 2005).

The negative attitude of the host nationals has its ups and downs and is sometimes even further stirred by the local media. As one of the respondents said, an "anti-MONUC campaign" began recently, triggered by the government" (Interview 23, 51). At that particular time in November 2009, during our field work, President Kabila requested MONUC to develop an exit strategy to be implemented on or around 30 June 2010. That is the day that the DRC would celebrate its 50th year of independence. Kabila wanted to show his people that his country can manage without any foreign troops. The local media, mostly owned by political parties, took hold of this wish for MONUC to leave, boosting it to the level of "hate speech" (Interview 23, 25).

In the eastern part of the country, MONUC's reputation tends to be better. Still, there have been incidents of aggression against MONUC in the east as well, although to a lesser extent and in another context compared to Kinshasa. For example, in North Kivu, there were demonstrations on 28 October 2008, where one UN car was burnt, because the protesters felt that MONUC had not dealt with a certain incident appropriately. According to a respondent in the east, the host nationals indeed sometimes protest, but the protesters are youth who do not understand MONUC's position. He recalled an incident when the local leaders were able to stop the protesters from throwing any more rocks at UN vehicles. One of the reasons for the demonstrations in the east is that "the local population has expectations from MONUC which actually concern the responsibilities of the Congolese government." For example, "they expect that MONUC will act as an effective police force" (Interview 33). So the motives for demonstrations in the east differ from those in Kinshasa, but they are both related to disinformation and differing expectations.

Obviously, there have been positive remarks about the mission as well, mostly from inside the UN organization. Actually, optimism is more often encountered than pessimism, especially in the east. This is probably because in the eastern provinces, the immediate effects of MONUC are more visible than in Kinshasa, where the mission deals more on the abstract political level. Most respondents from the North and South Kivu Brigade are convinced that the mission has a positive effect. However, if you ask them if MONUC is reaching its final stage, they think MONUC needs more time to really create a safe environment for the population and give full responsibility to the government. It may be part of the cultural background of some respondents not to criticize the organization for which they work. For example, when we asked what someone would like to change about the mission, most respondents from the North and South Kivu Brigade wanted to change things such as "security for the local population" or "more uniforms for the FARDC." These are external issues, but hardly any respondent wanted to change something within the mission.

Another possible reason why most positive comments come from within the organization is that there are two ways to respond to the negative feedback from the outside. Some reinforce the criticism. We have heard a comment coming from the logistical part of MONUC: "This is the worst organization I have ever worked for! I can't wait to leave!" (Interview 30). On the other hand, one can respond by defending his or her cause. "I would not improve anything" (Interview 46), or even better: "MONUC is used as an example for other missions" (Interview 25, 40).

Despite this optimism, triggered by the idealistic motivation of the UN personnel who risk their lives for peace, the negative responses of the host nationals to MONUC do have consequences. It does not matter whether MONUC is in fact doing a good job or not. The situation in the DRC is in accordance with the so-called Thomas Theorem: "If men define situations as real, they are real in their consequences" (Merton 1968). If the host nationals do not experience MONUC's contribution as something positive, they will not support it. This also works the other way round: if MONUC thinks it is doing a good job, they will keep on working the way they do. As long as the mission is not supported by the host nationals due to disinformation and differing expectations, no sustainable effort can be made and the goals of the mission remain far at the horizon. How to understand, and even better, solve this situation?

THE FOUR Ps OF CLASSICAL PRAGMATISM AND MONUC

We have seen that the context in which MONUC entered the stage in the DRC and the contested mandate render the acceptance and stability of MONUC problematic. The negative attitudes towards MONUC confirm that the relationship with the host nationals is strained and that this is related to disinformation and differing expectations. To understand how MONUC deals with this problem we will approach the mission from the angle of the four Ps of classical pragmatism—practical, pluralistic, participatory and provisional—in relation to public administration (Shields 2008). Within the framework of these four Ps, we are be able to identify the challenges of MONUC's struggle for acceptance and stability and propose possible solutions.

Practical: "At least the Chinese fill the potholes"

In line with the practical essence of classical pragmatism, one should "take mandates and translate them into working programs" (Shields 2008, 211). For a mission such as MONUC, this means that there needs to be a focus on the practical implementation of the mandate and rules of engagement. Now, MONUC mainly deals with "root problems" (Interview 40). These are the main problems that are considered to need most care; for example the introduction of human and gender rights, next to security and public order. However, in places such as Kinshasa where MONUC vehicles drive around the city without the local population understanding why, the presence of MONUC could be made more acceptable in the eyes of the population in the city. To accomplish this, the mission could focus more on concrete, tangible things for people ("atoms instead of bytes"). This is also in line with the argument of political scientist Séverine Autesserre when she says that, for international actors, "the best approach is to make a priority of treating core problems at the local level […] rather than focusing exclusively on managing their broader consequences" (Autesserre 2008, 110). A more visible representation may be needed. That way, the general population will be able to see, and indeed experience, the efforts of MONUC.

Some projects are indeed running, such as winning hearts and minds projects, financed by MONUC, and quick impact projects, carried out and financed by different nations, such as the Pakistanis and Indians. However, apart from MONUC, one can particularly see many Chinese efforts to conduct visible work, such as the construction of roads and buildings. The invisibility of MONUC in Kinshasa has led to remarks such as "At least the Chinese fill the potholes" (Interview 4).

Conducting visible projects, however, may be criticized for its effects or motives. Recent literature questions the effect of humanitarian aid (Moyo 2008; Polman 2010). There are three main points of critique that need to be taken into consideration before one can endorse the argument that MONUC needs to increase its efforts in concrete, tangible projects.

A major point of critique is that such projects may create too much dependency of the host nation's population. It is the task of the host government to provide good roads, education and welfare facilities. If a foreign party, MONUC in this case, takes over these responsibilities, it would undermine the government's responsibility and authority which it is actually trying to restore. So by conducting visible projects, the local authorities would further lose respect from the population and at the same time, the population would become more dependent on foreign parties as they do not learn how to deal with the problems themselves.

Second, it is argued by outsiders that visible projects do not really contribute to the local society. The problem is that often the projects are not tuned with the host nationals. What do the people really need and how can they maintain the projects? One respondent says that MONUC personnel does as much as possible concerning visible projects, but the problem is that "once they have been somewhere and done something, MONUC does not come back" (Interview 33).

The final point of critique concerns the memory of the host nationals. MONUC can invest a lot in filling potholes and other visible projects, but as one of the respondents says: "People have amnesia. If MONUC does something well, the population forgets this quickly" (Interview 40). It seems that the host nationals have a shared long term memory, looking back at their traumatic history. On the other hand, they easily forget on the short term, maybe because they lost trust in (current) authorities due to this traumatic history. This suggests that, for example, quick impact projects may be good to trigger a positive manifestation of MONUC, but if there is no follow-up, the effect won't be long lasting.

Despite the critiques on visible projects, MONUC may need to flavour its idealistic and oftentimes abstract western approaches to root problems with a more practical implementation of the mandate, leading to concrete solutions for nuisances in people's everyday life. MONUC may need to be more visible for the host nationals, not only symbolically, but also effectively. MONUC's approval of 41 projects worth more than a half million dollars, announced on 10 February 2010, might be a shot in the right direction (*MONUC approves 41 projects for more than a half million dollars 2010*).

Pluralism: "*Une voix pour tous!* [One voice for all!]"

To overcome the problems raised by the critiques on visible projects, we need to understand the importance of the other three Ps. The pluralistic approach of classical pragmatism underlines the impossibility to bind the diversity of human and natural phenomena to a single explanation (Brendel 2006, 30). It takes into account that there are different parties and stakeholders, but emphasizes the need to find unity of effort. As referred to earlier, a peace mission such as MONUC needs to operate with one voice (Onana and Taylor 2008, 514). However, MONUC is not the only party in the theatre. It operates in an environment where host nationals are the main stakeholders. Therefore, it has to find a way to represent itself without overpowering the authorities in place and, at the same time, committing itself to a durable dialogue with the host nation's politics and society at large.

Here, MONUC finds itself in a predicament again. It wants to open up to interaction on the one hand, but it does not consider itself to be in the position to develop relationships too closely with the local population. In 2004, there was upheaval in the international community about MONUC personnel accused of sexual abuse. This tarnished the reputation of the mission. MONUC responded to this with the creation of a Comport and Discipline Unit and a policy that absolutely banned any social contact between male UN personnel and local women. In the words of a respondent involved in the Comport and Discipline Unit, the areas around the camps needed to be "cleaned" (Interview 18), meaning that there should be no locals at all roaming near the camps. This way any case of sexual abuse of MONUC personnel could be avoided.

This reaction, however, brings about a second-order, unintended consequence. Although sexual abuse is avoided by the physical distance between MONUC and the local population, this also creates an emotional distance, a "fear of risky strangers" (Furedi 2006). Emotional distance makes it hard for MONUC to commit itself to a durable dialogue with the rich variety of stakeholders among the general population, including the people in the streets. The pluralistic approach is therefore undermined in such a policy. MONUC has to find a way to keep some distance from the population, while at the same time getting close enough to establish itself in the local discourse to create an environment of unity of effort. In other words, MONUC needs to develop its skills of *ambidexterity*, the same way as piano or percussion players need to be equally skilled with their right and left hands (Soeters 2008).

It is hard to find the balance in using both hands. Still, one would think that even with a certain level of physical distance, it should be possible for MONUC to become part of the discourse in the country. MONUC focuses on the dominant discourse, which is that of the authorities. This is an understandable focus, as MONUC's presence is dependent on Congolese politics. If Kabila wants MONUC out, MONUC is out. Additionally, influence on the dominant discourse also affects the host nationals. As the Congolese culture still has hierarchical tribal influences (Noorderhaven and Tidjani 2001) and is founded on oral communication, the host nationals very much depend on what is told by the leaders of the country. The effects of the "hate speech" about MONUC in the local mass media are a clear example of this. This means that if MONUC has a positive influence in and on the dominant discourse, this will affect all layers of society.

A way for MONUC to achieve this is by acting more prominently in the public sphere. As one respondent who deals with public information suggests, MONUC has to put more effort in getting itself invited to local television talk-shows (Interview 23). This is not an easy task, as more or less all Congolese television stations are owned by political parties. In Kinshasa, television is said to be the most popular medium (Interview 23), so if MONUC wants to transmit its message, it needs to try harder to become involved in the discussions broadcast through this medium.

Another important medium is radio. As said before, the Congolese culture is very much oral based. Radio is, therefore, important. A major radio station in the DRC is Radio Okapi. This radio station is a partnership between MONUC and the Swiss NGO Foundation Hirondelle. It is known for its impartiality and a lot of Congolese, especially in the east, rely on Radio Okapi as a source of information. One of the respondents even told us that, when Radio Okapi was planning to leave a certain area, the local population organized a demonstration. This resulted in the decision to keep the station located there. The slogan of Radio Okapi is significant: "*Une voix pour tous!*" ("One voice for all!" *Radio Okapi* 2010).

Radio Okapi offers an important platform for MONUC. However, according to some respondents, MONUC is not able to profit from Radio Okapi to the fullest. Understandably, Radio Okapi is afraid to lose its neutrality and will never run the risk of becoming a propaganda tool. However, in order to live up to its slogan, it needs to provide access to all facets of society. According to a respondent who is involved in military public information, Radio Okapi is not very eager to invite the military, as they are considered to be "too robust in their statements" (Interview 23).

Unfortunately, this fear influences the responses of the military, as another respondent from outside the mission claimed that once a military spokesperson from MONUC is on air, most critical questions are responded to with a "no comment" (Interview 38). So while one of the most powerful media is within its reach, MONUC seems to be either afraid to use it to the fullest, or Radio Okapi is too fearful to fully open its door. Still, without losing the neutrality of Radio Okapi, MONUC, including its military component, should be able to comment on itself and distribute information about its position and function in the DRC.

The Security Council has become aware of the importance of knowledge about the mission among the host nation population. In the recent Resolution 1906 (2009) it encourages MONUC to "enhance its interaction with the civilian population to raise awareness and understanding about its mandate and activities" (UN Security Council Resolution 1906 2009). MONUC responded to this by initiating an information campaign on the United Nations Charter and the functioning of the United Nations system. This campaign took place from 27 January to 20 February 2010. It consisted of a series of conference-debates involving teachers of civic education from secondary schools, opinion leaders, leaders of civil society organizations as well as students completing their secondary education. It was designed "to get social leaders to understand that the DRC is a

United Nations member and the UN is backing DRC's efforts to solve its basic problems. […] (*MONUC and Congolese Government launch information campaign in the UN in Kinshasa* 2010). This is a great step to do something about the disinformation of the host nationals and it will hopefully align mutual expectations.

One problem that has to be kept in mind is that it is not clear when MONUC is expected to reach its final stage. As Kabila asked for an exit strategy, this may result in MONUC no longer having enough time to get involved in the Congolese discourse.

In short, the pluralistic approach has very much to do with the involvement of the rich variety of host nation stakeholders in the country. Bringing in traditional African perspectives in developing the country seems highly needed (Maathai 2009). The Congolese authorities, the local politicians outside government, the various population groups and MONUC, all have their own visions and agendas, but in the end they all want to reach the same goal. A discourse of all with all is essential, since it will help to connect indigenous African perspectives and ambitions with the goals and activities of the international community, embodied in MONUC.

Participatory: "We communicate through drumming"

When the pluralistic approach takes into account the unity of effort of different stakeholders and joint participation in the Congolese societal discourses, the participatory approach concerns the involvement of the Congolese within the internal structure of the mission. Just like the pluralistic approach, the participatory approach of classical pragmatism tries to address those problems raised by practical visibility. MONUC cannot have the illusion that it will solve the DRC's problems on its own. It should involve the Congolese in the mission. As Shields explains: "community and participation facilitate a fuller and deeper understanding of the problematic situation" (Shields 2008, 213).

Regarding participation, four related areas of meaning can be distinguished (Musch 2002). The first is participation as a right to be involved in decision-making. The second is related to participation as autonomous action. The third is participation as development based on local knowledge, and finally, participation as a transfer of power. All of these forms of participation are important in MONUC, but they are not recognizable everywhere. For example, MONUC counts numerous Congolese employees in its staff, such as in Radio Okapi and the Joint Mission Analysis Centre (JMAC). In these departments, local knowledge is recognized and valued a lot, especially as the national staff has access to sensitive information. This way these departments can be in the loop of all different sources. By doing this, for example JMAC wants to advise leaders and support MONUC's decision-making process. However, in the strategic apex of the mission there are virtually no Congolese staff members. This means that there are no, or hardly any, host nationals directly involved in the development of MONUC's strategic decisions. That predominantly is a foreigner's affair, no matter how cosmopolitan, idealistic and highly qualified these people may be.

The absence of Congolese people in the mission's activities, particularly in the strategic decision-making process, has consequences. There are several motives for participation of stakeholders in a post-conflict situation, including local ownership, capacity building, sustainability, increased security, legitimacy of local authorities and the alignment of host nation perceptions with those of external actors (Khalil et al. 2008). All these motives are important contributors to the reputation and legitimacy of a mission. In the case of MONUC, the last motive seems to be most important. The participation approach can reduce the perception gap between the host nationals and MONUC. For example, MONUC and the host nationals can connote different meanings to important notions such as peace and security. Local participation can contribute to bringing these interpretations together as it contributes to aligning mutual expectations (ibid., 149), or "managing expectations," as General David Petraeus described it in relation to Iraq (Petraeus 2008, 4). On a strategic level, more involvement of the Congolese within the mission could thus ultimately result in better alignment between Congolese policies and MONUC's policies.

Language is an important aspect related to local participation. Being able to communicate in local languages is important to have the population involved in the mission. This implies that participation is not only a concern of the host nationals, but that MONUC personnel also need to be active in the Congolese society. After all, "the readiness to address people in their own language does not solely arise from a demonstration of sympathy or a gesture of courtesy. The choice of language, rather, rests on the presences of common objectives and the willpower 'to make things work'" (Loos 2007; van Dijk 2008, 77). A simple "Jambo!" can already open doors, but obviously that is not sufficient for a constructive dialogue.

In the east of the DRC, language is a difficult issue. For example, in the Kivu brigades, the Indians and Pakistanis hardly speak any French or local languages. As some of the respondents say, the language barrier can hinder the development of mutual trust (Interview 33, 36, 44). Somehow, these barriers need to be overcome. Remarkably, a Pakistani respondent pointed out that when communicating with the FARDC, they do not only use telecommunications. The FARDC units also use drumming and whistling during the night to signal the South Kivu Brigade if it needs support (Interview 43).

To a certain extent, the FARDC is part of the participatory approach. Although the FARDC is not part of MONUC, nor the other way round,

MONUC does support it as the national army of the host country. As discussed earlier, this is a struggle for MONUC. On the one hand, it needs to engage to a certain extent in the activities of the FARDC. On the other hand, it needs to distance itself from the misbehaviour of the FARDC. As mentioned earlier, the support to the FARDC can be misinterpreted easily by the population, showing that even the participatory approach has its limits. Taking into account the limitations of a participatory approach, the involvement of the host population in the activities and decision-making process of MONUC is important. It can contribute to closing the perception gap which is likely to pave mutual expectations and align MONUC's policies with those of the Congolese.

Provisional: *"Chhe Maheenai mein north bhi seedha nahi hota* [In six months the North cannot be ascertained]"

Knowledge is always provisionally valid, also in the field of public administration and security. As Shields reminds us, the "pragmatic public administrator must be able to tolerate unintended consequences and ambiguity in the policy environment. If nothing else, public administrators need a *provisional* orientation or risk losing their sanity" (Shields 2008, 215). In the DRC the environment is constantly changing. MONUC should be able to anticipate this environment by regular reflection. The provisional approach does not mean that MONUC should only focus on short-term goals. It does remind us that it is necessary to evaluate the goals and adjust them as necessary: "Unwillingness to acknowledge and accept that actions did not work would merely substantiate preconceived positions" (ibid.).

In particular, given MONUC's highly ambiguous and unclear task environment, it is even more important to search for actions that may turn out to be ineffective. If one knows what does not work, it may also become clear what, in fact, does work. This sorting out of what works and what does not may only come about if there is room for an attitude of (controlled) experimentation among the mission's staff (Sitkin 1996). This is what has become known as the steering principle of Variation and Selection. It may, to some extent, replace the principle of Analysis and Instruction, which is the dominating way of guiding bureaucracies, in particular military organizations and operations (Soeters, van Fenema, and Beeres 2010). Yet, it also seems that even this traditional way of analysis and instruction has not been fully developed in MONUC. One respondent in the east from outside the mission indicated that he never goes to a MONUC briefing because there is a load of information, but hardly any analysis of what is going on (Interview 38). Hence, MONUC's staff should try to improve this part of their job and stimulate policies of experimentation to ascertain which projects and efforts "pay," and which do not. This provisional essence of classical pragmatism also applies to the practical implementation of the mandate. By an attitude of experimentation and regular reflection on the outcomes, MONUC may find concrete and effective solutions.

Additionally, once different experiences have become part of the standard repertoire, the process of keeping track of an institutional memory is essential. In MONUC, however, there seems to be a lack of institutional memory. As a respondent says: "There is no corporate memory. Sometimes I think: we must have done that before; where are the lessons learned? Probably it is too chaotic" (Interview 29). Unfortunately, the differences in rotations between the military and the civilian components can frustrate this process. In fact, the continuous rotations, particularly among military personnel, inhibit the organizational learning process. This has led a Pakistani respondent in Kinshasa to share an Urdu saying with us: *"Chhe Maheenai mein north bhi seedha nahi hota* [In six months the North cannot be ascertained]" (Interview 20). This is not to say that organizational learning in UN missions is impossible. Morjé Howard (2008) has studied a number of UN missions that have been successful in learning from their experiences and in transmitting these experiences to the UN HQ in New York. Their lessons of integrating previous experiences in new approaches and attempts to achieve the mission's goals may also be fruitful for MONUC.

CONCLUSION

This chapter examined why it is possible that the relationship between MONUC and the host nationals in Congo has been strained over the years. We have seen that the answer to this question lies in the complexity of the traumatic historical background of the DRC, MONUC's difficulty dealing with dissimilar views about the implementation of the paradoxical mandate, disinformation in Kinshasa and unequal expectations in the east. A positive institutionalization that eases the strained relationship with the host nationals has not been accomplished yet.

By analyzing MONUC within the framework of the four Ps, we have been able to identify the challenges MONUC has to deal with in relation to its positive institutionalization. The practical approach shows that MONUC needs to transfer its idealism into a workable implementation of the mandate. Root problems have to be addressed, but not those merely underground. The host nationals desire to see the efforts of MONUC, not only symbolically, but effectively. The major points of criticism about visible projects can be balanced by the pluralistic and participatory approach. The pluralistic approach concerns the involvement of the locals in order to create a unity of effort among the different stakeholders in the DRC. A joint participation in the local discourse is therefore essential. Local media, especially Radio Okapi, are important in this regard. Participation also concerns involvement of the host nationals with the activities and decision-making process of MONUC. It can contribute to closing the perception gap, which will pave the way for mutual expectations and align MONUC's policies with those of the Congolese. The provisional approach has shown the importance of reflection and controlled experimentation in a constantly changing environment and that lessons learned need to be stored in the institutional memory of the mission.

As the Special Representative of the Secretary-General Alan Doss says, the host nationals need to understand that MONUC is not a "foreign presence but rather an expression of the United Nations" (*MONUC and Congolese Government launch information campaign in the UN in Kinshasa* 2010). Through the recognition of the four Ps, MONUC can generate this understanding and hopefully it will be able to relax the strained relationship with the host nationals before it has to carry out an exit strategy. The future of the mission is being discussed and under-Secretary-General for Peacekeeping Operations Alain Le Roy already stated that on request of the Congolese government, the first group of UN troops could leave the country before the end of June 2010 (UN News Centre 2010). If MONUC is not able to acknowledge the importance of the four Ps, the mission most likely will leave the country without having achieved its main goals. That would be a major loss of effort and willpower.

NOTES

1. Thanks to Francis Wilanga, staff member of the Dutch embassy in Kinshasa, DRC for providing this proverb. We also thank Dr. Patricia Shields (Texas State University) for offering us a great idea.
2. This quotation derives from Interview 2. The numbers behind the interviews refer to the list of interviews conducted in the DRC by the authors and reserve major Dr. Tom Bijlsma, (Netherlands Defence Academy). This fieldwork took place in the period from 21 November to 3 December 2009. The list is in the possession of the interviewers. We conducted a total of 54 interviews as part of our research on the organizational and corporate mission identity of MONUC. The majority of 45 respondents of over 20 nationalities were people from within the mission, mostly at the strategic level in the HQ in Kinshasa (26) and the command level of the Forward HQ and Brigade HQ in Goma and Bukavu (19). There were 27 respondents who were part of the military and 18 were part of the civilian component of the mission. We also spoke to nine people from outside the mission, such as personnel from the Dutch embassy. The respondents made us recognize the severity of MONUC's fragile reputation and legitimacy, on which this chapter is based.

REFERENCES

Aoi, C., C. de Coning, and R.C. Thakur. 2007. *Unintended Consequences of Peacekeeping Operations*. Tokyo: United Nations University.

Autessere, S. 2008. The Trouble with Congo. How Local Disputes Fuel Regional Conflict. *Foreign Affairs* 87 (3):94-110.

BBC. 2010. *Democratic Republic of Congo Country Profile*. At http://news.bbc.co.uk/2/hi/africa/country_profiles/1076399.stm#facts (accessed 3 February 2010).

Brahimi Report, 21 August 2000. Panel on United Nations Peace Operations. New York.

Brendel, D.H. 2006. *Healing Psychiatry: Bridging the Science/Humanism Divide, Basic Bioethics*. Cambridge, Mass. and London: MIT Press.

Bureau d'Etude de Recherches et de Consulting International (BERCI). 2005. *Peacekeeping Operations in the Democratic Republic of the Congo: The Perception of the Population*. Report commisioned by the Peacekeeping Best Practices Section of the Department of Peacekeeping Operations.

Coleman, K.P. 2007. *International Organisations and Peace Enforcement: The Politics of International Legitimacy*. Cambridge: Cambridge UP.

Deephouse, D.L., and M. Suchman. 2008. Legitimacy in Organizational Institutionalism. *The Sage Handbook of Organizational Institutionalism*, ed. R. Greenwood, C. Oliver, R. Suddaby, and K. Sahlin-Anderson, 49-77. Thousand Oaks: Sage.

Dijk, A., van, 2008. Tough Talk: Clear and Cluttered Communication during Peace Operations. In *Military Cooperation in Multinational Peace Operation: Managing Cultural Diversity and Crisis Response*, ed. J. Soeters and P. Manigart, 70-80. London and New York: Routledge.

Doorn, J.A.A., van, and J.H. Mans. 1968. United Nations Forces. On Legitimacy and Effectiveness of International Military Operations. In *Armed Forces and Society: Sociological Essays*, ed. J.A.A. van Doorn, 345-377. The Hague/Paris: Mouton.

Dunn, K.C. 2003. *Imagining the Congo: The International Relations of Identity*. New York and Basingstoke: Palgrave Macmillan.

Furedi, F. 2006. *Culture of Fear Revisited: Risk-taking and the Morality of Low Expectation*, 4th ed. London: Continuum.

Hochschild, A. 2006. *King Leopold's Ghost. A Story of Greed, Terror and Heroism in Colonial Africa*. London: Pan Books.

Holt, V.K., and T.C. Berkman. 2006. *The Impossible Mandate?: Military Preparedness, the Responsibility to Protect and Modern Peace Operations*. Washington DC: The Henry L. Stimson Center.

Khalil, M., S.F. Wahidi, S.J.H. Rietjens, and M.T.I.B. Bollen. 2008. Enhancing the Footprint: Civil-Military Cooperation and Local Participation. In *Managing Civil-Military Cooperation: A 24/7 Joint Effort for Stability*, ed. S.J.H. Rietjens and M.T.I.B. Bollen, 147-165. Hampshire: Ashgate.

Lawrence, Th., W.I. Winn, and P. Deveraux Jennings. 2001. The Temporal Dynamics of Institutionalization. *Academy of Management Review* 26 (4):624-644.

Loos, E. 2007. Language Policy in an Enacted World. *Language Problems and Language Planning* 31 (1):23-37.

Lusaka Agreement. 1999. At http://www.iss.co.za/af/profiles/drcongo/cdreader/bin/2lusaka.pdf (accessed 3 February 2010).

Maathai, W. 2009. *The Challenge for Africa. A New Vision*. London: William Heinemann.

Merton, R.K. 1968. *Social Theory and Social Structure. 1968 Enlarged Edition.* New York, etc.: The Free Press.

MONUC and Congolese Government Launch Information Campaign in the UN in Kinshasa. 2010. At http://monuc.unmissions.org/Default.aspx?tabid=932&ctl=Details&mid=1096&ItemID=7465 (accessed 3 February 2010).

MONUC Approves 41 Projects for More than a Half Million Dollars. 2010. At http://monuc.unmissions.org/Default.aspx?tabid=932&ctl=Details&mid=1096&ItemID=7674 (accessed 14 February 2010).

MONUC Facts and Figures. 2010. At http://www.un.org/en/peacekeeping/missions/monuc/facts.shtml (accessed 8 March 2010).

Morjé Howard, L. 2008. *UN Peacekeeping in Civil Wars.* Cambridge: Cambridge UP.

Moyo, D. 2008. *Dead Aid: Why Aid is Not Working and How there is Another Way for Africa.* London: Allen Lane.

Musch, A. 2002. *The Small Gods of Participation*, PhD diss., University of Twente, Enschede.

Noorderhaven, N., and B. Tidjani. 2001. Culture, Governance, and Economic Performance: An Explorative Study with a Special Focus on Africa. *International Journal of Cross Cultural Management* 1 (1):31-52.

Onana, R., and H. Taylor. 2008. MONUC and SSR in the Democratic Republic of Congo. *International Peacekeeping* 15 (4):501-516.

Petraeus, D.H. 2008. Multi-National Force-Iraq Commander's Counterinsurgency Guidance. *Military Review* 88 (September-October):2-4.

Polman, L. 2003. *We Did Nothing. Why the Truth Doesn't Always Come Out When the UN Gets In.* London: Penguin.

— 2010. *War Games.* London: Viking.

Pouligny, B. 2006. *Peace Operations Seen from Below. UN Missions and Local People.* Bloomfield, CT: Kumarian Press.

Prunier, G. 2009. *From Genocide to Continental War. The "Congolese" Conflict and the Crisis of Contemporary Africa.* London: Hurst and Company.

Radio Okapi. 2010. At http://www.radiookapi.net (accessed 3 February 2010).

Rodrigues, S. and J. Child 2008. The Development of Corporate Identity: A Political Perspective. *Organization Studies* 45 (5):885-911.

Roessler, P., and J. Prendergast 2006. Democratic Republic of the Congo. In *Twenty-First-Century Peace Operations*, ed. W.J. Durch, 229-318. Washington, DC: United States Institute of Peace and the Henry L. Stimson Center.

Rubbers, B. 2009. The Story of a Tragedy: How People in Haut-Katanga Interpret the Post-Colonial History of Congo. *Journal of Modern Africa Studies* 47 (2): 267-289.

Shields, P.M. 2008. Rediscovering the Taproot: Is Classical Pragmatism the Route to Renew Public Administration? *Public Administration Review* 68 (2):205-121.

Sitkin, S.T. 1996. Learning Through Failure: The Strategy of Small Losses. In *Organizational Learning*, ed. M.D. Cohen and L.S. Sproull, 541-577. Thousand Oaks: Sage.

Soeters, J. 2008. Ambidextrous Military: Coping with Contradictions of New Security Policies. In *The Viability of Human Security*, ed. M. den Boer and J. de Wilde, 109-124. Amsterdam: Amsterdam UP.

Soeters, J., P. van Fenema, R. Beeres, eds. 2010. *Managing Military Organisations: Theory and Practice.* London and New York: Routledge.

Soeters, J., and P. Manigart, eds. 2008. *Military Cooperation in Multinational Peace Operations: Managing Cultural Diversity and Crisis Response.* London and New York: Routledge.

Tessema, M.T., and J. Soeters 2006. Practices and Challenges of Converting Former Fighters into Civil Servants: the Case of Eritrea. *Public Administration and Development* 26 (4):359-371.

UN News Centre. 2010. *First Set of UN Troops Could Leave DR Congo by June, Says Peacekeeping Chief.* At http://www.un.org/apps/news/story.asp?NewsID=33993&Cr=democratic&Cr1=congo (accessed 29 March 2010).

UN Security Council Resolution 1856. 22 December 2008.

UN Security Council Resolution 1906. 23 December 2009.

PART 2: BUILDING COMMUNITIES IN SUPPORT OF INTERNATIONAL STABILITY

OF STRUCTURES, AMBITIONS AND NATIONAL CAVEATS: THE ESDP/CSDP AND AUSTRIA

FRANCO ALGIERI AND ARNOLD H. KAMMEL

With the Treaty of Maastricht, a new integration project became reality in the form of the Common Foreign and Security Policy (CFSP). However, quite early it became obvious that such a policy should also comprise a security and defence political dimension. This paper analyses the development, the structures and the operational ability of the European Security and Defence Policy (ESDP), with the Treaty of Lisbon renamed the Common Security and Defence Policy (CSDP). Having explained the institutional and procedural aspects of European security and defence policy, as well as the strategic ambitions of the EU, special attention is paid to Austria. This article argues that, even though an institutional and strategic framework for European security and defence policy exists, further improvements need to be made in order to fully develop the European Union (EU) into a security and defence political actor. Consequently, for a member state like Austria, the participation and performance in European security and defence depends, to a large extent, on the supranational policy arena. Moreover, as is explained in the Austrian case, specific national approaches and caveats can have a negative impact on the development of a genuine security and defence policy of the EU.

INTRODUCTION

On 1 December 2009 the *Treaty of Lisbon* came into effect and the European Union (EU) finally could overcome long-lasting reform stagnation. This treaty offered a more sophisticated but also more complex framework for

Mission Critical: Smaller Democracies' Role in Global Stability Operations, ed. C. Leuprecht, J. Troy, and D. Last. Montreal and Kingston: Queen's Policy Studies Series, McGill-Queen's University Press. © 2010 Queen's Centre for International Relations, Queen's University at Kingston. All rights reserved.

the system as such, as well as the policies of the Union. It is another milestone in the development of the European integration process; however, it will not be the last. Looking at the foreign security and defence policies of the European Union (EU), today's qualitative and quantitative level is the result of a lengthy development. With the *Treaty of Maastricht*, coming into effect on 1 November 1993, the European Political Cooperation (EPC) had come to an end after two decades of existence. Consequently, this way of coordinating the foreign policies of the member states of the European Community (EC) was replaced by the Common Foreign and Security Policy (CFSP) of the European Union. When the *Treaty of Amsterdam* came into effect on 1 May 1999, the legal provisions of the CFSP were modified in certain ways; nevertheless, the development of a common European defence policy was simply alluded to as an incremental process, the success of which was dependent on the willingness of the EU member states. The breakthrough towards a European Security and Defence Policy (ESDP) developed in parallel and outside the treaty framework in the second half of 1998. European Union internal, as well as EU external, developments had created a growing pressure on the EU member states to shape a more comprehensive foreign security and defence political profile.

ESDP cannot be considered as a stand-alone policy; on the contrary, it is an essential part of the CFSP. European Security and Defence Policy is a policy field of the EU that has been developed by consecutive political agreements and decisions of European states, due to the need to react to developments in the European as well as the international context. In the case of the ESDP, the legal form followed the political function. It took until the *Treaty of Nice*, enacted on 1 February 2003, that the ESDP was integrated into the overarching legal framework of the EU. With the *Treaty of Lisbon*, the ESDP has been renamed to the Common Security and Defense Policy (CSDP) and new legal changes have been introduced.

Looking at the time frame 2003 to 2009, the European Union has conducted 22 missions and operations, being of purely civilian, purely military and civil-military nature. Such a quantitative description of the ESDP at work can be used as an argument for the progressive development of European security and defence policy. However, whether such an approach is sufficient to understand the potential and the shortcomings of the ESDP can be doubted. Any analysis of European Union missions and operations thus needs to consider, first, the historic development, and second, the institutional and procedural regulations of the EU's foreign security and defence policies. Furthermore, apart from such considerations, the quality and the effect of operations and missions are highly dependent on the support of the member states of the EU. Therefore, the supranational level not only has to be taken into account, but also the national one.

This chapter will follow a two-level approach. First, the overarching supranational level will be discussed, beginning with an explanation of the development from the European Security and Defence Policy to the Common Foreign and Security Policy, including institutional and procedural aspects, followed by an overview of the strategic ambitions of the EU. Second, against this background, a detailed look will be taken at Austria as a European Union member state, which is participating in EU operations and missions, and a country which has very specific national preconditions that are determining Austria's contribution to the ESDP/CSDP.

Finally the chapter draws some lessons learned from the various ESDP/CSDP operations and concludes with an outlook concerning the future of the CSDP, with special emphasis on Austria and the future development of its security and defence policy within the European framework.

THE NATURE OF THE SECURITY AND DEFENCE POLICY OF THE EUROPEAN UNION

Creating the European Security and Defence Policy

Several dates are mentioned for the birth of the ESDP. Some argue that it was the joint British-French Declaration of Saint-Malo in December 1998, others regard the European Council of June 1999 as the relevant step. However, from another perspective it becomes clear that it is less a single date or event but rather an ESDP formative time frame that spans a one-year period from 1998 to 1999. The kick-off was the meeting of the heads of state and government of the European Union in Pörtschach during the Austrian EU presidency in October 1998. The then British Prime Minister, Tony Blair, argued for a stronger security and defence identity in NATO and for an integration of the Western European Union (WEU) into the EU. This signalled a remarkable development of the position of the United Kingdom in the debate about European security and defence. Shortly afterwards, the Franco-British meeting at Saint-Malo marked another milestone. At this occasion France and the United Kingdom demanded, in their joint declaration on European Defence, that the EU "must have the capacity for autonomous action, backed up by credible military forces, the means to decide to use them and a readiness to do so, in order to respond to international crises" (Franco-British Summit 1998). For both countries this did not imply a reduced concern for intergovernmental interest in security, defence, and political cooperation, nor an intent to weaken the North Atlantic alliance (NATO). Saint-Malo was an attempt to bring two different strategic histories and cultures of two major EU member states closer together. For the British motives it should also be remembered that the debate about a European defence component was part of a larger set of considerations about how the United Kingdom could get a stronger role in the European integration process (Grant 1998; Howorth 2000; Lindley-French 1998).

These dynamics became part of the reform negotiations amongst the EU member states. It soon became clear that, in order to strengthen the global role and credibility of the Union, reliable security, defence, and political capacity was needed. The German-French security and defence council declared in Toulouse in May 1999 that the integration of the WEU into the EU was necessary (Deutsch-Französischer Sicherheits- und Verteidigungsrat 1999). Facing the war in the Balkans and the military engagement in Kosovo, the reflections about security and defence policy in a European context were intensified during the German EU presidency in the first half of 1999. At the Cologne European Council in June 1999 the member states of the EU agreed to establish the ESDP (European Council Cologne 1999). Also with regard to the experiences made on the Balkans, the United Kingdom and Italy made a common proposal in July 1999 aiming at the improvement of European defence capabilities (British-Italian Joint Declaration 1999). What had been achieved at the Cologne European Council was further developed during the subsequent Finnish presidency. The European Council of Helsinki focused on developing military capabilities, improving non-military crisis management and on decision-making (European Council Helsinki 1999).

This one-year period can be seen as the creation phase of the ESDP. It has to be put in context with the changing security situation in Europe in the late 1990s. The disintegration of the former Yugoslavia and the war in Kosovo became a catalyst for the further strengthening of the CFSP with the help of the ESDP (Report Lalumière 2000). While the development of the European Defence and Security Policy had started, the integration of this new policy field in the treaty-based legal framework followed with the *Treaty of Nice*, beginning on 1 February 2003. In the years that followed more and more specific arrangements about procedures, instruments, but also about ambitions, were developed. And finally, the member states of the EU had to re-consider their national security and political approaches in a European context.

Institutional and procedural aspects

The decision-making and shaping of EU operations and missions took place in a highly institutionalized setup.[1] The number of actors involved in the process had increased steadily. On the ministerial level the foreign ministers and the defence ministers played a major role. However, there was still a clear separation of competencies, i.e., defence ministers' meetings were not on the same level as the formal meetings of foreign ministers. The Political and Security Committee (PSC) is the central institutional forum for all aspects related to the CFSP. With respect to civil-military operations, other institutional bodies do need to be mentioned.

The European Union Military Committee (EUMC) is the highest military body of the EU, responsible for conducting military operations of the EU. The committee supports and advises the Political and Security Committee and, in case of a crisis, it drafts—together with the EU Military Staff (EUMS)—recommendations for the PSC. The EUMC is the forum for military consultation and cooperation among EU member states in the fields of conflict prevention and crisis management. The EUMC is supported by the EUMS and the latter acts in the area of early warning, situation assessment and strategic planning. The EUMS is in constant contact with the Situation Center (SitCen), the military staffs on the national level, as well as with NATO, exchanging information and assessing security and defence political developments. In case of a crisis, the EUMS can develop strategic options as well as contribute to corresponding non-military aspects.

Inside the European Union Military Staff, further support comes from the Civil-Military Cell (CivMilCell), coordinating civil and military activities. The EU Operations Center (OpsCen) can be set up by the European Council for autonomous EU operations, but this does not equal a permanent Operational Headquarters (OHQ). The Civilian Planning and Conduct Capability (CPCC) is under the authority of the Political and Security Committee and, in close cooperation with the European Commission, is responsible for planning and coordinating civil missions in the framework of the ESDP. The Committee for Civilian aspect of Crisis Management (CIVCOM) informs and advises the PSC on respective matters concerning crisis management.

Of course, the overview described above does not comprise all actors involved. Apart from the Council-related institutional actors and structures, the European Commission and the European Parliament need to be mentioned. Taking into account the legal framework of the *Treaty on European Union*, both institutions do have clearly defined roles to play in the intergovernmental ESDP. The European Commission has, however, a considerable weight when recourse is made to civilian capabilities and resources, which are communitarized, such as the European Instrument for Democracy and Human Rights (EIDHR) or the European Neighbourhood Policy (ENP). Furthermore, the European Commission has financial resources that can be used for crisis management tasks, like humanitarian aid, development policy, or the Instrument for Stability. Herewith the measures undertaken by the Council can be supplemented and consequently the institutional interplay between the intergovernmental and the community field of foreign security and defence policy are essential for the success of the EU's crisis management.

The European Parliament has a rather limited range of competencies in the CFSP and especially the ESDP. Regular information and consultation of the parliament by, for example, the Presidency and the High Representative for CFSP is nevertheless an important tool for improving the democratic development of the EU. Inside the European Parliament the standing committee on foreign affairs (AFET), with its subcommittee on security and defence (SEDE), do not just analyze and comment on the EU's CFSP and ESDP. Moreover, these committees frequently draft proposals and recommendations concerning the development of foreign security and defence policy in general, as well as specific, aspects linked herewith.

With the *Treaty of Lisbon*, far-reaching restructuring processes began inside and between institutions. The new High Representative of the Union for Foreign Affairs and Security Policy, Catherine Ashton, is not only part of the intergovernmental sphere of the Council. She is also a vice-president of the Commission and, as such, the interaction between intergovernmental and communitarized policy fields will become more relevant. A further remarkable novelty introduced by the Lisbon treaty is the European External Action Service in which the member states of the EU, the Council Secretariat, as well as the Commission, will be represented.[2]

For ESDP operations and missions, a final crucial topic concerns financing. In the 2008 CFSP budget of around €285 million, the major part was linked to civilian crisis management, in particular €120 million for EULEX Kosovo, €45 million for EUPOL Afghanistan and €35 million for EUMM Georgia (EUR) (Council of the European Union/Secretariat General 2009, 36). Against the background of the international financial and economic crisis, the former High Representative for the Common Foreign and Security Policy, Javier Solana, made a link between challenges, common acting, and financing: "The challenges we face require collective action which is cheaper through collective financing. With scare resources, and in the current economic crisis, we have to develop the right capabilities to meet our challenges, we must be cost-effective in doing so and we must ensure that the result is greater flexibility and interoperability" (ibid., S066/09). Nevertheless, demands for a common financing system for security and defence political activities are less easily answered. Through the Community budget, it is only possible to finance the civilian dimension. Article 28(3) of the *Treaty on European Union* (Nice version) and subsequently Article 41(2) (Lisbon version) stipulates that operational expenses with military or defence political implications cannot be financed by the Community or, respectively, the Union budget. Since 2004 the financing of military operations is done by the so-called "Athena mechanism." Through a new procedure, the Lisbon treaty now offers the possibility to get faster access to the Union budget (Art. 41(3) *Treaty on European Union*).

To sum up: In the first decade of ESDP, the institutional setup had been extended and more actors became involved. In this setup, the dualism between intergovernmentalism, on the one hand, and common policies on the other, became clearly reflected. With the Lisbon Treaty some changes occurred; however, the general pattern was not changed radically. New institutional arrangements and procedures need time to work efficiently. Future CSDP operations and missions will be determined by the two spheres of European foreign security and defence policy-making. This has to be kept in mind when the strategic ambitions of the European Union are considered.

Strategic ambitions

Looking at the EU with respect to two areas, i.e., concerning, on the one hand, the institutional nature of the Union with all its related complexity, and on the other hand, the Union's ambition to be a relevant international actor, it soon becomes clear that the analysis of the first cannot be conducted without considering the other. The member states of the EU have developed an increasing and ambitious list of what should be fulfilled on the supranational level. These ambitions have been put into a strategic framework offered by the European Security Strategy (ESS) of 2003 (European Security Strategy 2003). However, the transformation of the strategy into concrete operational steps shows that a range of improvements is necessary to overcome shortcomings. Looking at the European Security Strategy of 2003 two major aspects need to be mentioned.

First, the ability of European states to agree upon a document like the European Security Strategy can be described as a remarkable breakthrough in European foreign policy coordination. It proves a growing self-confidence of the member states to commonly define political threats and security interests. At the same time it is an expression of the EU's political, economic and the still somewhat limited defence power. Looking at a set of key threats, the ESS approaches them using a comprehensive understanding of security. Consequently, it is considered important to apply a set of instruments in order to act and react. High importance is given to a preventive policy, in order to avoid the escalation of a crisis or conflict. Even though a global perspective can be recognized in the ESS, the geographic priority is placed upon the EU's neighbourhood. Cooperation with major powers and international organizations is understood as an essential part of European foreign policy.

Second, the European document underlines the importance of an effective multilateralism, international law and the role of the United Nations. This is based on the conviction that no state is able to effectively cope with the old and new challenges of global dimension. The ESS therefore favours an international system offering inclusive opportunities to all states.

Shortly after the European Security Strategy had been published in December 2003, critical comments claimed that the document was too descriptive rather than strategic. It was also unclear about the conditions under which the EU would act, as well as when and how they would do so. Published in December 2008, the Report on the Implementation of the European Security Strategy can be described as an assessment and adaptation of the 2003 document (Report on the Implementation of the European Security Strategy 2008). There is no doubt that the ESS of 2003 remains fully relevant as the central strategic document of the EU. As a consequence, the contents of the Implementation Report echoes, in large part, what was established five years earlier in the European Security Strategy. New challenges are mentioned, enlarging the comprehensive dimension of security. With respect to the resources at hand, the report is consistent with the widespread demand for improving them. Multilateralism and cooperation with other actors remains important. In this context, it is interesting to note that the United States is regarded as the "key partner" of the EU. Furthermore, it states "the EU and US have been a formidable force for good in the world" (ibid., 16). Even though the ESDP gets greater attention in the Implementation Report, it is still not clearly expressed under which conditions the EU will use military force and where military engagement starts. Concerning the link between civilian missions and military operations, the document also remains less precise. For those, having expected a qualitative leap forward, the Implementation Report is a rather disappointing document. However, taking the 2003 and the 2008 documents together, a reference framework is formed that expresses political ambitions, but without binding characteristics for the EU member states.

Such a broad political declaration of ambitions needs to be supported in practical operational terms. This brings the analysis back to the above-mentioned institutional and procedural aspects. Without a functioning system and effective procedures, operations and missions cannot be brought to the described level of ambition. Apart from that, institutional, procedural, as well as strategic, ambitions depend on the support of national governments. For example, it is up to them to support European security and defence policy with sufficiently trained civilian personnel and military troops, to bring them together in a short time and to sustain interoperability even over a longer period of time. Even though the EU member states have started to adapt national planning and national structures, there are still shortcomings recognized, for example, in the case of making national staff and experts available for the EU, or for budgeting and procurement concerns. In the past, one of the most critical issues was the fast and timely availability of equipment. As mentioned earlier, the Lisbon treaty addresses some of these shortcomings; however, it has to be seen whether the member states of the Union will act correspondingly. In this context it should also be mentioned that calls for the development of a European strategic culture are noble, but as long as the member states of the EU cannot find a commonly accepted definition of what this means, it will have no added value for the quality of European policies.

AUSTRIA: NON-ALLIED BUT COMMITTED TO EUROPEAN SOLIDARITY

General remarks

Generally speaking, Austria's security policy has to be seen in a historical perspective. Having lost World War II, Austria was trying to establish a new identity and role on the international stage. In the course of negotiations towards its independence, one of the preconditions, set especially by the Soviet Union, was the declaration of neutrality on 26 October 1955. This declaration has to be seen in the wider context of the *State Treaty* of 15 May 1955 restoring the independent and democratic state of Austria. The Federal Constitutional Law on Neutrality stipulates in its Article 1 that the neutrality should be of a permanent nature, and in its second paragraph, that Austria will not join any military alliance nor allow the deployment of foreign troops on its territory. Austrian permanent neutrality was a product and a result of a Soviet peaceful coexistence policy that created a neutral Alpine wedge, together with Switzerland, cutting the NATO northern flank from the southern flank (Hauser 2007, 46). In the beginning, Austria's neutrality was intended to be comparable with the concept of Swiss neutrality, but quite soon, Austria's neutrality changed and developed in its own way. The concept of Austrian neutrality was the subject of heavy debate in Austria, due to the fact that the country joined the UN in December 1955 and the European Council in April 1956. According to the opinion of Karl Zemanek, there were already at that time contradictions between the Austrian concept of neutrality and the obligations deriving from UN membership (ibid., 46). Compared to the international dimension of Austrian foreign policy, the European dimension was underdeveloped. In 1959, Austria was a founding member of the European Free Trade Association (EFTA), because at that time an EC membership was rather illusory as a consequence of the restrictions set by the neutrality.

In 1956, the Austrian armed forces were called on to deal with the first of two border crises. It was in that year that the Hungarian uprising was crushed by the Soviet Union, and 170,000 Hungarians fled into Austria. The second crisis took place in 1968 when Warsaw Pact troops invaded neighboring Czechoslovakia. Austria's experiences during the Hungarian and Czechoslovak crises helped clarify the nature of the potential threat to the nation's neutrality and led to a reorientation of defence policy and a revised definition of the military's mission. These crises also lead to irritations with Russia, which were resolved by a visit of the Russian Deputy Prime Minister Mikojan in April 1957 in Vienna. At the beginning of the 1960s, Austria actively engaged in UN peacekeeping operations, such as the operations in Congo (1960–1963) and Cyprus 1964 (Kramer 2006, 813). During the Cold War period, Austrian neutrality became important within the framework of a very active and peaceful neutrality policy as stated by Chancellor Kreisky during his governments from 1970 to 1983. All major parts of Austrian foreign policy were considered as part of Austria's neutrality policy (Skuhra 2006, 843). Austria was actively involved in the drafting and adoption of the Helsinki Final Acts in 1975 in the framework of the Conference on Security and Cooperation in Europe (CSCE) and was still an active member of international organizations. This engagement was seen in a very positive light and lead to the appointment of Kurt Waldheim to the post of UN Secretary General in 1971 and his re-appointment in 1976. Consequently Austria's neutrality policy and attitudes changed to an active neutrality policy.

With the fall of the Iron Curtain and the entrance of the Austrian Freedom Party (FPÖ) into a coalition government with the Austrian Socialist Party (SPÖ) in May 1983, a reorientation of Austria's security policy took place and the defence policy became a matter of interest again. Especially with the Austrian membership to the EC/EU in 1995, the security policy changed significantly and it was linked directly with the developments on the European level. When Austria joined the EU together with Finland and Sweden, no exception was made for the new "neutral" members. On the contrary, they had to sign a joint declaration being added to the Final Act of the Accession Treaty that they would be ready and able to participate fully and actively in the Common Foreign and Security Policy (CFSP) of the EU and that their legal framework would be compatible with the rules and traditions of the CFSP (Hey 2003, 102).

When the EU Treaty entered into force on 1 November 1993, the creation of a CFSP became one of the main objectives of all EU member states, including the *de jure* neutral countries of Austria, Finland, Ireland, and Sweden. With the Austrian membership to the EU, the understanding of neutrality changed completely and the importance of the concept diminished. Article 23f of the Austrian Federal Constitution (Bundesverfassungsgesetz, B-VG), which was introduced in the course of the Austrian accession to the EU, allows the Austrian participation within the CFSP in the whole spectrum of the Petersberg tasks, including crisis management and peace-making operations. Therefore, in the academic opinion of the countries' leading constitutional law experts, the concept of neutrality has been derogated materially (Öhlinger 1999, 96; Walter and Mayer 2000, 168).

In 1995, Austria also became a member of NATO's Partnership for Peace (PfP) program and in 1996, Austria and Sweden were founding members of the UN Multinational Standby High Readiness Brigade of United Nations Operations (SHIRBRIG) with its headquarters in Copenhagen. This brigade also included the following NATO members: Canada, Denmark, the Netherlands, Norway, and Poland. Austria took the SHIRBRIG presidency in 2004, coordinating UN operations. Austria's contingent to SHIRBRIG consisted of a transportation company (Hauser 2007, 47). Furthermore, Austria plays an active role in the context of Central European Nations' Co-operation in Peace Support (CENCOOP), as there are common interests between Austria and its neighbours in the field of security policy. The political dimension of CENCOOP is an example of regional cooperation having the potential to be used in the future to share not only a common analysis, but also a part of the burden related to European security (Wosolsobe 2006, 9).

The legal and political framework of Austria's security policy

In the course of a revision of the B-VG in 1975, Article 9a B-VG was introduced declaring the comprehensive national defence[3] as a national objective. The aim should be to guarantee the independence of the republic and to defend the neutrality of Austria. The concept of a comprehensive national defence comprises elements of a military, psychological, civil and economic national defence. In addition, Article 9a B-VG lays down the basis of the Austrian conscript system in its third paragraph. Article 79, paragraph 1 B-VG stipulates that the Austrian armed forces have to be developed as a militia system (Walter, Mayer and Kucsko-Stadlmayer 2007, 361). According to Article 80 B-VG, the President of the republic is also commander-in-chief of the armed forces. The supreme command is held by the Minister of Defence, through the officers and military commanders. According to Article 79, paragraph 2 B-VG, the armed forces, i.e., the Austrian Bundesheer, have to protect the constitutionally established institutions and the population's democratic freedoms; to maintain order and security inside the country; to render assistance in the case of natural catastrophes and disasters of exceptional magnitude (ibid., 364).

Due to its foreign engagements and the duties deriving from membership in the UN, it was necessary to regulate the practice for the deployment of Austrian troops abroad. Therefore the National Assembly adopted a constitutional law act, the so-called KSE-BVG[4] in 1997. In its Article 1, this law permits the deployment of Austrian troops for peace-ensuring missions within the framework of international organizations, the OSCE or the CFSP as well as in the case of humanitarian aid and international crisis management exercises. Article 4 KSE-BVG determines the principle of voluntariness as the core principle for foreign deployment of Austrian troops.

As a consequence of EU membership and due to a change of government in Austria, a new security and defence doctrine was adopted by the center-right coalition. The strongest reference to the doctrine is related to the European Union, but also NATO/PfP and the Euro-Atlantic Partnership Council (EAPC) remain key elements of Austria's security. In 2001 NATO was more visible in the political debate in Austria, but membership is still illusory. The document clearly states that there is no immediate military threat against Austria's territory and sovereignty in the foreseeable future. The security of the EU is considered a key reference point for Austria's security. A closer look at this assessment shows a paradigm shift in Austria's security policy can be detected. National and territorial defence are increasingly focused on a protective role, in many cases playing a subsidiary role supporting other state actors (Wosolsobe 2006, 7).

Austria and ESDP

As already stated above, the Austrian Security and Defence Policy determines the European Union as the cornerstone of Austrian security policy. Austria was one of the obstetricians to the birth of the European Security and Defence Policy. The primary aim of Austrian security policy should be to promote Austria's role as an active and solitary player within ESDP in order to preserve national and European security interests, as well as maintaining Austria's position in the group of European financial core contributors and policy shapers (Reiter and Frank 2004, 1).

Austria's international commitments are directed towards the EU. Approximately 2,000 troops were pledged to the European Union's 1999 Headline Goal, but lowered to 1,500 in 2003. The level of ambition has been defined as two battalions plus support forces for unlimited deployment on stabilization and reconstruction missions of low to medium intensity. In addition, a framework brigade at 30-day readiness, sustainable for one year, was planned for high-end missions such as separation of forces, and the government aimed to develop the ability to maintain a classical peacekeeping deployment similar to its mission in the Golan Heights (Giegerich and Nicholl 2008, 66). In total, the Austrian armed forces comprised approximately 39,600 troops and a reserve staff of approximately 66,000 (IISS 2008, 166). During the last Austrian EU Presidency in 2006, Austria fully supported the development of the ESDP by declaring ESDP operations, the development of military capabilities, civil-military coordination, as well as the developments in the Balkans, to be key issues of the Austrian program in the field of ESDP.

Looking more closely at Austria's participation in EU crisis management, the picture is rather ambivalent. The EU's activities in crisis management constitute an important element of the EU´s external action. The European Council of Laeken of 2001 already declared ESDP to be operational, but it took two more years to launch the first operations within the framework of ESDP. From the beginning Austria has been strongly committed to these crisis management exercises and participated in civilian, as well as military, crisis management operations. Two regions can be identified as fields of action, namely the Western Balkans and Africa, being both of strategic importance for the EU as well as for its member states. Considering the importance of the Western Balkans for Austria's security, it seems rather obvious that there was always a need to engage in the neighbourhood. As the front garden of the EU, stability in the Western Balkans is decisive for Europe's security. Therefore the failure to solve the Balkan Wars in the mid-1990s led indirectly to the creation of the CFSP and its ESDP.

Furthermore, Africa is of particular interest for the European Union. The large number of crises and vital interests that the EU takes in Africa renders this region crucially important for its CFSP. Consequently, Austria will not be able to shirk the common responsibility of the EU, which means that missions in Africa will become more and more likely (Segur-Cabanac 2006, 17). Austria already has lengthy experience with peacekeeping missions in Africa within the framework of the UN, which date back to the year 1960 when Austria participated in ONUC[5] in the Democratic Republic of Congo with a medical contingent. Moreover Austria participated in UNEF II[6] in Egypt from 1973 to 1974 and sent military observers to Cambodia, Somalia and Rwanda.[7]

Looking at the continuing and finished military ESDP operations[8] from an Austrian point of view, the picture is rather ambivalent. While the engagement in the ESDP operations Concordia, Artemis and the Congo was of a rather symbolic nature by deploying staff officers, Austria played an important role in EUFOR Althea and EUFOR Tchad/RCA.

Lessons learned from E(C)SDP operations

As regards the lessons learned from the EU military operations, the following characteristics have to be mentioned.

1. The procedures on the political level ought to be clarified. In all operations the legal framework should be defined by the political authorities in cooperation with lawyers and issued to the force before its deployment. Political considerations should never jeopardize the military principles, the force protection and the operational coherence of unit deployment. The lack of experience of troops from some nations in regard to military operations, or the difference in national caveats from one state to another were perceived. In spite of some imperfections in procedures, the decision-making process enables better reactivity, especially for EUFOR RD Congo from now on. But the European forces on the ground should constantly adapt (Ducastel 2007, 119).

2. The European Union should assert its military might in becoming more self-sufficient with respect to NATO. Since its first military operation Concordia in FYROM, benefits from the "Berlin-Plus" agreement could be seen, while differing markedly from NATO. However, as regards a more efficient transfer of authority between NATO and the EU for the operations to come, Berlin-Plus stresses the necessity of a better definition of the chain of command. Bosnia

aspires to join NATO, but also the European Union. Like other west-Balkan countries, all of them perceive Brussels as the ultimate strategic perspective. EUFOR relaying SFOR has not generated any significant change.

The number of remits that EUFOR shares with NATO takes away any possibility of full self-sufficiency. This is stressed, as there was a risk during the transition period to see the Alliance retaining all the positive aspects of an operation and leaving the less prestigious duties to the European Union (ibid., 119).

3. Improving European planning and command capabilities is unavoidable. The framework-nation concept has been rather successful, but the relationships between the operational and force headquarters (OHQs-FHQs) still need to be improved. This concept has the advantage of a higher reactivity compared to the usual multinational concept. Nevertheless, the limited number of possible framework-nations calls for other forms of planning and command capabilities. As the European Union does not have a European OHQ at its disposal (having no permanent structure at the operational military strategic level[9]), the ability of the EU to plan and conduct military operations at that level is reduced, which affects the European Union's effectiveness and credibility. On launching an operation, the credibility of the action relies first on the credibility of the chain of command, i.e., the capability for the upper layer to assess and control at any time what the subordinate layers are doing. This would be a great asset in particular for small member states that are unable to use staff officers in the various ad hoc OHQs by deploying them to a permanent Brussels-based OHQ. Therefore, a clear military need for a permanent structure at the operational strategic level exists (Hochleitner 2008, 4).

4. The cooperation between the UN and the EU has to be strengthened. Three main challenges can be identified in this respect (Major 2008, 38): intra-organizational questions need to be solved in order to improve inter-organizational cooperation; there is a high degree of structural, organizational and cultural divergence between the two organizations; and multinational deployments display, by definition, a high degree of heterogeneity. Thus, the EU and the UN could engage in joint contingency planning which would allow the development of a common coordinated planning culture and enhance the mutual understanding of both organizations.

5. The mandate and the operative range are key factors for the success of the operation. In this context, any engagement has to be evaluated individually. Moreover, in particular, the goals and means to achieve have to be defined. A short-term military operation to guarantee peace and stability during a crucial period of time might make sense, but

only if it is embedded in a long-term strategy for the development of a region.

6. A decisive and well-equipped force is obligatory. The force generation process, especially in the case of EUFOR Tchad / RCA, has shown the European weakness in critical resources such as the lack of helicopters. Only by combining sufficient military force with soft power means, can success be achieved in these critical areas. In particular the combination of military and civil means is a unique asset of the European Union.

7. Interoperability of the forces is a precondition for a successful outcome of operations. The reality of integrating different national contributions into small EUFOR missions proves more difficult. Therefore, establishing training mechanisms might help to overcome interoperability problems. This also applies for the use of different and often incompatible equipment and armament by the participating countries. However, it leads to extra costs and diminishes efficiency. In this context the European Defence Agency (EDA) should play a central role in defining and harmonizing defence equipment.

8. Acceptance by the local population is a key factor for success. Confidence-building measures and cooperation are therefore of utmost importance.

9. Communicating the necessity of an operation to the population at home is vital. Therefore, prior to launching an ESDP operation, it is necessary to develop a media plan containing the command structures, the key messages and possible questions and replies to the most burning issues. The initial entry force should, therefore, also be supported by a press officer who is responsible for internal communication, as well as the documentation of the mission (Prantl 2006, 546).

10. Intelligence capabilities have to be strengthened. If there is a fault, the operation will need to be resumed once this fault has been ironed out, and not when the clashes cease, as seems to be the intention of those in charge (Arteaga 2008).

11. A suitable financial mechanism is needed. The so-called Athena mechanism provides a sound budgetary basis for operations and constitutes a first step towards sharing the increasingly heavy financial burden for external operations among member states, and strengthens EU integration in the field of defence and external intervention policy. The question of whether the financial burden should be transferred to the EU or whether national responsibility should prevail needs to be resolved.

12. Sustainable engagement in crisis areas is a precondition for long-term success. Three to twelve months for a European mission is little time to stabilize an area, and especially in the case of Africa, the regional

resources do not appear to be plentiful enough for a handover once that period has ended (Arteaga 2008). Showing real commitment to solve the problems of a region would facilitate local public support. This would also strengthen the perception of the EU as a comprehensive and credible global actor.

13. Effective parliamentary control over ESDP operations is required. The intergovernmental body of the Council of the European Union decides when to start and conclude an ESDP operation. But there is a number of parliaments, and neither the EP nor EU national parliaments hold the collective power to approve of, or put an end to, an ESDP operation. In brief, there is an acute problem of parliamentary scrutiny over ESDP civilian and military operations (Security and Defence Agenda 2007, 21). Consequently, close cooperation between the European Parliament and the parliaments of the member states is essential to provide this effective parliamentary control.

The way ahead for CSDP and implications for Austria

Concerning security and defence policy the respective provisions laid down in the *Treaty on European Union* leave no doubt that consensus and intergovernmentalism were, and will remain, the guiding cornerstones. Looking at the different reform stages from Maastricht to Lisbon on the one hand, a progressive development of foreign security and political defence integration has taken place. But on the other hand, member states keep control of the process and national interests or constitutional aspects are of lasting importance. Even though a rather sophisticated legal framework could be developed, the political will of the member states offering the needed practical—and not just rhetorical—support is often missing. This affects the progress, effect and success of ESDP/CSPD in a negative way. With the growing number of interests in the EU, due to the enlargement process, and increasingly more actors involved in ESDP, as well as the expansion of the described growth of the institutional setup, finding an answer to the question of how to bring ambitions in line with effective operations and missions will be crucial for the EU in general and the CSDP in particular.

Looking back at the first ten years with the ESDP,[10] a positive conclusion would be that this young policy field of the EU has developed in a dynamic way. The regular reports of the EU presidency on ESDP offer an image of multifaceted security and defence political activities (see e.g., Council of the European Union 2009). Considering the development path of the European integration process, the ESDP was described as a policy in the making (Marchetti 2009, 305). And because the integration process is continuing, the CSDP could become a decisive policy. Such decisiveness can be deduced from the sum of the civilian and military capabilities the

EU has developed. Whether this might trigger a common defence policy one day cannot be answered today.

However, there are still huge discrepancies between the capabilities of the single member states of the EU (IISS 2008). There is obviously no lack of proposals and policy recommendations pointing towards the pooling of different national capabilities and resources, but in the end it is a matter of national interests and corresponding governmental decisions to take the necessary steps (Bertelsmann Foundation 2004; Keohane and Valasek 2008). Thus a critical assessment has to accompany the positive conclusion. Nick Witney has listed a number of essential shortcomings of the ESDP (2008, 39-50):

1. Member states of the European Union and the actors on the supra-national level act in a strategic vacuum, i.e., operations do not follow common conceptualization and execution.
2. Be it with respect to military, or be it with respect to civil-military operations and missions, member states tend to declare their support, but when it comes to the actual input of personnel or assets they become hesitant, which leads to substantial shortcomings.
3. The Athena financing mechanism has turned out to be insufficient.
4. The lack of a permanent OHQ of the EU, responsible for military and civilian operations and missions, makes the planning and the conduct of such activities more difficult.
5. The lessons learned, from the process of ESDP operations and missions, are not adequate.

Against that background Witney soberly concludes as follows: "ESDP has got through five years of operations on a wing and a prayer, thanks to good luck, ingenuity on the part of many individuals who have found ways to work the unworkable, and a collective readiness to settle for the relatively safe and unambitious" (ibid., 50).

Does this lead to the final conclusion that ESDP is in crisis? The answer would be "no," but at the same time an extensive celebration of this first decade of the EU's security and defence policy would not be appropriate. It will need to be determined how comprehensive civilian and military crisis management can be developed. The former head of the EU Military Committee, Henri Bentégeat, has described a vast area: "In the coming decade, the focus of missions under the ESDP will … remain the management of crisis outside the Union, from their 'hot phase' to their stabilization" (2009, 93). This demands an approach of combining military with non-military capabilities. However, while it is easier for the EU member states to commit themselves to non-military missions, they are more hesitant with respect to military operations. A concept such as battle groups can be used by the member states of the European Union to show political good will. Whether they will ever be used, and which operational problems will turn out in practice, remains open.

ESDP was, and CSDP will be, an essential test for the political deepening of the European integration process. If time and learning processes are considered important factors, and if this policy is understood in an incremental way, the following assessment can be taken to underline it: "… the Union's general approach to security and defence cooperation might be characterized as a cautious way of achieving the general goal by promoting so-called 'evolutionary changes,' e.g., emphasizing smooth and slow development, both functionally and institutionally" (Kernic 2006, 18). But such a development can reach its limits if the member states of the European Union do not support ESDP/CSDP with the same level of ambition and when differences between states are apparent. Combined with increasing external pressure on the European Union to act, this might lead to a stronger development of group-building. As could be witnessed for example with operation ARTEMIS in the Democratic Republic Congo, in which France, Belgium, Germany and Sweden participated, group-building has already become part of the ESDP pattern. The Lisbon treaty offers new means for group-building, for example through permanent structured cooperation, and this underlines the fact, inside the security and defence policy, that the differentiation of European integration can be manifested.

Differentiation might become the tool for avoiding a marginalized role of the EU in comparison to the major powers of the 21st century. The National Security Council argues that "Europe will face difficult domestic challenges that *could* constrain its ability to play a larger global role, especially in the security realm" (National Intelligence Council 2008, 94). Robert Kagan does not see European capabilities as necessary for shaping events: "The future of international order will be shaped by those who have the power to shape it. The leaders of a post-American world will not meet in Brussels but in Beijing, Moscow, and Washington" (2007, 4). In this context, the ideal of a European integration process is rejected: "International order does not rest on ideas and institutions. It is shaped by configurations of power" (ibid., 6). It has to be seen in the years to come whether such an assumption will prove to be right or wrong. In the meantime, the European Union is moving between structures and ambitions. The more the ambitious strategic outline can be put into practice by the assistance of corresponding working structures, the more the European Union can remain relevant as a foreign security and defence political actor.

With regard to Austria, it is obvious that Austria's security is indivisibly bound up with the security of the European Union. Security policy in Austria today continues along the lines of pragmatic neutrality by participating in EU Petersberg and NATO PfP tasks (Hauser 2007, 54). For a country of Austria's size, a coordinated approach with partners sharing common values and interests has become an absolute necessity. CFSP and ESDP are important pillars for a strong Union in a globalized world. The future developments within the EU regarding its external action and security policy is closely linked to the future of Austria's foreign policy. Austria supports all developments that contribute to strengthening the EU's security policy (Reiter and Frank 2004, 2). The Austrian contribution to peace support operations has been very ambitious so far and will remain on the agenda for the foreseeable future. The present international missions reflect the picture laid down in Austria's strategic objectives. The majority of the Austrian forces are deployed in the Balkans, but Austria, alone, also responded to the new challenges in Africa. The Austrian efforts to strengthen its contribution to the European Union and, at the same time, to improve its military capabilities to reach a level that facilitates participation in a future and more demanding European defence context (Wosolsobe 2006, 11) can be used as evidence that, consequently, Austria will continue to take an active part in crisis management operations and missions of the European Union, be they of a civilian, military or civil-military nature.

NOTES

1. For a detailed description see Grevi (2009).
2. By the time of writing this article, the discussion concerning the concrete setup of all the institutional novelties caused by the Lisbon treaty was still at an early stage.
3. In German: umfassende Landesverteidigung.
4. BVG über die Kooperation und Solidarität bei der Entsendung von Einheiten und Einzelpersonen ins Ausland, BGBl I 1997/38, Constitutional Law on the cooperation and solidarity in the case of deploying troops abroad.
5. Opérations des Nations Unies au Congo.
6. United Nations Emergency Force II.
7. Austria participated e.g., in MINURSO in the Western Sahara, in UNAMIC/UNTAC/UNMLT in Cambodia or UNOSOM I in Somalia.
8. The distinction between civilian and military ESDP operations is rather artificial. A clear differentiation is not possible. For the purpose of this chapter only the purely military operations will be taken into consideration. Civil-military operations, such as EUSSR Guinea-Bissau, EUSEC RD Congo and the Support to AMIS II mission will not be considered. The same counts for the first naval ESDP operation, EUNAVFOR Atalanta on the coast of Somalia.
9. Within the Berlin-Plus arrangement, the EU could use SHAPE as an OHQ. Furthermore five framework-nations' HQs are at the EU's disposal as well as the EU Operation Centre. Nevertheless, there is no really autonomous EU planning and command capability available being able to conduct several missions in the upper range of the Petersberg tasks at the same time and providing for the necessary institutional memory and lessons learnt mechanism.
10. See for a comprehensive assessment Grevi, Helly and Keohane (2009).

REFERENCES

Arteaga, F. 2008. The Chad Conflict, United Nations (MINURCAT) and the European Union (EUFOR). *ARI Papers* 20. Madrid: Real Instituto Elcano. At http://www.realinstitutoelcano.org/wps/portal/rielcano_eng/Content?WCM_GLOBAL_CONTEXT=/elcano/elcano_in/zonas_in/international+organizations/ari20-2008 (accessed 8 April 2010).

Bentégeat, H. 2009. What Aspirations for European Defence? In *What Ambitions for European Defence in 2020?* ed. A. Vasconcelos, 91-99. Paris: Institute for Security Studies.

Bertelsmann Foundation. 2004. *A European Defence Strategy*. Gütersloh.

British-Italian Joint Declaration. 1999. *Declaration Launching European Defence Capabilities Initiative*. London 19/20 July 1999.

Council of the European Union. 2009. *Presidency Report on ESDP*. 10748/09. Brussels, 15 June.

Council of the European Union/Secretariat General. 2009. *2008 Annual Report from the Council to the European Parliament on the Main Aspects and Basic Choices of the CFSP*. Brussels.

Deutsch-Französischer Sicherheits- und Verteidigungsrat 1999. *Erklärung von Toulouse*. 29 May.

Ducastel, C. 2007. Roles and Lessons Learned from European Union's Military Operations. *Doctrine #13*. October.

European Security Strategy 2003. *A Secure Europe in a Better World*. Brussels. 12 December.

European Council Cologne. 1999: *Presidency Conclusions*. Annex. 3–4 June.

European Council Helsinki. 1999. *Presidency Conclusions*. Annex IV. 10–11 December.

Franco-British Summit. 1998. *Joint Declaration on European Defence*. Saint-Malo, 4 December. At http://www.ena.lu/francobritish-saint-malo-declaration-december-1998-020008195.html (accessed 21 November 2007).

Giegerich, B., and A. Nicholl 2008. *European Military Capabilities. Building Armed Forces For Modern Operations*. London: IISS.

Grant, C. 1998. *Can Britain Lead Again in Europe?* London: Center for European Reform.

Grevi, G. 2009. ESDP Institutions. In *European Security and Defence Policy. The First Ten Years (1999–2009)*, ed. G. Grevi, D. Helly, and D. Keohane, 19-67. Paris: EU Institute for Security Studies.

Grevi, G., D. Helly, and D. Keohane, eds. 2009. *European Security and Defence Policy. The First Ten Years (1999–2009)*. Paris: EU Institute for Security Studies.

Hauser, G. 2007. Austrian Security Policy—New Tasks and Challenges. *Defence and Strategy* 1:45-56.

Hey, J.A.K., ed. 2003. *Small States in World Politics. Explaining Foreign Policy Behavior*. Boulder: Lynne Rienner.

Hochleitner, E. 2008. *Permanent Planning and Command Structures for Autonomous EU Operations. A Capacity Deficit to be Addressed*. AIES: Maria Enzersdorf.

Howorth, J. 2000. European Integration and Defence. The Ultimate Challenge. *Chaillot Papers* 43. Paris: Institute for Security Studies.

International Institute for Strategic Studies (IISS). 2008. *European Military Capabilities. Building Armed Forces for Modern Operations*. London.

Kagan, R. 2007. *End of Dreams, Return of History*. Hoover Institution. At http://www.hoover.org/publications/policyreview/8552512.html (accessed 3 August 2007).

Keohane, D., and T. Valasek. 2008. *Willing and Able? EU Defence in 2020*. London: Center for European Reform.

Kernic, F. 2006. European Security in Transition. The European Security Architecture Since the End of the Second World War—An Overview. In *European Security in Transition*, ed. G. Hauser and F. Kernic, 5-21. Aldershot: Ashgate.

Kramer, H. 2006. Strukturentwicklung der Außenpolitik (1945–2005). In *Politik in Österreich*, ed. H. Dachs, et al., 807-838. Wien: Manz.

Lindley-French, J. 1998. Time to Bite the Eurobullet. *New Statesman*, 26 June, pp. 38-39.

Major, C. 2008. EU-UN Cooperation in Military Crisis Management: The Experience of EUFOR RD Congo in 2006. *Occasional Paper No. 72*. Paris: EU Institute for Security Studies.

Marchetti, A. 2009. Die Europäische Sicherheits- und Verteidigungspolitik. *Politikformulierung im Beziehungsdreieck Deutschland-Frankreich-Großbritannien*. Baden-Baden: Nomos.

National Intelligence Council. 2008. *Global Trends 2025. A Transformed World*. Washington, DC.

Öhlinger, T. 1999. *Verfassungsrecht*. Wien: WUV.

Prantl, M. 2006. EUFOR Tschad/RCA—Öffentlichkeitsarbeit & Kommunikation. *Truppendienst* 6 (2008):540-546.

Reiter, E., and J. Frank 2004. *The European Security Strategy—Austrian Perspective*. Paper prepared for the Ministry of Defence, Vienna.

Report on the Implementation of the European Security Strategy. 2008. *Providing Security in a Changing World*. Brussels, 11 December.

Report Lalumière. 2000. European Parliament. 20 November. A5-0339/2000. Part 2.

Security and Defence Agenda. 2007. The EU's Africa Strategy: What Are the Lessons of the Congo Mission. *SDA Discussion Paper*. Brussels.

Segur-Cabanac, C. 2006. Austria's Strategic Objectives for Foreign Missions of her Armed Forces. *Truppendienst International* 1:12-17.

Skuhra, A. 2006. Österreichische Sicherheitspolitik. In *Politik in Österreich*, ed. H. Dachs, et al., 838-861. Wien: Manz.

Walter, R., and H. Mayer 2000. *Bundesverfassungsrecht*. Wien: Manz.

Walter, R., H. Mayer, and G. Kucsko-Stadlmayer. 2007. *Bundesverfassungsrecht*. Wien: Manz.

Witney, N. 2008. *Re-energising Europe's Security and Defence Policy*. London: European Council on Foreign Relations.

Wosolsobe, W. 2006. Austria's Security and Defence Policy. *Truppendienst International* 1:6-11.

NEW MISSIONS AND EMERGING POWERS: BRAZIL, PEACE OPERATIONS AND MINUSTAH

KAI MICHAEL KENKEL

This chapter investigates the engagement of a strong emerging power from the developing world—Brazil—with the debate on, and participation in, missions of the new type discussed here. The first section examines the normative, political and juridical bases of Brazil's position on peace operations, as well as a short history of its contributions to such missions, before illustrating how the new mission in Haiti has required thorough-going changes in soldiers' training for deployment. The second section examines directly Brazil's contributions to MINUSTAH. Here the analysis brings to light the effects of regional, historical and cultural specificities and outlines the features of an emergent Brazilian model for peace-building. This is followed by a final section on MINUSTAH's role as a "laboratory" for South American diplomatic, military and development cooperation.

The advent of new, complex integrated peace operations in the international community's conflict resolution toolbox has been accompanied by the concomitant emergence of new contributors to these missions, many from the global South and the post-colonial sphere. As these countries gain in importance as executors of new-mission mandates in ever more difficult environments, such troop donors' motivations, constraints and capabilities are of growing interest. In this volume's spirit of examining how states face the novel challenges brought about by participation in new types of interventions, this chapter investigates the engagement of a strong emerging power from the developing world—Brazil—with the debate on, and participation in, missions of the new type discussed here. This perspective will be broadened to include further-reaching conclusions about the Southern Cone countries where appropriate.

The Brazilian case is presented here as representative of the experiences of several of the important emerging actors in new missions. In doing so, it provides examples of how, as a result of involvement with a specific new mission—the United Nations Stabilization Mission in Haiti, or MINUSTAH—one such state has faced increasing tensions in its policy objectives surrounding the debates on sovereignty and intervention. For Brazil, participation in MINUSTAH represents a fundamental rupture with a number of its previously cherished foreign policy tenets.

The chapter is divided into three sections. The first examines the normative, political and juridical bases of Brazil's position on peace operations, as well as a short history of its contributions to such missions. The second section examines directly Brazil's contributions to MINUSTAH, bringing to light the effects of regional, historical and cultural specificities and outlining the features of an emergent Brazilian model for peacebuilding and the training needs connected to this effort. This is followed by a final section on MINUSTAH's role as a "laboratory" for South American diplomatic, military and development cooperation.

BRAZIL AND PEACEKEEPING

This section aims to give an outline of Brazil's past involvement in peace operations prior to its first engagement with a modern complex mission in the case of MINUSTAH. It first presents briefly Brazilian foreign policy principles and the constitutional precepts which govern the country's conduct as an international actor before outlining the historical conditioning factors for Brazilian, and more broadly Latin American, attitudes towards issues of sovereignty and intervention. Following this, Brazil's past involvement in traditional peace operations is reviewed and the contours of an emerging "Brazilian way of peacekeeping" explored.

Foreign policy principles

Brazilian foreign policy, as crafted and implemented by the Foreign Ministry, is characterized by three main guiding principles, each of which, in apposition to the dominant reading of sovereignty outlined below, contributes pressure towards increasing Brazil's participation in United Nations peacekeeping missions, more specifically peace-building missions with a strong economic development component. Firstly, the Ministry of External Relations has, since the days of the iconic Baron Rio Branco, established a strongly Grotian profile (Goffredo 2005), banking on the legal guarantees of state equality inherent in multilateralism as a guarantee against the exploitation of what is seen as the country's subordinate position in the international system (Pinheiro 2000, 323). This results in the sovereigntist and normativist (Fonseca 1998, 359) view of statehood outlined briefly above, which defines sovereignty exclusively as the inviolability of borders (non-intervention) and is coupled with a distinct preference for the peaceful (particularly legalist) resolution of disputes. This has also resulted in occasional recourse to the notion of "soft power" in advancing Brazilian foreign policy goals (Goffredo 2005, 101; on "soft power" see Nye 1990a, 1990b, 2004).

Former Foreign Minister Celso Lafer embodies the view that this is the best means for Brazil to maximize its voice: "Brazilian diplomacy exercises the potential for the generation of power, inherent to the role of *soft* power at the international level, with the objective of assuring space for the defence of its national interests" (Lafer 2001, 77). This led to the country's consistently taking an active role in international fora such as the United Nations (Hirst and Soares de Lima 2006). This predilection for multilateralism is the locus of more fundamental tension as international institutions move increasingly away from the identity of sovereignty with mere inviolability. The second principle is an emphasis on economic development both within Brazil and the wider region, which has long been identified within the Foreign Ministry as the key to Brazil's advancement from a subordinate position in the international system.

The soft power idea is further reflected in the third guiding principle, which reflects Brazil's preponderance at the continental and regional levels: the country prefers to limit its action predominantly to the South American sphere, and, where applicable, to offer its services as a mediator between larger powers at the international level. The balance between these ambits has been affected by the current government's increasing desire to play a strong role in global-level institutions, sometimes expressed as a "middle power" role.

The origin of these tensions, particularly as related to the intervention debate, lies within the juridical framework of the country's foreign policy, which in part creates, and then fails to resolve, these tensions. Article 4 of the Brazilian Constitution encapsulates this duality by constructing as competing *and inherently equal* various components of sovereignty:

> [t]he international relations of the Federative Republic of Brazil are governed by the following principles:
> I – national independence;
> II – *prevalence of human rights*;
> III – self-determination of the peoples;
> IV – *non-intervention*;
> V – equality among the States;
> VI – *defence of peace*;
> VII – peaceful settlement of conflicts;

VIII – repudiation of terrorism and racism;
IX – cooperation among peoples for the progress of mankind;
X – granting of political asylum. (Constitution of Brazil 1988)

Principles II, IV and V have equal status in determining Brazilian foreign policy priorities; however, emerging intervention norms such as the responsibility to protect, have exacerbated the friction between them as defining elements of sovereignty as regards intervention. In practice, this tension has been resolved according to the continental preference for non-intervention, giving primacy to the horizontal component of sovereignty. As a result, until recently Brazil's participation in active conflict resolution has been limited by this interpretation, ruling out contributions to Security Council action under Chapter VII of the Charter. This Chapter's provisions are seen as a violation of the principle of non-intervention established in Article 2(7) of the UN Charter, a value which, in keeping with historical legacy, comes to the fore very evidently in the 1996 (Brazil 1996, para 2.3) and 2005 National Defence Policies (PDN) (Brazil 2005c, para 2.3, 4.12).

These latter two documents illustrate important progress in the country's engagement with, if not the normative, at least the military requirements of new missions: whereas the 1996 PDN called for Brazil to "participate in the [sic] international peacekeeping operations, in accordance with national interests" (Brazil 1996, para 5.1[e]), the 2005 version connects this specifically to the Security Council and, embryonically, to the need to develop increased expeditionary capacity: [Brazil should] "dispose of [sic] capacity of [sic] projection of power, seeking the [sic] eventual participation in established or authorized operations by [sic] the UN Security Council (Brazil 2005c, Guideline XXIII).

This is of some consequence to the country's role as a troop contributor for new missions, and is inextricably intertwined with an emerging Brazilian approach to complex peace operations, which will be outlined in greater detail below. These three principles come together in Brazil's leadership of MINUSTAH, the United Nations' only peace operation in the Western Hemisphere, composed largely of South American troops and containing a strong element of support for Haiti's economic development as the key to a lasting peace.

Views on sovereignty and intervention

In analyzing Brazil's response—and that of its Latin American neighbours—to the challenges posed by complex missions, the region's history, and the traces it has left on the continent's place in the international system, is of paramount importance. A number of after-effects of the colonial legacy remain strong, and this is reflected in the importance of the principle of sovereignty in Latin America and the particular interpretation it is given. Broadly speaking, Latin American states, including

Brazil, interpret sovereignty almost exclusively in its "horizontal" manifestation, embodied in the inviolability of borders. This is a reaction to a perceived subordinate position in the international system, against the negative effects of which this aspect of state sovereignty is seen as a form of protection.

In addition, the principle of inviolability and non-intervention is viewed as playing a fundamental role in keeping the peace on a continent that has seen no notable interstate armed conflict for over a century and a half. The "vertical" or contractual aspect of sovereignty which highlights state responsibility towards citizens decidedly takes a back seat in this conception, leading to attendant effects on the reception of the norms of intervention on which modern complex missions are based.

Concepts such as human security and R2P have, with a very few notable exceptions, been roundly rejected by the states of the region as yet another iteration of Northern *ingérence*. In this sense, as the states of the region emerge as ever more important troop contributors to United Nations peace operations, the motivation for this shift in behaviour must be sought elsewhere than in acceptance of the new intervention norms which increasingly underpin complex humanitarian interventions, and accordingly of their larger-order objectives.

One oft-cited motivation for Brazil's prominent role in MINUSTAH is that its Haitian involvement presents an opportunity to demonstrate its aptitude to occupy a seat in an eventual reformed United Nations Security Council, which has been elevated to one of the principal diplomatic goals of the current Lula administration. Herein lies the fundamental tension currently facing Brazilian foreign policy: the norms underlying modern peace operations—participation in which is a putative prerequisite for permanent membership—clash with foreign policy traditions rooted in the country's colonial past and "peripheral" position in the international system (Kenkel 2008).

That this tension remains fundamentally unresolved is echoed, *inter alia*, in the official Brazilian response to the R2P norm. Brazilian officials have not yet engaged with the concept's links to the vertical contract underlying state sovereignty, underscoring the country's commitment to human rights without actually incorporating this into a broader guideline on intervention:

> In our view, the General Assembly could examine in detail the new concept of a "collective responsibility to protect" … Brazil has a historic and sound commitment to human rights, democracy and the rule of law. We are parties to all main human rights treaties and we have significantly cooperated with and benefited from the international human rights machinery. It is this context that we welcome the proposals contained in the report of the SG towards the strengthening of the system. We believe that the debate on this issue is also necessary and positive and we intend to actively participate in the exercise. (Brazil 2005a)

This stance is rooted in a reluctance to view military means as an adequate answer to internal problems, which is in turn rooted in the particular interpretation of sovereignty that prevails on the continent, which favours diplomacy and non-violent means:

> We have been called upon to deal with new concepts such as "human security" and "responsibility to protect." We agree that they merit an adequate place in our system. But it is an illusion to believe that we can combat the dysfunctional politics at the root of grave human rights violations through military means alone,[1] or even economic sanctions, to the detriment of diplomacy and persuasion. (Brazil 2005b; Amorim 2007, 63-66)

Foreign Minister Celso Amorim has publicly rejected R2P, dubbing it "the *droit d'ingérence* ... in new clothes" (Amorim 2004, 140) and laying out in classic terms the apprehension of marginalization prevalent in the region:

> The most questionable section of the Report is that which refers to the question of who decides whether or not there should be an intervention. While the authority of the United Nations Security Council is not questioned, different more or less heterodox courses of action are examined for those cases in which that body may be paralyzed by the threat of a veto by a permanent member. ... The door is thus left open for certain countries to arrogate to themselves the right to intervene, without the express authorization of the Council or monitoring by a truly multilateral body. (Ibid., 140)

Thus, while rejecting some of the fundamental normative underpinnings of modern interventions, Brazilian policymakers have concomitantly highlighted the country's desire to participate more actively in the United Nations Security Council and thus these same new types of missions (of which MINUSTAH is an example):

> It is within this context that Brazil's aspirations for an enlarged Security Council with new members, permanent and non-permanent, with developed and developing countries in both categories, should be seen. Brazil has already indicated its willingness to assume immediately its responsibilities as a permanent member, alongside other countries that are equally capable of acting on the global level and contributing to international peace and security. (Amorim 2005, 12)

Brazil is a cogent example of the importance of regional context in evaluating smaller states' engagement with new forms of intervention and complex peace operations. As will be shown in the following section, several of the fundamental precepts in which these new missions find their normative basis present fundamental differences with the underpinnings of foreign policy conduct in the "periphery" of the international system.

Accordingly, when looking at the engagement of the global South as a source of troop contributors for modern interventions, one must bear in mind the strong possibility that participation in these missions might occur without "buy-in" into the higher-order normative tenets that underpin such missions politically and conceptually, with attendant effects on mission effectiveness and political coordination. This is evident in the interplay between the traditional tenets of Brazilian foreign policy and its role in Haiti as well.

Past participation in peace operations

As a result of this multilateralist foreign policy, Brazil has a long history of consistent, if not extensive, participation in the peacekeeping operations established by the UN. In fact, Brazil's commitment to multilateral conflict management measures even predates the UN, beginning with measures established by the League of Nations in the 1930s (Fontoura 1999, 195). Over the period from 1957 to 1999, Brazil deployed a total of over 11,000 troops, and more than 300 policemen, on UN duties.

However, with the exception of the "Suez Battalion," which reached a maximum strength of approximately 600 men during UNEF I (United Nations Emergency Force—Suez) and an 800-man battalion which served with UNAVEM (United Nations Angola Verification Mission) III from 1995 to 1997, this participation consisted largely of small teams of military observers, staff officers and liaison officers. Brazilian general officers served as commanders of UNEF I (1964), the United Nations Operation in Mozambique (UNOMOZ, 1993-1994), of the military observer corps of UNAVEM I (Fontoura 1999, 201-203).

This pattern of deployment clearly shows the marked predilection for Brazilian troops to be deployed in lusophone African countries (an integral part of the "Brazilian way" discussed below) and other former Portuguese colonies, the exception being a steady stream of military observers present in missions in the Middle East. As a result, while Brazil can claim to have participated in a majority of the peace operations established by the United Nations, due to the limited nature of that participation (with exceptions noted) before the advent of MINUSTAH, this pattern has not resulted in a large percentage of troops, and particularly commissioned officers, accumulating experience in such environments.

Although Brazil's leadership of MINUSTAH clearly reflects the guidelines for Brazilian foreign policy outlined above, it breaks in two ways from the practice of participation in UN PKOs as catalogued by diplomat Paulo Roberto Fontoura. As will be shown below, MINUSTAH is a very robust Chapter VII peace enforcement mission, and Haiti is neither lusophone nor situated on the African continent. As such a mission, and because it has been commanded by a string of Brazilian general officers, preparation for the deployment of Brazilian soldiers to MINUSTAH has become a considerably more complex enterprise, involving the creation of a specific training centre for Brazilian peacekeeping troops. There has been a similar evolution in the other major MINUSTAH troop contributors from the Southern Cone, although the latter tends to consist of the improvement and expansion of existing centres which predate their Brazilian counterparts.

Civil-military relations and the "Brazilian way of peacekeeping"

Civil-military relations, particularly as they relate to "secondary missions," are of fundamental importance in understanding the nature of all Southern Cone troop contributors' involvement in complex and integrated missions.[2] Southern Cone armed forces' effectiveness in missions with humanitarian and development components is increased by these forces' experience with such missions in their home countries. Viewed by Northern civil-military relations theory as indicators of incomplete civilian control due to their nefarious effects on political autonomy, these domestic secondary missions actually give a comparative advantage to South American troops in contexts such as Haiti and Congo.

The Brazilian Army played a fundamental role in the settlement and economic development of the country's vast Amazon region; Argentine and Chilean troops have long had internal missions, and such deployments have come to represent the bulk of tasks for some Andean militaries. South American militaries thus possess extensive pre-existing experience with the development components of modern peacebuilding missions. Civilian politicians' inability or reluctance to become involved in mission definition has also left many of these militaries with an institutional culture which affords field commanders considerable autonomy in designing and carrying out activities oriented towards the local population.

However, depending on the severity of past violations of democratic government by the military, there is significant variation in the extent to which certain countries are willing to carry out these tasks. For example, troops from Chile, where democratic control is more of an issue following the relatively severe violations of the Pinochet regime, seek to minimize involvement in these types of tasks and limit themselves to the civilian-defined mission mandate.

This differs significantly from the Brazilian approach to new peacekeeping missions, which combines, among others, three elements: high contact with the local population, cultural affinity, and the application of development and humanitarian experiences from domestic rural contexts. There is a widespread belief in Brazil that Brazilians possess a particular affinity for developing close, caring personal relationships with the local population during complex peace operations. This leads to increased security and greater efficiency in humanitarian tasks, thanks to a positive operational environment, higher-quality information sources and improved relationships with local actors.

As a result of this dependence upon a high level of interaction with the target population, there is a consensus among decision-makers in Brazil that deployment of the country's troops in complex missions of this type should be limited to contexts where this advantage can be brought to bear. In other words, cultural affinity is used as a criterion for selecting missions on which to deploy. There is a preference for lusophone countries, countries with an Iberian colonial past, and countries whose development contexts are similar to those encountered in Brazil's own interior areas. Within the—not necessarily easily exportable—confines of this selection criterion, it is possible to bring to bear an incipient Brazilian peace-building model of humanitarian aid and economic development, whose determinants are described below in the context of the country's leadership of MINUSTAH. The success of this model is an important component of the "soft power" side of Brazil's strategy of increasing its global clout through participation in peacekeeping missions.

Training for a new mission

The subject of training for "new missions" is one in which larger conclusions can be drawn across the South American continent, particularly as it relates to these countries' cooperation on the ground in Haiti. Because of its role as the supplier of the lead contingent for MINUSTAH, and because of that mission's importance in Brazil's bid to show the world its readiness to assume a larger role in world affairs and its support of the United Nations' efforts at conflict resolution, it became necessary to augment Brazilian peacekeepers' training, in terms not only of overall military effectiveness but of coordination with United Nations training modules and tactics and strategies specific to urban warfare (the "three-block war") and high in-combat interaction with the local population (the "strategic corporal"). This went hand in hand with a certain improvement in *matériel*.

In a development symbolic of the country's persistent problems with inter-service rivalry, exacerbated by a young and weak Ministry of Defence, Brazil actually possesses two training centres for peace operations. Within the Brazilian MINUSTAH contingent, the Brazilian Army and Marine Corps deploy separate companies, which are trained separately as well. The larger of the two schools is the Army's Sergio Vieira de Mello Peacekeeping Training Centre; the Navy maintains its own Peace Operations Training School, which is part of the Marine Corps' Instruction Centre (CIASC). The country's National Defence

Strategy calls for the creation of one joint training centre, but attempts to do this have been repeatedly foiled due to inter-service rivalry. Most recently (late 2009), the Army obtained a large increase in funding for this centre, with an eye to making its pre-eminence a *fait accompli*. The Army and Marine Corps Training Centres tend, where possible, to follow channels of cooperation with sister institutions in other countries, with cooperation occurring between Army centres and between those associated with Marine Corps, although both work with the integrated centres that have been established in other countries. The Army centre possesses more resources than that of the Marine Corps, and has in the past trained closed companies of Paraguayan soldiers for service as an integral part of BRABATT, the Brazilian MINUSTAH contingent. Small Paraguayan as well as Uruguayan units are housed within the BRABATT compound at Camp Charlie in Port-au-Prince.

In the case of the Army, pre-deployment training takes a total of six months; units are chosen on the basis of geographical rotation and the 1,200-man[3] Army component of the MINUSTAH Brazilian Battalion (BRABATT) is assembled and given advanced mission-specific training. Typically, officers and some sergeants spend a longer time in Rio de Janeiro at the PTC, undergoing training which is later passed on to the enlisted at their home base.

The Army PTC offers the following courses:

1. Preparation Course for Commanders of Military Organizations and Joint Staff (one week, rank of Colonel and Lieutenant Colonel), designed to train staff officers, with a strong C3M and civilian interaction component;
2. Subunit and Platoon Commanders' Course (two weeks), designed to familiarize these ranks with the functioning of the UN and with C3M;
3. Advanced Peace Operations Exercise (one week, all troops deployed participate); largely for mental preparation; also contains a strong C3M component;
4. Preparation Course for Individual Military Observers and Staff Officers, (two weeks, ranking from Captain to Colonel);
5. Course for (Civilian) Journalists in Conflict Zones (two days);
6. Basic PKO Course for Civilians (largely university students, two days);
7. Integrated DDR Course (experts, police, military officers, three days);
8. Senior Mission Leader Course (Force Commander, Police Commissioner, SRSG; two weeks.[4]

It is important to note that both in designing the course modules taught at the Training Centre and in the didactic schooling given its instructors, normative cues are taken based on a mixture of Brazilian Army tactical doctrine and elements gleaned from cooperation with the Association of Latin American Peacekeeping Training Centres (ALCOPAZ); the Pearson Peacekeeping Training Centre in Canada; the German UN Training Centre; SWEDINT in Sweden; the PKO section of the Portuguese Army Infantry Practical School; and Guatemala's CREOMPAZ.

One of the major differences between the Brazilian peacekeeping training centres and homologous institutions in neighbouring countries is the level to which each responds to the integrated nature of the tasks called for by participation in new missions. While Brazil has been unable to complete a fusion of the Army and Marine Corps training centres, Argentina's Centre for Joint Training for Peace Operations (CAECOPAZ) integrates all the country's armed forces, as does Uruguay's *Escuela Nacional de Operaciones de Paz* (ENOPU); Chile's *Centro Conjunto para Operaciones de Paz* (CECOPAC) is integrated, joint and combined.

Perhaps the region's most advanced and well-funded[5] peacekeeping training centre is Chile's CECOPAC, founded in July 2002. While all of the region's training centres except the Brazilian ones incorporate to some degree other forces, police and civilians into their activities, CECOPAC has the distinction of being the only one in the region whose permanent staff includes representatives of army, navy, air force, investigative police and gendarmerie (*Carabineros*). The Chilean centre also maintains an extensive web of contacts, exchanges and flow of didactic information with centres both within and outside the region, having signed alliance agreements with the United Nations' Department of Peacekeeping Operations (DPKO) and homologous centres in Argentina, Canada, Germany, France, the Netherlands, the United Kingdom, Sweden, Australia, the Republic of Korea, Australia, New Zealand, Bangladesh, India, Kenya, Ghana and Nigeria.

Argentina's CAECOPAZ was founded in June 1995 and is also joint and integrated in nature, preparing contingents and individuals for deployment primarily to MINUSTAH. All five regional centres have the same focus: training closed groups of troops and their officers for service in MINUSTAH, as well as training individual officers for duty as Military Observers and Staff and Liaison Officers with DPKO.

Of some importance in the context of peacekeeping training and deployment in the Southern Cone is the Southern Cross Peacekeeping Force (*Fuerza de Paz Cruz del Sur*), a binational force constituted by Chile and Argentina in December of 2006— after 16 months of negotiations—for deployment under the United Nations' Standby Arrangement System (UNSAS). The Southern Cross force rotates its headquarters between Buenos Aires and Santiago and is presided over by a Combined Joint General Staff (EMCC). The Force's current strength is at 800 men for the terrestrial force, one frigate, one transport vessel, four patrol boats and two corvettes. It further has at its disposal four helicopter platoons. The Cruz del Sur force is the region's most advanced military cooperative effort to date; however, due to its recent date of foundation, little more factual information about it is available at this time.[6]

The situation in Uruguay is somewhat different from that of its larger neighbours. As the Uruguayan armed forces' budget is heavily dependent upon resources gained from participation in United Nations peacekeeping operations, the country not only participates with a large contingent in MINUSTAH, but also remains one of the larger contributors to MONUC, the United Nations Mission in the Democratic Republic of the Congo. Due to the country's small size and relatively even smaller armed forces, this means that at any given time, between 15–20 percent of Uruguay's military are deployed on United Nations peace operations.

As a result, peacekeeping training takes on even more institutional importance in Montevideo; Uruguay was one of the first countries to found a separate training centre, during the deployment of peacekeepers to the Sinai Peninsula in 1982. The Army Peace Operations School (EOPE), founded in 1998, was in 2009 integrated with the other forces and renamed the Uruguayan National Peace Operations School (ENOPU). In addition, the National Peace Operations Support System, SINOMAPA, retains a prestigious position within the military establishment. Despite, or perhaps even due, to the fact that 70 percent of Uruguayan military officers have experience in peace operations, ENOPU and SINOMAPA remain more closed to cooperation with foreign militaries than the centres of the rest of the Southern Cone. The School does integrate, through modules received from DPKO's Integrated Training Service, predominantly Scandinavian content into its preparatory courses, but its exchanges are limited at the level of personnel to interactions with staff from Spain and Chile and instructors from France and the United Kingdom.[7]

At Argentina's prompting, the peacekeeping training centres of the Southern Cone, together with their peers from Ecuador, Peru and Guatemala, joined together in October 2007, in the interstices of the annual meeting of the International Association of Peacekeeping Training Centres (IAPTC), to found the Latin American Association of Peacekeeping Training Centres (ALCOPAZ). The organization was formalized in December of the same year and began to work on the following goals:

- The promotion of exchange between training centres in the region;
- support to standardization of educational procedures;
- facilitating fluid and efficient contact between members;
- promoting mutual knowledge of different institutional perspectives and cultures between personnel participating in peace operations (ALCOPAZ 2009).

As ALCOPAZ remains at this time in its beginning stages, it remains to be seen what role it will play in cooperation in peacekeeping training between the region's militaries; as with its sister institution the IAPTC, it possesses strong potential to increase information flows and personnel exchange in the years to come.

It can be concluded, then, that the states of the Southern Cone region, including to an extent Brazil, have reacted to the challenges posed by new missions in three ways: by seeking to integrate, at the level of training, all the institutions involved in complex missions; by augmenting their curricula, previously oriented exclusively around national doctrine, to courses developed at DPKO and in largely Northern states with extensive experience in new missions; and by taking advantage of the close cooperation in MINUSTAH to institutionalize relationships across borders in the region.

It is very important to note, once again, that while DPKO and foreign inputs have been added to training in an effort to better prepare soldiers operationally for deployment, this does not necessarily extend to acceptance of the broader normative underpinnings of new missions such as R2P and human security. Another commonality across these centres is that training for new missions is tailored to regional specificities. Brazilian forces, for example, despite a marked lack of connection to the high-tech approaches now gaining ground in the North Atlantic ambit, attain during their training a level of mission effectiveness akin to that of US and NATO troops by making full use of contextually-dependent comparative advantages. These are outlined in the following section.

NEW MISSION, NEW CHALLENGE: MINUSTAH

Torn between historical tradition and future aspirations: Brazil, Chapter VII and the MINUSTAH mandate

Brazil's participation in, and leadership of, MINUSTAH provides clear examples of the unresolved tensions in the country's foreign policy brought about by the emergence of "new missions." The tension between the country's continental and regional foci here intersect trenchantly with the pull towards new global-level norms of intervention such as the responsibility to protect (R2P), mediated through the aims of the United Nations in Haiti. Importantly, participation in MINUSTAH presents a very strong challenge to Brazil's traditional adherence to the principle of non-intervention and its previous self-limitation to Chapter VI missions.

The confusion begins with MINUSTAH's mandate. Security Council Resolution 1542 unequivocally establishes the mandate for MINUSTAH under Chapter VII, and certain elements have clearly been inspired by R2P, in terms both of preventive action and the characteristics of the intervention itself:

I. Secure and Stable Environment:
(*a*) in support of the Transitional Government, to ensure a secure and stable environment within which the constitutional and political process in Haiti can take place;

(*b*) to assist the Transitional Government in monitoring, restructuring and reforming the Haitian National Police, consistent with democratic policing standards, including through the vetting and certification of its personnel, advising on its reorganization and training, including gender training, as well as monitoring/mentoring members of the Haitian National Police;

(*c*) to assist the Transitional Government, particularly the Haitian National Police, with comprehensive and sustainable Disarmament, Demobilization and Reintegration (DDR) programmes for all armed groups, including women and children associated with such groups, as well as weapons control and public security measures;

(*d*) to assist with the restoration and maintenance of the rule of law, public safety and public order in Haiti through the provision inter alia of operational support to the Haitian National Police and the Haitian Coast Guard, as well as with their institutional strengthening, including the re-establishment of the corrections system;

(*e*) to protect United Nations personnel, facilities, installations and equipment and to ensure the security and freedom of movement of its personnel, taking into account the primary responsibility of the Transitional Government in that regard;

(*f*) to protect civilians under imminent threat of physical violence, within its capabilities and areas of deployment, without prejudice to the responsibilities of the Transitional Government and of police authorities;

II. Political Process:

(*a*) to support the constitutional and political process under way in Haiti, including through good offices, and foster principles and democratic governance and institutional development;

(*b*) to assist the Transitional Government in its efforts to bring about a process of national dialogue and reconciliation;

(*c*) to assist the Transitional Government in its efforts to organize, monitor, and carry out free and fair municipal, parliamentary and presidential elections at the earliest possible date, in particular through the provision of technical, logistical, and administrative assistance and continued security, with appropriate support to an electoral process with voter participation that is representative of the national demographics, including women;

(*d*) to assist the Transitional Government in extending State authority throughout Haiti and support good governance at local levels;

III. Human Rights:

(*a*) to support the Transitional Government as well as Haitian human rights institutions and groups in their efforts to promote and protect human rights, particularly of women and children, in order to ensure individual accountability for human rights abuses and redress for victims;

(*b*) to monitor and report on the human rights situation, in cooperation with the Office of the United Nations High Commissioner for Human Rights, including on the situation of returned refugees and displaced persons;

> The Council also requested that MINUSTAH cooperate and coordinate with the Organization of American States (OAS) and the Caribbean Community (CARICOM) in carrying out its mandate. (S/RES/1542)

Not only is the focus on preventive action, but the emphasis is on capacity-building within Haitian state institutions rather than ongoing foreign intervention. This not only aligns the mandate with R2P,[8] it also brings the mission's goals more closely into line with the developmentalist precepts that partially underpin established Brazilian foreign policy objectives. However, sources of fundamental tension remain within Brazil, particularly with regard to the aims underlying the use of military force and the legal basis of the mandate. The Foreign Ministry has staunchly maintained that MINUSTAH does not represent a rupture with the tradition of rejecting Chapter VII missions, asserting that only a section of the preamble fell under that provision:

> [t]he interpretation of the Brazilian government is that there is no inconsistency. In Resolution 1529, the reference to the fact of the Security Council "acting under Chapter VII" of the Charter is already made in the preamble to the Resolution, whereas in Resolution 1542 this reference to Chapter VII of the Charter is made only in paragraph 7 which would indicate, in the interpretation of the Brazilian government, that only this paragraph of Resolution 1542 is based on Chapter VII and not the whole resolution. According to this interpretation, therefore, MINUSTAH would not be based on Chapter VII and would be a peacekeeping operation.(Diniz 2005, 95; see also Fishel 2008)

However, these dialectic contortions aside, the "secure and stable environment" section of the MINUSTAH mandate is consensually recognized to be explicitly established under Chapter VII (S/RES 1542, operative paragraph 7). One leading interpretation, however, minimizes the extent to which this represents a rupture with Brazilian traditions by pointing out that while the mission is indeed authorized under Chapter VII, as opposed to some other operations mandated under that provision, it enjoys the explicit consent of the host government (Zuccaro 2005, 24).[9]

The problems with this flight into the byzantine are the strongest section of Diniz' outstanding recent treatment of the subject (2005, 100-102); he illustrates thoroughly the intricate balance Brazil must strike between the damage to the continuation of its traditions represented by participation in a Chapter VII mission, and the damage to the advancement of its quest for increased profile, including a UNSC seat, that would result from non-participation. This debate highlights once again the fact that while Brazil and other states in the postcolonial mould are emerging as increasingly important contributors to new missions, they do so without necessarily endorsing the normative objectives of these missions, and often in contravention of their own foreign policy traditions.

Brazil in MINUSTAH: leadership and the "Brazilian model"

Since the creation of MINUSTAH in June of 2004, Brazil has supplied both the mission's lead contingent and, in a break with previous UN procedures, its Force Commander. Prior to the 12 January 2010 earthquake, the Brazilian Battalion (BRABATT) consisted of approximately 1,400–1,500 troops, divided into three components. The largest by far was the regular Army contingent, consisting of about 1,000 men and composed of three companies and the accompanying battalion infrastructure. This is followed by the approximately 250-man Marine Corps task group, which is housed and controlled separately from the Army contingent, and finally the ca. 200-man Army engineering company. These numbers were increased following the earthquake by about 700 men from the regular Army and an extra 70 from the Marine Corps.

BRABATT is based in the Haitian capital of Port-au-Prince; its area of responsibility encompasses about 1.6 million people in the city's most economically disadvantaged and initially most insecure areas, such as Cité Soleil, Bel-Air and Cité Militaire. The main tasks faced by BRABATT have evolved as the mission has progressed in carrying out its mandate. The early contingents, deployed between 2004 and 2006, were primarily charged with the robust use of military force to pacify these areas, rooting out opposition and bringing about a situation conducive to the re-establishment of a state presence. Later contingents have, again prior to January 2010, dedicated themselves more intensively to foot and mechanized patrols and a number of humanitarian activities such as food and water distribution. These latter, while illustrating the importance attached to the image Brazil projects in its participation in MINUSTAH, have met with criticism from UN agencies charged with the country's long-term development prospects.

Nonetheless, Brazil has been very actively involved in supporting projects for long-term development in Haiti, both within and outside the auspices of the UN. In doing so, a model of assistance has emerged that can be said to represent the nascent stages of a Brazilian model of peace-building.[10]

This approach is based first on a high level of contact with the local population, in order to make use of common cultural experiences and affinities. It is assumed that as Brazilian enlisted soldiers often come from the country's economically disadvantaged and more rural interior, they will be familiar with the social context of underdevelopment faced by the local population. Additionally, the selection criteria for deployment assure a certain level of cultural and linguistic affinity, which are known to be key factors in mission success across complex operations.

This high-contact, light-footprint approach is coupled with a specific form of project support. Funding is given only to purchase materials necessary to carry out specific projects, which are chosen based on sustainability criteria. Workers are paid only for work carried out, and there is a strong emphasis on avoiding the corruption that afflicts development projects in Haiti. Projects are calibrated to local needs, avoiding major, more visible projects in favour of more effective small-scale endeavours. An emphasis on training further increases the lasting sustainability of these projects, which are financed from a dedicated budget that prior to the events of January 2010 amounted to just under US$3 million.

According to Brazilian officials, this approach bears similarities to the way Brazilian government agencies conduct development assistance projects in the country's own interior. Similarly, small-scale projects such as the transfer of rural technologies such as seeds and saplings with their attendant cultivation skills from geo-climactically similar areas of Brazil have met with some success. In the case of Haiti, this approach is coordinated under the auspices of the Foreign Ministry and involves a broad range of government agencies, including the government development bureaucracy, public services providers and the ministries of Defence, Finance, Mines and Cooperation. This cooperation is steered by an Interministerial Working Group chaired by the Foreign Ministry. In the case of MINUSTAH and Haiti, well-established and effective cooperation takes place not only within Brazil, but between the countries of the Southern Cone in general, all of whom are major troop contributors to MINUSTAH.

LATIN AMERICAN COOPERATION IN MINUSTAH

Increased participation in MINUSTAH and other missions has created what has become the most visible and intensive forum for diplomatic and military cooperation among the countries of the Southern Cone. Indeed, Haiti has become a reluctant "laboratory" for Southern Cone military and development cooperation in the context of a modern integrated peacebuilding mission. In a sense, many Latin American countries have long been dealing with security challenges considered "new" by Northern powers in the context of a new type of intervention. These include largely issues treated under the rubric of public security (police tasks) in the global North, but whose extent below the equator render them larger societal problems, including drug production and trafficking, small arms and urban violence, and organized crime. While there have been few successful attempts to institutionalize cooperation in the region on these issues within the sending countries, this cooperation has gained marked impetus in the case of South American contributions for peace-building in Haiti.

The "2x9" mechanism

Given the predominance of Latin American troops contributing countries in MINUSTAH, and Haiti's role as a "laboratory" for South American integration in the military, diplomatic and development spheres, it became necessary soon after the establishment of the mission to coordinate foreign and defence policies better before the region's states took their places in international fora to speak and act on Haiti. As a result, a year after the creation of the mission, on 13 May 2005, the vice-ministers of Foreign Affairs and Defence of the four main Southern Cone MINUSTAH troop contributors, as well as Panama (the then-representative of the region in the Security Council), met in Buenos Aires. Their aim was to coordinate development efforts in Haiti, as well as those designed to foster the democratic process in the impoverished Caribbean nation. The vice-ministers met again on 19 August 2005, 16 January 2006 and 4 August 2006, for meetings at which they were joined by their colleagues from three further South American contributing states: Ecuador, Peru and Guatemala. Finally, they were joined *inter alia* on 12 February, 4 September and 26 October 2007, 29 August 2008, 28 September 2009, by colleagues from Bolivia and Peru, and frequently by, notably, the Haitian Foreign Minister, as well as the heads of CARICOM, MINUSTAH and the OAS.

Although tied to a specific, time-limited context of cooperation, the "2x9" mechanism is a clear step forward in defence policy coordination in the context of the Southern Cone and the broader region. It represents a further large step in the democratization of military cooperation, in the sense that it subordinates fully the military cooperation involved in the efforts in Haiti to an overarching civilian-set foreign policy goal. It should be noted that the emphasis of this coordination mechanism is on integrating all aspects of participation in this complex new mission, in fact placing an emphasis on political and economic aspects of the peace-building goal:

> The bureaucrats made clear that the objective of the policy coordination was not centred on the military aspect of the mission, but on obtaining better democratic conditions on the island. The convocation and the coordination mechanism both were determinedly political, and accordingly, the central topic of debate was the elections in Haiti. (Diamint 2005, 5)

In this respect, the collaboration between the countries of the Southern Cone in preparing their troops for MINUSTAH and potential other deployment with the United Nations has already borne fruit in the field. Brazilian and Argentine troops jointly conducted the operation to capture the noted Port-au-Prince drug lord Dread Wilme; integrated in BRABATT, Paraguayan troops continue to serve integrated in BRABATT; Brazilian troops and the Uruguayan Navy work together to patrol Haiti's maritime borders; and extensive cooperation takes place within MINUSTAH's higher military command structure.

UNASUL and the South American Defence Council

Inspired by the successes achieved under the aegis of regional integration in the European Union, the cornerstone for the Community of South American Nations was laid in Cuzco, Peru on 18 December 2004, and the organization was formalized at the Brasília Summit on 30 September 2005. On 23 May 2008 it was renamed the Union of South American Nations (UNASUL, in Portuguese). The organization has been greeted with both enthusiasm and criticism in other institutions in the region. Criticism has come primarily from the OAS, to which it is a seen as an alternative way for regional integration to go ahead without fears of US hegemony. Conversely, in the absence of American dominance, fears have risen that UNASUL might be used as a tool for Brazil to assert its own dominance in the region,[11] as many of its institutional advancements have come at Brasília's prompting.[12]

One of these initiatives is the Defence Council, proposed by Brazilian President Luis Inácio Lula da Silva in 2008 and formalized in March 2009. In the short time since its founding, there has been consistent debate about the Council's role—whether it should take on a proactive role modelled after NATO, given that UNASUL is modelled after the EU, or take second place to existing institutions such as the OAS. In deciding its future role, the states of the region have attributed to the Council the following declared objectives:

> a) to consolidate South America as a zone of peace, and as the basis of democratic stability and overall development of [its] peoples and as a contribution to world peace;
> b) to construct a South American identity in matters of defence, which takes into account subregional and national characteristics that contribute to the strengthening of the unity of Latin America and the Caribbean;
> c) to generate consensus in order to strengthen regional cooperation in matters of defence. (Serbin 2009, 151)

It is clearly this last point that is of most interest here. Venezuela-based analyst Andrés Serbin points out the larger objectives behind the creation of the Council:

> Even if this proposal is still in the process of being formulated, it dilutes any militarist aspiration in regional integration. Its fundamental objective is conflict prevention and resolution and the creation of a forum for promoting dialogue between the Ministers of Defence of each country, to reduce lack of confidence and lay the foundation for a common defence policy—excluding the United States—that is based on civilian control of the armed forces. (Ibid., 151)

In this sense, one of the consequences of increased Brazilian and South American involvement in new missions is the potential for a subtle shift in the tenor of civil-military relations, whose effects and legacy have been described above. Where armed forces on the tail end of a transition to democracy once had the autonomy to conduct most of their direct cooperation in pursuance of parochial institutional interests, the increasing integration of regional civilian politics has increasingly subordinated this type of cooperation to broader policy goals. These goals, at the level of regional security policy integration, are increasingly centered upon cooperation in the preparation and deployment of troops to MINUSTAH and other eventual modern complex interventions.

What conclusions can be drawn, then, from the above brief analysis of Brazil's response to the challenges brought on by new peacekeeping and peace-building missions? Foremost, there is the realization of the importance of historical context and the legacy of colonialism. States such as Brazil see state sovereignty, narrowly defined, as a form of protection against a repetition of past experiences of exploitation and intervention.

Yet, at the same time, several of the states in this category have begun to strive for increased global influence, and view participation in new missions as a means to this end. As a result, these states find themselves participating—often decisively and with significant success—in these missions without commitment to the normative tenets that underpin this type of mission, whether they be R2P or the more classic reconstruction of the neoliberal state, post-conflict.

Furthermore, the debate within these states on their participation often takes place in a context of strong tensions between competing objectives in state policy with respect to intervention. Participation in these missions often represents a rupture with previous tradition. However, not all regional specificities necessarily bring with them difficulties when it comes to participation in new missions. Specific forms of civil-military relations in post-colonial, particularly South American and African societies, while viewed as problematic in a Northern context, can in fact provide distinct advantages in terms of mission success for missions with a strong humanitarian component.

As emerging Southern states such as Brazil are taking on increasing importance as suppliers of troops to new missions, the gap between the normative foundations for such missions—a modern conception of sovereignty and a concern for human rights—and more traditional motivations, such as international influence and military prestige, must be addressed. Concomitantly, however, the learning process with respect to intervention is by no means a one-way street—Brazil's peacebuilding model and cultural approach to new missions such as MINUSTAH can serve as a source of fruitful insights for the established Northern peacekeeping powers. Openness to the responses developed by states such as

Brazil to the difficulties of new missions is an important key to meeting the challenges these interventions will bring in the future.

NOTES

1. Note that this appears to belie an understanding of R2P that responds only to the provisions of the "responsibility to react" and omits entirely the responsibility to prevent and to rebuild, both of which are considerably better adapted to Brazilian foreign policy precepts.
2. For more on this see Kenkel (2009).
3. Prior to the January 2010 earthquake, after which the unit currently in training was sent to Haiti to bring the total number of Brazilian Army troops to approximately 1,900.
4. Information provided in response to a questionnaire submitted to the Brazilian Army Peacekeeping Training Centre by the author, 19 June 2008.
5. A situation assisted by Chilean law giving the armed forces a share in all proceeds from the country's extensive copper production.
6. For more analysis on the binational force, see María Inés Ruz (2008) and Gonzalo Garcia Pinto (2008).
7. Interview with Colonel Carlos Delgado, Commandant, ENOPU and Captain (N) Gabriel Vaccarezza, Commandant, Uruguayan Marine Corps, Montevideo, 17 July 2009.
8. For the official presentation of this concept see ICISS (2001); Further interpretation is available from the norm's creators in Weiss (2004, 2006, 2007) and Evans (2006).
9. On this point, see also André Luís Ramos Figueiredo Simões (2007).
10. The information that follows is the fruit of interviews and communication with civilian and military Brazilian officials.
11. On the potential for the Council to work as a platform for Brazilian hegemony, see Susanne Gratius (2008).
12. For more information, see, *inter alia*, Alex Sánchez (2009).

REFERENCES

Amorim, C. 2004. Conceitos de Segurança e Defesa—implicações para a ação interna e externa do governo. In *Reflexões sobre defesa e segurança : uma estratégia para o Brasil*, ed. J.R. de Almeida Pinto, A.J. Ramalho da Rocha, and R. Doring Pinho da Silva, 135-157. Brasília: Ministry of Defence.

— 2005. Política Externa do Governo Lula: os dois primeiros anos. *Análise de Conjuntura OPSA*. n. 4. At http://observatorio.iuperj.br/pdfs/5_analises_Artigo%20Celso%20Amorim.pdf (accessed 1 November 2008).

— 2007. Discurso… da abertura do Seminário de Alto Nível sobre Operações de Manutenção da Paz, Brasília, 5 de fevereiro de 2007. Brazil. Ministry of External Relations. *Resenha de Política Exterior do Brasil* 100: 63-66.

Brazil. 1996. Ministry of Defence. *National Defence Policy*. Brasília: Ministry of Defence. At http://merln.ndu.edu/whitepapers.html (accessed 15 May 2009).

— 2005a. Permanent Mission to the United Nations. *Cluster III: Freedom to Live in Dignity. Statement by Ambassador Roanldo Sardenberg, Permanent Representative of Brazil to the UN. New York, 19/20 April 2005.* At http://www.reformtheun. org/index.php?module=uploads&func=download&fileId=307 (accessed 15 May 2009).

— 2005b. Ministry of External Relations. Statement by H.E. Ambassador Celso Amorim, Minister of External Relations of the Federative Republic of Brazil, at the Opening of the General Debate of the 60th Session of the United Nations General Assembly. New York, 17 September 2005. At www.un.org/webcast/ga/60/statements/bra050917eng.pdf (accessed 15 May 2009).

— 2005c. Ministry of Defence. *National Defence Policy.* Brasília: Ministry of Defence. At http://merln.ndu.edu/whitepapers.html (accessed 15 May 2009).

Constitution of Brazil. 1988. At http://www.v-brazil.com/government/laws/titleI.html (accessed 31 October 2008).

Diamint, R. 2005. El "2X9": ¿Una incipiente comunidad de seguridad en América Latina?. Policy Paper No. 18. Buenos Aires: Friedrich Ebert Foundation, Programa de Cooperación en Seguridad Regional.

Diniz, E. 2005. O Brasil e a MINUSTAH. *Security and Defense Studies Review* 5 (1):90-108.

Evans, G. 2006. From Humanitarian Intervention to the Responsibility to Protect. *Wisconsin International Law Journal* 24 (3): 703-722.

Fishel, J.T. 2008. Latin America: Haiti and Beyond. In *Peace Operations: Trends, Progress, and Prospects,* ed. D.C.F. Daniel, P. Taft, and S. Wiharta, 153-186. Washington: Georgetown University Press.

Fonseca Júnior, G. 1998. *A legitimidade e outras questões internacionais - Poder e Ética entre as Nações.* São Paulo: Paz e Terra.

Fontoura, P.R.C.T. da. 1999. *O Brasil e as Operações de Manutenção da Paz das Nações Unidas.* Brasília: FUNAG.

Garcia Pinto, G. 2008. Força de paz combinada Cruz do Sul. In *Segurança internacional. Um diálogo Europa-América do Sul,* ed. W. Hofmeister. Rio de Janeiro: Fundação Konrad Adenauer.

Goffredo Júnior, G.S. de. 2005. *Entre poder e direito: A tradição grotiana na política externa brasileira.* Brasília: Instituto Rio Branco/FUNAG.

Gratius, S. 2008. ¿Hacia una OTAN sudamericana? Brasil y un Consejo de Defensa Sudamericano. Comentário FRIDE abril 2008. Madrid: Fundación para las Relaciones Internacionales y el Diálogo Exterior.

Hirst, M., and M.R. Soares de Lima. 2006. Brazil as an intermediate state and regional power: actions, choices and responsibilities. *International Affairs* 82 (1):21-40.

International Commission on Intervention and State Sovereignty (ICISS). 2001. *The Responsibility to Protect: Report of the International Commission on Intervention and State Sovereignty.* Ottawa: International Development Research Centre.

Kenkel, K.M. 2008. *Global Player,* or Sitting on the Fence? The "Responsibility to Protect": definition e implications for Brazil. *Revista da Escola de Guerra Naval* No. 12.

— 2009. Civil-Military Interaction and Latin American Troop Contributors: A Comparative Perspective. In *Revisiting Borders between Civilians and Military: Security and Development in Peace Operations and Post-conflict Situations,* ed. E. Hamann, 110-114. Rio de Janeiro: Viva Rio.

Lafer, C. 2001. *A identidade internacional do Brasil e a política externa brasileira.* São Paulo: Perspectiva.

Latin American Association of Peacekeeping Training Centres (ALCOPAZ). 2009. ALCOPAZ website, at http://www.alcopaz.org/missao.htm (accessed 17 December 2009).

Nye, J.S.1990a. *Bound to Lead: The Changing Nature of American Power.* New York: Basic Books.

— 1990b. "Soft Power." *Foreign Policy* 80:153-171.

— 2004. *Soft Power: The Means to Success in World Politics.* New York: PublicAffairs.

Pinheiro, L. 2000. Traídos pelo Desejo: Um Ensaio sobre a Teoria e a Prática da Política Externa Brasileira Contemporânea. *Contexto Internacional* 22 (2):305-335. At http://publique.rdc.pucrio.br/contextointernacional/media/Pinheiro_vol22n2.pdf (accessed 15 May 2009).

Ruz, M.I. 2008. La Fuerza de Paz Cruz del Sur: cooperación chileno-argentina. *Estudios Internacionales* 41 (160):107-118.

Sánchez, A. 2009. The South American Defense Council, UNASUR, the Latin American Military and the Region's Political Process. Washington, DC: Council on Hemispheric Affairs. At http://www.coha.org/the-south-american-defense-council-unasur-the-latin-american-military-and-the-region%E2%80%99s-political-process/ (accessed 17 December 2009).

Serbin, A. 2009. América del Sur en un mundo multipolar: ¿es la Unasur la alternativa? *Nueva Sociedad* 219:151.

Simões, A.L.R.F. 2007. Apreciação juridical sobre o emprego da força militar de paz no Brasil na MINUSTAH. Thesis, Curso de Estado-Maior para Oficiais Superiores, Escola de Guerra Naval, Rio de Janeiro.

Weiss, T.G. 2004. The Sunset of Humanitarian Intervention? The Responsibility to Protect in a Unipolar Era. *Security Dialogue* 35 (2):135-153.

— 2006. R2P after 9/11 and the World Summit. *Wisconsin International Law Journal.* 24 (3):741-760.

— 2007. *Humanitarian Intervention: Ideas in Action.* Malden: Polity Press.

Zuccaro, P.M. 2005. A participação das forças armadas brasileiras em operações de manutenção da paz como instrumento da política externa brasileira e seus reflexos para o Poder Naval. C-PEM Thesis, Escola de Guerra Naval, Rio de Janeiro.

BUILDING A RESEARCH COMMUNITY TO SUPPORT NEW MISSIONS: THE ROLE OF DEFENCE UNIVERSITIES

DAVID LAST[1]

The challenge of complex missions is not to defeat military enemies, but to combine the political, economic, and social policies of diverse small states, each with modest expeditionary forces, in order to support stabilization and development. To achieve this, synergies will not be achieved by training, but by research and education. This chapter considers the nascent International Society of Military Sciences, a consortium of small defence universities, as a potential model for research and university collaboration, comparing it to the governance structures of successful international medical and social science collaborations. Considering the structures of security education, national and international research collaboration, and university governance, this chapter suggests that defence universities in small countries may be well placed to build research and education networks that will improve transnational cooperation in operations if they behave more like universities.

Here I make the argument that the missing piece in achieving this long-sought level of synergy is not training, but education. Furthermore, we have to build the institutions to meet that educational need, and we cannot do it within any one state, especially a superpower with national interests and arcane domestic motives. This is a job for an international "middle class" of capable states with a vested interest in the larger community. Armed forces, police forces, governmental and non-governmental

Mission Critical: Smaller Democracies' Role in Global Stability Operations, ed. C. Leuprecht, J. Troy, and D. Last. Montreal and Kingston: Queen's Policy Studies Series, McGill-Queen's University Press. © 2010 Queen's Centre for International Relations, Queen's University at Kingston. All rights reserved.

organizations, and key individuals of all descriptions have long sought to become an effective community of practice, and the effectiveness they seek can only be built on experimentation and evidence, on research and education. The hundreds of think tanks and research establishments doing good work in isolated stovepipes all over the world have made important contributions, but their contributions are the work of Sisyphus. Time and staff turnover, budgets and barriers to dissemination, changing environments and new rules for operating will keep rolling the rock back downhill. There is no panacea for this human condition, but the venerable and evolving institution of the university as repository of knowledge, pursuer of truth, and shaper of future generations, can be the wedge that saves Sisyphus, and the lever that pushes back.

As I began to read the latest round of academic books about reconstruction and stabilization, and the latest insights from the field about solving the problems of Iraq and Afghanistan, I was struck by a depressing sense of déjà vu. We saw a lot of this literature in the mid-1990s. More striking still is the extent to which such works eschew empiricism, and fail to cite that which has gone before. I have been guilty of this myself. We seem stuck in a cycle of six-month epiphanies, as bright young leaders go off to face new challenges, are moved to present solutions, write a few papers, and move on. Where is the accumulation of professional knowledge? Universities evolved to serve this function. The best of them have become, in Clark Kerr's phrase, "multiversities"—embodying the functions of research, teaching, housing and disseminating knowledge through specialized institutions, and developing and evaluating policies in collaboration with government (Kerr 2001). Kerr was writing about the American university, but I want to apply the concept here to the challenge facing small countries trying to shape their security environment by reaching out to other defence universities. I am consciously stretching the concept of defence, associated with military forces, to encompass the wider security community, including police and gendarme and intelligence services.

The International Society of Military Sciences (hereafter ISMS or "the Society") is a nascent exercise in international institutional cooperation, and it bears examination to determine the extent to which it might become a research community to support new missions. Beyond the narrow function of a research community to support operations, the concept of an international network for professional education has potential ramifications for the way future generations of security professionals—police as well as gendarmes and soldiers—approach their responsibilities to deal with collective action problems like demographic shifts, climate change, pandemic disease, social collapse, and security challenges we have not yet begun to contemplate.

In this chapter, I consider the way in which a network of defence universities can help to support challenging new missions for small states.

The International Society of Military Sciences is a new organization, which might learn from other successful university and research networks in order to support the development of a coherent security profession that transcends state boundaries.

HURDLES FOR NEW MISSIONS

Today, it is possible to conceive of a coherent security profession, consisting of all armed and uniformed services—police, paramilitary, and military—and all other branches of state that seek to build and preserve human security, national security, and international security. But it is hard to find such a community in practice, and easier to isolate the military profession as we look back at the evolution of security thinking. For soldiers it is easier to think in terms of their own tribes—army, navy, air force—or even the families within—infantry, armour, and artillery. It is at this microscopic level that we find it easiest to trace the evolution in the use of practical knowledge: gunpowder, cannon, field artillery, indirect fire, and so on. But let us try to think in broader terms, of the contribution of knowledge to the pursuit of security in the twentieth century, in which winning wars was the focus of the military profession, and cleaning up after them was the task of other parts of an evolving security community—diplomats, police, development aid, and so on.

The functional separation of military and civilian, diplomacy and development, and so on, is related to hurdles for contemporary operations, which might be surmounted with the help of new evolutions in the security universities in small countries. The first hurdle is the prevalence of stovepipes and isolated enclaves of professional knowledge. We know that military forces cannot and should not operate in isolation, yet on the academic side, we find strategic studies departments that have no truck or trade with peace studies scholars, and on the practical side we find counter-insurgency doctrine that is widely rejected by the development community (The Network of Concerned Anthropologists 2009).

The second hurdle is that these isolated enclaves interact most under the pressure of operational necessity. Civil-military cooperation evolved in European and American colonies from the 1890s, maritime-land cooperation evolved in peripheral theatres, land-air cooperation evolved for continental operations. The American *Goldwater-Nichols Act* is the epitome of shotgun weddings to force joint-ness on unwilling services, but its prominence obscures that fact that the barriers to cooperation are smaller where forces and operations are smaller. This gives a comparative advantage to small, developed countries with well-educated professionals.

The third hurdle is an occasional non-academic tendency amongst field operators, who may choose not to make time for professionally relevant study, or may be unaware of fields of study that would be relevant. To be fair, many academics have been unwilling to constrain themselves to practical matters or the rigors of operational fieldwork. This two-way barrier has limited the application of university knowledge to security problems typically found at the tactical and operational levels. This tendency in the army, foreign service, and development world has waxed and waned over time, and has sometimes been reduced by cross-cutting cleavages of the headquarters-field divide, or technical-humanistic ideologies, which seek their academic champions.

The fourth hurdle for contemporary operations has been the slow pace of adopting knowledge from new disciplines. This is related to separation of domestic and foreign operations, and of thought and practice relevant to war and operations other than war. Police science, for example, has made great strides in understanding the correlates of domestic order, but this has not always been applied to expeditionary operations in which artillery and air strikes hit enemies, while strategists puzzle about "hearts and minds" and patrols frequently operate without interpreters. Treating "war" and "operations other than war" as separate has resulted in resistance in some military communities to the serious study of many of the missions in which armies have actually been engaged. Some professionals prefer to focus on the history of big wars, and the putative next big war. Military history therefore has a special place in military academies and staff colleges, while sociology, social psychology, anthropology, and even political science and international relations have been less well represented. These disciplines have evolved in civilian universities faster than in military establishments.

Finally, the fifth hurdle for contemporary operations has been the intellectual model of war, which has dominated military thinking, separating it from the other security professions, which now must collaborate to achieve security (Keegan 1993). War is about defeating an enemy, and the mental constructs of enemy, victory, and defeat led through the course of European civil wars of the nineteenth and twentieth centuries to a dawning understanding on the part of many states that security could not be achieved through the defeat of enemies. The stronger is the military establishment of a state, the weaker is the presence of this understanding amongst the intellectual community that pursues security. Again, smaller and weaker states may have a comparative advantage, being less tempted by coercive solutions.

These five hurdles—stovepipes, reluctant integration, the intellectual-practical gap, the slow pace of integrating new knowledge, and the crippling dominance of Eurocentric notions of war—have created the urgent need for an international intellectual community that pursues professional knowledge relevant to security for the common good, but they are also hurdles that might be more easily surmounted by agile small countries than by big powers with large and anonymous research communities linked to defence industries. How are the defence universities of smaller states positioning themselves to overcome these problems?

AN INTERNATIONAL SOCIETY OF MILITARY SCIENCES

Since the end of the Cold War, the staff colleges and defence academies of the world have been increasingly focused on education for the new unknowns, rather than training for the certainties that passed with the fall of the Berlin Wall. As more of them sought to offer bachelor's and master's degree programs, many institutions found themselves without a comfortable peer group, being unlike the civilian universities to which they looked for models and degree accreditation. As the civilian and military faculty of these institutions came under pressure to research and publish, they needed contacts with a larger military academic community. The progress from "student to scholar" is not the same in civilian and military establishments, whether the candidate is in camouflage or tweed (Cahn 2008). Moreover, those who would be academics in support of security recognize the difference.

Eight institutions representing ten small countries have joined to form an International Society of Military Sciences (ISMS or the Society), with the aim to "build a network for the creation and diffusion of research and knowledge about war, conflict management and peace support efforts" (ISMS 2008). The member institutions are listed in Table 2.

What sort of a community is this Society? The narrative of its establishment parallels that of any other nascent academic society of mutual interest, but there are some important differences. The Society actually has elements of three distinct types of academic networks, which serve different purposes for communities seeking to develop and propagate knowledge.

It is, primarily, an association of national institutions (in one case a multinational institution), rather than autonomous academics or independent universities or disciplinary departments. Secondarily, it permits individual members to participate. The governing body of the Society is a council made up of representatives of institutions. In this it resembles bodies like the councils of universities that accredit their members in many countries. Civilian universities in Canada have been permitted since confederation to grant degrees by provincial statute, and are regulated by provincial ministries of education, but also belong to the Association of Universities and Colleges of Canada, which speaks for their collective interests, and on which they are represented by their executive heads. Similar arrangements exist for the unitary states whose defence educational establishments belong to the Society, most of which offer university degrees.

Individuals from any country or institution are free to join the Society, and in this it resembles disciplinary associations like the International Sociological Association (ISA), or its more specialized and often multidisciplinary cousins like the European Research Group on Military and Society (ERGOMAS) or the Inter-University Seminar on Armed Forces and Society (IUS). These are bodies of scholars in pursuit of their personal academic and professional interests; they are self-managing professionals. The model for academic disciplines goes further: to establish standards of evidence through peer review, venues for debate and publication, and a platform for leadership in the direction of the discipline. The American Political Science Association (APSA), for example, has been instrumental in maintaining the quantitative preference in American political science (Jacobsen 2005). ISMS could evolve as a disciplinary association for the study of military sciences with the attendant debate about what "military sciences" are and are not.

On the other hand, ISMS purports to serve a military profession, and so might have some elements of professional associations like the American Medical Association, in which practitioners meet in both conference and committee to evaluate their peers and the progress of their profession. It does not have the goal of regulating or disciplining national institutions, but like international associations of professional associations, it provides an opportunity to compare national approaches and reconcile divergence when there is a common interest in standards and practices that transcend national boundaries. The European Organization of Military Associations (EUROMIL) is an umbrella organization for national military associations and trade unions, which promotes the social and professional interests of European military personnel. It is interesting because these interests include the democratic control of armed forces, and the Association has been a vehicle for spreading democratic values to post-Soviet states and emerging democracies, through vehicles like the *OSCE Handbook on Human Rights* (2008). In the case of ISMS, the transcending goal is the pursuit of professional knowledge in the service of peace and security. To understand this, we turn to the discussions surrounding the foundation of the Society.

The point paper that formed the basis for discussion at the first meeting, argued for the need to:

> ...create an association of research institutions interested in the academic study of war, conflict management and peace support. This association creates a network for the diffusion of scientific knowledge through synergetic cooperation and efforts of its members. (Wagemaker 2008)

Not stated, but inherent in the process, was that the participating institutions were military. The phrase, "military arts and sciences in the broadest senses" reflects the different meanings evidently associated with the original aims as they were interpreted by military educational cultures of the founding countries. The label "war, conflict management and peace support" was intended to imply the full spectrum of conflict, but also reflects a common perception amongst the founding institutions' representatives that military professionalism entails the management of violence rather than just the successful prosecution of wars. This is a key point. Losing a war is a failure of the military profession, but for most of the world's professional armies in developed countries, being forced into a war is also a failure.

European military institutions have moved beyond being colleges that teach the skills to win wars against each other, and seem to treat military arts and sciences in terms that are compatible with the goals of the Stockholm International Peace Research Institute (SIPRI), or the International Peace Research Assocation (IPRA).

Since 1964 IPRA has been pursuing interdisciplinary research into the most pressing issues related to sustainable peace around the world today. As a network of scholars, practitioners and decision-makers from all continents, we strive to stay at the cutting edge of the state of the art of peace. IPRA is about building communities of inquiry (IPRA Website 2009).

The main distinction between these organizations lies in their membership and their assumptions about the utility of military force, with defence colleges and academies clearly committed to preserving the relevance and utility of the military instrument.[2]

The eight institutions making up the Society do not have common trajectories. Austria's is the oldest tradition dating back to 1751, while the Baltic Defence College is the youngest, established in 1998. The membership includes cadet academies, staff colleges, and research institutes with varying connections to universities. Some grant degrees, and others provide only cadet or staff training, so it is helpful to develop a common language or taxonomy to situate their roles in the development of professions.

The Bologna process has helped to formalize comparability among European universities, primarily with the aim of enabling greater transferability of university credits, permitting an internationalization of the business of education through the European Credit Transfer and Accumulation System (ECTS). More student mobility under the Bologna process will help to solidify a European identity and common citizenship (Fejes 2008), and this might also result from more interaction in security education. Three cycles of education are described in the Bergen Declaration (2005), which is related to the Bologna process, and these are illustrated in Table 1. There is no particular pressure to standardize the 3ième cycle, because these graduates are evaluated on their own merits under special circumstances, usually by universities or research institutions to which they are applying for employment. Considerable progress has been made towards standardizing the first two cycles, and these correspond closely to the levels of professional education typically undertaken by military officers.

TABLE 1
Comparison of Security Education

Bologna Process	Degrees	Academic Institutions	Professional Stages	Professional Institutions
1ière cycle	BA 180–240 ECTS 3–4 years	Accredited colleges or universities	Initial officer formation	Commissioning schools or colleges
2ième cycle	MA 90–120 ECTS 1–2 years	Graduate schools	Officer Mid Career	Command and Staff Colleges
	MPhil		Senior Leaders	War College or National Defence College
3ième cycle	PhD No ECTS equivalency 3 yrs or more		Some specialists, e.g., Finnish PhD in Military Pedagogy	

Source: Author's compilation from various sources.

Table 1 compares the three cycles of the Bologna process with the professional stages of development common to military forces around the world. Initial officer formation brings recruits (or in some cases soldiers) to the stage of commissioning as junior officers. The year equivalency is based on 60 ECTS per year, which assumes about 1,500 to 1,800 hours of study. The two common patterns in European civilian universities are a three-year BA followed by a two-year MA, or a four-year (honours) BA followed by a one-year MA. These are significant benchmarks for military institutions, because time spent on a rifle range, obstacle course, or route march does not earn academic credit, and the pressure to award degrees therefore either lengthens time to commissioning, or restricts time available for core military training.

Table 1 implies that initial formation normally corresponds to the 1ière cycle, and staff colleges to the 2ième cycle, but that there is no equivalence between senior leader courses and the 3ième cycle. This is not to say that all commissioning schools and colleges offer university degrees, the Sandhurst model of commissioning emphasizes training in practical military skills, leadership, fitness and sport. But there has been increasing pressure on military commissioning schools to offer university degrees, all over the world, and it has become common since the nineteen-sixties to grant a university degree with the initial officer commission. Today, more than 80 percent of Sandhurst cadets are already university graduates. Australia, Austria, Argentina, Belgium, Canada, Japan, Germany, and the Netherlands, are just some of the countries that began to offer accredited university degrees as part of the officer commissioning process since the Second World War. (The author is in the process of compiling a global comparative database of security education.) Others, like Finland, Norway, and Sweden, have begun to offer university degrees through their initial officer intake programs, partly motivated by competition for quality candidates in labour markets (Warner 1990). Economic and recruiting motivations to link commissioning to degrees have fluctuated, but the demand for an educated officer corps has risen consistently. It has paralleled demand for education in other social elites, to which military professionals often compare themselves (Janowitz 1960).

Mid-career command and staff colleges prepare officers to command formations or to work in higher headquarters, and are normally undertaken after about ten years of commissioned service. It is increasingly common for these mid-career courses to include elective academic courses and to offer—more rarely to require—a thesis or original research contribution to professional study. Following America's lead, an increasing number of command and staff colleges around the world are offering master's degrees. The US Army Command and General Staff College began to offer the Master of Military Art and Science in 1991, was accredited by the North Central Association of Colleges and Schools in 1995, and graduate degree-granting authority was extended to nine other American defence schools and colleges in 2009 (Duncan Hunter 2009). The Masters of Defence Studies, awarded by the Royal Military College to officers undertaking additional work at the Canadian Forces College, was first awarded in 2002, and accredited by the Ontario Council of Graduate Studies in 2005, although RMC had been awarding Master's degrees unrelated to the staff college since 1981. Other institutional members of the Society have begun to offer degrees of the 2ième cycle within the last five years. In this process there has been constant bargaining over the benchmark quality lines for graduate degrees.

Courses for senior leaders, often labelled War College or National Defence College, are the pinnacle of professional education, usually undertaken after more than twenty years of service, by only the most successful officers, typically at ranks equivalent to colonel or general. Evaluation on these "terminal" courses is normally by peer assessment, and while assignments may be demanding, dropout or failure is highly unusual because of the care taken in the selection and institutional investment in the students.

There is no suggestion that military senior leader courses are the equivalent of doctoral studies, aimed at generating new knowledge, or that doctoral degrees could replace senior leader development. When Congress broadened the degree-granting authority in American military schools and colleges, it caused Dr. Jack Kem at the US Army Command and General Staff College to speculate on the future of a PhD in operational art, probably building on the School of Advanced Military Studies, rather than targeting successful commanders. The United States probably leads the field in the number of senior officers with good doctoral degrees already.

The pursuit of degrees is a common theme in status-conscious military hierarchies; successful commanders and general officers feel less pressure to earn higher degrees for their terminal professional courses, while those seeking additional prestige, career opportunities, or personal satisfaction may seek out the opportunity for academic advancement (Auge 2009). Each of the ten states involved in the Society has some mechanism for preparing senior leaders, and there is, as yet, no discernable pressure in general to offer doctoral degrees to generals.

Within this taxonomy, then, we can describe the institutions that make up the Council of the International Society of Military Sciences. Table 2 lists the institutions and the focus of their educational programs. Although this requires some explanation, the members focus primarily on higher officer education, for which some research and original contribution to professional knowledge is required, but for which coordination of curricula is also necessary if officers are to be effective in international operations. Although I stress below the evolution of degree-granting authority, it is important to note that the primary function of all of these institutions is to prepare professional officers for national service, and requires competence in multinational and civil-military operations. These are precisely the areas in which officers from small states are most likely to have to work with officers and civilians of other states.

TABLE 2
ISMS Council Members' Educational Focus

Institution	Cycles
Austria's Bundesheer Landesverteidigungsakademie (www.bundesheer.at)	2
Baltic Defence College – Latvia Lithuania and Estonia (www.bdcol.ee)	2
Royal Military College of Canada (www.rmc.ca)	1, 2, 3
The Royal Danish Defence College (www.fak.dk)	2
Finland's National Defence University (www.mil.fi)	1, 2, 3
Royal Netherlands Defence Academy(www.nlda.nl)	1, 2
Norwegian Defence Staff College (www.fss.mil.no)	1, 2
Swedish National Defence College (www.fhs.se)	2

Source: Author's compilation.

The most common pattern amongst the ISMS members is for initial officer formation and commissioning to occur at one institution, sometimes divided by service (army, navy, air force), and for all higher officer training and education to be combined at another institution.

Institutions responsible for higher officer education, offering or seeking to offer master's degrees, form the core of ISMS membership. The relationship between the two levels of a military educational institution varies. Austria's *Landesverteidigungsakademie* is charged with research and support to teaching, with some military academics specializing in research and others in teaching. Research has become more of a concern at institutions for higher professional education as accreditation is sought for university status, but the capacity to do research has also made these institutions more useful to commanders and staff who need to answer difficult operational questions on the basis of some expertise. There is inevitably some tension between the utility of "research on demand" and the desirability of academic freedom for researchers.

For Austria, initial formation is provided by the Theresian Military Academy in Wiener Neustadt, which began offering bachelor's degrees in 1998. Austria's National Defence College in Vienna (Bundesheer Landesverteidigungsakademie) provides most higher officer education, including research and training to support senior officer development, and the editorial offices of the *Austrian Military Journal*, which is considering making the transition from a professional to a peer reviewed journal.

Amongst the three Baltic states, the Baltic Defence College has served for senior officer education in a joint environment since 1999, with master's degrees offered since 2008. In addition to the joint Baltic Defence College, Latvia, Lithuania and Estonia have their own national institutions, which offer officer training and education at all of the levels described on the right side of Table 1. To the extent that their curricula aim to support joint and combined operations in a NATO context, there is some coherence and commonality as there is for other NATO states.

Like other Nordic countries, Finland adjusted its policy of conscription after the Cold War, and increased the focus on education for long-service officers. It has one national military university, which dates back to 1933, and offers Bachelor's and Master's of Military Science, a General Staff Officer's Degree, and a Doctor of Military Science. It has been awarding bachelor's and master's degrees since 1992, and doctoral degrees in military pedagogy since 1997.

Canada's Royal Military College is something of an outlier in the ISMS membership. It was established as a nation-building institution in 1876, before there was a significant regular army or navy into which to commission its graduates. It began offering bachelor's degrees in 1959, and master's degrees in 1981. The junior staff college for the army has also been located in Kingston, as was the National Defence College until 1995. The Canadian Forces College for joint command and staff training, however, was established in Toronto during the Second World War, and since 2002 has offered three levels of professional officer training, including a master's degree concurrently with the Joint Command and Staff Program (JCSP) mentioned above. The academic staff for this degree constitute a department of the Royal Military College, and RMC remains the degree granting authority, making the Master of Defence Studies one of four non-technical master's degrees offered to meet Canadian Forces needs.

We can draw several conclusions from this summary of ISMS and a survey of its membership. First, military educational institutions in Europe are evolving to become more like civilian universities, concerned with accreditation, research and teaching as well as professional education. This is about preserving and generating knowledge relevant to security. Along with the renewed academic focus comes an expectation of academic integrity, hence academic freedoms. There is an emerging consensus, not yet consummated everywhere in regulations, that even military researchers in uniform must be free to investigate important questions and report honestly with minimal restrictions.

Second, outreach across national boundaries, not limited to these countries, has become a normal part of national approaches to developing a favourable security environment. Sometimes this is guided and funded by defence and foreign affairs staff, and sometimes it follows the more serendipitous path of individual research interests, which national authorities are nevertheless happy to harness. There is a widespread awareness that the skills taught in mid-career staff colleges are fundamentally international rather than national in focus.

Third, part of the response to the less predictable post-Cold War security environment has been higher education, in which mid-career and senior officer education is combined with pursuit of master's degrees, for which officers are expected to conduct research. Anecdotally, this seems to be most effective when entry-level and mid-career academic education is combined, allowing more concentration of resources for research.

Because ISMS has elements of several different kinds of academic associations, and because civilian universities have been in the business longer, it is worth examining the ways in which civilian university and research networks contribute to the sort of knowledge and expertise that might support new missions.

THE SOCIETY AS A UNIVERSITY NETWORK

If a university is a community that supports scholarship, a university network is a community that supports scholarly communities. Professions rely on these communities of schools, colleges, and universities to preserve existing knowledge, and to conduct original research, which expands the boundaries of the known (Van Creveld 1990; Janowitz and Wesbrook 1983; Masland and Radway 1957).

What do civilian university networks do that a security university network could learn from, to support the security professions in new missions? I will limit myself here to three issues: peer institutional review and accreditation, evidence-based teaching, and specialised bibliometry.

The Council of Ontario Universities was established in 1962, at the time of the growth of new universities (Ross 1966), to improve the quality and accessibility of higher education in Ontario—a jurisdiction about the size of some of the ISMS partners.[3] It began as a committee of university presidents and steadily expanded to address issues of management, information, responsiveness to the market for higher education, and preservation of traditional institutional autonomy. The Ontario Council on Graduate Studies (OCGS) conducts quality reviews of proposed and existing graduate programs in Ontario universities, including the Royal Military College of Canada, and RMC's Master of Defence Studies (MDS) taught through the Canadian Forces College in Toronto. RMC is an Associate Member of the Council of Ontario Universities; it voluntarily submits to program reviews by OCGS, and provides faculty to support reviews of other institutions. This institutional "peer review" helps to preserve and enhance academic standards, as universities compare their programs to those of a larger community, which is a natural administrative extension of the disciplinary communities that professors normally frequent: historians in history conferences, engineers in engineering conferences, and so on. For RMC, voluntary associate membership provides added justification to bolster academic rigour against the occasional demands of military expediency—no, we can't offer a BA in two years, because it would not be accredited, and we would lose good candidates; no, we can't admit everyone to our MA programs, but we can offer alternatives to make up educational shortfalls.

It may make no sense for military universities or police academies to seek accreditation from a peer group of security institutions in other countries. From a recruiting and employment perspective, a Swedish Major wants to know that his degree is recognized in Sweden, rather than by an international association which has little impact on his post-service employment prospects. The benefit to the institution comes from having a peer group that understands its needs and constraints. Academics who have never worked in military staff colleges or academies may not recognize the forms that scholarship can take there. Classified reports, operational research, and field service are not unique to security environments, but are more familiar to those who operate under similar circumstances. Thus, when the Swedish or Danish Defence Colleges are asked by their national ministries or university associations for names of academics who can competently review their programs, they can draw on the faculty of sister institutions in other countries. This mutual evaluation is the beginning of a self-aware international community, which will be able to develop common approaches and mutually reinforcing research programs to support new missions. Those who do the reviews take good points back to their own institutions.

This brings me to the problem of evidence-based teaching. As police or military professionals, do we really know what we need to know to pursue security effectively? Do we ask relevant questions, seek the answer with sound sources and methods, and apply those answers to teaching the next generation, or are we still bound to antiquated curricula and assumptions of cause and effect that are more ideological or doctrinal than empirical? University networks help to keep the faculty members of each institution grounded in the general advance of knowledge. Small colleges will not be at the forefront of relevant research in every discipline, but can draw on new research at other universities; indeed, they are expected to. Again, we can look to other disciplines to see how this might work for military sciences, and how it might support new missions.

NATO's Partnership Action Plans on Defence Institution Building (PAP-DIB), developed common curricula addressing three major themes: public administration and governance, defence management and economics, and ethics and leadership (Emelifeonwu 2008). There are common professional standards and references that accompany much of the relevant course material. National staff colleges and defence universities in new NATO member countries prepare their own teaching material and find their own sources and evidence to support the broad themes identified in the curricula. There has been no concerted research program or systematic review of evidence to support this teaching; it is more doctrinal than empirical—based on belief more than evidence. In contrast, medicine and social work draw on systematic reviews of evidence, described below. If we assume that empirical evidence can contribute to new operations, then we should expect that security education should endeavour to incorporate sound research and systematic reviews in the material that they teach to future leaders. Perhaps even more importantly, they might strive to model critical empiricism in their approaches to new missions.

This returns us to the question of "military science" and what sort of a field of study it is. What is being taught in defence colleges and academies in the world, based on what evidence, what academic disciplines, and to what end? Police science, almost anywhere in the world, is a fairly consistent combination of law, criminology and sociology, with the majority of police academies focused on practical preparations for professional police work. Where gendarme schools and colleges exist, they tend to combine practical policing with light infantry weapons skills and tactics. The interior ministry universities of the former Soviet Republics have more expansive intellectual ambitions, which include masters' degrees in public management, social science and pedagogy, business and law. The Kharkiv National University of Internal Affairs in Ukraine is an example of such a "multiversity" in the paramilitary domain, although more than two thirds of their graduates serve out of uniform. In its expansive interpretation of policing science, Kharkiv reflects the broad understanding of military science practiced in the former Soviet Union, and widely understood in Eastern Europe.

Austria's military education establishment is arguably the oldest in Europe, and its concept of military science is perhaps the broadest, encompassing all branches of human knowledge and practice applied to the conduct of war (and now, the pursuit of peace and stability). The idea that military studies must be "scientific" lives on in post-enlightenment nineteenth century institutions like the US Military Academy West Point, which offers only Bachelor of Science degrees.

In entry-level military colleges, it is common to find departments of leadership and military studies, as well as other departments that approximate those of a civilian university. At the mid-career level, the most common divisions of staff colleges address some combination of leadership and management, defence policy, and military operations and strategy. Both entry-level academies and staff colleges are affected by the operations of the day: the Cold War in the 1980s, the Balkans in the 1990s, Afghanistan in the first decade of the 2000s. This is more evident in mid-career staff colleges than entry-level colleges where traditional disciplines are often well entrenched. Surprisingly, many security education establishments have not evolved as repositories of learning, as have medical or law schools. In most countries, military academies and staff colleges tend not to be the first point of enquiry for puzzled practitioners, nor are they at the forefront of research on professional and operational matters. Evidence-based teaching, then, is not a strong point for security education in small countries, and this is presumably something that could be improved by more cooperation and sharing.

The evolution of libraries has been a central feature of evolving universities that preserve and expand knowledge (Clark 2007). Bibliometry permits us to understand better the patterns and quality of scholarship emerging from published materials (Giske 2008). University data servers, no less than library shelves, are increasingly important means to preserve access to the growing volume of electronic journals, reports, and datasets, partly because they have specialised university librarians who can often track and access material more effectively than researchers. Libraries, indices, and bibliometric tools, however, reflect academic usage, and security institutions are comparative late-comers to twentieth century library tools. To take a few examples, Ulrich's Periodical Directory—reporting on more than 300,000 periodicals in 200 languages—does not list security, criminology, defence, war studies, or peace studies as subject headings. "Military" and "Civil Defence" are the only two of 950 subject headings that capture these fields. Periodicals are categorized as scholarly/academic, peer reviewed, or general. The 2009 Directory listed 158 scholarly and 44 peer reviewed journals under the military subject heading. Another indicator is the distribution of military subject areas in the Web of Science Social Science Citation Index. Table 3 lists the seven largest military categories by discipline, according to the number of articles cited. Book holdings, of course, would present a different picture, as would actual library holdings of serials.

TABLE 3
Military Subject Areas, Web of Science, November 2009

Web of Science "Military" Subject areas in Social Science Citation Index	No. of Articles
Political Science	1,119
International relations	1,057
Sociology	460
Area studies	450
Economics	324
Psychiatry	323
History	221

Source: Compiled by Sarah Toomey and Clarinda Olsen.

University libraries form a network within the university network, and are part of a research community that supports the advance of knowledge within disciplines. Research centres concerned with secrecy and training centres without academic libraries are generally not part of this network. Anecdotally, staff colleges in many countries are more aware of the need for library resources than they were a decade ago, but are not under the same compulsion to acquire them as are colleges or academies that seek university status or that offer degrees, particularly within recognizable disciplines. The Canadian Forces College in Toronto has about 100,000 volumes, RMC Kingston has about 330,000, US Military Academy West Point about 608,000, and the US Air Force Academy about 1.7 million volumes. Better capacity for searching and sharing library holdings should be a high priority for smaller institutions.

Building a research community amongst small states to support new missions can benefit from security education institutions that behave more like a university network. While we would expect them to continue to be accredited nationally, the individuals doing the accreditation could be drawn from a wider international community, and this will help facilitate the spread of useful ideas and practices. The development of coherent bodies of shared study, evidence-based teaching, and supporting research libraries will also enhance the professional prospects of soldiers no longer primarily focused on winning wars against each other. Even more important than a university network, however, is the concept of an international research network to support security professions.

THE SOCIETY AS A RESEARCH NETWORK

> Engineers can build bridges that stay up; social scientists can't build countries that stay together. What's wrong with you guys?
>
> *Al Stewart, Dean of Engineering, RMC, 2005*

> Politics is more difficult than physics.
>
> *Albert Einstein, Physicist, 1879–1955*

Institutions like Canada's Royal Military College were established to produce leaders with the technical expertise to build the British Empire—roads, bridges, railways, and administrative skills. But today's domestic and international operations are challenged more by human, rather than technical, difficulties and the social sciences have not arrived at many clear solutions, as RMC's Dean of Engineering facetiously but accurately suggested (above). Nevertheless, there are examples of successful research networks that have made dramatic progress on complex social problems. By considering some of the generic characteristics of these networks, we might deduce ways in which ISMS or comparable networks could contribute to security knowledge for new missions.

What does it mean for a research community to be successful? Good research results in changed practice in a timely way (Tash 2006). It responds to the changing demands of practitioners, but also moderates practitioners' expectations and demands in accordance with the interests of society. For example, medical research does not focus just on better cures for heart disease, but also on prevention. The evolution of medical "general practice" and "public health" as specialties provide examples of the symbiosis between research and practice (Duffin 2000). Medicine, social policy, and workplace health and safety therefore provide a rich pool of examples with which to compare security research in support of new missions. In all these fields, social choices must be made about the allocation of resources, and public and private costs and benefits. The aim here is not to describe these in detail, but illustrate some of the characteristics and structures of research communities that might inform the evolution of a new multi-national security research community, not led or dominated by major military powers, or dominated by commercial interests.

We like to think that medical knowledge is closer to the precision and accuracy of engineering than the rather shaky record of the social sciences. Yet as recently as 1991, the editor of the prestigious *British Medical Journal* asked, "where is the wisdom?" He pointed to a study showing that only about 15 percent of medical practice was based on sound evidence, with antiquated teaching, "common knowledge," a colleague's recommendations, drug company studies, and other dubious sources accounting for the rest (Smith 1991). For military practice (beyond studies of weapons effects), we have no comparable data. A major effort to enhance evidence-based practice ensued, and spread in UK policy circles under successive governments. In medicine, it was embodied by the Cochrane collaboration, which aimed to increase the availability of reliable evidence about common medical procedures. The Cochrane collaboration aims at "improving healthcare decision-making globally through systematic reviews of the effects of healthcare interventions, published in the Cochrane Library" (Cochrane Library Press Releases). It is a global network of more than ten thousand volunteers that accepts grants and donations, but does not accept funding from commercial sponsors with interests in health practice. The scope of evidence-based military practice is potentially much broader than weapons effects and combat tactics, but the national and human security implications are also more complex.

The Cochrane collaboration consists of collaborative review groups, centres, methods groups, fields, a consumer network, an elected steering group, and a small professional secretariat. The major source of funding for the secretariat and website is royalties on sales from the Cochrane Library, which reports the findings from systematic reviews. Other activities are funded by grants from non-conflicted sources. Funding is not accepted from drug companies, for example. Collaborative review groups produce systematic reviews of studies that evaluate health interventions. Recent reviews range from small questions to larger health issues: vitamin D supplementation can reduce falls in nursing care facilities; combined drug and radiotherapy improves survival of cervical cancer; four major reviews of arthritis find insufficient evidence to support a previously common treatment, and evidence of efficacy for new treatments; new drugs have better cure rates for malaria, and so on. The last mentioned is the work of the Cochrane Collaboration Infectious Diseases Working Group, which has been conducting collaborative systematic reviews since 1994. Collaborative Review Groups are supported by research centres in each geographic region (for example, the Australasian Centre at Monash University in Melbourne), which usually have the resources of a major university, teaching hospital, and research laboratories. The Methods Group evaluates the soundness of systematic review techniques, and has developed standards for inclusion of studies, which have in turn influenced granting agencies, and the design of testing for drugs and procedures. Fields and networks identify health issues that are important to various populations. They then help to concentrate resources to conduct reviews that are relevant to these groups. The Consumer Network represents the interests of patients, who have an interest in the priority of work and use of results of the systematic reviews.

Governance of the Cochrane Collaboration is a good example of democratic scientific management, which is relevant to defence universities in small powers. The steering group sets policy, and the secretariat implements it. The steering group consists of 17 elected members—six elected by review groups, four by centres, two by the consumer network, one each by fields and methods groups, and the final three are the Trials Search Coordinator and two co-chairs representing no specific entity. The electoral process for each position is by proportional representation, but each cluster of seats has requirements. For example, of the four centre representatives, one must be a Centre Director who is not a Branch Director, one must be a member of centre staff (who is neither a Director nor a Branch Director) and two must be members of centres (without restriction on their position) (Cochrane Collaboration 2009).

The Cochrane Collaboration's governance mechanism is significant because it puts control of the collaborative scientific enterprise effectively beyond the reach of corporate or government interests. Any defence scientist or military officer who has been involved in the machinations of the NATO's International Military Staff or the NATO Command, Control and Communications Agency (NC3A) will recognize the merits of democratic management from the perspective of smaller states, and the drawbacks from the perspective of larger powers, which expect a measure of control (at least commensurate to their funding). An organization that is capable of pronouncing with authority that this or that instrument is effective would be a very valuable organization to influence.

The systematic reviews of the Cochrane Collaboration are most effective for biomedical problems that approximate engineering in the precision and reproducibility of cause and effect. Any problem involving free will and human behaviour, particularly collective human behaviour, presents difficulties around experimentation, non-reproducibility, and value expectations. This encompasses almost every serious question related to defence and security policy. Equity is one such issue in medical care, and the Cochrane Collaboration has recently joined with another project that addresses social policy questions. The Cochrane Equity Field became the Campbell and Cochrane Equity Methods Group in February 2010 (Cochrane Review Press Release 2010).

Like the Cochrane Collaboration, the Campbell Collaboration produces systematic reviews, but focused on the effects of social interventions, which have much more in common with security problems: education, crime and justice, and social welfare. In each of these broad areas, the Campbell collaboration asks, "What helps? What harms? Based on what evidence?" A new initiative to identify "burning questions" seeks input on "what works and what harms in the development of stable and inclusive societies and states. What policies and programmes contribute to welfare and wellbeing, and what policies do not?" (Campbell Collaboration website) These questions have more in common with the sort of security problem facing contemporary military forces, particularly when they are engaged in protracted social conflicts, insurgencies, and post-conflict reconstruction.

Some of the headlines from recent Campbell Collaboration reviews include findings that: anti-bullying programs in schools are often effective; formal processing of juvenile delinquents does not reduce delinquency, but treating serious juvenile offenders in secure facilities does; and problem-oriented policing and closed-circuit television both have modest impacts on crime and disorder. The evidence for these statements comes from reviewing many studies, each of which meets stringent criteria. The findings about problem-oriented policing, for example, were based on rigorous review of ten studies of police services in the US and UK using the SARA (Scanning-analysis-response-assessment) model for problem-oriented policing on a variety of different problems ranging from school victimization and vandalism through to dangerous neighbourhoods and drug markets. Although all ten programs in the UK and US followed the same model, the review reported a lot of variation in implementing the model—some focusing on "problem places" and some on "problem people" (the latter seemed more effective). In addition to the ten programs for which rigorous analyses were available, a further 45 studies did not meet the required standard; some did not include a control group, many were merely descriptive, others did not provide adequate data for comparison (Weisburd et al. 2010). The review concludes: "Across such a small number of studies, then, it is difficult to draw any firm conclusions." Major military interventions such as peacekeeping, counter-insurgency, security sector reform, and security assistance are rarely followed by systematic data-collection or evaluation, and standards of evidence about their consequences are correspondingly even lower than for the studies mentioned above.

The problem with any social intervention, including new missions for small states' armies, is that causality is not simple or direct. Causal chains are densely populated, inter-related, and tend to loop back on themselves. The expectation that something will happen can affect individual and collective behaviour in surprising ways. Rather than accumulate systematic reviews that may or may not reflect unique circumstances, social researcher Ray Pawson (2006) argues that policy should be understood in its proper context: an intervention produces an outcome in a specific context. In a different context, the same intervention should be expected to produce a different outcome. The implication is that pooled data sets and aggregation of study results from different contexts cannot be definitive. Indeed, the language of the Campbell Collaboration reports is consistently more circumspect than that of the Cochrane Collaboration. Only in the realms of value judgement (like equity) and method are the two collaborations on equal footing.

These two collaborative research networks and Pawson's critique of social policy research help to map the functions of a defence and security research network. Most importantly, they provide a framework for consistent collaboration and evaluation of research results. As with other academic associations, they provide a common set of standards, and a peer group for review. They provide a network that draws from and contributes to a set of academic journals, but they also help to break down the stovepipes of disciplinary affiliation by bringing science back to the practical questions—what should be done? (Becher 1989).

Military research has sometimes benefited from international collaboration, defying expectations that national security fears would prevent it. Britain's decision to share sensitive technical research with the United States at the height of the Second World War, before America committed to the fight against the axis powers, was the forerunner of The Technical Cooperation Programme (TTCP) in 1940. Snow (1961) describes the anxieties surrounding that decision and the ultimate benefits. The American, British, Canadian, Australian and New Zealand Armies' Program (ABCA), established in 1947, is a doctrinal equivalent of scientific cooperation, aiming to achieve effective integration of five nations' army capabilities to permit the full spectrum of coalition operations. TTCP and ABCA offer different models for research cooperation. While the Cochrane and Campbell Collaborations are democratic associations of individual researchers and autonomous centres, TTCP and ABCA are creations of participating governments, which host events in rotation, provide national staff officers to manage communications, and vet participation in events. It is common for contributions to be classified, because they build on national defence research networks, for which security of information is an important consideration.

National research on security matters does involve civilian universities, often in clusters and centres that reflect patterns of funding and expertise. Defence Research and Development Canada (DRDC), for example, is organized in seven centres with technical specialties ranging from chemical and biological defence to submarine warfare, intelligence systems, and explosives. Like the Second World War and the Cold War, the War on Terror has spurred joint research with other government departments and agencies, and money for civilian research. The Centre for Security Science in Ottawa is a joint endeavour with Public Safety Canada, which has collaborative projects with researchers in civilian universities, the Royal Military College of Canada, and the US Department of Homeland Security.

The Chemical-Biological-Radiological-Nuclear-Explosives Research Technology Initiative (CRTI) is an outgrowth of multi-agency collaboration in Canada, which involves a network of researchers at civilian universities. Its origin lay in the sudden availability of research funds after the 9/11 terrorist attacks, and it is now in its second five-year funding cycle. The focus of its research has expanded and shifted since 2001 to adapt to evolving perceptions of threat. Major events influencing its direction included a weak national response to severe acute respiratory syndrome (SARS) in 2003, the evident failures of American response to Hurricane Katrina in New Orleans in 2005 (and planning for a Vancouver earthquake), and the emergence of home-grown terror cells in Toronto in 2006. The common factor in all these events was a large psychosocial component and the broader question—what permits or impedes successful mobilization of resources appropriate to deal with these threats? The CRTI had spent $150 million on 79 research projects between 2002 and 2007. Most of these addressed technical capabilities: could labs detect bio toxins? Could samples be transmitted safely and analyzed quickly? Was protective clothing for first responders adequate? In November 2007, a new psychosocial research cluster was launched within CRTI to address the broader questions prompted by events like SARS, Katrina, and the "Toronto 18."

Governance of the CRTI research clusters is centralized and responsive to government funding, which competes with other government priorities. The Director of CRTI is a government appointee, who oversees portfolio directors in each of the five science clusters: chemical, biological, radiological-nuclear, forensic and explosives. The Director is guided by the Program Management Board of the Public Security Science and Technology Program, which is co-chaired by the Director General of the Center for Security Science, and the Assistant Deputy Minister for Science and Technology of the Department of National Defence. In contrast to the Campbell and Cochrane collaborations, this is a top-down model, however there is scope for private sector and public university application for funding, and funding applications are reviewed by panels of government officials and university academics according to criteria that include feasibility, innovation, and alignment with security priorities.

I have described two different governance models for collaboration in research networks. If autonomous researchers and scientists are at the working level, and government-directed management and funding is at the "top" level, then we can describe the Cochrane and Campbell collaborations as democratic, bottom-up research collaborations in the public interest, with minimal opportunity for either government or corporate interference. DRDC, CSS, and CRTI on the other hand (and other national analogues of the same) are top-down, government directed collaborations in the pursuit of public interest as seen by the government of the day. The main advantage of the top-down approach is the ability to throw money at problems quickly, while the main advantage of autonomous researchers is the self-correction of focus by a larger community of researchers.

CONTRIBUTIONS TO NEW MISSIONS

Research cooperation always raises questions about sharing knowledge, sometimes because of intellectual property, sometimes due to national security. But in top-down defence research cooperation, there is the added fear of losing privileged access. An officer serving at US Military Academy West Point presented work on social network analysis in support of operations, but the presentation came with the stricture (from DRDC, not from the presenter) "Do not distribute outside DND." Thus, it could not be easily shared with research partners in Canada's national police force, the RCMP, or the national agency responsible for tracking money used by terrorists and organized crime—FINTRAC. In contrast, analysis of the resilience of covert social networks was presented at the first ISMS conference, and freely shared amongst the civilian and military participants at ISMS (Lindelauf, Borm and Hamers 2009). Anecdotally, one might deduce that smaller players working with bottom-up academic governance models have a greater incentive to overcome stovepipes and share research. This is another illustration of the "boundary" position of small countries' defence universities. Operating on the boundaries between military and civilian scholarship, they can bridge to each other, to other government departments, and to professional communities demanding trustworthiness and discretion.

The International Society of Military Sciences is in an interesting boundary position for both top-down and bottom-up forms of research collaboration. Its members are therefore well placed to collaborate on research to support new missions, in which small countries have a stake. The Society, as a network of defence universities, might present a model for managing and developing research support to new missions, maximizing the impact of scarce research funds, and sharing the burden of building a more effective evidence-based security practice that serves the security interests of small countries.

NOTES

1. I am grateful to the organizers of the workshop *New Missions and New Challenges*, particularly Franz Kernic and Christian Leuprecht. Christina Last provided research assistance. Sarah Toomey and Clarinda Olsen assisted with the section on research library resources. Christian Leuprecht, Jodok Troy and anonymous reviewers improved the quality of the original submission. I am responsible for any errors and omissions.
2. A search of IPRA and all its regional chapters reveals no connections with military organizations, and no members with military rank. This suggests that there are no institutional ties, but does not preclude individual contributions.
3. Ontario has a population of 11 million, Austria 8 million, Denmark and Finland both about 5 million, Latvia-Lithuania-and-Estonia 7 million together, Netherlands 16 million, Norway almost 5 million, and Sweden 9 million.

REFERENCES

Auge, A. 2009. Military Culture and University Degrees: The Hidden Side of French Officers. Presented at IUS, 23 October.

Becher, A. 1989. *Academic Tribes and Territories: Intellectual Enquiry and the Cultures of Disciplines*. Milton Keynes: The Society for Research into Higher Education and the Open University Press.

Bergen Declaration. 2005. *The Framework of Qualifications for the European Higher Education Area*.

Cahn, S.M. 2008. *From Student to Scholar: A Candid Guide to Becoming a Professor*. New York: Columbia University Press.

Campbell Collaboration. At http://www.campbellcollaboration.org/ (accessed 2 November 2009).

Clark, W. 2007. *Academic Charisma and the Origins of the Research University*. Chicago, IL: University of Chicago Press.

Cochrane Collaboration. 2009. *Process for Elections to the Cochrane Collaboration Steering Group*. Updated 21 December.

Cochrane Library Press Releases. At http://www.cochrane.org/press/releases. htm (accessed 2 November 2009).

Cochrane Review Press Release. 2010. Cochrane Equity Field Becomes the Campbell and Cochrane Equity Methods Group, 24 February. At http://news. cochrane.org/view/item/review_one.jsp?j=1801 (accessed 2 May 2010).

Duffin, J. 2000. *History of Medicine: A Scandalously Short Introduction.* Toronto: Palgrave Macmillan.

Duncan Hunter National Defense Authorization Act for Fiscal Year 2009. 2009. Public Law 110-417, October 14.

Emelifeonwu, D. 2008. *Partnership Action Plan on Defence Institution Building Reference Curriculum: Public Administration and Governance; Defence Management and Economics; Ethics and Leadership*. Kingston: Canadian Defence Academy. Draft.

Fejes, A. 2008. European Citizens Under Construction—The Bologna Process Analysed from a Governmentality Perspective. *Educational Philosophy and Theory* 40 (4):515-530.

Giske, J. 2008. Benefiting from Bibliometry: The Use and Misuse of Bibliometric Indices in Evaluating Scholarly Performance. *Ethics in Science and Environmental Politics* 8:79-81.

International Society of Military Sciences (ISMS). 2008. Letter of Intent, signed at Copenhagen, 22 October.

IPRA website. At http://soc.kuleuven.be/iieb/ipraweb/index.php?action=home& cat=hom (accessed 16 March 2010).

Jacobsen, K. 2005. Perestroika in American Political Science. *Post-autistic economics review* 32, 5 July:article 6. At http://www.paecon.net/PAEReview/issue32/ Jacobsen32.htm (accessed 5 February 2010).

Janowitz, M. 1960. *The Professional Soldier: A Social and Political Portrait*. Glencoe, ILL: Free Press.

Janowitz, M., and S.D. Wesbrook 1983. *Political Education of Soldiers*. London: Sage.

Keegan, J. 1993. *A History of Warfare*. New York: Knopf.

Kerr, C. 2001. *The Uses of the University.* Cambridge, MA: Harvard University Press.

Lindelauf, R., P. Borm, and H. Hamers 2009. Understanding Terrorist Network Topologies and Their Resilience Against Disruption. Discussion Paper No. 2009-85, November, University of Tilburg.

Masland, J.W., and L.I. Radway 1957. *Soldiers and Scholars: Military Education and National Policy.* Princeton, NJ: Princeton University Press.

OSCE. 2008. *Handbook on Human Rights and Fundamental Freedoms of Armed Forces Personnel.* Geneva: OSCE Office for Democratic Institutions and Human Rights (ODIHR).

Pawson, R. 2006. *Evidence Based Policy: A Realist Perspective.* London: Sage.

Ross, M.G., ed. 1966. *New Universities in the Modern World.* New York: St Martin's.

Smith, R. 1991. Where is the Wisdom? The Poverty of Medical Evidence [editorial]. *British Medical Journal* 303:789-799.

Snow, C.P. 1961. *Science and Government.* Cambridge, MA: Harvard University Press.

Tash, W.R. 2006. *Evaluating Research Centers and Institutes for Success! A Manual and Guide with Case Studies.* Fredericksburg, VA: WT and Associates.

The Network of Concerned Anthropologists. 2009. *The Counter-Counterinsurgency Manual, or Notes on Demilitarizing American Society;* especially D. Price, Faking Scholarship, 59-76. Chicago, IL: Prickly Paradigm Press.

Van Creveld, M. 1990. *The Training of Officers: From Military Professionalism to Irrelevance.* New York: Free Press.

Wagemaker, A. 2008. Point Paper. Unpublished document circulated at the first meeting of the International Society of Military Sciences in Amsterdam, Netherlands, 8 May.

Warner, J.T. 1990. Military Recruiting Programs During the 1980s: Their Success and Policy Issues. *Contemporary Economic Policy* 8 (4)47-67.

Weisburd, D., C.W. Telep, J.C. Hinkle, and J.E. Eck. 2010. The Effects of Problem-Oriented Policing on Crime and Disorder. At http://gunston.gmu.edu/cebcp/OnePageBriefs/CampbellPOP.pdf (accessed 15 February 2010).

PART 3: COMPETENCIES FOR NEW MISSIONS

COOPERATIVE AND LEARNING-ORIENTED LEADERSHIP RELATED TO CIVIL-MILITARY RELATIONS IN INTERNATIONAL MISSIONS? A RELATIONAL APPROACH[1]

Bo Talerud

International peacekeeping missions have gone through radical changes over the last decades, both in number and nature, from monitoring ceasefires to supporting the re-creation of fragile or damaged states. In efforts to combine security and development in international missions, civil-military cooperation has become increasingly important. The involvement of civilian actors from many different organizations has resulted in a very complex mixture of military and civilian players on different organizational levels, illustrated by a "matrix" in the article. The diversity among all those players results in constraints of different kinds: structural, ideological, cultural as well as power-related.

Is it possible to develop the conditions for more symmetrical and elaborate civil-military cooperation? — And if so, how? What are the implications for military leaders and leadership? Could competencies for handling civil-military cooperation be developed? — And if so, how?

In this article I will describe a relational and learning-oriented leadership approach and suggest that this approach might be helpful in developing the conditions for elaborate civil-military cooperation and comprehensive approaches for international missions.

CIVIL-MILITARY RELATIONS – A SHORT BACKGROUND

Relations between civil society and its military organization have been a crucial question for as long as military organizations have existed. Plato,[2] maybe, was the first to theorize about the issue. After World War II there was a discussion about civil-military relations on a societal or system level with Samuel P. Huntington's *The Soldier and the State* (1957) as a starting point, and with Morris Janowitz's *The Professional Soldier* (1960) expressing another view. Both agreed on an ideological gap in civil-military relations. Huntington argued that this gap must be managed and tolerated by the civil society, while Janowitz argued that the military must lessen the gap. This discussion has continued ever since within military sociology, military history and political science (see e.g., Wong, Bliese and McGurk 2003 or Feaver 1999). Civil-military relations here refer to relations between the civil *society* and the military *system*.

A more down-to-earth and operational approach to civil-military relations comes from experiences with counter-insurgencies. Peter Dahl Thruelsen (2008) gives an account of what he calls "classic counter-insurgency theories" and some of the thoughts of a French colonel, David Galula (1964). Drawing experiences from counter-insurgency (COIN) campaigns after World War II, Galula, as early as 1964, argued that to gain active support from the majority of the population in such campaigns, the counterinsurgencies must provide the population with basic security and in particular a legitimate government. A civilian population's support cannot be won by military means alone; there must be some civil-military cooperation. That goes for numerous COIN campaigns, but also has relevance for peacekeeping operations in modern times.

International peacekeeping missions have gone through radical changes over the past decades, both in number and nature, from monitoring ceasefires to supporting the re-creation of fragile or damaged states. If those peace-restoring operations are important for international society, then it is crucial to develop civil-military relations at different levels. In an effort to combine security and development in international missions, civil-military cooperation has become increasingly important. The involvement of civilian actors from many different organizations (UN, NATO, EU, ICR, NGOs, local authorities, etc.) has resulted in a very complex mixture of military and civilian players on different organizational levels. I have tried to just hint at this complexity by designing a matrix regarding different kinds of relationships in peace-building operations (Appendix A). The diversity of all those players is likely to result in constraints of different kinds: structural, ideological, cultural, as well as power-related.

In light of all these actors involved in international peacekeeping missions, we can realize the importance of developing the cooperation, coordination and collaboration among all parts in this complex and disparate mixture involved in peacekeeping operations.

> Integration is critical for linking the different activities involved in contemporary post-conflict activity (political, developmental, humanitarian, human rights, rule of law, social and security. (UN 2007, 33)

There have been different concepts articulated in order to develop such integration. The Canadian concept of "3D" requires that the various agents of government—Development, Diplomacy and Defence—work together to achieve a set of common all-embracing goals concerning security and development (Cooter 2007; Okros 2007). Different national concepts of "Provincial Reconstructing Teams" (PRTs) seem to have the same approach at the local level in Afghanistan.[3] Another similar concept is the *comprehensive approach*.

> CA /comprehensive approach/ is about combining military, political and developmental actors to create stability, conducting security sector reform (SSR) and especially to capacity build local authorities to perform governance tasks in the area. (Dahl Thruelsen 2008, 9)

NATO describes "comprehensive approach" in the following way in the Bucharest Summit Declaration of April 2008:

> Effective implementation of a comprehensive approach requires the cooperation and contribution of all major actors, including that of Non-Governmental Organisations and relevant local bodies. To this end, it is essential for all major international actors to act in a coordinated way, and to apply a wide spectrum of civil and military instruments in a concerted effort that takes into account their respective strengths and mandates. (Bucharest Summit Declaration 2008, para. 11)

I think that a "comprehensive approach" will have different outcomes, whether it is handled from a top-down perspective (focusing on state security) or a bottom-up perspective (focusing on human security) or a combination of both perspectives.[4]

Both civilian and military players seem to be convinced that different kinds of peace operations can rarely be achieved by military or civilian means alone. There must be different kinds of cooperation with civilian and military actors involved.—But on whose conditions?

Being the strongest part mostly, military presence, perspective and culture, seeing the cooperation mostly as a military operation, tends to dominate (Olson and Gregorian 2007),[5] and is also due to the military's stronger leadership—and "command and control" traditions. There are some tendencies that traditional "warrior ethos" tends to dominate over a "softer" military peacekeeper identity (Okros 2007; Cooter 2007; Olson and Gregorian 2007). Some civil players, especially NGOs, experience power asymmetries when it comes to cooperation efforts and planning, especially towards military participants. Some actors also feel a lack of sensitivity over those power asymmetries. Some NGOs and IOs (e.g., the Red Cross) have difficulties with, or even refuse closer cooperation with, military units, as they think that their security decreases, rather than increases if they become mixed up with military forces (Olson and Gregorian 2007).

Is it possible then to develop the conditions for more symmetrical and elaborate civil-military cooperation?—And if so, how? What will the implications be for military leaders and leadership? Could competencies to handle civil-military cooperations be developed?—And if so, how?

In the following I will try to outline a relational and learning-oriented leadership approach and suggest that this approach might be helpful to develop the possibilities for more elaborate and symmetrical civil-military cooperation in international missions.

AN OUTLINE OF LEARNING-ORIENTED LEADERSHIP

When it comes to leadership for civil-military cooperation, there are at least three ways of considering a learning-oriented process: To develop a collaborative learning culture for the education of officers in a "community of inquiry"[6] is desirable during an international mission as well as towards one's own organization and subordinates. You can alter between production/performance leadership and development leadership, in order to facilitate the learning conditions for co-workers by encouraging conscious learning activities in formal, non-formal and informal daily settings, while stressing reciprocal interactions between leader and co-workers, as well as between co-workers and colleagues—in order to, among other things, facilitate co-workers' and colleagues' ability to develop civil-military relationships. I will develop the concepts of "production/performance leadership" and "development leadership" as well as the differences between formal, non-formal and informal settings later in this article.

When it comes to meetings with representatives from other organizations in order to develop civil-military cooperation on terms—as equally as possible—there is a need for a complementary leadership and learning orientation. Non-hierarchical leadership, sensitive to other ways of seeing the world, but equally important, able to develop the ability as conscious *learners* having the ability to utilize critical reflection, not least to question one's own taken-for-granted assumptions. It is a matter of being interested in other ways to understand the world, of being curious and conscious of the restrictions of one's own worldview. It is a question of developing a leader/mediator/facilitator approach to upcoming more or less problematic situations.[7]

I think that many officers and soldiers in international missions do have many of these qualities, like curiosity of other cultures and world-views, a willingness to learn and a consciousness that says my own way to consider the world is not always the only truth. Maybe those traits should be made more explicit in the socialization of officers and soldiers, among other things; a more conscious and reflective approach to the concept of learning should be encouraged.

DIFFERENT APPROACHES TO LEARNING

As with "leadership" there are numerous definitions of, and approaches to, "learning." I will start with the changing role of learning in educational research.

During the last few decades, educational research has moved its focus from processes of teaching to processes of learning, especially in the case of adult education. Moreover, there has been an increased focus on lifelong and life-wide learning and non-formal and informal learning. Traditional connotations in the field of education to schooling and learning in formal settings have become too narrow.

According to World Encyclopaedia and Oxford References Online, *Education* is: *"Processes, either formal or informal, of acquiring knowledge and skills."*—Education, as I see it, refers both to educational performances and to a field of (scientific) studies. Education as (social) science deals with questions about influences on *learning*, ranging from education in formal settings to learning in non-formal and informal settings, including processes of socialization and enculturation. Learning is both a process and a product.

There are at least two different approaches concerning perspectives on learning: A cognitive perspective that learning occurs within the individual and, on the other hand, is situated or, for socio-cultural perspectives, that learning is embedded in historical, cultural and social contexts. Knud Illeris (2003, 170) tries to encompass both of those perspectives in his definition of learning:

> [L]earning must be understood as all processes leading to permanent capacity change—whether they be physical, cognitive, emotional or social in nature—that do not exclusively have to do with biological maturation or ageing.

Per-Erik Ellström (1992, 67) has formulated a similar definition: "Learning is regarded as relatively lasting changes in an individual as a result of the individual's interaction with his/her environment."

Even as learning has its cognitive and emotional aspects, learning occurs when a person interacts with his/her environment, be it a text, another person, an organization, a situation, physical surroundings, etc.

As mentioned above, there has been an increased interest during the past decades on life-long and life-wide learning as with non-formal and informal education and learning. In his Annotated International Bibliography of *Non-Formal Education* (1972) Rolland Paulston outlines the distinctions between formal, non-formal and informal education. *Formal education* is the "age-graded hierarchy of elementary, secondary and higher education." He described *non-formal education* as "systematic, non-school educational and training activities of relatively short duration in which sponsoring agencies seek concrete behavioural changes in fairly distinct populations." It can be provided in the workplace or by organizations and groups in civil society i.e., popular adult education. Maybe parts of military training and courses can be seen as non-formal education. In *informal education* people learn "in a non-systematic manner from generally unstructured exposure to cultural facilities, social institutions, political processes, personal media, and the mass media." Kjell Rubenson (2007) makes a similar description regarding formal, non-formal and informal learning.

It is, however, important to stress the differences in learning conditions regarding formal, non-formal and informal settings. Overall, we can argue that the learners have responsibility for their own active learning. "You can lead a horse to water, but you can't make him drink." In the case of *self-directed* informal learning, learners have the full responsibility for what, why and how they will learn. Learning in formal settings, however, is also directed by the government and governmental agencies that have goals for the education of, for example, engineers, medical doctors, psychologists—and military officers. Also educational leaders and teachers have their own intentions with respect to those settings.[8] As with learning in non-formal settings, arranged by non-governmental organizations, there is a similar situation where organizers, teachers and learners have their respective interests, goals and responsibilities. Most learning, however, takes place in informal, less conscious or non-conscious situations when we are socialized to different cultural traits.[9] The responsibilities for those learning situations are more complicated and complex.

In connection with *self-directed learning*, Philip C. Candy (1991, 22-23) makes a slightly different division of different learning conditions. He distinguishes four distinct (but related) phenomena: "self-direction" as a personal attribute (personal autonomy); "self-direction" as the willingness and capacity to conduct one's own education (self management), "self-direction" as a mode of organizing instruction in formal settings (learner-control); and "self-direction" as the individual, non-institutional pursuit of learning opportunities in the "natural social setting (autodidaxy)."

The focus during recent decades on lifelong, life-wide, non-formal and informal learning has contributed to increased emphasis on the importance of learning within modern organizations (e.g., learning at work) and the management of such learning processes. Leadership and continuous learning are seen as the two most important factors critical to achieving organizational goals. Modern trends toward process-oriented, knowledge- and team-based organizations make new demands on leaders to lead and facilitate (knowledge-based) processes among their staff. Guiding and facilitating learning processes are essential for this kind of modern leadership.[10] Learning though can be of different kinds. In his classical study, Jean Piaget (1969) distinguished between assimilative and accommodative learning processes. Jack Mezirow's (2000) theory of transformative learning describes how learners learn by integrating new knowledge with their existing knowledge in such a way that their frames of reference are developed in a transformative way:

> Transformative learning refers to the process by which we transform our taken-for-granted frames of reference (meaning perspectives, habits of mind, mind-sets) to make them more inclusive, discriminating, open, emotionally capable of change, and reflective so that they may generate beliefs and opinions that will prove more true or justified to guide action. (Ibid., 7-8)

Central to his theory is the ability of critical reflection and self-reflection. The theory of transformative learning is influenced by Paulo Freire's concept of "conscientizacao"[11] and of Jurgen Habermas's delineation of the concepts of communicative competence and instrumental learning as the major domains of learning.

Also, according to Ellström (2002), learning processes could be of at least two kinds, connected to two logics of activity and learning connected to workplace learning:

1. *Production-oriented learning and the logic of production* with emphasis on routinized, effective action, problem solving through application of given rules/instructions, consensus, standardization, stability and avoidance of uncertainty, adaptive learning oriented towards the mastering of procedures and routines.
2. *Developmental learning and the logic of development* with emphasis on thought and reflection, alternative thinking, experimentation and risk taking, tolerance for ambiguity, variation and mistakes, and development oriented learning.

You can find some similarities between Piaget's distinction between assimilative and accommodative learning as with Argyris and Schön's (1978) distinction between single loop and double loop learning. You can also find some similarities between Mezirow's transformative learning and Ellström's developmental learning.

Ellström's distinction between production-oriented and developmental learning could be questioned and he underlines the complementarities of those two logics. The challenge for modern organizations according to Ellström is, both to convince the value of integrating learning and production, and to show how to organize both production-oriented and developmental learning in an effective way:

> Accomplishing this is of course not a simple matter. In order to do that management strategies are of great importance, as are perceptions of the leading actors with regard to the possible, desirable and for the time being appropriate way of running the business of the organization. These perceptions are in turn linked to a number of economic, ideological and structural conditions on the societal level. The influence of management in this context depends to a great extent on their ability to put development issues on the agenda. (Ellström 2002, 92)

My interpretation of this is that the greatest challenge for modern leadership is to facilitate a constructive combination and dynamic between production-oriented and developmental learning, according to both leaders and their co-workers, in such a way that it strengthens the successful development of the organization and its members' ability to fulfil their tasks according to its mission. Concerning Ellström's two types of logic, we can describe two (complementary) types of leadership: *Production-oriented leadership*, where the leader acts as a "coach" inspiring co-workers to perform better and more effectively according to ongoing production, and *development-oriented leadership*, where the leader inspires reflection, alternative/critical thinking and developmental learning (see also Talerud 2007a). Could these two complementary types of leadership, as well as knowledge about the different aspects of learning, give some contribution to an elaborated civil-military encounter as part of a comprehensive approach?

An important aspect of learning, especially developmental learning, is the ability for communication. When it comes to civil-military cooperation, the capacity for communicative/dialogical competence is even more crucial.

COOPERATIVE LEADERSHIP AND COMMUNICATIVE/DIALOGICAL COMPETENCE

I will use a tentative definition of *cooperation* as common actions with varying degrees of agreement and understanding. It could range from restricted coordination by interchange of necessary information to more elaborated and reciprocal forms of cooperation and collaboration.

Even a restricted coordination of actions and information could be a problem in civil-military relations if the military have a tendency to want to have information but are not equally ready to share information with their civilian counterparts.[12]

A crucial aspect when developing some degree of common understanding is that the participants interpret the situation in similar ways, and try to develop some collective sense of what is going on and what needs to be done—a process of sensemaking.

> Communication is a central component of sensemaking and organizing: We see communication as an ongoing process of making sense of the circumstances in which people collectively find themselves and of the events that affect them. The basic evolutionary process assumed by sensemaking is one in which retrospective interpretations are built during interdependent interaction. (Weick, Sutcliffe and Obstfield 2005, 413)[13]

In order to come to some kind of agreement and understanding, we must communicate. I will here superficially touch upon Jürgen Habermas's theory of "communicative action" from his monumental *Theorie des kommunikativen Handelns* (1981/1984) (see also Mezirow and Associates 2000). Habermas argues that every statement can be analyzed whether it is

1. *Intelligible/comprehensible*—i.e., Do we understand the statement in the same way?
2. *True* i.e., What evidence or proof of the statement can be found?
3. *Legitimate* i.e., Appropriate to the context of the statement?
4. *Sincere* i.e., Genuinely meant and without a hidden agenda?

If we regard those claims of Habermas, as not digital (i.e., true/not true) but as relative positions on a scale, I will argue that if a statement is intelligible, true, legitimate and sincere to a greater degree, the communicative act has a bigger chance to succeed than if there is a lesser degree of it. The degree of agreement and understanding is determined—among other things—whether the statement is comprehensible, true, legitimate and sincere in a higher or lower degree. The four elements suggested by Habermas could be used to measure *the degree* of communicative rationality by thoughtful meta-communication.

An *ideal speech situation* in Habermas's sense is free from domination and has an equal distribution of power. Of course this is seldom the case and Habermas argues for compromises where communicative rationality dominates over diverse interests and power. Even conflicting opinions, *dissensus,* can be a way to uncover different ways to see the world.

Lena Wilhelmsson in her doctoral thesis "Learning dialogue" (1998) talks about *"The symmetric/co-operative discourse"* (patterns of speech) where all speakers learn from each other's different perspectives. That is, those with less power are able to speak freely and those superiors, or those with more power, learn to be more competent in dialogical discussions when they critically reflect on their own powerful position. "The asymmetric competitive discourse type" implies that each speaker learns to argue his or her own opinion. *The asymmetric co-operative discourse type"* implies that all participants adopt the perspective of the most dominant actor(s) and *"the asymmetric competitive discourse type"* implies that the participants hold to their own assumptions. The superior actor actively dominates others in the communication process and the others instead develop silent opposition and resistance (ibid., 266).

Cooperative leadership in my sense must incorporate educational competencies like explaining, clarifying, arguing and convincing in order to influence others to understand and agree to common actions with an appropriate degree of agreement and mutual understanding. But it must also exceed those educational competencies ranging from abilities to have a true dialogue near to Habermas's ideal type of *communicative action* to asymmetric persuading from a power position in order to facilitate cooperation.

A cooperative leadership must be able to analyze what kind of discourse that is at hand in each situation and what discourse most likely will lead to optimal cooperation and the ability to act accordingly. That implies also the ability to analyze the relationship in terms of power, status, prestige, ideology, cultural differences, fear, uncertainty to the possibility of hidden agendas, etc. In order to acquire such competencies, a cooperative leadership must also develop a conscious ability to learn and to reflect over the different conditions of learning.

IMPLICATIONS FOR LEADERSHIP IN NEW MISSIONS

In his *Leadership in Organizations,* Gary Yukl (2006, 8) quotes R.M. Stogdill that "there are almost as many definitions of leadership as there are persons who have attempted to define the concept."—After a discussion of different concepts Yukl ended up with a rather broad definition, taking into account "several things that determine the success of a collective effort by members of a group or organization to accomplish meaningful tasks."

> *Leadership* is the process of influencing others to understand and agree about what needs to be done and how to do it, and the process of facilitating individual and collective efforts to accomplish shared objectives. (Ibid., 8)

A common trait in most modern definitions is that leadership is considered to be processes of social interactions, rather than a set of individual traits as in more conservative approaches to leadership. Trait-approaches to leadership tend to be top-down and leader-oriented, while process approaches to leadership take into account more the interactive process between leader and "followers."

How about *leadership for co-operation*? Yukl's "process of influencing others to understand and agree about what needs to be done and how to do it" can be interpreted in different ways. My approach to leadership/ co-worker relations (the "others") is to regard it very much as a mutual interactive process, a relational approach. If the purpose is to influence others to understand and agree about more elaborated cooperation in the negotiation of what "shared objectives" that could be agreed upon—what competencies are needed? What constitutes a "cooperative leadership"?

According to Habermas (1984), there are two major domains of learning: *Instrumental learning* to control, manipulate the environment or other people, as in task-oriented problem solving to improve performance, and *communicative learning*—learning what other people mean when they communicate with you. Most learning involves elements of both domains and a cooperative leadership needs elaborated learning capacities in both domains. How does this approach correspond with common approaches to *military* leadership in general?

Wong, Bliese and McGurk (2003) review research on military leadership in order to highlight further research opportunities for leadership scholars. They distinguish between two complementary ways in which military leadership research can be defined: (1) a context-free orientation (e.g., transformational leadership) examined within a military context but applicable to organizations other than the military, and (2) a context-specific orientation focusing on *military* leadership.

The authors distinguish between different kinds of military leadership according to organizational levels/domains within the (US) military system: Systems leadership (at the generals level), organizational leadership levels (colonels to two-star generals) and direct leadership levels (battalion level and below). At each level they distinguish between, and comment on, external environment, critical tasks, individual capability and organizational culture. The review focuses mainly on officers at the upper two levels—I will, however, focus on their direct leadership level.

According to Wong et al. (ibid.), direct leadership is the most widely studied of the three levels/domains in the military, "most likely because it provides access to the largest number of leaders" (ibid., 675). Concerning the external environment they differ among three contexts: (1) training/ garrison context, (2) deployment/combat context, and (3) schooling/ evaluation context and argue that "[e]ach of these contexts carries different implications for the critical tasks, individual capabilities, organizational culture and mission effectiveness aspects of leadership research" (ibid., 676).

Concerning "critical tasks," direct level leaders have two main tasks: executing orders from higher levels and assuming responsibility for all aspects of the soldiers' well-being corresponding to task-related versus HR-related leadership. In the schooling/evaluation context, focus on their own individual performance will dominate, while leadership in garrison and combat settings will have a more collective focus.

> Given that many leadership researchers have backgrounds in psychology or other individual-oriented disciplines, it is not surprising that a great deal of research has been focused towards understanding individual capabilities of leaders. (Ibid., 679)

From my point of view this is an important statement. It could strengthen a rather conservative view focusing merely on the leader alone, favouring trait approaches to leadership instead of the reciprocal process between leaders and "followers"/collaborators/co-workers.

Coming to "leadership skills" the authors noticed that "the current dominant paradigm for leadership skills is transformational-based theories. One would expect that the transformational leadership findings conducted in nonmilitary settings would generalize in military settings, and this appears to be the case (ibid., 682). This is confirmed for example in the Swedish military setting, where a Swedish modified version of transformational leadership has become The Leadership Doctrine within the Swedish Armed Forces.

According to Bass (1998), transformational leadership moves the follower beyond self-interest and is charismatic, inspirational, intellectually stimulating, and/or individually considerate. Furthermore, he argues, it leads to a whole new mode of leadership training. The components of transformational leadership are: The leader is charismatic, is a role model, gives inspirational motivation to his/her subordinates or followers as well as intellectual stimulation and individualized consideration.[14] Intellectual stimulations involve the stimulation of followers' ideas, attitudes and values. Through intellectual stimulation, transformational leaders help followers think about old problems in new ways.

Even if transformational leadership has several constructive elements, there is, however, still a one-sided focus and emphasis on the single leader. Storey (2004) noticed that "inspirational motivation" holds forth the idea of ordinary people achieving extraordinary things through the influence of the leader. Storey reports several researches, critical to the idea of transformational leadership and concludes:

> People are beginning to look for alternatives to the charismatic transformational leader. There is a growing realization that there are no easy answers and that an alternative mode of leadership must be one which promotes learning and is more capable of being sustained than the quixotic heroic concept normally allows. (Ibid., 33)

Even Yukl and Lepsinger (2004) criticizes the one-sided focus and emphasis on the single leader as "the myth of the heroic leader" and links it to other stereotyped pictures of heroes in our culture:

> Depicting a senior executive as a heroic individual is a dramatic, romantic notion of leadership, similar to that of other stereotyped heroes in our culture, such as the lone cowboy who single-handedly vanquishes the bad guys or the secret agent who acts alone to save the world from nuclear destruction by terrorists. (Ibid., 4)

If military leaders are fostered in the rather leader-centric approach of transformational leadership and in a rather hierarchical military culture characterized more of instrumental than of communicative learning, there could be some major problem when it comes to civil-military cooperation when representatives from different organizations, both civil and military, meet on equal terms to develop and implement elements of a comprehensive approach, as important steps in a peace-operating process. Regarding leadership more as a social and reciprocal process according to my interpretation of Yukl's leadership definitions could make such meetings more constructive—that is, if the players, especially the dominant military ones, could adopt a more "relational" approach. Maybe a "Team Leadership" (Kogler Hill 2007) or even "Shared Leadership" (Pearce and Conger 2003) as a mixed responsibility between "leader" and "co-worker" would be more appropriate.

Maybe the ordinary socialization of military leaders needs to be complemented with more of a "collegial," "collaborative" or "peer leadership" or even be a part of a "community of inquiry" (see note 6), that is, dealing with problematic situations with a scientific attitude in an atmosphere of participatory democracy. This is the ideal ethos at least partially of the academic culture. There could maybe also be some training in communicative/dialogical competencies.

COOPERATIVE AND LEARNING-ORIENTED LEADERSHIP FOR ELABORATED CIVIL-MILITARY RELATIONS?—SOME CONCLUSIONS

Wallo (2008) develops the concepts of "production-oriented" and "development-oriented" leadership. He starts with arguing that a learning-oriented leadership has three roles: as supporter to learning opportunities, as educator and as a confronter. A production- or performance-oriented leadership focuses mostly on formal education as a means for reaching goals of production, while a development-oriented leadership, in addition to formal and non-formal education, also accentuates informal learning that occurs daily in the work place. A development-oriented leadership influences

> the co-worker to think in new ways. Similarly, by pairing co-workers in new constellations, opportunities are created for exposure to alternative perspectives. Instead of assimilating the newcomer to the prevailing order of things,

> learning from each other implies using the outsider's perspective and curi-
> ous questions to find new ways of understanding the practice. (Ibid., 155)

You can notice some resemblance with parts of transformational leadership especially its focus on intellectual stimulations, learning opportunities and a supportive climate. Pairing co-workers in new constellations
and sensitivity to outsiders' perspectives could indicate a less leader-
centered view compared to transformational leadership. But I will once
more stress the importance for a cooperative (military) leader in new
missions to develop his/her relational leadership approach and communicative learning.

In their *International Operations in Focus* Nørgaard and Holsting
(2006, 116) discuss the complementarities of *combat skills* and *contact
skills*. Contact skills are based on "mutual respect, communication ability, holistic understanding, cooperativeness, flexibility and the ability to
de-escalate conflict situations." They argue for a better balance in military
training and education between those two skills. Of course development
of "combat skills" is crucial for the military profession, but in relation to
a comprehensive approach and the different kinds of civil-military relations connected to it, it could improve those relations if "contact skills"
also were made more explicit in training and in the education of officers
and soldiers as in other parts of the military socialization process. That
could also include those communicative/dialogical competencies and the
different approaches to learning and leadership discussed in this article.

An obstacle for this kind of development could, of course, be those
collective inherited social constructions, formed through cultural pattern
and perceptions of the military ethos as mainly a warrior's ethos[15] as with
military leaders' relative lack of experience (at least at lower levels) to
negotiate with representatives from other (civilian) organizations with
divergent organizational culture, mandate, aims, power-structure, etc.

A main problem though in regards to leadership and civil-military
relations, as I see it, could be the dominate conception of a focus on
the leader alone, in a hierarchical system rather than the relational
processes within a group of "leaders" or representatives from different
organizational cultures where leadership may be altered depending on
what issues are in hand. Structured groups for self-directed learning and
better group-development over time (see e.g., Wheelan, Davidson and
Tilin 2003) could be part of a development together with more training
in "team leadership" and "shared leadership."

Personal experiences of reciprocal learning in connection with
civil-military relations could be another complement by "peer leadership coaching."[16] This concerns different mind-sets to "leadership,"
learning and a communicative/dialogical competence. It deals not only
with different leadership and learning contents but also different views
concerning leadership-coworkers relations and ways to understand the
conditions for learning, communication and dialogue. This could lead to

a reframing of parts of the education and training of soldiers and officers for international operations. In the long run it might change and reframe the military mind-set, ethos, and culture more appropriately to handle civil-military cooperation and coordination in the new missions.

NOTES

1. A relational approach: An approach stressing mutual social interactive processes.
2. In *The Republic*, Plato discuss the division of power between the rulers, the soldiers and the rest of the people.
3. See e.g., Jacobsen (2005) for a description of the US, German and British concepts of PRT.
4. On the concept of "human security," see e.g., Human Security Centre (2005). See also about the narrower and broader concept of Human Security: Talerud (2007b) or Kostovicova (2008).
5. This was confirmed—at least in regards to Afghanistan PRTs—by Torbjörn Pettersson, chairman of the Swedish Committee for Afghanistan in a meeting 15 May 2009 within "The Swedish Inter-Agency Working Group on Civil-Military Relations." In practice, the objectives for PRTs are to win "hearts and minds"—for military reasons.
6. The concept "community of inquiry" was developed by Charles Sanders Peirce for the scientific discussion but extended to educational and social matters by Jane Adams and John Dewey. Patricia Shields points out that the concept also could be very useful in Public Administration. See e.g., Shields (1999, 2003).
7. Shields (2003, 526) referred to Jane Adams for this approach.
8. For a critical examination of the concepts of "education" and "learning," see e.g., Biesta (2005).
9. For some connections between education, learning and culture, see e.g., Talerud (1985).
10. There have been some research studies in Sweden on knowledge and team-based organizations in connection with learning, e.g., Ellström (2001).
11. For the process of developing critical consciousness, see Smith (1976). See also e.g., Freire (1972a, 1972b, 1974).
12. As discussed at the Swedish Joint Working Group on Civil-Military Relations. Report from seminar 15 May 2009 at Kista/Stockholm.
13. The concept "sensemaking" has been used as an important concept in several academic disciplines, e.g., in educational science by Bron and Lönnheden (2005, 44): "Learning as an act of sensemaking will help adults to understand and change themselves and their surroundings" (my translation). In social anthropology by Ulf Hannerz (1992, 3): "*Homo sapiens* is the creature who "makes sense." She literally produces sense though her experience, interpretation, contemplation, and imagination, and she cannot live in the world without it. The importance of this sensemaking in human life is reflected in a crowded conceptual field: ideas, meaning, information, wisdom, understanding, intelligence, sensibility, learning, fantasy, opinion, knowledge, belief, myth, tradition … culture has been taken to be above all a matter of meaning."

14. A somewhat more elaborated description is:
  - Charismatic; that is, being a role model; so that the follower seeks to identify with the leader and emulate him/her.
  - Inspirational motivation; by providing purpose, understanding and challenge to their followers' work.
  - Intellectual stimulation; by being innovative, creative and by questioning assumptions, reframing problems, and approaching old situations in new ways.
  - Individualized consideration; special attention to each individual follower's need for achievement and growth by acting as coach or mentor. Followers and colleagues are developed to successively higher levels of potential. Individualized consideration is practiced when new learning opportunities are created along with a supportive climate. (Bass 1998, 5-6)
15. For a comparison and discussion of the military ethos in Canada, Sweden and the US see Talerud (2007b).
16. Maybe one can get some inspiration from Robertson (2009) or Sabo, Duff and Purdy (2008).

REFERENCES

Argyris, C., and D. Schön. 1978. *Organizational Learning: A Theory of Action Perspective*. Reading, MA: Addison-Wesley.

Bass, B. 1998. *Transformational Leadership—Industrial, Military and Educational Impact*. New Jersey, London: Lawrence Erlbaum Associates.

Biesta, G. 2005. Against Learning—Reclaiming a Language for Education in an Age of Learning. *Nordisk Pedagogik* 25:54-66.

Bron, A., and C. Lönnheden. 2005. Lärande utifrån symbolisk interaktionism. (Learning from the perspective of symbolic interactionism). In *Läroprocesser i högre utbildnin*, ed. Bron/Wilhelmson, 36-50. Stockholm: Liber Publisher.

Bucharest Summit Declaration Issued by the Heads of State and Government participating in the meeting of the North Atlantic Council in Bucharest on 3 April 2008. At http://www.nato.int/cps/en/natolive/official_texts_8443.htm (accessed 20 July 2010).

Candy, P.C. 1991. *Self-Direction for Lifelong Learning. A Comprehensive Guide to Theory and Practice*. San Fransisco, Oxford: Jossey-Bass.

Cooter, C. 2007. A Canadian Perspective on Civilian-Military Co-operation: Making a Good Idea Better. *Civil-Military Co-operation in Multinational Missions*. Conference Report, Forum for Security Studies, 18–19 January, pp. 18-25. Stockholm: Swedish National Defence College (SNDC).

Dahl Thruelsen, P. 2008. *Implementing the Comprehensive Approach in Helmand—Within the Context of Counterinsurgency*. Royal Danish Defence College, Faculty of Strategy and Military Operations.

Ellström, P.-E. 1992. *Kompetens, utbildning och lärande i arbetslivet* (Competence, education and learning in working life). Stockholm: Publica.

— 2001. Integrating Learning and Work: Problems and Prospects. *Human Resource Development Quarterly* 12 (4):421-435.

— 2002. Time and the Logics of Learning. *Lifelong Learning in Europe* (2):86-93.

Feaver, P.D. 1999. Civil-Military Relations. *Annual Review of Political Science* (2):211-241

Freire, P. 1972a. *Pedagogy of the Oppressed*. Essex, United Kingdom: Penguin Books.
— 1972b. *Cultural Action for Freedom*. Essex, United Kingdom: Penguin Education.
— 1974. *Education for Critical Consciousness*. New York: Seabury Publisher.
Galula, D. 1964. *Counterinsurgency Warfare: Theory and Practice*. London: Praeger Security International.
Habermas, J. 1984. *The Theory of Communicative Action*. Mansfield: Beacon Press.
Hannerz, U. 1992. *Cultural Complexity—Studies in the Social Organization of Meaning*. New York: Columbia University Press.
Human Security Centre. 2005. *Human Security Report 2005—War and Peace in the 21st Century*. University of British Columbia, Canada/Oxford University Press.
Huntington, S.P. 1957. *The Soldier and the State: The Theory and Politics of Civil-Military Relations*. Cambridge, MA: Harvard University Press.
Illeris, K. 2003. Workplace Learning and Learning Theory. *Journal of Workplace Learning* 15:167-178.
Jakobsen, P.V. 2005. *PRTs in Afghanistan—Successful but not Sufficient*. DIIS Report 2005:6. Copenhagen: Danish Institute for International Studies.
Janowitz, M. 1960. *The Professional Soldier: A Social and Political Portrait*. New York: Free Press.
Kogler Hill S.E. 2007. Team Leadership. In *Leadership—Theory and Practice*, 4th edition, P.G. Northouse, 207-235. London and New Delhi: SAGE Publications.
Kostovicova, D. 2008. Ahtisaari Settlement for Kosovo from a Human Security Perspective. *International Peacekeeping* 15:631-647.
Mezirow, J. and Associates. 2000. *Learning as Transformation*, 631-647. San Francisco: Jossey-Bass.
Nørgaard, K., and W.S. Holsting. 2006. *International Operations in Focus*. Copenhagen: Royal Danish Defence College.
Okros, A. 2007. 3D Security: The Implications of Integrating Defence, Diplomacy and Development in Multi-national Missions. *Civil-Military Co-operation in Multinational Missions*. Conference Report, Forum for Security Studies, 18–19 January, pp. 7-17. Stockholm: Swedish National Defence College (SNDC).
Olson, L., and H. Gregorian. 2007. Interagency and Civil-Military Coordination: Lessons from a Survey of Afghanistan and Liberia. *Journal of Military and Strategic Studies* 10 (1). At http://www.jmss.org/jmss/index.php/jmss/issue/view/9 (accessed 13 May 2010).
Paulston, R.G. 1972. *Non-Formal Education. An Annotated International Bibliography*. New York: University of Pittsburgh.
Pearce, C.L., and J.A. Conger, eds. 2003. *Shared Leadership—Reframing the Hows and Whys of Leadership*. London, New Delhi: SAGE Publications.
Piaget, J. 1969. *Psychologie et pédagogie*. Paris: Édition Denoel.
Robertson, J. 2009. Coaching Leadership Learning through Partnership. *School Leadership & Management* 29 (1):39-49.
Rubenson, K. 2007. *Determinants of Formal and Informal Canadian Adult Learning—Insights from the Adult Education and Training Surveys*. Prepared for Learning Policy Directorate, Strategic Policy and Research, Human Resources and Social Development Canada.
Sabo, K., M. Duff, and B. Purdy 2008. Building Leadership Capacity through Peer Career Coaching: A Case Study. *Nursing Leadership* 21 (1):27-35.
Shields, P.M. 1999. *The Community of Inquiry: Insights for Public Administration from Jane Adams, John Dewey and Charles S. Peirce*. Department of Political Science, Texas State University.

— 2003. The Community of Inquiry: Classical Pragmatism and Public Administration. *Administration & Society* 35:510-537.

Smith, W.A. 1976. *The Meaning of Conticientizacao: The Goal of Paulo Freire's Pedagogy.* Center for International Education, University of Massachusetts.

Storey, J., ed. 2004. *Leadership in Organizations—Current Issues and Key Trends.* London and New York: Routledge.

Talerud, B. 1985. *Kulturpedagogik i tekniksamhälle* (Cultural Pedagogy in a Technological Society). Doct. thesis, University of Stockholm, Department of Education.

— 2007a. Educational Aspects of Swedish Military Leadership. In *Military Pedagogy in Progress,* ed. H. Annen and W. Royl, 273-288. Internationaler Verlag der Wissenschaften: Peter Lang.

— 2007b. Ethos and Ethics for Today's Armed Forces in the Western Societies. In *Ethical Education in the Military—What, How and Why in the 21ˢᵗ Century?* ed. T. Jarmo, 63-84. Helsinki, Finland: National Defence University.

United Nations (UN). 2007. UN Peacekeeping Operation Principles and Guidelines, Capstone Doctrine Draft 3, 29 June.

Wallo, A. 2008. *The Leader as a Facilitator of Learning at Work—A Study of Learning-Oriented Leadership in Two Industrial Firms.* Diss., Linköping Studies in Behavioral Science. Linköping University, Department of Behavioral Sciences and Learning.

Weick, K., K.M. Sutcliffe, and D. Obstfeld. 2005. Organizing and the Process of Sensemaking. *Organization Science* 16 (4):409-421.

Wheelan, S.A., B. Davidson, and F. Tilin. 2003. Group Development Across Time: Reality or Illusion? *Small Group Research* 34:223-245.

Wilhelmson, L. 1998. *Lärande dialog—Samtalsmönster, perspektivförändring och lärande I gruppsamtal* (Learning Dialogue. Discourse patterns, perspective change and learning in small group conversation). Doct. Thesis, Stockholm University, Department of Education.

Wong, L., P. Bliese, and D. McGurk. 2003. Military Leadership: A Context Specific Review. *The Leadership Quarterly* 14:657-692.

Yukl, G., and R. Lepsinger. 2004. *Flexible Leadership: Creating Value by Balancing Multiple Challenges and Choices.* San Francisco: Jossey-Bass.

Yukl, G. 2006. *Leadership in Organizations,* 6ᵗʰ edition. New Jersey: Pearson Prentice Hall.

APPENDIX
A Matrix For the Complexity Regarding Civil-Military Relations in Peace-Building Operations

Decision in UN Security Council Leading to a UN-Mandate for a Peace-Building Operation

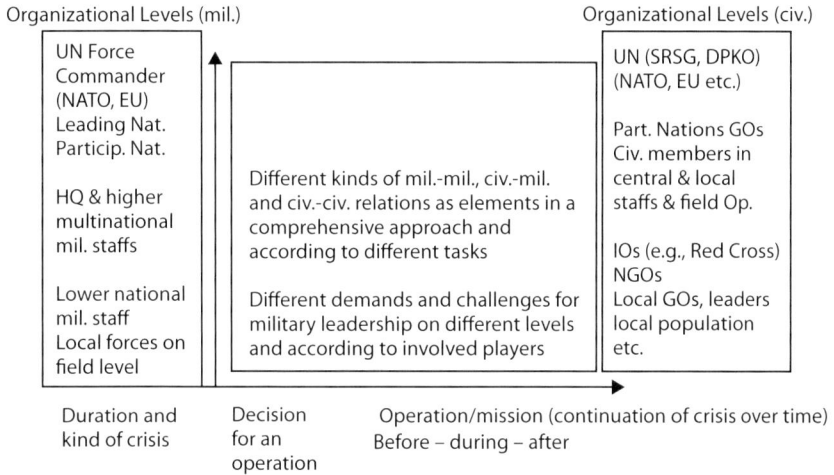

Organizational Levels (mil.)   Organizational Levels (civ.)

| UN Force Commander (NATO, EU) Leading Nat. Particip. Nat.

HQ & higher multinational mil. staffs

Lower national mil. staff Local forces on field level | Different kinds of mil.-mil., civ.-mil. and civ.-civ. relations as elements in a comprehensive approach and according to different tasks

Different demands and challenges for military leadership on different levels and according to involved players | UN (SRSG, DPKO) (NATO, EU etc.)

Part. Nations GOs Civ. members in central & local staffs & field Op.

IOs (e.g., Red Cross) NGOs Local GOs, leaders local population etc. |

Duration and   Decision   Operation/mission (continuation of crisis over time)
kind of crisis   for an   Before – during – after
                       operation

PRIVATE-MILITARY INTERFACES: COOPERATION AND NON-COOPERATION BETWEEN PRIVATE MILITARY AND SECURITY COMPANIES AND THE ARMED FORCES

GERHARD KÜMMEL

For quite some time, international relations and, especially, international conflict situations have been influenced by a phenomenon that came to be termed the privatization of security, which is reflected in the rise and growing number of private security and military companies (PSMCs). This means that activities that are located, in one way or another, in the area of producing and maintaining security have increasingly been commissioned to private enterprises by governments and other institutions of the state throughout the world that are hoping to get more for less. When it comes to the contacts between PSMCs and the military, the stereotypical image is one of a smooth relationship and functioning cooperation between state actors and PSMCs. Yet, this need not be the case. And indeed, quite often this is not the case, as is most dramatically and tragically illustrated by contractors dying due to "friendly fire" and by soldiers being left in the lurch by contractors who do not live up to their contractual commitments. This chapter, then, is organized in three large sections: While the first section will explicate the theoretical context of the chapter, the second section will give a brief and condensed overview of the PSMC business, including a balance sheet of the pros and cons of using and employing PSMCs. The third section will explore the interfaces of soldiers and contractors in order to come up with

Mission Critical: Smaller Democracies' Role in Global Stability Operations, ed. C. Leuprecht, J. Troy, and D. Last. Montreal and Kingston: Queen's Policy Studies Series, McGill-Queen's University Press. © 2010 Queen's Centre for International Relations, Queen's University at Kingston. All rights reserved.

working solutions to coordination and cooperation problems. Here, the United States of
America will be taken as the object of study because the US is the most important client
of PSMCs, and because, in the case of the United States, some information is available.

INTRODUCTION

For quite some time already, international relations and, especially, international conflict situations have been influenced by a phenomenon that
came to be termed the privatization of security which is reflected in the
rise and the growing number of private security and military companies
(PSMCs). This means that activities that are located, in one way or another,
in the area of producing and maintaining security have increasingly been
commissioned to private enterprises by governments and other institutions of the state throughout the world hoping to get more for less.

To cite a quite uncommon example to illustrate the general trend:
Even Germany, a country that is usually not considered when talking
about privatization and outsourcing in the military and related spheres,
is quite deeply engaged in such endeavours which, to be sure, do not
reach to genuine military tasks such as combat or close-to-combat tasks
(Petersohn 2006; Marischka 2009). These endeavours have basically taken
two avenues:

1. One avenue is what could be termed "managed privatization." Crucial
    here is that about ten years ago, in 2000, the German Department of
    Defense established some kind of privatization agency, a company
    named Gesellschaft für Entwicklung, Beschaffung und Betrieb
    (g.e.b.b.) which solely belongs to the Department of Defense. The
    g.e.b.b. has meanwhile created various public-private partnerships
    that are working in different fields. The most well-known public-
    private partnerships are the Bw Fuhrpark Service, a joint venture of
    the Deutsche Bahn AG (24.9 percent) and the g.e.b.b. (75.1 percent)
    that was established in 2002 and manages the (civilian and, in the
    future also partly-military) vehicle fleet, and the Lion Hellmann
    Bekleidungsgesellschaft, also established in 2002. This latter company
    unites the g.e.b.b. (25.1 percent) and a consortium of Lion Apparel
    Deutschland and Hellmann Worldwide Logistics (74.9 percent) to pro-
    vide a more efficient clothing management system to the Bundeswehr.
    In both cases, the shares of the g.e.b.b. were transferred directly to
    the federal government in 2006. Further public-private partnerships
    include the Heeresinstandsetzungslogistik (HIL GmbH) and the
    Herkules IT Projekt. Within HIL, a tripartite consortium consisting
    of Rheinmetall, Krauss-Maffei Wegmann and Industriewerke Saar
    (51 percent) is partner to the federal state (49 percent). Whereas the

objective of the HIL is to manage the maintenance of army equipment in such a way that 70 percent of this equipment is available daily, the multi-billion Euros for the Herkules IT Projekt is nothing less that the single largest public-private partnership throughout Europe. Here, Siemens IT Solutions and Services and IBM Germany which hold 50.1 percent of the company's shares, are the partners of the federal government (49.9 percent). Lastly, public-private partnership projects in the planning stage include, for example, the broad area of logistics.[1]

2. The second avenue is outright outsourcing, i.e., the complete contracting out of certain services. Examples include private security companies that provide site protection to military sites both within Germany and in the areas of operation abroad, companies that provide the management of military sites within Germany (such as the Gefechtsübungszentrum in Altmark), corporations such as Lufthansa that provide training facilities for pilots of the Bundeswehr, or, in a similar vein, MTU or EADS that provide the education and training of technicians for the new Eurofighter as well as companies like Israel Aerospace Industries (IAI) that train German soldiers in the use of the new UAVs HERON-1. Next to this, there are companies such as Antonov Airlines or Ruslan SALIS that sell strategic air transportation capacities to the Bundeswehr, another 13 companies providing the maintenance of equipment abroad or companies building and managing military camps abroad. All these services are crucial and vital for the Bundeswehr's mission in Afghanistan.

Thus, it does not come as a surprise when official German security policy documents endorse the idea of privatizing security even further. The following paragraph taken from the *White Paper* of the German Department of Defense serves to illustrate the rationale that governs this trend in official wording:

> The Bundeswehr will consistently concentrate on its core tasks. Cooperation with trade and industry on service tasks, extending as far as the outsourcing of complete task packages that the private sector can provide more economically, is being pursued further. This will ease the work burden of the Armed Forces, boost cost efficiency, and reduce operating costs and tied-up capital. Private investor capital will be mobilized, new sources of revenue opened up and opportunities to strengthen investments for the Bundeswehr thereby created. (Federal Ministry of Defense 2006, 62-63)

The stereotypical image subcutaneously woven into sentences like this is that of a smooth relationship and a functioning cooperation between state actors and PSMCs. Yet, this need not be the case, and, indeed, quite often this is not the case as is most dramatically and tragically illustrated by contractors dying due to "friendly fire" and by soldiers being left in the lurch by contractors who do not live up to their contractual com-mitments. Effective and mutually beneficial cooperation, then, needs empathy, willingness, effort and care. A starting point formulated like this implies a pronounced premise that should be apparent right from the beginning, namely, that it is indeed worthwhile to explore issues like this which, in turn, does not denigrate PSMCs per se as something that should be marginalized, abolished and rooted out, but to view PSMCs differently and take them as potential and actual valuable assets and in-struments in today's and tomorrow's international relations and security politics. Indeed, it can safely be assumed that PSMCs are by no means a transitory and temporary phenomenon, but a phenomenon that is here to stay. Private security and military contractors will increasingly become a permanent feature of present-day and future conflicts, so that it is even more important to look at the military-contractor interface.

This chapter, then, is organized in three large sections: While the first section will explicate the theoretical context of the chapter, the second section will give a brief and condensed overview of the PSMC business, including a balance sheet of the pros and cons of using and employing PSMCs. The third section will explore the interfaces of soldiers and con-tractors in order to come up with working solutions to coordination and cooperation problems. Here, the United States of America will be taken as the object of study because the US is the most important client of PSMCs and because in the case of the US some information is available. In gen-eral, the military-contractor interface is an issue area that is only rarely been dealt with because of the difficulties in accessing and obtaining the necessary information. Thus, the chapter, by necessity, has a preliminary, even incomplete character.

THE THEORETICAL FRAMEWORK

The starting point of this chapter is the theoretical contextualization of our topic. This rests in principal-agent theory (Jensen and Meckling 1976) that models the relations between an actor commissioning a certain task (the principal) and an actor that takes over this task (the agent). Our as-sumption here is that the relationship and the interactions between PSMCs and their clients—irrespective of whether the client is a government or another state institution, a transnational corporation, a non-governmental organization or a (group of) private person(s)—matches the construct of principal-agent theory: the PSMC's client is the principal, the PSMC is the agent. According to the theory, the principal and the agent act accord-ing to their interests, they both act opportunisticly and egoistically. This means that in the basic interaction structure, the client principally aims to get as much payment for as few services as possible, while the principal aims to get as many services for as little payment as possible. The actors' interests, then, are by no means identical which implies that conflicts may arise within the interaction. These conflicts may be ameliorated or even be circumvented, if one clearly recognizes the potential points of tension within a principal-agent relationship. The most important points of tension are as follows (Figure 1):

FIGURE 1
Points of Tension within the Principal-Agent-Relationship

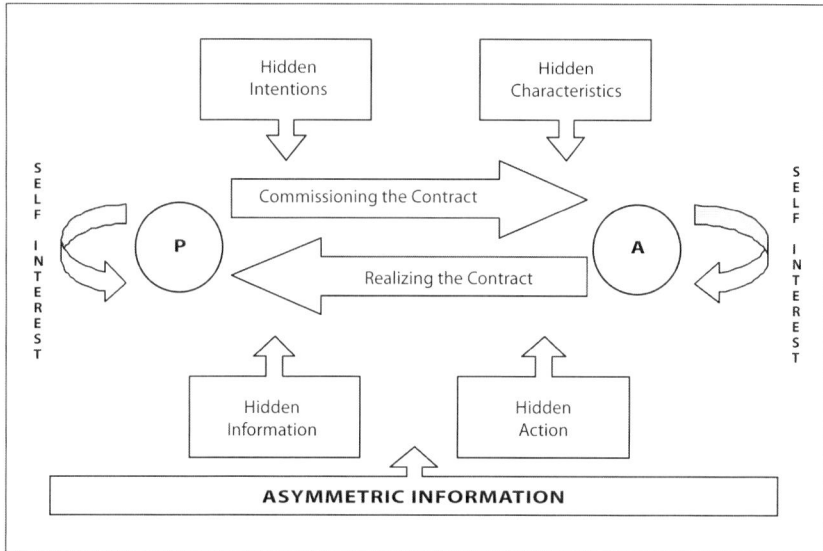

Prior to contracting:

- Hidden characteristics: A principal looking for an agent to deliver certain services wants to be quite sure that the agent actually disposes of the requested competences and capabilities in order not to choose the wrong client which may result in an unwelcome outcome (adverse selection). A PSMC, for example, that has violated human rights in a post mission may find it appropriate not to mention this to a potential principal in order to be awarded the present contract. Such a constellation can be detrimental to the new principal if this information is somehow leaked to the public.

After contracting:

- Hidden action: This problem arises when the principal is not fully capable of supervising, overseeing and controlling the agent's performance. In such a case, the agent disposes of substantial discretionary leeway of action that may be opportunistically exploited (moral hazard) and remain unknown to the principal. To illustrate this: A PSMC may sub-contract parts of the original contract to another PSMC without telling the principal. Such a move usually leads to an additional benefit for the PSMC because the sub-contractor generally receives less payment than the prime contractor negotiates from the principal. By doing so, however, the prime contractor carries the risk that the practical realization of (parts of) the contract may rest with people of less expertise that may not have up-to-date equipment which may result in a sub-optimal outcome. A further illustration is that the PSMC may be induced to employ dubious methods and instruments (such as torture) to improve effectiveness which, in turn, may backfire for the principal once knowledge about these methods and instruments spreads.

- Hidden information: Even if the principal is able to oversee the agent's performance, it may very well be that the principal, for lack of specific expertise, is not in a position to judge the quality of the performance. Often, principals issue so-called cost-plus contracts which guarantee the agent the reimbursement of the entailed costs plus the payment of a profit of X percent without fully determining the scope of the services and products. Since the PSMC's gain correlates with turn-over, an agent working in the field of logistics is induced to increase turnover, e.g., by delivering certain goods such as gas or food as much as possible. Given the complexities of the conflict environment, the principal may then find himself in a situation in which he is not fully able to specify the exact number of goods actually delivered. Reality shows that this is not a hypothetical case only; indeed, PSMCs have overcharged their clients.

- Hidden intention: In the end, the principal is not able to fully judge the agent's intentions. This means that there exists an asymmetric distribution of information within the principal-agent constellation. An argument put forward rather often by critics of PSMCs says that a given PSMC may have a latent low interest only in completing the task and may, to the contrary, even be seduced to perpetuate the conflict since this means business.

THE WORLD OF PSMCS

What is a PSMC?

The phenomenon of security privatization itself is nothing new to scholars of the history of war and conflict because private actors in general and mercenaries in particular are familiar elements within this history. Yet, the analogy to the mercenary of the past in order to describe the rise of PSMCs is quite misleading as the definition of the mercenary in inter-national humanitarian law establishes quite a threshold that cannot easily be passed. In its Article 47, the *Protocol Additional to the Geneva Conventions of 12 August 1949, and relating to the Protection of Victims of International Armed Conflicts* of 8 June 1977 defines a mercenary as follows:

> A mercenary is any person who: (a) is especially recruited locally or abroad in order to fight in an armed conflict; (b) does, in fact, take a direct part in the hostilities; (c) is motivated to take part in the hostilities essentially by the desire for private gain and, in fact, is promised, by or on behalf of a Party to the conflict, material compensation substantially in excess of that promised or paid to combatants of similar ranks and functions in the armed forces of that Party; (d) is neither a national of a Party to the conflict nor a resident of territory controlled by a Party to the conflict; (e) is not a member of the armed forces of a Party to the conflict; and (f) has not been sent by a State which is not a Party to the conflict on official duty as a member of its armed forces.

This definition is a cumulative one, as all six criteria have to be met simultaneously to call somebody a mercenary.

This, in turn, means that the notion of mercenarism may be suitable to describe some aspects within the large universe of PSMCs, but is inappropriate to serve as an encompassing depiction of this universe as such. What basically sets PSMCs apart from the mercenary is what Singer (2003, 45) has termed "corporatization": PSMCs are not individuals like mercenaries, but corporations and, as such, collective entities aiming not for individual, but for corporate profit; one can buy—contrary to mercenaries—shares of these companies which operate under the imperatives of the market, are often parts of larger business networks, recruit their people much more systematically, have a considerably broader variety of different actors as their clients, and offer a much more elaborate spectrum of services to their clients (Singer 2003, 45-47). If history provides some parallel to the present PSMCs at all, one may look at entities like the British East-India Company or the Dutch East-India Company (Ortiz 2007; Kramer 2007).

Within the literature, there is a variety of attempts to categorize the PSMC-universe which can broadly be defined as encompassing companies that provide services, manpower, hardware and/or software in the field of security and the military for both state and non-state actors such as single governments or state agencies, international organizations, transnational corporations, international non-governmental organizations, humanitarian relief organizations and various groups of individuals or even single individuals. One such attempt tries to establish a good-versus-bad dichotomy and separates the (good) private security companies from the (bad) private military corporations. Yet, this differentiation is somewhat misleading and not persuasive: Given the fluidity and, sometimes, volatility of today's conflict and crisis situations a neat distinction between security-only and military-only settings is not convincing. Instead, the following typology which resorts to similar endeavours by Shearer (1998, 25-26), O'Brien (2000, 59-64) and Singer (2003, 91-100) might be more appropriate as it proposes three broad categories of PSMC activity: Providing, consulting and supporting with each category comprising both the military and the security dimension. *Military and security provider firms* conduct direct military and security implementation and command functions and operations for their clients; *military and security consultant firms* offer a broad range of consulting, intelligence and training services; and *military and security support firms* provide logistics, transportation, and technical support. One must add that this typology is an ideal-typical one, which means that a given company may be found in more than one segment.

The PSMC business is a growth business that dates back to the 1960s with companies like David Sterling's WatchGuard International, founded in 1967 and consisting of former elite soldiers of the British Special Air Services (SAS) who trained various armed forces in the Persian Gulf. In the 1970s and 1980s companies like Kulinda Security Ltd., KAS Enterprises, and Saladin Security emerged which were active in African countries (O'Brien 2000). The exponential growth, however, occurred in the 1990s. To take Africa as an example, a list of PSMC operations shows 15 entries for the period 1950 to 1989, but 65 entries for the period 1990 to 1998 (Musah and Fayemi 2000, appendix 1). Such growth is also reflected in the substantial increase of business turnover and revenues. Although the data given varies depending on the respective author, the general trend is clear: While reasonable estimates for the global PSMC industry show some tens of billions of US dollars annually in the 1990s, the numbers now are in the range of US$2–300 billion. Finally, the fact that security sells is underlined by the growing interest of investors and large holding companies to buy shares or even fully acquire PSMCs.

WHY IS THERE A PSMC BOOM?

Broadly speaking, the privatization of security and the emergence of PSMCs resonate with notable shifts in state-society and state-individual relations, with broader socio-cultural trends and developments and with shifts in the macro- and security-political fabric of the world. The catchwords here are (a) the Zeitgeist and (b) the end of the East-West conflict which provided significant windows of opportunity for PSMCs.

The Zeitgeist

The Zeitgeist has changed. These four words encompass the overall interpretation of more complex processes. One is the course the political debate has taken in Western countries in the last quarter of the 20th century to the present day. This debate was triggered by developments in the world of business in the 1960s. At that time, large companies started to outsource certain parts of their business to increase efficiency, effectiveness and profit, a process that transmuted into the political sphere. What was, and still is being discussed here, is a basic question about the functional reach of the state, i.e., the question of which tasks and functions the state should assume and perform and which should not—or not any longer. Fearing state over-extension, and perceiving an impending ungovernability of political systems, the discursive mainstream turned out to argue that the state and particularly the Western welfare state had reached its limits. The solution presented turned to the market as the ordering principle and resorted to neo-liberal economic thinking. Thus, outsourcing and privatization, the medicine that had worked for business, suggested that for the state to survive and to remain functional, it was absolutely necessary for the state to retreat, trim, shrink and downsize (Feigenbaum, Henig and Hamnett 1999). This privatization euphoria singing the song of "cheaper and better" spread from the United Kingdom of Margaret Thatcher to most parts of the world and, eventually, did not leave security issues and the military unaffected (Edmonds 1999). Defence, security, and the military got into the "zest for privatization," a process that "spread around the world like wildfire" (Mandel 2001, 129).

Another process—not fully separate from what has just been sketched and, so to speak, the flip side of this coin—is marked by well-known sociological keywords like risk society, value shift, individualization and informalization (Beck 1986, 2007). Since in an increasingly turbulent and complex world the individual bears more and more responsibility for the contingencies of life, these keywords, in the end, boil down to expecting less and less of the state and demanding more and more of oneself. This, to be sure, is by no means purely negative because the individual might also enjoy more freedom in the course of these normative and socio-cultural shifts. But the point here is that such a normative or cultural setting is a fertile ground for PSMCs to grow because it favours private over state approaches and solutions and suggests less concern for state sovereignty in general and the state's monopoly of the legitimate use of force in particular.

The end of the East-West conflict

The end of the East-West conflict was conducive to the surge in the privatization of security in several ways: First, the collapse of the bipolar world order nourished hopes for a less militarized, even peaceful "One World" in broad segments of society as well as in politics. As a result, a peace dividend was broadly expected and materialized in the notable demobilization of literally millions of regular soldiers worldwide and substantial cutbacks in defence budgets and armaments expenditures. The International Institute for Strategic Studies provides data according to which global defence expenditures and the number of regular soldiers declined from US$1.171 billion and 28 million soldiers respectively in 1985 to US$842 billion and 20.5 million soldiers respectively in 2002 (IISS 2003, 335-340). Next to this, a number of states moved on to considerably reduce their military equipment in the 1990s. The—unintended—result of these processes, however, was that, on the supply side, both military expertise and military equipment were available for PSMCs on the market in larger quantities than before and at relatively modest prices.

Next to this, the global conflict map was conducive to the rise of PSMCs. This has to do with the evaporation of the significant taming and disciplining effect of the East-West conflict in international relations. Since the East-West conflict was the structural, defining and dominant conflict in international relations for most of the time in the second half of the 20th century, both Washington and Moscow had a big say in conflicts and the escalation level of conflicts all over the world. With the East-West conflict gone, the degree of control on old and newly developing conflicts was reduced, implying that international relations were marked by increasing turbulence. In the former Soviet hemisphere various state- and nation-building projects emerged and were sometimes accompanied by a good portion of conflict and violence. In other parts of the world such state- and nation-building endeavours including secessionist movements felt free from superpower tutelage and felt encouraged by these shifts in world politics as well. At times, this also led to violent conflicts, even wars, as is the case with various precarious attempts at state- and nation-building in what came to be termed failed or failing states.

As a consequence, in many countries, areas, and regions of the world, security turned more precarious for both state and non-state actors: Governments, humanitarian organizations, international organizations, non-governmental organizations, transnational corporations, groups of individuals and individuals were increasingly lured into the process of security privatization by the PSMCs' siren song (Bryden and Caparini 2006). Regular armed forces and defence ministries all over the world hopped onto this train which was gaining pace and increasingly resorted to using contractors because of the military's extended task profile and capabilities requirements due to the diffusion of military operations into peacekeeping, peace-enforcement, peace-building and nation-building (Kümmel 2003).

In a similar vein, the Balkans, Iraq and other manifestations of collective violence demonstrated that war and violent conflict were very much alive. This image of war at the end of the 20th and the beginning of the 21st century, however, successively moved away from resembling the traditional notion of war as a business between states with at least two regular armed forces confronting each other, to violent conflicts in which non-state actors emerged to challenge a state's military and made up for patterns of power asymmetries by resorting to unconventional means of warfare often in contradiction of the international rules of the game (i.e., war) (Kaldor 2006). Such a constellation is also conducive to the growth and the increasing usefulness of private security and military companies, because, at least until the terrorist attacks of 11 September 2001 and perhaps only temporarily reversed by 9/11, modern Western societies can be conceived as casualty sensitive, casualty shy and post-heroic and as such willing to let others do the dangerous "dirty jobs" (*inter alia*, Mandel 2004).

THE PSMC BALANCE SHEET

Pro-PSMC arguments begin with the well-known cocktail of attributes that is generally applied to privatization endeavours: quick, flexible, cost-efficient, effective. PSMCs are increasingly able to provide their services ad hoc everywhere in the world. They offer what can be termed on-time production of military and security services which need no storage producing additional costs. In addition, they allow governments and state agencies to clandestinely participate in a conflict situation thus circumventing one's official presence. They are appropriate instruments of "foreign policy, by proxy" (Mandel 2001, 134) and as such politically fungible. At the same time, they are socially acceptable as functional equivalents of regular armed forces in cases of operations which entail political risks and are difficult to assess in terms of their outcome.

Yet, there is a flip side of the coin and these contra-PSMC arguments cannot easily be dismissed or ignored. A very important aspect is the question of the control of the use of force. Contracting is the executive's domain; parliaments usually do not have a say in this. Also, in a historical perspective, the emergence of the state and the establishment of the state's monopoly of the legitimate use of force means some civilizational progress because this considerably reduced the level of violence in society. Privatizing parts of the state's monopoly of the use of force not only means that security becomes a commodity that is asymmetrically available depending on money, but may also lead to an undermining of the state's sovereignty that may be detrimental to both democracy and human rights (Wulf 2005; Uesseler 2006). Further on, there are problems of accountability, both with respect to the question of whether the contractor will actually live up to his contractual commitments and with respect to the billing policy of PSMCs that has been shown to be questionable in various cases.

From my perspective, the record—the balance sheet—of PSMCs is a mixed and ambivalent one (see Jäger and Kümmel 2007). It is not as unequivocally negative as the critics argue nor is it an exclusively positive one. On a very general level, one would surely have to say that yes, there are human rights violations committed by PSMCs; yes, such privatization of security implies a commodification of security; yes, these companies do not necessarily produce sustainable solutions to a given conflict; yes, there is relatively little democratic control over the employment and use of these enterprises so that foreign policy by proxy is tempting and even practiced; yes, the state's monopoly of the legitimate use of force is scratched, is undermined, by them; and yes, the accountability of these firms is, at times, problematic and regular armed forces might become too dependent upon them. Yet, PSMCs are also effective, useful for their various clients, quick in reacting, flexible and cost-effective. Since PSMCs, most likely, are here to stay, the problem is how to have less of the former and more of the latter, i.e., to shift the balance from the problems and pitfalls to the prospects and chances.

TAMING THE BEAST

If the trend definitely is: More of them, since both the conflict constellation of the time and the socio-cultural fabric of modern Western societies point in this direction, this first of all calls for a more intense debate about PSMCs in politics, the media, public opinion and academia. For governments (as well as for other clients of PSMCs), then, to employ these agents carries both chances and risks. Therefore strategies for the intelligent use of this instrument are in high demand.

This is helped by the fact that the PSMC industry is currently characterized by a search for respectability, solidity and legitimacy. The champions in this business seek for broad political and social legitimacy and are concerned about their reputation in order to increase their chances in this market. Advocating corporate responsibility, they employ strategies that basically have self-binding effects. They develop codes of conduct in which they make the respect for national and international law and for human rights obligatory for themselves. They also increase the level of transparency displayed to the broader public by institutionalizing ethics committees which sometimes incorporate non-company members as well and decide upon accepting or rejecting a task or a mission. Given this striving for legitimacy and responsibility, it may be expected that, in single cases, social scientists will be allowed access to these companies to analyze and evaluate their work more easily and more often than in the past. Such permission to become the object of social scientific research would clearly be driven by the contractor's self-interest as the companies allowing such access would surely hope to be certified, so to speak, as a trustworthy firm by the researchers. Yet the insights derived from such a research perspective from within could be substantial and promises to significantly enlarge our knowledge of these companies. They might also help to further the theorizing and the theoretical work on this topic.

The existence of such an attitude in large and influential segments of this business suggests that the various attempts at regulating this industry, at the national level as well as at the international level, might be more effective in the future. Although this process is not a very swift, but, quite to the contrary, a rather slow one, more and more countries could move to develop national legislation to regulate these firms. To register them, to develop criteria and procedures to certify them and, perhaps most important, to establish a working control and supervision of the realization of the contracts, are to be mentioned in this regard as well. On the international level, within the United Nations and beyond, there also is some new momentum to establish an international legal framework to deal with this business with the Montreux Document being the most recent and perhaps most promising one (Cockayne 2009).

Nevertheless, such regulation, at both the national and international level, cannot be complete because not all countries of the world, for various reasons, seem to be willing to follow suit. This implies that there will still be quite a few escape routes for the "black sheep of the family" that are certainly out there. No matter how limited this market may be, there is a market for these not so respectable firms because of their fungibility; there is a market for operations better kept secret, for clandestine politically dubious and morally questionable security, military and, particularly, combat operations. Thus, the supply side can be expected to follow this demand side, so that there are and will be PSMCs willing to provide the requested services. Whether the general public will learn about these operations remains an open question and will surely often depend on an individual's willingness to leak such information to the media.

THE MILITARY-CONTRACTOR NEXUS: THE CASE OF THE UNITED STATES

The starting point for the argument advanced here is that military-contractor interfaces have to be analyzed on two qualitatively different levels: One is the literal cooperation between the military and the contractors that follows from the wording of the contracts; the second level is a meta-level, so to speak, that looks at the military-contractor relationship from the angle of contract supervision. The focus of analysis for both levels will almost always be the case of Iraq. We start, however, by sketching the impressive extent to which the US armed forces resort to contractors and which is seen as an "unprecedented scale of dependence on contractors" by the US Department of Defense itself (Department of Defense Program for Planning, Managing, and Accounting for Contractor Services and Contractor Personnel during Contingency Operations 2008, 2).

THE SCOPE OF THE MILITARY-CONTRACTOR NEXUS

The use of private actors by the US military has a long history and, indeed, dates back to even before the Civil War. During the East-West-conflict contracting was particularly revived following the Office of Management and Budget (OMB) Circular 1-76 in 1967 (Shields 1990, 21-23). By now, as has already been stressed, the United States is the single most import-ant client of PSMCs in the world and has advanced the privatization of security much further than (continental) Europe by reaching out to the areas of combat support and combat. The wars in Afghanistan and Iraq serve as vivid examples: According to the Los Angeles Times that cited information by the US Department of State, the US Agency for International Development (USAID) and the US Central Command (CENTCOM) "private contractors outnumber US troops in Iraq" (Miller 2007). In recent years, the numbers have not been subject to major change despite the change in the administration from George W. Bush, Jr., to Barack Obama. By February 2007, there were some 160,000 US soldiers in Iraq plus a couple of thousand civilian employees from the American government. They faced about 182,000 private contractors and private sub-contractors that were financed by American governmental institu-tions, among them about 21,000 Americans, 118,000 Iraqis, and 43,000 foreigners. The Pentagon had some 130,000 contractors, USAID some tens of thousands and the State Department had the rest under contract (ibid.).

Meanwhile, according to the May 2009 report of the Office of the Assistant Deputy Under Secretary of Defense, Program Support (ADUSD (PS)) (2009, 1), the US Department of Defense alone pays 132,610 contract-ors in Iraq and 68,197 contractors in Afghanistan as of 31 March 2009. Within CENTCOM's total area of responsibility, the number is 242,657. These numbers imply that in Afghanistan and in Iraq the ratio of deployed American soldiers and Department of Defense contractors are roughly the same as is illustrated in Figures 2 and 3.

The ADUSD (PS) report categorizes the contractors in three groups: US citizens, third country nationals and local/host country nationals. Comparing the respective numbers for Iraq and Afghanistan notable differences come to the fore. In Iraq, the relative involvement of and the number of US citizens (36,061) is markedly larger than in Afghanistan (9,378). The biggest group of contractors in Afghanistan is made up by local/host country nationals (51,776; Iraq: 36,305) whereas it is third country nationals in the case of Iraq (60,244; Afghanistan: 7,043) (ibid.).

As is illustrated by Figure 4, these people operate in a high-risk environment; the situation is complex, fluid and challenging and contains a multitude of actors of different kinds. Given this com-plexity of the situation, the services provided by the Department of Defense Contractor Personnel in Iraq show a remarkable variance as is shown in Table 1.

By May 2009, 10,743 out of 12,942, i.e., most of the Department of Defense's private security contractor personnel in Iraq performing either personal security, static security or convoy security missions are armed. These personnel break down into 681 US citizens, 1,665 local/host country nationals and 10,596 third country nationals and imply a

FIGURE 2

The Military–Department of Defense Contractor Ratio in Historical Perspective

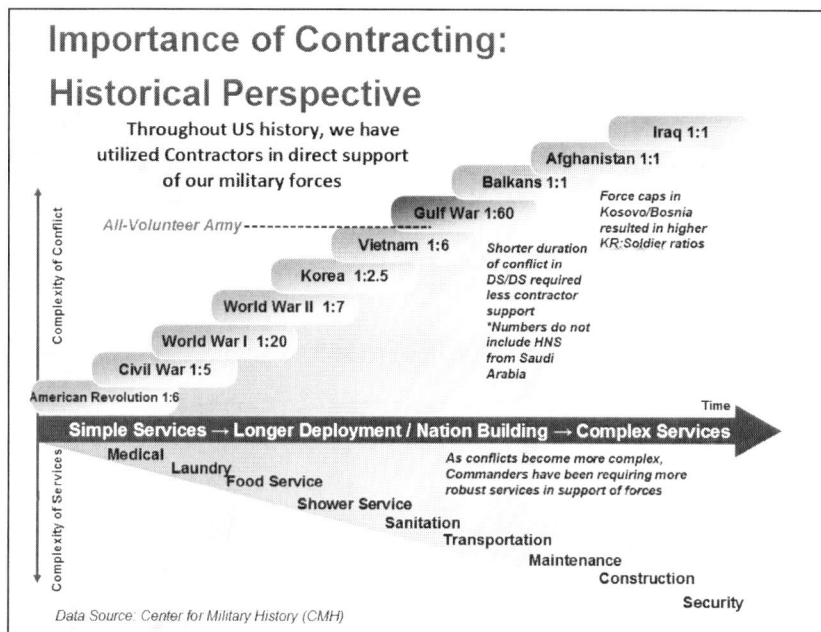

Importance of Contracting:
Historical Perspective

Throughout US history, we have
utilized Contractors in direct support
of our military forces

Iraq 1:1

Afghanistan 1:1

Balkans 1:1

Gulf War 1:60

Force caps in
Kosovo/Bosnia
resulted in higher
KR:Soldier ratios

All-Volunteer Army

Vietnam 1:6

Korea 1:2.5

World War II 1:7

World War I 1:20

Civil War 1:5

American Revolution 1:6

Shorter duration
of conflict in
DS/DS required
less contractor
support
*Numbers do not
include HNS
from Saudi
Arabia

Complexity of Conflict

Time

Simple Services → Longer Deployment / Nation Building → Complex Services

Medical
Laundry
Food Service
Shower Service
Sanitation
Transportation
Maintenance
Construction
Security

As conflicts become more complex,
Commanders have been requiring more
robust services in support of forces

Complexity of Services

Data Source: Center for Military History (CMH)

Source: Reproduced with permission from the Commission on Wartime Contracting (see
Commission on Wartime Contracting in Iraq and Afghanistan 2009, 21).

FIGURE 3

The Military–Department of Defense Contractor Comparison for Afghanistan and Iraq

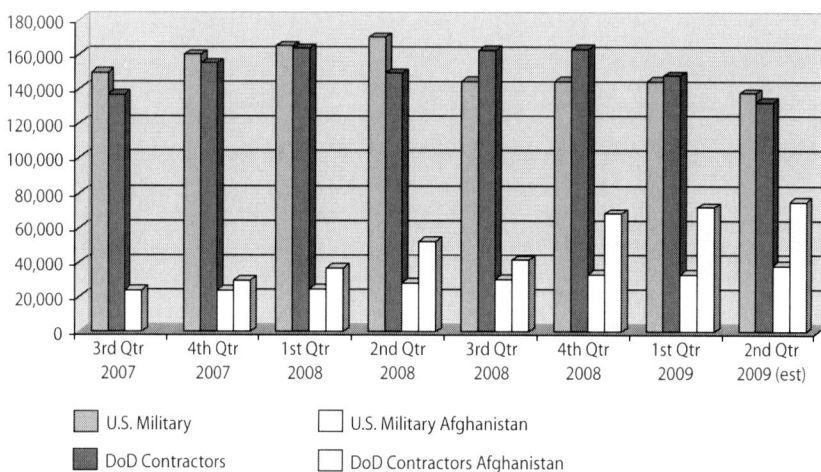

| | 3rd Qtr 2007 | 4th Qtr 2007 | 1st Qtr 2008 | 2nd Qtr 2008 | 3rd Qtr 2008 | 4th Qtr 2008 | 1st Qtr 2009 | 2nd Qtr 2009 (est) |

Legend:
- U.S. Military
- DoD Contractors
- U.S. Military Afghanistan
- DoD Contractors Afghanistan

Source: Motsek 2009, 9.

FIGURE 4
The Complex Battle Space in Iraq

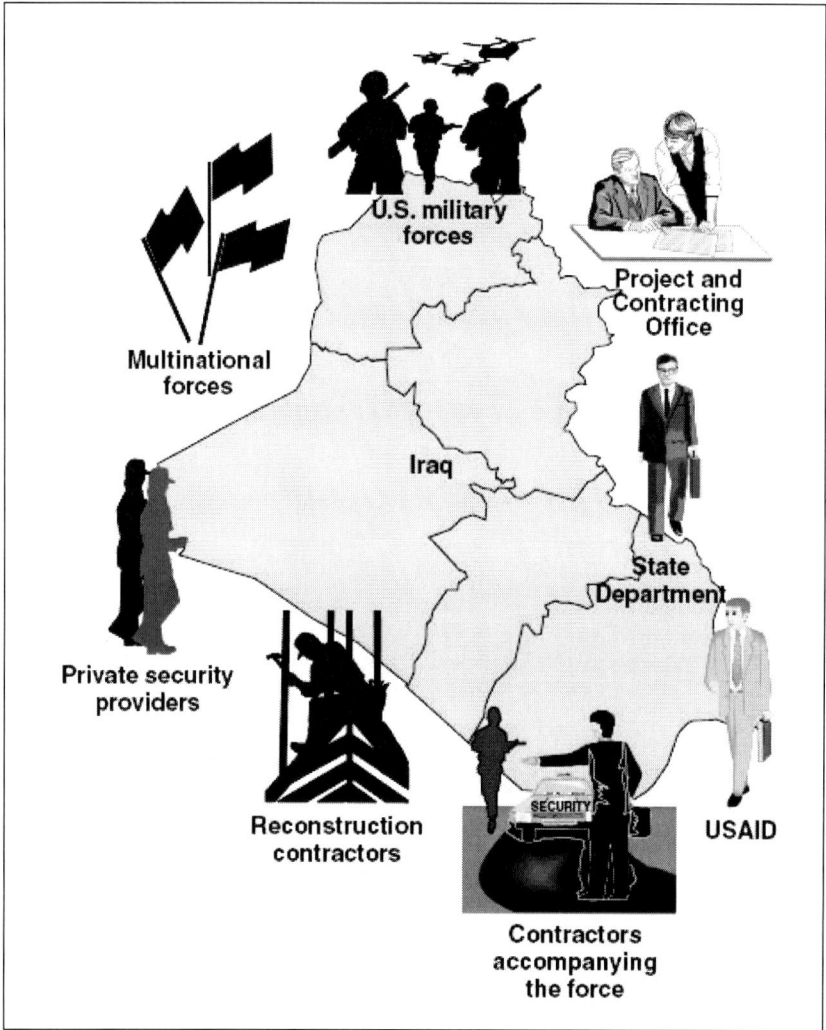

Source: Government Accountability Office 2005, 12.

23 percent increase compared to earlier this year which is explained by the "improved ability to account for subcontractors who are providing security services" (Office of the Assistant Deputy Under Secretary of Defense, Program Support (ADUSD (PS)) 2009, 3). To these have to be added 3,321 private security contractor personnel working under the Department of State Worldwide Personal Protective Services (WPPS)

TABLE 1
Department of Defense Contractor Personnel by Type of Service Provided in 2009

Type of Service	Number of DoD Contractors	Percentage of Total DoD Contractors
Base Support	77,669	58
Construction	19,941	15
Security	10,422	8
Translator/Interpreter	9,241	7
Transportation	2,383	2
Communication Support	1,460	1
Other	11,494	9

Source: Office of the Assistant Deputy Under Secretary of Defense, Program Support (ADUSD (PS)) 2009, 2.

and Baghdad Embassy Security Force contracts; 1,250 of these are United States or coalition citizens, 1,921 are third country nationals and 150 are local/host country nationals (Commission on Wartime Contracting in Iraq and Afghanistan 2009, 62). According to a Congressional Budget Office (CBO) paper, the total number of private security contractor personnel is still higher and is estimated to be 25–30,000 people working for about 60 companies contracted by various US agencies, the Iraqi government, coalition governments and US contractors and others (Congressional Budget Office 2008, 2, 14).

The Congressional Budget Office estimates the costs for private security contractors to be in the order of US$6–10 billion from 2003 through 2007. This represents about 10 percent of total US spending for all contractors, i.e., prime contractors and subcontractors in this period: "From 2003 through 2007, US government agencies obligated a total of $85 billion for contracts principally performed in the Iraq theater […] The $85 billion in obligations for contracts performed in the Iraq theater accounts for almost 20 percent of the $446 billion of U.S. appropriations for activities in Iraq from 2003 through 2007" (Congressional Budget Office 2008, 2). Sometime in 2008, then, US spending for contractors had reached the number of US$100 billion. This is tantamount to saying that "today America's military cannot function effectively without" them (Kelty and Segal 2007, 216).

MILITARY-CONTRACTOR ENCOUNTERS I: THE LEVEL OF LITERAL COOPERATION

Since the beginning of operations in the Iraqi theatre, a number of problems have emerged with regard to the military-contractor relationship and cooperation. They include the following:

- Military-contractor encounters may be dangerous, even lethal, for the contractors. Events in Iraq have illustrated that "the presence of armed contractors introduces the possibility of shooting incidents between contractor personnel and military or local civilian personnel" (Congressional Budget Office 2008, 15). The US Government Accountability Office (GAO) gives more details: "One of the coordination issues that contractors and the military continued to be concerned about is blue on white violence. Blue on white violence is the term used by contractors and the military to describe situations when the military fires at friendly forces (such as contractors) or, as happens less frequently, when private security employees fire at military forces. An analysis of incident reports completed by the ROC [Reconstruction Operation Centers, G.K.] indicates that these incidents happen most frequently when contractors encounter a military checkpoint or a military convoy. Private security providers have told us that they are fired upon by U.S. forces so frequently that incident reports are not always filed with the ROC" (Government Accountability Office 2005, 27). To give a hint of the problem: From January to May 2005 alone, 20 reports of blue on white incidents were sent to the Reconstruction Operation Centers (ROC).
- Military-contractor encounters may be dangerous, even lethal, for the military as well. The recent report by the Commission on Wartime Contracting in Iraq and Afghanistan, i.e., a bipartisan legislative US commission established to study wartime contracting, perceived some increased risk due to the fact that static security services for almost all of the more than 300 forward operating bases are rendered by third-country nationals from countries like Uganda or Peru. The Commission thus raises concerns "that some contractors in Iraq may be limiting training and not providing basic equipment. The adequacy of weapons and equipment, the number of vehicles available, and the type of night-vision equipment used are a few areas of performance that gave us cause for concern" (Commission on Wartime Contracting in Iraq and Afghanistan 2009, 71). Furthermore, contractor activity, especially with regard to private security contractors, may lead to increased risk for the military. After the Nisour incident in September 2007, i.e., when Blackwater personnel shot 17 and wounded 24 Iraqi civilians, the situation became more dangerous not only for Blackwater, but also for the US military.
- To some extent, there are irritations among and even animosities between contractors and soldiers which are grounded in some structural issues. The pay differential, with some contractors making considerably more money than military people, is an example. Another is the detention of a number of contractors working for Zapata Engineering at the end of May 2005 by US marines as reported in the media in June 2005. The Zapata employees were taken into custody to an American

prison for three days. While the US Marines argued that the Zapata convoy had shot at them and some civilians, thus putting the lives of American soldiers at risk, the Zapata employees state that they had been humiliated, tortured and abused by the American soldiers who had made taunts about the contractors' salaries and had called them rogue mercenaries. Next to this, soldiers sometimes complain about contractors behaving like "trigger-prone cowboys" who are a law unto themselves. The fact that American soldiers were tried by the courts for misconduct at Abu Ghraib, while private security contractors were not, since they practically enjoyed immunity following from CPA Order 17, was cause for substantial resentment. In addition to this, military-contractor encounters and cooperation suffered from communication problems as communication systems often lack interoperability; from the fact that contractors usually are outside the military's chain of command; from mutual ambiguity concerning the roles and particular responsibilities; from differing company standards and cultures; and from the fact that the military personnel "deployed to Iraq received no guidance or training regarding the relationship between private security providers and the military prior to deploying" (Government Accountability Office 2005, 29). For most of the time since the beginning of military operations in Iraq, the situation was like this:

> According to military officials, contractors, and security providers coordination between the military and security providers was initially done informally. When a private security provider arrived in a unit's area of operation, the security provider would try to meet with key officials of the unit and establish a relationship. A private security provider we spoke with told us that the results of this informal coordination varied based on the individual personalities of the military and provider personnel. According to some security providers, although many military commanders were very interested in establishing a relationship with the security providers, others were not. Additionally, coordination was inconsistent. For example, one officer who had served with the 4th Infantry Division in Iraq told us that coordination in his area was mixed. According to the officer, some security providers, such as the one providing security for the Iraqi currency exchange program, would always coordinate with the division before moving through the division's area of operations but another contractor rarely coordinated with the division. (Government Accountability Office 2005, 22)

MILITARY-CONTRACTOR ENCOUNTERS II: THE META-LEVEL OF CONTRACT SUPERVISION

Right from the start, the issue of contract supervision, which is a central steering mechanism to shape military-contractor relationship and cooperation, was a problematical one. If one looks at various reports of the Government Accountability Office, one will find numerous examples of waste, fraud and abuse by individual, even well-known and prestigious PSMCs. The general impression from the American case is that the United States, for a very long time, did too much privatization and outsourcing in much too little time implying that the military organization (and other contracting agencies like the Department of State and USAID) had serious problems in keeping pace institutionally, in particular with regard to its contract oversight capabilities. It looked like it was not the dog wagging its tail, but the PSMCs wagging the dog. The recent report by the Commission on Wartime Contracting in Iraq and Afghanistan (2009) cites these findings of earlier reports and provides a neat summary of the situation in recent years:

Management and accountability

- Neither the military nor the federal civilian acquisition workforces have expanded to keep pace with recent years' enormous growth in the number and value of contingency contracts.
- Contracting agencies must provide better and more timely training for employees who manage contracts and oversee contractors' performance. In particular, members of the military assigned to perform on-site performance oversight as contracting officer's representatives often do not learn of the assignment until their unit arrives in the theater, and then find insufficient time and Internet access to complete necessary training.
- Contract auditors are not employed effectively in contingency contracting.
- Contracting officials make ineffective use of contract withhold provisions recommended by their auditors, and many contract audit findings and recommendations are not properly resolved.
- The government still lacks clear standards and policy on inherently governmental functions. This shortcoming has immediate salience given the decisions to use contractors in armed-security and life-support tasks for military units.

Logistics

- Contractors provide critical support to U.S. military personnel in Iraq and Afghanistan, yet the Department of Defense cannot provide a complete accounting of all the contracted support it relies upon. The absence of definitive information affects commanders' ability to understand and make best use of the support they receive, and impedes policy makers' ability to address the appropriate balance between contractors and military personnel.
- The Department of Defense has failed to provide enough staff to perform adequate contract oversight. Inadequate oversight, poorly written statements of work, lack of competition, and contractor inefficiencies have

contributed to billions of dollars in wasteful spending in the Army's largest contract for support services, the Logistics Civil Augmentation Program or LOGCAP contract.
- Contractors are playing a key role in the drawdown of U.S. military forces in Iraq. As military units withdraw from bases, the number of contractor employees needed to handle closing or transfer tasks and to dispose of government property will increase. Strong government oversight will be required, but preparations for this major shift out of Iraq and into Afghanistan or other areas are sketchy.

Security

- The Rules of Engagement for the military differ significantly from the Rules for the Use of Force for private security contractors. The Rules for the Use of Force for private security contractors guarding forward operating bases may not adequately protect military personnel.
- Documented problems with the selection, training, equipping, arming, performance, and accountability of private security-contractor employees will require policy and regulatory changes to provide more effective oversight.

Reconstruction

- Attempts to achieve unity of effort and more measurable results are hampered by weaknesses in the planning, organizing, coordinating, and oversight of reconstruction and development projects.
- Reconstruction, stabilization, and development activities in contingency-operation zones can involve numerous government agencies, private sector, and nongovernmental organizations. Yet there is no locus of planning, coordination, and information—a situation that undermines the goals of the total effort, and one that should be corrected.
- The lack of coordination between USAID projects and the Department of Defense's Commander's Emergency Response Program funded projects is a serious problem that needs to be addressed to maximize capacity building and avoid cross-purpose efforts." (Commission on Wartime Contracting in Iraq and Afghanistan 2009, 2-3)

The bonanza, the gold rush, however, seems to have turned towards a more modest character within the last two years. The reason for this is that both politics and public opinion became increasingly aware of the issues involved when dealing with the PSMC industry. The watershed event was the above-mentioned Blackwater incident at Nisour Square in September 2007 that persuaded the American public and American politics to take some steps to increase oversight of contractor activity, including, *inter alia*:

- ending PSMC immunity following from CPA Order 17;
- improving interagency-coordination by (a) the December 2007 Memorandum of Agreement between the Defense and State departments (Memorandum of Agreement 2007), and (b) the July 2008 Tripartite Memorandum of Understanding between the State and Defense Departments and USAID (Memorandum of Understanding 2008);
- building up oversight competencies and capabilities including tackling the problem of understaffing;
- improving institutional knowledge-sharing processes; and
- establishing law enforcement possibilities for contractors.

To reach this will definitely take a few years, difficult years, because PSMC contracting cannot be suspended meanwhile due to the existing contingencies. And it is not yet fully clear whether the United States will indeed stay the course. It is quite disturbing that some of the improvements done with regard to the Iraqi theatre have not been transferred to the Afghanistan operation, so far.

CONCLUSION

In recent years, the PSMC industry has advanced to considerable size, strength and importance. Although the development pace may not be as dynamic as it has been in the past, it may safely be assumed that PSMCs are here to stay and that they are a relevant element in international relations and conflict situations. This has raised the issue of military-contractor relations and cooperation which will be decisive in present and future mission performance and mission success. The present chapter has looked at this issue by presenting an overview of the PSMC phenomenon and by looking somewhat more deeply into the case of the United States being the largest commissioner of PSMC contracts in the world. The war in Iraq, in particular, has served to illustrate both the potential for military-contractor conflict and for insights into practices that should not be followed. The PSMC business is too ambivalent in character to unleash it from contract supervision and oversight. Just the opposite needs to be done in order to turn PSMCs into a useful and reliable instrument of the state and/or the military. Here, the approach of (continental) Europe and Germany to go for a "managed privatization" approach as indicated at the beginning of this chapter might be worthwhile to consider.

In the end, then, we may thus argue that Principal-Agent Theory has much to say on how to achieve the principal's effective oversight of his agent's activities by tackling the basic problem of information asymmetry (Macho-Stadler and Perez-Castrillo 2001). Though this entails transaction costs, both parties may be interested in achieving more symmetry in information. Yet, it is also clear that the incentives for information symmetrification should be stronger. Such information symmetrification may take place even prior to the signing of the contract. The point of tension, termed hidden characteristics, may be circumvented by signalling and screening strategies. Whereas signalling means, for example, that the agent conveys a profile of his capabilities and competencies that is as realistic as possible, the principal compares, analyzes and checks the profiles of the various agents offering themselves for hire (screening). Next to this, the problem of hidden intentions may be alleviated by the principal by establishing certain incentive structures. This may be a bonus in case the task is accomplished faster than envisaged. Lastly, the points of tension of hidden information and hidden action may be ameliorated by employing contract oversight, control, monitoring and evaluation instruments much more rigorously than in the past which also entails the use of sanctioning instruments (Fredland and Kendry 1999).

This being said, it also becomes clear that research efforts need to be intensified. As of now, the empirical access to the object of analysis is difficult to realize. Nevertheless, the methodology of future research efforts are quite clear: Access contractors and access soldiers through qualitative or quantitative research; look at the diversity of contractors and at the diversity within the military to determine where and why military-contractor relations and cooperation are easier to achieve; and identify best practices with regard to contract oversight.

NOTE

1.   All data taken from the website of the g.e.b.b.: www.gebb.de.

REFERENCES

Beck, U. 1986. *Risikogesellschaft. Auf dem Weg in eine andere Moderne*. Frankfurt am Main: Suhrkamp.

— 2007. *Weltrisikogesellschaft. Auf der Suche nach der verlorenen Sicherheit*. Frankfurt am Main: Suhrkamp.

Bryden, A., and M. Caparini, eds. 2006. *Private Actors and Security Governance*. Wien – Berlin: Lit Verlag.

Cockayne, J. 2009. Regulating Private Military and Security Companies: The Content, Negotiation, Weaknesses and Promise of the Montreux Document. *Journal of Conflict & Security Law* 13 (3):401-428.

Commission on Wartime Contracting in Iraq and Afghanistan. 2009. *At What Cost? Contingency Contracting in Iraq and Afghanistan. Interim Report*. Arlington, VA: Commission on Wartime Contracting in Iraq and Afghanistan.

Congressional Budget Office. 2008. *Contractors' Support of U.S. Operations in Iraq, August 2008*. Washington, DC: Congressional Budget Office. At http://www.cbo.gov/ftpdocs/96xx/doc9688/08-12-IraqContractors.pdf (accessed 5 May 2009).

Department of Defense Program for Planning, Managing, and Accounting for Contractor Services and Contractor Personnel during Contingency Operations. 2008. *Report to the Congress of the United States, April 2008*. Washington, DC: Department of Defense Program for Planning, Managing, and Accounting for Contractor Services and Contractor Personnel during Contingency Operations. At http://www.acq.osd.mil/log/PS/p_vault/final_section854_report_Congress_Apr08.pdf (accessed 5 May 2009).

Edmonds, M. 1999. Defence Privatisation: From State Enterprise to Commercialism. *Cambridge Review of International Affairs* 13 (1):114-129.

Federal Ministry of Defense. 2006. *White Paper 2006 on German Security Policy and the Future of the Bundeswehr*. Berlin: Federal Ministry of Defense.

Feigenbaum, H., J. Henig, and Ch. Hamnett. 1999. *Shrinking the State. The Political Underpinnings of Privatization*. Cambridge et al.: Cambridge University Press.

Fredland, E., and A. Kendry, 1999. The Privatization of Military Force: Economic Virtues, Vices and Government Responsibility. *Cambridge Review of International Affairs* 13 (1):147-164.

Government Accountability Office (GAO). 2005. *Rebuilding Iraq. Actions Needed to Improve Use of Private Security Providers, July 2005*. Washington, DC: GAO.

International Institute for Strategic Studies (IISS). 2003. *The Military Balance 2003–2004*. London: Oxford University Press for the IISS.

Jäger, Th., and G. Kümmel, eds. 2007. *Private Military and Security Companies: Chances, Problems, Pitfalls and Prospects*. Wiesbaden: VS Verlag für Sozialwissenschaften.

Jensen, M., and W. Meckling. 1976. Theory of the Firm: Managerial Behaviour, Agency Costs, and Ownership Structure. *Journal of Financial Economics* 3 (4):305-360.

Kaldor, M. 2006. *New and Old Wars. Organised Violence in a Global Era*, 2nd edition. Cambridge: Polity Press.

Kelty, R., and D.R. Segal. 2007. The Civilianization of the US Military: Army and Navy Case Studies of the Effects of Civilian Integration on Military Personnel. In *Private Military and Security Companies. Chances, Problems, Pitfalls and Prospects*, ed. Th. Jäger and G. Kümmel, 213-239. Wiesbaden: VS Verlag für Sozialwissenschaften.

Kramer, D. 2007. Does History Repeat Itself? A Comparative Analysis of Private Military Entities. In *Private Military and Security Companies. Chances, Problems, Pitfalls and Prospects*, ed. Th. Jäger and G. Kümmel, 23-35. Wiesbaden: VS Verlag für Sozialwissenschaften.

Kümmel, G. 2003. A Soldier is a Soldier is a Soldier!? The Military and Its Soldiers in an Era of Globalisation. In *Handbook of the Sociology of the Military*, ed. G. Caforio, 417-433. New York: Elsevier.

Macho-Stadler, I., and J.D. Perez-Castrillo. 2001. *An Introduction to the Economics of Information. Incentives and Contract*, 2nd edition. Oxford–New York: Oxford University Press.

Mandel, R. 2001. The Privatization of Security. *Armed Forces & Society* 28 (1):129-151.
— 2004. *Security, Strategy, and the Quest for Bloodless War*. Boulder, CO: Lynne Rienner.

Marischka, Ch. 2007. Marktradikales Militär. Die privatwirtschaftliche Basis einer Armee im Einsatz. *Wissenschaft & Frieden* (3):10-14.

Memorandum of Agreement (MOA) Between the Department of Defense and the Department of State on USG Private Security Contractors. 2007. At http://www. acq.osd.mil/log/PS/p_vault/signed_MOA_5Dec07.pdf (accessed 5 May 2009).

Memorandum of Understanding (MOU) Between the U.S. Department of States (DOS) and the U.S. Department of Defense (DOD) and the U.S. Agency for International Development (USAID) Relating to Contracting in Iraq and Afghanistan. 2008. At http://www.acq.osd.mil/log/PS/p_vault/MOU_Signed_July2008.pdf (accessed 5 May 2009).

Miller, T. Ch. 2007. Private Contractors Outnumber U.S. Troops in Iraq. New U.S. Data Show How Heavily the Bush Administration Has Relied on Corporations to Carry out the Occupation of the War-Torn Nation. *Los Angeles Times,* 4 July, p. A1.

Motsek, G. 2009. *Operational Contract Support "State of the Union."* Washington, DC: Office of the Assistant Deputy Under Secretary of Defense (Program Support)—ADUSD (PS).

Musah, A.-F., and J.K. Fayemi, eds. 2000. *Mercenaries. An African Security Dilemma.* London – Sterling, VA: Pluto Press.

O'Brien, K.A. 2000. PMCs, Myths and Mercenaries: The Debate on Private Military Companies. *Royal United Service Institute Journal* 145 (1):59-64.

Office of the Assistant Deputy Under *Secretary* of Defense (Program Support)—ADUSD (PS). 2009. *Contractor Support May 2009.* Washington, DC: Office of the Assistant Deputy Under Secretary of Defense (Program Support)—ADUSD (PS). At http://www.acq.osd.mil/log/PS/hot_topics.html (accessed 12 June 2009).

Ortiz, C. 2007. Overseas Trade in Early Modernity and the Emergence of Embryonic Private Military Companies. In *Private Military and Security Companies. Chances, Problems, Pitfalls and Prospects*, ed. Th. Jäger and G. Kümmel, 11-22. Wiesbaden: VS Verlag für Sozialwissenschaften.

Petersohn, U. 2006. *Die Nutzung privater Militärfirmen durch US-Streitkräfte und Bundeswehr.* Berlin: SWP.

Shearer, D. 1998. *Private Armies and Military Intervention (Adelphi Paper 316).* Oxford et al.: Oxford University Press for The International Institute for Strategic Studies.

Shields, P.M. 1990. *Military Privatization: The Normative/Affective Context (Faculty Publications-Political Science 4).* San Marcos: Texas State University. At http:// ecommons.txstate.edu/polsfacp/4 (accessed 29 January 2010).

Singer, P.W. 2003. *Corporate Warriors. The Rise of the Privatized Military Industry.* Ithaca, NY–London: Cornell University Press.

Uesseler, R. 2006. *Krieg als Dienstleistung. Private Militärfirmen zerstören die Demokratie.* Berlin: Ch. Links Verlag.

Wulf, H. 2005. *Internationalisierung und Privatisierung von Krieg und Frieden.* Baden-Baden: Nomos.

PART 4:
COLLABORATION VS. IMPOSITION

THE ROLE OF TRUST IN WHOLE OF GOVERNMENT MISSIONS

MEGAN M. THOMPSON AND RITU GILL

The increased complexity of modern-day operations is reflected in the new focus on whole of government (WoG) responses that seek to integrate various government agencies within a single mission space and mandate. Here teams of diverse partners contribute distinct yet complementary expertise, skills, and resources. However, getting these various partners "organized on battlefields, after disasters, and during crises can be like herding cats" (Carafano 2008, 135). This chapter will define the complexities of current missions that have resulted in a new emphasis on integrated WoG responses. We next explore the role of trust and its importance in collaborative tasks, especially those arising from complex, uncertain and high-risk environments. We then integrate key results from the existing inter-organizational trust research with the realities of WoG approaches, focusing on key considerations and selected strategies, referencing the Canadian experience, for establishing trust with WoG missions.

NEW MISSION CONTEXTS

Contemporary global conflict increasingly occurs in the context of failed and failing states in which governments have become incapable of, or uninterested in, providing for the basic needs and governance of its people (Patrick and Brown 2007). These settings are often characterized by severe resource degradation and scarcity, poverty and desperation, disease, famine, and abrupt demographic shifts. Such factors, especially when occurring within a governance void, leave the population at extreme

Mission Critical: Smaller Democracies' Role in Global Stability Operations, ed. C. Leuprecht, J. Troy, and D. Last. Montreal and Kingston: Queen's Policy Studies Series, McGill-Queen's University Press. © Her Majesty the Queen in Right of Canada, as represented by the Minister of National Defence, 2010.

risk and thus vulnerable to civil war, asymmetric conflict, the influence of nonstate actors, hegemons, and insurgencies (Gizewski 2007; Metz 2007). Moreover, the disorder inherent in such settings provides the potential for significant increases in organized crime (Mair 2008). Transnational terrorists also exploit these areas as safe havens from which to mount their strikes with relative ease and then retreat into the relative anonymity of the local population (ibid). The underlying causes of such conflicts are multiply determined and inexorably interconnected (Gizewski and Rostek 2007; Leslie, Gizewski and Rostek 2008), and all contribute to significant concerns, both nationally and within the international community.

Clearly establishing and maintaining security remains a key goal in the face of such widespread damage and volatile instability. However, the scale of devastation and deprivation and the lack of crucial governance capacity and infrastructure mean that providing humanitarian relief and development opportunities, and supporting the creation and sustainment of all lines of good governance, are also integral to the success of such missions (Olson and Gregorian 2007; Patrick and Brown 2007; Simms 2008; St-Louis 2009). These realities have led to a comparatively new and explicit focus on Whole of Government (WoG) responses conducted within the context of the comprehensive approach (CA) to operations. The goal of WoG approaches is to integrate the activities and efforts of various government agencies within a single mission space and mandate (Leslie, Gizewski and Rostek 2008; Olson and Gregorian 2007; Patrick and Brown 2007). Usually centered on the 3D triad of defence, diplomacy, and development, comprehensive approaches may also incorporate other governance functions such as justice, border and corrections services, and civil security, as is the case within the current missions in Afghanistan and Haiti (Geddes 2010).

Ideally, an integrated or comprehensive approach should reflect an alignment of purpose among national (and/or international) agencies (Leslie, Gizewski and Rostek 2008; Simms 2008). Working together within one unified purpose is also undertaken to provide a range of other benefits such as increased situational awareness by all players in a complex operational space, proactive sharing of accurate and timely information, and the elimination of a duplication of effort, or worse, the potential for working at cross purposes (Wentz 2006; Spence 2002; Van der Kloet 2006). Such comprehensive approaches to operations are being actively pursued in many countries, notably Canada, the United Kingdom, the United States, Australia, France, Germany, and Sweden (Patrick and Brown 2007; Morcos 2005). NATO and the UN, too, have endorsed the comprehensive approach as most appropriate to address the complexity of modern operations[1] (de Coning 2008; Patrick and Brown 2007; Olson and Gregorian 2007), as does Canada's 2005 International Policy Statement (Leslie, Gizewski and Rostek 2008).

Although developed as the optimal response to the challenges of these new missions, there is a wide array of potential barriers to effective WoG collaboration. These include conflicting political agendas, or at least incompatible objectives; disparities in organizational structures (e.g., hierarchical and centralized vs. flat and decentralized); incompatible financial and knowledge management and communication systems; little or no corporate memory; few formal lessons-learned mechanisms; poor funding and personnel shortfalls; and "competition for resources and agency profile" (Olson and Gregorian 2007, 13, see also de Coning 2008; Morcos 2005; Patrick and Brown 2007; Spence 2002; Stephenson and Schnitzer 2006; Winslow 2002). Reviews of recent comprehensive missions have concluded that while individual successes do occur, these appear to be ad hoc in nature and consistent, effective collaboration has not yet been attained in such settings (Olson and Gregorian 2007; Patrick and Brown 2007; Rietjens 2008).

ORGANIZATIONAL ALLIANCES: THE IMPORTANCE OF TRUST

Recently, organizational psychology, too, has become keenly interested in the establishment and development of effective diverse teams, mainly due to the increase in multinational and inter-organizational alliances. This nascent literature is directly pertinent to the WoG context in that both multinational and WoG alliance formation involve the formal linkage of discrete organizations that remain distinct from a legalistic framework, yet which contribute complementary expertise, skills, resources and technologies to produce potentially synergistic effects (Jennings et al. 2000; Leslie, Gizewski and Rostek 2008). The term "potentially" is used specifically here: despite the opportunities offered by alliances, not all of them meet their goals or objectives, nor do all alliances continue (Das and Teng 1998; Jennings et al. 2000; Olson and Gregorian 2007; Patrick and Brown 2007; Rietjens 2008).

Trust is a critical factor in alliance formation (Krishnan, Martin and Noorderhaven 2006; Dyer and Chu 2003; Mohr and Spekman 1994; Zaheer, McEvily and Perrone 1998), and is believed to be particularly important for success in complex environments characterized by high ambiguity and uncertainty (Child et al. 2007, 153). There is no doubt that the hallmarks of complexity, ambiguity, and uncertainty are readily apparent in situations that demand a WoG/comprehensive response, arguably to an even greater degree than in typical organizational alliance contexts. Certainly WoG alliances entail greater risks and costs should the mission fail, giving rise to the possibility of further state or regional collapse as well as trans-state terrorism and crime, all of which may contribute to international instability.

Given the importance of such missions, and the centrality of trust in such settings, we apply key results from the organizational trust literature to the issue of optimizing WoG alliances. First, we begin by defining trust, and then review the relevant literature to highlight the specific ways in which trust might manifest itself and be of benefit within such settings.

Trust is generally defined as a willingness to be vulnerable to another based on the confident expectation that the other will behave in a manner that will meet, or at least not betray, our needs (Holmes 1991; Mayer, Davis and Schoorman 1995). Meeting those needs may involve demonstrations of competence, predictability, benevolence and/or integrity, depending upon the situation (Mayer, Davis and Schoorman 1995; Rousseau et al. 1998). Importantly, this willingness to be vulnerable exists even in the absence of controls or monitoring that would compel the other to act in a trustworthy manner. Trust is assumed to be critical in situations that are characterized by interdependence, uncertainty, ambiguity, and risk (Holmes 1991; Mayer, Davis and Schoorman 1995; Stouffer et al. 2008). Indeed, many theorists argue that it is only under these conditions that real trust occurs (Mishra 1996). As trust is always a judgment based on incomplete information, it represents both a probability estimate (Gambetta 2000) and, ultimately, "a leap of faith" (Boon and Holmes 1991; Holmes 1991).

The research literature indicates the various benefits associated with high trust. For instance, trust promotes the ability to establish new and maintain existing associations (Lewicki and Bunker 1996; Mayer, Davis and Schoorman 1995), and has been termed "a foundation of social order" (Lewicki, McAllister and Bies 1998, 438). Higher trust reduces the likelihood of exploiting another's vulnerabilities (Barney and Hansen 1994; Mayer, Davis and Schoorman 1995). When trust is conferred, people are less vigilant to signs of inconsistency, and less likely to attend to the specifics and details of another's behaviour; therefore, fewer opportunities exist for potential exposure of disconfirming information. Thus, trust makes partners less likely to invest time in monitoring the relationship and protecting against opportunistic behaviours (Bromiley and Cummings 1995; Dore 1983). Indeed, with fewer concerns about one's partner(s) in an endeavour, trust facilitates the taking of other risks, reducing demands for controls and "protections against the possibility of betrayal, and the insistence on costly sanctioning mechanisms to defend their interests" (Tyler and Kramer 1996, 4).

By bringing about positive beliefs concerning the competence, reliability, benevolence and/or the integrity of another's behaviours (Zaheer, McEvily and Perrone 1998), trust reduces the incidence of conflict, and also helps defuse its potential, because trusting partners are more likely to interpret each other's equivocal actions in a constructive manner conducive to the stability of the relationship (Uzzi 1997; Zaheer, McEvily and Perrone 1998). Should perceived trust violations occur, higher pre-existing levels of trust mean that the responses of the injured party tends to be less intense or more limited in terms of the attributions made (Robinson 1996;

Benton et al. 1969). Higher levels of trust are also associated with greater feelings of shared identity and a higher incidence of spontaneous communication and increased efforts to promote the welfare of the group, even in instances where team or group members are not co-located (Brewer and Miller 1996; Hinds and Mortenson 2005). Such findings led Fisher and Brown to conclude that trust was perhaps the "single most important element of a good working relationship" (1988, 107).

However, trust not only facilitates the tone or effect in relationships, but has also been found to have positive effects on performance outcomes (Dirks 1999; Dirks and Ferrin 2001). For instance, higher levels of trust in managers have been shown to be related to increased sales, profits, and reduced employee turnover (Davis et al. 2000). Within and across organizations, trust is thought to relate directly to efficient information dissemination and processing, as there is less concern regarding sharing proprietary or sensitive information (Krishan, Martin and Noorderhaven 2006). Moreover, the reduction in a reliance on procedures and controls also allows for more efficient and timely decisions and actions. Trust-based relationships are also conducive to the discovery of mutually beneficial, integrative solutions (Walton and McKersie 1965), also increasing the likelihood of effective transactions.

Importantly, under crisis conditions, high trust works to keep authority and decision-making structures decentralized, to maintain honest and open communication, and to lead to the sharing of scarce resources (Mishra 1996). Trust also leads to the extension of goodwill when unforeseen contingencies arise (Krishan, Martin and Noorderhaven 2006). Also critical in an interagency context, trust:

> encourages partners to be aware of the processes and procedures that each partner follows (Gulati and Singh 1998). Thus, trust encourages partners to remain flexible when managing their interface in the face of interdependence. … Under high interdependence, inter-organizational trust is therefore essential for alliance performance, as it facilitates mutual adjustment and allows the smoother synchronization of critical tasks. (Krishnan, Martin and Noorderhaven 2006, 896)

Overall then, there appears to be a general consensus in the field that trust is important and useful in a range of organizational processes and outcomes (see Brockner et al. 1997; Dirks and Ferrin 2001; Elangovan and Shapiro 1998; Mayer, Davis and Schoorman 1995; McAllister 1995; Morris and Moberg 1994; Rich 1997), all of which play important roles in the ultimate effectiveness and viability of an organizational alliance (Fukuyama 1995). As the risk, complexity, interdependence of a mission increases, as is often the case when WoG responses are adopted, trust is expected to play a fundamental role in mission effectiveness, efficiency and success.

BUILDING TRUST WITHIN WOG ALLIANCES

Up to this point, we have outlined the complexity of contemporary international missions and the integrated responses that have evolved in order to meet the complexities associated with them. We have also defined trust and established the importance of trust in organizational alliances. We then reviewed the ways in which trust is expected to facilitate operational effectiveness in organizational alliances. Having set the stage, we now present five key considerations based on the organizational trust literature relevant to establishing interagency trust within the challenge of whole of government missions.

Consideration of the role of situational strength

First, it is imperative for government partners to understand how situational aspects such as risk, uncertainty, and ambiguity factor into WoG missions and the important role of trust in ameliorating these situational effects. All situations are assumed to vary along a continuum referred to as situational strength. Situational strength is said to be strong in cases where the cues for appropriate attitudes and behaviours are overt and apparent (Dirks and Ferrin 2001). Cues such as rules, norms, and rewards, serve as important guides to behaviour. Thus, where situational strength is very strong, behaviours are more or less predetermined by other factors, and trust is expected to play less of a role in behaviours. Where situational strength is moderate, other cues will begin to exert more of an effect on outcomes such as cooperative behaviours. Trust will act as a moderator primarily by shaping the nature of the attributions we make for another's somewhat ambiguous actions and intentions "… affect[ing] the extent to which the action is salient, the conclusions one draws about the factors motivating one's action, and ultimately one's psychological and behavioural responses to the action" (ibid., 459). Weak situational strength is associated with higher levels of ambiguity, where such other factors do not play as strong a role. Accordingly, where situational strength is quite weak, trust will be an important direct determinant of whether positive behaviours such as cooperation and information-sharing will occur.

Many WoG missions will have weak situational strength for a variety of reasons. First, WoG responses are a relatively new approach, at least in terms of being an explicit goal or approach of a national government toward a crisis. Second, as noted, WoG responses mean that agencies and departments that have very different purposes, cultures, and reporting structures must somehow meld into a unified approach, suggesting a high degree of diversity among players. These differences mean that common procedures and structures are less likely to exist. Third, WoG responses are increasingly being adopted in complex, ambiguous, uncertain, and dangerous circumstances, or at least circumstances entailing dynamically shifting demands. Thus, the "messy playing fields" (Olson and Gregorian 2007) that characterize many WoG missions indicate that weak situational strength will often be the norm, meaning that trust will be a defining feature of success. As noted above, however, one way in which to augment situational strength within any given alliance is through pre-existing organizational links, leading to...

Organizational structural considerations within WoG alliances

In particular the focus here needs to be on building organizational structures that promote collaboration, communication, and trust which, in turn, will support WoG effectiveness. As is the case in many other countries, the Canadian government has realized the importance of coordinating structures to facilitate a WoG approach. These structures begin at the highest governmental levels. For instance, the Cabinet Committee on Afghanistan comprises all relevant government department ministers including the ministers of Foreign Affairs, International Trade, National Defence, Public Safety, and State (Agriculture). The goal of this committee is to consider the defence, development, diplomatic and security concerns related to Afghanistan and to monitor progress with respect to Canadian priorities in Afghanistan (Canadian Committee on Afghanistan 2010). Another interorganizational structure within the Government of Canada's WoG strategy is the Stabilization and Reconstruction Task Force (START) within the Department of Foreign Affairs and International Trade (DFAIT). Stood up in the fall of 2005, the purpose of START is to lead the coordination of WoG policy and programs within fragile states. In particular, within START's mandate is the facilitation of "coordinated responses to crises (conflicts and natural disasters) requiring whole-of-government action, deploy[ing] Canadian experts when and where required, and provid[ing] support for international partners working in these contexts" (START 2010; Abbaszadeh et al. 2008).

The Canadian government's integrated approach to operations continues in-theatre. Perhaps the most well-known of these organizational structures is the Provincial Reconstruction Team (PRT) construct that is ascribed to by several nations within the Afghanistan mission. Since its inception in 2005, the Canadian PRT in Kandahar province has undergone a number of reconfigurations and advancements. In general, however, the PRT structure comprises roles for members of the Canadian Forces (CF), the Canadian International Development Agency (CIDA), DFAIT, the Correctional Service of Canada (CSC), and civilian police (CIVPOL) elements. The PRT is led by a board of directors, who are representatives of the contributing organizations, meeting at least once a week to confer on matters related to the mission. Despite the numerous challenges to effectiveness posed by the security situation in Kandahar province, and the understandable growing pains associated with a new and integrated approach, the PRT continues to be an explicitly whole of government entity (Abbaszadeh et al. 2008; Patrick and Brown 2007). Moreover, the Canadian Forces Battlegroup also incorporates an interagency structure, having a Development and a Political Officer (and other subject matters experts as necessary) as positions working with the battlegroup headquarters in order to maximize opportunities for ready consultation and collaboration among government partners in planning battlegroup activities.

TRUST AND ORGANIZATIONAL CONTROL PROCESSES

There is no doubt that the complexity and diversity inherent in organizations that contribute to WoG missions will give rise to a requirement for formal structures and processes that promote coordination and cooperation, streamline efficiencies, aid in reporting, and provide requisite oversight to such interactions. Certainly, research in this area suggests that organizational structures and processes can support or facilitate trust in cases where interpersonal trust may be lacking (Zaheer, McEvily and Perrone 1998). Indeed, the institution of additional controls (e.g., contracts, bureaucratic procedures, or legal requirements) is often an organizational response when trust appears to be an issue (Sitkin and Roth 1993). Paradoxically, however, the organizational trust literature demonstrates that it is often the case that these very control structures, processes and procedures instituted in an attempt to instill or restore trust can actually do much to undermine it (Reed 2001; Shapiro 1987). At its worst, such efforts can lead "to an inflationary spiral of increasingly formalized relations, such as when negotiations break down due to haggling over procedures by which mutually acceptable procedures will be determined" (Sitkin and Roth 1993, 367).

Although no magic bullet exists with respect to this issue, what the organizational trust literature can provide are some guiding principles that should be considered in the development of such formal controls and structures. For instance, bureaucratic and legalistic procedures, policies, rules and processes that emphasize social distance (i.e., the perceived interpersonal space between individuals or groups) will work to undermine trust. Similarly, legalistic mechanisms that focus on or increase the salience of the impersonal relative to the personal aspects of relationships will also cause trust to suffer. In particular, it seems that the specificity of many bureaucratic and legalistic approaches makes them applicable to only specific issues and very constrained situations. However, when trust issues are tied to value-based assumptions, legalistic structures will undermine trust by not addressing underlying trust issues (Sitkin and Roth 1993).

A critical question then is what are the relative merits of trust versus control structures and mechanisms in organizational outcomes? Das and

Teng (1998) have sought to address this question, noting that while trust refers to positive expectations about partners' motives, control refers to regulatory processes that make a system more predictable via the creation and maintenance of common standards (Leifer and Mills 1996). Moreover, they articulate a model in which trust and control are related in that together they form different ways of achieving confidence in the behaviour of others, where confidence is defined as the degree of certainty concerning the cooperative behaviours of others (Das and Teng 1998). Accordingly, confidence can be achieved, even under conditions of low trust, if sufficient and appropriate controls are in place that regulate and reward cooperative behaviour. Confidence can also be achieved in the absence of controls under conditions of high trust. Finally they suggest that trust can moderate the effect of control structures. That is, high trust will set the stage for control mechanisms and structures to work maximally. It is clear, then, that formal controls should be used as needed in ways that facilitate coordination and trust and that support, without undermining, interpersonal and organizational bonds, the latter occurring with the creation of additional bureaucracies, operating delays and negative attitudes, all of which will interfere with the strategic goals of interagency collaboration (Sitkin and Roth 1993). However, even with the institution of appropriate organizational structures and processes, having the right people in roles that promote coordination and cooperation will remain vital in order to foster effective continued interagency collaboration.

Consideration of the role of interpersonal trust within the WoG paradigm

Governments hoping to optimize WoG approaches to operations must recognize that interpersonal trust will continue to play a role in WoG effectiveness and thus must give due consideration to the personnel selected and placed in roles that will act as organizational links between WoG partners. Within the organizational alliance literature, the interpersonal level of trust is considered to be largely the purview of *boundary spanners* between organizations. Boundary spanners are those individuals whose organizational role (and so in this sense could also be termed an organizational structure) provides them with the opportunity to have contact with or to seek out their counterparts in another organization (Zaheer, McEvily and Perrone 1998; Katz and Kahn 1978; Friedman and Podolny 1992). The literature regarding boundary spanners continues to grow as organizations increasingly come to rely on diverse teams that aim to tackle complex problems. Several formulations have been applied to understanding this crucial role (Challis 1988; Engel 1994; Friend, Power and Yewlett 1974; Trist 1983; Webb 1991; as cited in Williams 2002); however, some clear themes of particular relevance to the current issues have emerged. Among these are the common key attributes associated with excelling in the role of boundary spanner. These attributes include the abilities to cultivate "interpersonal relationships, effective communication skills, an interest in an appreciation of the interdependencies" (Williams 2002, 109) among the players, sufficient knowledge of organizational structures to facilitate linkages and problem resolution, a recognition and value of differences, the capacity to invite and entertain the perspectives of others, and the ability to use social engagement and influence to achieve a common good rather than an over-reliance on formal organizational structures and power dynamics. In fact, some researchers (Beresford and Trevillion 1995; Faitlough 1994; cited in Williams 2002) summarized the requisite personal attributes associated with successful boundary-spanners as involving "diplomacy, tact, dispassionate analysis, sincerity, honesty, commitment and reliability"—notably all attributes associated with trustworthy individuals. In summary then, the current relevant organizational literature strongly suggests that boundary spanning roles and the individuals who fill them play a crucial role in inter-organizational trust and effectiveness (Williams 2002).

The thinking concerning boundary-spanners and their role in facilitating inter-agency collaboration is entirely consistent with the role of positive personal interactions that have been identified by researchers in the area of civil-military relations. For instance, Olson and Gregorian (2007) noted that some "… individuals, whether military or humanitarian personnel, or diplomats, who by their energy and initiative and communication skills had been very effective at coordination in the field. In fact, good people can often overcome bad systems" (86). Stephenson and Schnitzer (2006) concur, linking the role of personal level relationships directly to trust, and to inter-organizational cooperation in the field.

> [P]ersonal knowledge, when it exists, may be critical to decisions to extend trust and therefore to cooperate across organization lines. Aid workers may be skeptical or even jaundiced about a specific organization, but if they believe their counterpart there is competent and trustworthy, they are likely to agree to coordinate anyway. (219)

This ability of particular individuals to prevail given the various challenges associated with the comprehensive approach is echoed in other literature that also explored interagency collaboration (Patrick and Brown 2007; St-Louis 2009; Winslow 2002). Moreover, the abilities of these boundary-spanning individuals may be particularly important in the initial stages of interagency coordination and cooperation, prior to the working out of more formal organizational structures.

As just one Canadian example, a notable interagency collaboration developed between Brigadier General Denis Thompson, the Canadian Commander of Task Force Kandahar and Ms. Elissa Golberg in her capacity as the Representative of Canada in Kandahar (RoCK), the senior civilian Canadian government representative in Kandahar province. Ms. Golberg continues fostering Canadian interagency collaboration with the CF and with other Canadian government agencies in her capacity as Director General START (Geddes 2010). Similarly, within the Canadian Land Force, the human dimension is considered to be increasingly significant, and there is a clear acknowledgement that "future soldiers must be able to interact with a multitude of players—other services, multinational coalition partners and, increasingly, other government agencies and a widening range of public players" (Thatcher 2007; Leslie, Gizewski and Rostek 2008; Simms 2008).

Thus, due consideration needs to be given to the skills and aptitudes that are required to excel in interagency alliances. Olson and Gregorian (2007) have eloquently summarized a number of these attributes.

> … Recruitment should emphasize consensus-building abilities and interpersonal and communication skills if agency personnel are to bridge major organizational divides and foster coordination. The cultivation of "good people" in these roles can also be supported through dedicated training in the necessary skills (negotiation, conflict management, consensus-building) and through rigorous screening to be sure the right people are situated in the right positions. It is imperative that properly vetted and trained personnel, who can exercise the kind of leadership that cross-organizational and cross-cultural collaboration requires, be placed in leadership positions at all levels. … An additional consideration is that international agencies are staffed with people from a very wide range of cultural backgrounds and perspectives on power, authority, and coordination, and these differences need to be dealt with in trying to support a more inclusive, consensus-seeking process of interagency dialogue on if and how to collaborate. (86-87)

Having the right key people in the right key places will be of great benefit. Note, however, that relying only on selected personal relationships in the absence of an organizational culture that supports and promotes interagency collaboration will always place additional heavy burdens on the people placed in boundary-spanning roles. This fact leads to our next focus on the wider role of social mechanisms in complex environments such as interagency collaboration.

Socialization considerations

Das and Teng (1998) contend that social influences are at least as powerful a form of influence as those embodied in formal controls. These "soft" measures include shared organizational values and norms that encourage appropriate and desired behaviours. One chief distinction between formal and social mechanisms in terms of trust is that formal controls usually restrict autonomy, because behaviours are strictly specified and often monitored, suggesting a lack of trust. Conversely, social mechanisms do not include explicit restrictions on members' behaviours, and do not limit autonomy. That is, the most successful social controls are implicit, pervasive, and inherent, resulting in voluntary behaviours that are consistent with group norms, rather than being based on rules or the fear of sanctions. As a result, trust and respect are assumed to be inherent in these social mechanisms. Presumably, in complex, evolving situations such as those inherent in missions that require a comprehensive approach, unity based on shared commitment and values and mutual understanding would be one key. Two such social influences include norms related to communication, not only the amount of information shared but, where possible, especially proactive communication is considered to be integral to establishing and maintaining trust. Norms concerning the degree to which the constructive airing of differences of opinion are shared are also assumed to promote trust in alliances (ibid.; Mohr and Spekman 1994). Results such as these speak to the importance of socialization processes as additional means to increase trust within WoG approaches.

The literature suggests that such social influences occur primarily through opportunities for socialization, including meetings, conferences, and joint education and training (Das and Teng 1998). These opportunities allow for information sharing and the development of shared understanding of each others' cultures, norms, priorities and constraints before hitting the high risk and stress of operations. A note of caution regarding education and training opportunities is warranted, however. These opportunities must be well thought out, focused, and coordinated to the needs of all relevant players in the WoG domain, so that smaller agencies and their personnel do not become overwhelmed by the number of golden training opportunities, lest golden opportunities become thought of as additional demands, some of which may be perceived as having limited value (ibid.). Thus, it is of particular importance to promote and support attendance at training exercises directed at the needs of all WoG/comprehensive players, especially those that serve as final mission rehearsals. Opportunities such as that offered by the Canadian Land Force to members of Canadian Other Government Departments (OGDs) within Exercise Maple Guardian, for example, provide excellent chances to interact in realistic field training highly relevant to the Afghanistan mission. Similarly, within START, operational debriefings have been routinely conducted after the missions to Pakistan (2005), Indonesia (2006), Peru (2007) and China (2008) to compile best practices for interagency missions (Geddes 2010).

An additional social mechanism that fosters trust is termed *cultural blending*. This term speaks to the process of the development of shared value-based assumptions (Das and Teng 1998). Relying largely on emergent and shared cultural values and norms, the process of cultural blending develops and provides important signals as to how individuals in alliances should behave. Ideally, such cultural blending should begin with the socialization and training of senior personnel from partner organizations, as a particularly potent strategy in cases where an alliance may involve partners having vastly different organizational cultures (ibid.). Interviews with individuals working in civil-military realms echo the importance of common organizational values as an essential basis for extending trust as well as the linkages between the organizational and interpersonal levels (Stephenson and Schnitzer 2006). "I would say it's around clarity, in terms of different roles and responsibilities. It's respect for each other's particular competencies and it's a confidence in each other that we will act consistently in the best interest of those who we seek to help" (218). In general then, it is important to encourage activities like these which bring together interested and motivated parties from each of the contributing WoG partners, and these activities need to be actively pursued.

Planning considerations

Recognition of the challenging and complex mission space, selecting and placing the right people in the right positions, the institution of appropriate processes and procedures, and opportunities for joint training, education, and mutual awareness and influence can do a great deal to foster a climate of trust within WoG missions. However, another crucial consideration will be the role of a unifying goal for WoG approaches overall and for individual missions. The organizational literature regarding alliance formation indicates the crucial influence of goal setting among alliance partners, not only in terms of the content of the mission goals but also, importantly, in terms of how mission goals are established among the government partners.

For instance, alliance success has been linked to setting a list of specific, achievable, congruent, and appropriate goals. This is also thought to assist in establishing control within an alliance. Equally important, however, is engaging in a process of goal-setting that is based on participatory decision-making among alliance partners. This participatory process is especially important in instances where goals may be difficult to formulate, in new strategic partnerships, and in highly complex and ambiguous settings, as would be the case in many WoG missions. This approach to the process of goal-setting conveys flexibility and adaptation on the part of alliance partners, but also develops collective norms and shared understanding, relating back to the notion of social influence discussed earlier. The goal-setting process itself is seen as a form of social influence. However, it should also facilitate clear and effective formal control mechanisms that reflect an appropriate match between task characteristics and control forms which are assumed to be key to facilitating or impeding trust (Ouchi 1979).

Such thinking underscores the importance of carefully and thoughtfully setting the stage for interagency operations as a collaborative activity wherever possible. Consistent with the literature on successful alliance formation, there should be an overarching plan that guides all players within the comprehensive approach. There is no reason to expect that they must or will have identical missions or tasks; but all need to be understood with regard to how they are expected to assist in the achievement of an overarching goal. Notably, the necessity of beginning with an effective and well articulated collaborative strategy that is contributed to, agreed upon, and managed by the different governmental partners has been called for in recent assessments of integrated approaches by recent in-theatre military commanders (Capstick 2008; Simms 2008).

Concerning the process of goal setting in alliances, some researchers have also advocated that the focus should be on maintaining feelings of equity and fairness among contributors, with partners contributing the most resources receiving the most benefits or playing a leading role in the alliance (Das and Teng 1998). That being said, it is important to note that one of the greatest ways to promote trust would be for the larger partner to deliberately allow smaller partners an equal say in decisions and directions and to provide needed resources to smaller partners whenever possible (ibid.). Further to this point, Das and Teng (1998) note the importance of adopting a trusting stance within the context of interagency alliances. These contributions, offered freely by partners, signal a commitment to the importance of the alliance and each partner's willingness to take risks and make itself vulnerable for the sake of the alliance, and presumably the alliance partners as well (e.g., the power of generosity, see Klapwijk and Van Lange 2009). This further demonstrates that all partners within the alliance are thought of as competent and worthy of respect (Das and Teng 1998; Ouchi 1979). Indeed, militaries, being the largest organizations, and often having the most dominant, assertive reputations within comprehensive approaches, can do much to establish the elements that will facilitate trust by bringing an openness and participatory decision-making culture to WoG/comprehensive missions. Moreover, efforts to make overt adjustments in behaviours and practices that are clearly directed toward benefiting the alliance and its partners—termed *interfirm adaptation* (Hallén, Johanson and Seyed-Mohamed 1991; Das and Teng 1998)—also signal and enhance trust. Finally, to demonstrate their commitment to the WoG mission, the military can offer resources to other constrained government departments, thereby establishing the conditions for increasing trust (ibid.).

Lessons learned and after action reviews, that include interpersonal human and organizational dimensions of WoG missions, should become standard. The Canadian military's Land Force has been conducting a Land Operations After Action Review (AAR) of the Afghanistan mission for three years and has included a comprehensive operations working group as one of its three themes. The participation and input of representatives of OGDs has been actively sought. The results of this AAR are used to brief the Chief of the Land Staff and to inform training, doctrine and planning that can facilitate future WoG missions (Roy 2010). Most recently, several questions tapping WoG issues have been included in the OP HESTIA (the military contribution to the Canadian mission in Haiti) Joint Lessons Learned Cell Information Collection Plan. These questions assess the amount and frequency of the communication and coordination among Canadian WoG partners within the Canadian government's response to the earthquake in Haiti. Explicit efforts such as these to capture the social and organizational aspects of WoG missions and their integration into LL feedback mechanisms to facilitate planning for future missions can only work to further strengthen the WoG approach.

SUMMARY AND CONCLUSION

In this chapter we have briefly reviewed key findings from the existing organizational literature on alliances to highlight the numerous benefits of trusting relationships (e.g., greater cooperation, higher productivity, conflict reduction, shared identity), all of which contribute to organizational viability and effectiveness. As we suggest here, trust is and will remain an important feature in the establishment of successful whole of government missions. Indeed, we believe that the notion of trust to be particularly critical in WoG/comprehensive settings. Trust can often involve high levels of interdependence among agencies that diverge along many fundamental philosophical, structural, and procedural lines. Moreover, that the missions undertaken from within a WoG/comprehensive approach are among the most challenging, involving high levels of ambiguity, uncertainty and risk, also speaks to the importance of trust in these contexts.

The interpersonal and the organizational will always be inexorably linked in WoG missions. Certainly, organizational structures and processes are necessary in WoG settings. However, as the literature suggests, the particular organizational control structures and processes must be developed with an eye to maximizing trust and collaboration in interagency contexts. Such processes and structures must be well thought out in order to avoid the pitfalls of an over-reliance on bureaucratic and legalistic responses that may in fact undermine trust and long-term success in these demanding interagency contexts. Ideally, trust-building and control mechanisms should be "employed simultaneously, in full awareness of the role and efficacy of each other" (Das and Teng 1998, 496). As noted, the organizational trust literature relevant to inter-organizational alliances is in the early stages, particularly with respect to the formal controls that provide efficiency and effectiveness while not undermining trust. Thus, additional and more in-depth research is required in this area as it will allow a better understanding and more exacting specification of the structures, processes and procedures that can facilitate or undermine trust. However, even at their best, formal organizational structures, processes and mechanisms will only ever act as facilitators.

Ultimately, this "environment is about people and relationships— building understanding, respect, and trust" (Simms 2008, 23). People are and will remain critical of establishing and maintaining interagency trust within WoG/comprehensive missions. Moreover, "… this approach of coordinated action needs to be agile and versatile enough to cater to a host of possibilities" (ibid., 13). The organizational trust literature shows that optimal effectiveness and efficiency is best facilitated by relationships that are based upon the notion of trust (positive expectations of the good will and intent of other players), as supported, rather than overtaken, by formal structures and process. Ideally, trust requires a continuum of careful building beforehand, through thoughtful planning, through opportunities for socialization, and through joint education and training to avoid those crisis situations where government agencies would have no choice but to "trust blindly, … because the alternatives are worse" (Gambetta 2000, 223).

NOTE

1. Our thanks to the insightful comments from all members of the Comprehensive Approach Line of Inquiry at the Land Ops After Action Review, held at CFB Kingston, 26–28 May 2009.

REFERENCES

Abbaszadeh, N., M. Crow, M. El-Khoury, J. Gandomi, D. Kuwayama, C. MacPherson, M. Nutting, N. Parker, and T. Weiss. 2008. *Provincial Reconstruction Teams. Lessons and Recommendations*. At http://wws.princeton.edu/research/pwreports_f07/wws591b.pdf (accessed January 2010).

Barney, J.B., and M.H. Hansen. 1994. Trustworthiness as a Source of Competitive Advantage. *Strategic Management Journal* 15:175-190.

Benton, A., E. Gelber, H. Kelley, and B. Liebling 1969. Reactions to Various Degrees of Deceit in a Mixed-Motive Relationship. *Journal of Personality and Social Psychology* 12:170-180.

Boon, S.D., and J.G. Holmes. 1991. The Dynamics of Interpersonal Trust: Resolving Uncertainty in the Face of Risk. In *Cooperation and Prosocial Behaviour*, ed. R.A. Hinde and J. Groebel, 190-211. Cambridge, UK: Cambridge University Press.

Brewer, M.B., and N. Miller. 1996. *Intergroup Relations*. Pacific Grove, CA: Brooks/Cole Publishing.

Brockner, J., P.A. Siegel, J.P. Daly, T. Tyler, and C. Martin. 1997. When Trust Matters: The Moderating Effect of Outcome Favorability. *Administrative Science Quarterly* 42:558-583.

Bromiley, P., and L.L. Cummings. 1995. Transaction Costs in Organizations with Trust. In *Research on Negotiations in Organizations*, Vol. 5, ed. R.B. Bies, B. Sheppard, and R. Lewicki, 219-247. Greenwich, CT: JAI Press.

Canadian Committee on Afghanistan. 2010. At http://www.afghanistan. gc.ca/ canada-afghanistan/approach-approche/ccoa-ccsa.aspx?menu_ id=72&menu=L (accessed January 2010).

Capstick. M. 2008. Renewing Canada's Afghan Mission. *Policy Options* (April):22-25.

Carafano, J.J. 2008. Managing Mayhem: The Future of Interagency. At http:// www.heritage.org/Press/Commentary/ed030308b.cfm (accessed May 2009).

Child, J., G. Dietz, N. Gillespie, P. Li, M.N.K. Saunders, and D. Skinner. 2007. Building, Maintaining and Repairing Trust across Cultures. *Management and Organizational Review* 4:153-154.

Das T.K., and B.S. Teng. 1998. Between Trust and Control: Developing Confidence in Partner Cooperation in Alliances. *Academy of Management Review* 23:491-512.

Davis, J.H., F.D. Shoorman, R.C. Mayer, and H.H. Tan. 2000. The Trusted General Manager and Business Unit Performance: Empirical Evidence of a Competitive Advantage. *Strategic Management Journal* 21:563-576.

de Coning, C. 2008. *The United Nations and the Comprehensive Approach*. DIIS Report 2008:14. Copenhagen, Denmark: Danish Institute for International Studies.

Dirks, K.T. 1999. The Effects of Interpersonal Trust on Work Group Performance. *Journal of Applied Psychology* 84:445-455.

Dirks, K.T., and D.L. Ferrin. 2001. The Role of Interpersonal Trust in Organizational Settings. *Organization Science* 12:450-467.

Dore, R. 1983. Goodwill and the Spirit of Market Capitalism. *British Journal of Sociology* 34:459-82.

Dyer, J.H., and W. Chu. 2003. The Role of Trustworthiness in Reducing Transaction Costs and Improving Performance: Empirical Evidence from the United States, Japan, and Korea. *Organizational Science* 14:57-68.

Elangovan, A.R., and D.L. Shapiro. 1998. Betrayal of Trust in Organizations. *Academy of Management Review* 23:547-566.

Fisher, R., and S. Brown. 1988. *Getting Together: Building Relationships as We Negotiate*. London: Penguin.

Friedman, R.A., and J. Podolny. 1992. Differentiation of Boundary Spanning Roles: Labor Negotiations and Implications for Role Conflict. *Administrative Science Quarterly* 37:28-47.

Fukuyama, F. 1995. *Trust: The Social Virtues and the Creation of Prosperity*. New York: Free Press.

Gambetta, D. 2000. Can We Trust? In *Trust: Making and Breaking Cooperative Relations*, electronic edition, ed. D. Gambetta, 213-237, Department of Sociology, University of Oxford.

Geddes, J. 2010. Yes, We Have a Plan: Canada's Speedy Response to the Haiti Crisis Was No Accident. *MacLean's*, 15 February, pp. 18-19.

Gizewski, P. 2007. The Future Security Environment: Threats, Risks and Responses. International Security Series. *Canadian Institute of International Affairs* (March):1-7.

Gizewski, P., and M. Rostek. 2007. Toward a JIMP-Capable Land Force. *Canadian Army Journal* 10:55-72.

Gulati, R., and H. Singh. 1998. The Architecture of Cooperation: Managing Coordination Costs and Appropriation Concerns in Strategic Alliances. *Administrative Science Quarterly* 43:781-814.

Hallén, L., J. Johanson, and N. Seyed-Mohamed. 1991. Interfirm Adaptation in Business Relationships. *The Journal of Marketing* 55:29-37.

Hinds, P.J., and M. Mortenson. 2005. Understanding Conflict in Geographically Distributed Teams: The Moderating Effects of Shared Identity, Shared Context, and Spontaneous Communication. *Organization Science* 16:290-307.

Holmes, J.G. 1991. Trust and the Appraisal Process in Close Relationships. In *Advances in Personal Relationships*, Vol. 2, ed. W.H. Jones and D. Perlman, 57-104. London: Jessica Kingsley.

Jennings, D,F., K. Artz, L.M. Gillin, and C. Christodouloy. 2000. Determinants of Trust in Global Strategic Alliances: AMRAD and the Australian Biomedical Industry. *Competitiveness Review: An International Business Journal Incorporating Journal of Global Competitiveness* 10:25-44.

Katz, D., and R. Kahn. 1978. *The Social Psychology of Organizations*, revised edition. New York: Wiley.

Klapwijk, A., and P.A.M. Van Lange. 2009. Promoting Cooperation and Trust in "Noisy" Situations: The Power of Generosity. *Journal of Personality and Social Psychology* 96:83-109.

Krishnan, R., X. Martin, and N.G. Noorderhaven. 2006. When Does Trust Matter to Alliance Performance? *Academy of Management Journal* 49:894-917.

Leifer, R., and P.K. Mills. 1996. An Information Processing Approach for Deciding Upon Control Strategies and Reducing Control Loss in Emerging Organizations. *Journal of Management* 22:113-137.

Leslie, A., P. Gizewski, and M. Rostek. 2008. Developing a Comprehensive Approach to Canadian Forces Operations. *Canadian Military Journal* 9:11-20.

Lewicki, R.J, and B.B. Bunker. 1996. Developing and Maintaining Trust in Work Relationships. In *Trust in Organizations, Frontiers of Theory and Research*, ed. R.M. Kramer and T. Tyler, 114-139. Thousand Oaks, CA: Sage Publications.

Lewicki, R.J., D.J. McAllister, and D.J., Bies. 1998. Trust and Distrust: New Relationships and Realities. *The Academy of Management Review* 23:438-458.

Mair, S. 2008. The Need to Focus on Failing States. *Failed States* 29. At http://hir.harvard.edu/index.php?page=article&id=1708 (accessed January 2009).

Mayer, R.C., J. Davis, and F.D. Schoorman. 1995. An Integrative Model of Organizational Trust. *Academy of Management Review* 20:709-734.

McAllister, D. 1995. Affect and Cognition-Based Trust as Foundations for Interpersonal Cooperation in Organizations. *Academy of Management Journal* 38:24-59.

Metz, S. 2007. *Rethinking Insurgency*. Strategic Studies Institute, United States Army.

Mishra, A.K. 1996. Organizational Responses to Crisis: The Centrality of Trust. In *Trust in Organisations*, ed. R.M. Kramer and T.R. Tyler, 261-287. London: Sage.

Mohr, J., and R. Spekman. 1994. Characteristics of Partnership Success: Partnership Attributes, Communication Behaviour, and Conflict Resolution Techniques. *Strategic Management Journal* 15:135-152.

Morcos, K. 2005. *Principles for Good International Engagement in Fragile States.* Organisation for Economic Co-operation and Development. DCD(2005)8/REV2. At http://www.oecd.org/dataoecd/61/45/38368714.pdf (accessed December 2009).

Morris, J.H., and D.J. Moberg, 1994. Work Organizations as Contexts for Trust and Betrayal. In *Citizen Espionage: Studies in Trust and Betrayal*, ed. T. Sarbin, R. Carney, and C. Eoyang, 163-187. Westport, CT: Praeger.

Olson, L., and Gregorian, H. 2007. *Side By Side or Together? Working for Security, Development and Peace in Afghanistan and Liberia*. The Peacebuilding, Development and Security Program (PDSP), Centre for Military and Strategic Studies, University of Calgary. At http://www.ucalgary.ca/pdsp/files/pdsp/sidebysideortogether_oct2007.pdf (accessed March 2009).

Ouchi, W.G. 1979. A Conceptual Framework for the Design of Organizational Control Mechanisms. *Management Science* 25:833-848.

Patrick, S., and K. Brown. 2007. *Greater than the Sum of Its Parts? Assessing "Whole of Government" Approaches to Fragile States*. New York: International Peace Academy.

Reed, M.I. 2001. Organization, Trust, and Control: A Realist Analysis. *Organizational Studies* 22:201-228.

Rich, G. 1997. The Sales Manager as a Role Model: Effects on Trust, Job Satisfaction, and Performance of Salespeople. *Journal of the Academy of Marketing Science* 25:319-328.

Rietjens, S.J.H. 2008. Managing Civil-Military Cooperation: Experiences from the Dutch Provincial Reconstruction Team in Afghanistan. *Armed Forces & Society* 34:173-207.

Robinson, S.L. 1996. Trust and Breach of the Psychological Contract. *Administrative Science Quarterly* 41:574-599.

Rousseau, D.M., S.B. Sitkin, R.S. Burt, and C. Camerer. 1998. Not So Different After All: A Cross-Discipline View of Trust. *Academy of Management Review* 23:393-404.

Roy, LCol. R. 2010. Personal communication, 8 February.

Schumacher, C.R. 2006. Trust—A Source of Success in Strategic Alliances? *Schmalenbach Business Review* 58:259-278.

Shapiro, S.P. 1987. The Social Control of Impersonal Trust. *American Journal of Sociology* 93:623-658.

Simms, J. 2008. *The Joint, Interagency, Multi-National, and Public (JIMP) Environment: Making Sense of a Crowded Battlespace*. Toronto, ON: Canadian Forces College. At http://wps.cfc.forces.gc.ca/papers/nssc/nssc10/simms.doc (accessed June 2009).

Sitkin, S.B., and N.L. Roth. 1993. Explaining the Limited Effectiveness of Legalistic remedies for Trust/Distrust. *Organization Science* 4:367-392.

Spence, N. 2002. Civil-Military Cooperation in Complex Emergencies: More than a Field Application. *Journal of Peacekeeping* 9:165-171.

Stephenson, M., and M.H. Schnitzer. 2006. Interorganizational Trust, Boundary Spanning, and Humanitarian Relief Coordination. *Nonprofit Management & Leadership* 17:211-233.

St-Louis, M-H. 2009. The Strategic Advisory Team in Afghanistan—Part of the Canadian Comprehensive Approach to Stability Operations. *Canadian Military Journal* 9:58-67.

START. 2010. At http://www.international.gc.ca/START-GTSR/start-definition-gtsr.aspx (accessed February 2010).

Stouffer, J., B. Adams, J. Sartori, and M. Thompson. 2008. Trust. In *The Military Leadership Handbook*, ed. B. Horn and R.W. Walker, 525-542. Kingston/Toronto: Canadian Defence Academy Press/Dundurn Press.

Thatcher, C. 2007. Future Force: Incorporating More than the Military. At http://www.vanguardcanada.com/FutureForceThatcher (accessed 28 May 2010).

Tyler, T., and R.M. Kramer. 1996. Whither Trust? In *Trust in Organizations: Frontiers of Theory and Research*, ed. R.M. Kramer and T.R. Tyler, 1-15. London: Sage.

Uzzi, B. 1997. Social Structure and Competition in Interfirm Networks: The Paradox of Embeddedness. *Administrative Science Quarterly* 42:35-67.

Van der Kloet, I. 2006. Building Trust in the Mission Area: A Weapon Against Terrorism? *Small Wars and Insurgencies* 17:421-436.

Walton, R.E., and R.B. McKersie. 1965. *A Behavioural Theory of Labor Negotiations: An Analysis of a Social Interaction System*. New York: McGraw-Hill.

Wentz, L. 2006. *An ICT Primer: Information and Communication Technologies for Civil-Military Coordination in Disaster Relief and Stabilization and Reconstruction*. Center for Technology and National Security Policy, National Defense University. At http://www.ndu.edu/ctnsp/Def_Tech/DTP31%20ICT%20Primer.pdf (accessed 10 January 2010).

Williams, P. 2002. The Competent Boundary Spanner. *Public Administration* 80:103-124.

Winslow, D. 2002. Strange Bedfellows: NGOs and the Military in Humanitarian Crises. *The International Journal of Peace Studies* 7(2). At http://www.gmu.edu/academic/ijps/vol7_2/cover7_2.htm (accessed March 2008).

Zaheer, A., B. McEvily, and V. Perrone. 1998. Does Trust Matter? Exploring the Effects of Interorganizational and Interpersonal Trust on Performance. *Organization Science* 9:141-159.

ANTHROPOLOGY AND CULTURAL AWARENESS FOR THE MILITARY

Donna Winslow

Anthropology arose from situations that required practical management of cultural differences. Out of the practical considerations of colonialism—administration, mission, policing and counterinsurgency—emerged methods and images of otherness that informed anthropological notions of cultural difference. Today anthropologists are being hired to support counterinsurgency efforts in Iraq and Afghanistan. This chapter focuses on the relationship between anthropology and the security sector, particularly in counterinsurgency operations. The examples are from the United States where the relationship has been most contested. I also discuss the US Army's 2010 Culture and Foreign Language Strategy and the framework it offers for training in smaller (non US) forces.

INTRODUCTION

The introduction to the influential US Army *Counterinsurgency Field Manual* (2007) tells us that "Throughout its history the US Military has had to relearn the principles of counterinsurgency." A key element of counterinsurgency doctrine as outlined in the manual is an understanding of the human terrain in the theatre of operations. To this end the Pentagon has enlisted the help of social scientists and particularly anthropologists to map the human terrain and support commanders in their dealings with the local population.

Anthropology, also known as ethnology, refers to the scientific study of cultures. It arose from situations that required a practical management

Mission Critical: Smaller Democracies' Role in Global Stability Operations, ed. C. Leuprecht, J. Troy, and D. Last. Montreal and Kingston: Queen's Policy Studies Series, McGill-Queen's University Press. © 2010 Queen's Centre for International Relations, Queen's University at Kingston. All rights reserved.

of cultural differences. Out of the practical considerations of colonialism—administration, mission, policing and counterinsurgency—emerged methods and images of otherness that inform anthropological notions of cultural difference to this day (Pels and Salemink 1999).

Today anthropologists are being hired to support counterinsurgency efforts in Iraq and Afghanistan.

In this chapter we will focus on the relationship between anthropology and the security sector, particularly in counterinsurgency operations. The examples are from the United States since this is where the relationship has been most contested. In the words of Gusterson (2007b, 164) "Not since World War II had military consulting been endorsed so publicly; not since Vietnam had it been condemned so fiercely." We will also discuss the US Army's 2010 Culture and Foreign Language Strategy (ACFLS) and the framework it offers for training in smaller forces.

ANTHROPOLOGY AND THE SECURITY SECTOR

In this section we briefly examine the role of ethnographic data and ethnographers in war and counterinsurgency. By the end of the 19th century, we begin to see the distinction emerge between "pure" (academic) anthropology, relatively autonomous from historical circumstance, and practical use or "applied" anthropology. As anthropology struggled to build its professional identity in the academy, it disavowed those who found employment outside the walls of the ivory tower. It was felt that "the average practical man" was incapable of good ethnographic analysis (Malinowski 1922, 5).

The early years

The US Department of Defense first recognized culture as a factor in warfare during the Indian Wars of 1865–1885. The American military had a special interest in the native peoples of the trans-Mississippi west because these battles provided the sole opportunities for combat experience, career advancement and military fame. "The investment in the existence of hostiles, as worthy opponents against which to test personal and cultural mettle, was heavy" (Hinsley 1999, 182). Military officers were charged with collecting ethnographic data for the war effort. For example, in the summer of 1881, Lieutenant John Bourke was freed from military duties by General Philip Sheridan, provided with assistants and supplies, in order to conduct full-time study of various Indian tribes of the West.[1]

Military personnel were valued ethnographic observers. Both the Smithsonian Institution and its predecessor, the National Institute, relied upon soldiers, explorers and missionaries to fill out questionnaires and vocabulary lists in their efforts to comprehend the native peoples of North America[2] (Hinsley 1999, 183). After the Civil War, Major John Wesley

Powell, who later headed the Bureau of American Ethnology, argued for the use of ethnographic knowledge as the basis for efficient military and political control of defeated Indian tribes. When Powell founded the Bureau of American Ethnology in 1879 he brought with him military men who had campaigned in the Civil and Indian wars.

However, since anthropologists were considered the "real" experts, they were also recruited into war efforts. During World War I, important and gifted ethnographers such as Richard Burton and Snouk Hurgronje worked as spies for the British and Dutch Armies (Pels and Salemink 1999, 26). Archaeologist Crawford used his talents to photograph and map battles and trenches at the front. European social scientists such as Emile Durkheim wrote propaganda pamphlets for the French government. On the other side of the trenches, German anthropologists were busy taking measurements and photographs of soldiers in POW camps, in order to identify specific national racial features (Price 2008, 5-6).

Franz Boas, founder of the first American academic department of anthropology at Columbia University in 1898, condemned anthropologists recruited by the US government for espionage during WWI.[3]

> [A] number of men… have prostituted science by using it as a cover for their activities as spies. … They merely accept the code of morality to which modern society still conforms. Not so the scientist. The very essence of his life is the service of truth… [They] have also done the greatest possible disservice to scientific inquiry. In consequence of their acts every nation will look with distrust upon the visiting foreign investigator who wants to do honest work, suspecting sinister designs. (Boas 1919)

For his efforts Boas was expelled from the American Anthropological Association.

Price tells us that the First World War established new relationships between American anthropologists and military and intelligence agencies that would remain important, if not problematic, in the wars waged throughout the twentieth century. "The First World War showed anthropologists to be able assets who were familiar with regions that were to become battlefronts or of strategic importance" (2008, 14).

The genie is out of the bottle

Anthropological contributions to the First World War paved the way for the next generation of ethnographers during World War II. González, Gusterson and Price maintain that "It was during World War II that American anthropology was formally organized to meet military and intelligence needs" (2009, 8-9). Many prominent anthropologists such as Clyde Kluckhohn, Margaret Mead, Ruth Benedict and Gregory Bateson[4] assisted the war effort. Some wrote pocket guides for GIs, gave classes to GIs on "primitive societies," worked on war problems related to refugees, domestic war production problems, intelligence analysis and the internment of Japanese Americans (González, Gusterson and Price 2009, 8-9; Price 2008, 39-41).

The Strategic Bombing Survey used psychologists, anthropologists and other social scientist to analyze the impact of Allied bombing on enemy military and civilian populations (Price 2008, 39). Anthropologists collaborated with the Office of Strategic Services (which later became the CIA) while others worked for Army and Navy Intelligence and the Office of War Information which was particularly interested in understanding the Japanese enemy through culture and personality studies (Price 2008, 19, 223).

In December 1941, the American Anthropological Association (AAA) passed a resolution stating: "Be it resolved that the American Anthropological Association places itself and its resources and the specialized skills of its members at the disposal of the country for the successful prosecution of the war" (AAA 1942 cited in Price 2008, 23). Between 1942 and 1945 the Smithsonian published 21 volumes of War Background Studies. These reports covered areas of interest such as Egypt, India, China, Indochina, the Soviet Union and Japan (Price 2008, 96).

The Ethnographic Board was established in 1942 as a Smithsonian think tank that used anthropologists, linguists and cultural geographers to generate information relevant to anticipated theatres of war. The Board also compiled an index of 5,000 anthropologists according to linguistic and geographical expertise and maintained a roster of anthropologists living in Washington, DC who could be contacted if the need arose (Price 2008, 97-99).

Meanwhile German wartime anthropologists reinforced the pseudo-scientific racial philosophy of the Nazi regime. Gretchen Schaff's 2004 work *From Racism to Genocide: Anthropology in the Third Reich* documents how anthropometric research was adapted to justify Nazi policy. The most notorious Nazi anthropologist was Joseph Mengele (Shaff 2004, 183). German archaeologists also shaped their findings to support the war needs of the Nazis, particularly the state's need to justify territorial claims to Poland and Czechoslovakia as prehistoric homelands (Price 2008, 64).

In Japan anthropologists supplied information that aided in the occupation of China and the Japanese Institute of Ethnology coordinated efforts to assist the nation's ethnic and national policies. As the Japanese moved across Southeast Asia and the Pacific, anthropologists studied and helped manage the natives. In fact, the war provided new opportunities for Japanese ethnologists to conduct field research among indigenous peoples (Price 2008, 65-71).

During World War II, anthropologists often stood on ethically shaky ground when working for military and intelligence agencies, and some of them came to regret the long-term consequences of their participation. In 1944 anthropologist Laura Thompson worried that the war had turned fellow social scientists into technicians for hire to the highest bidder (González, Gusterson and Price 2009, 9). In addition, Price's book reveals that during World War II, military officials had a tendency of selectively ignoring and selectively commandeering social scientists' recommendations. "Anthropological intelligence was deployed only when its findings fit the narrow paradigms of civilian and military commanders, and it was neglected when its knowledge was outside these world views regardless of its usefulness" (Price 2008, 197).

The Cold War

Price (2004) shows how US Cold War surveillance damaged the field of anthropology. He reveals how dozens of activist anthropologists were publicly and privately persecuted during the Red Scares of the 1940s and 1950s. It was not Communist Party membership or Marxist beliefs that attracted the most intense scrutiny from the FBI and congressional committees but rather social activism, particularly for racial justice—something anthropologists have traditionally defended.

During the Cold War, anthropologists and intelligence agencies such as the CIA also interacted. For example, Frank Hibben has reported how he used the cover as an archaeologist to plant secret devices to report on Chinese nuclear tests from Mongolia during the 1950s (Price 2002, 16). During this time anthropologists shuffled between the academy and intelligence agencies with apparently little notice or concern on the part of their colleagues. The CIA openly funded anthropological projects such as the Human Relations Area Files.[5]

University centres such as the Centre for International Studies at MIT also received CIA funding and famous anthropologists such as Ruth Benedict accepted hundreds of thousands of dollars from defence and security agencies.[6] Another anthropologist, Clyde Kluckhohm, was involved with a survey research centre which interviewed Russian immigrants to the USA and secretly shared this information with the FBI and CIA. The CIA also funded anthropology research using dummy research foundations as a cover (Price 2002, 19-20). In this way the CIA could fund projects that were of interest to the agency.[7] Price also describes how anthropology research was funded through the Human Ecology Fund and used by the CIA. But the Human Ecology Fund was not alone in receiving CIA funding. Other foundations such as Rockefeller, Ford and Carnegie received nearly half their grants in the field of international relations from the CIA (2002, 21).

Price (2007, 18-21) goes into great detail as to how research on stress during the 1960s under Human Ecology Fund sponsorship found its way into the CIA's Kubark interrogation manual.[8] Alfred W. McCoy's 2006 book, *A Question of Torture: CIA Interrogation, From the Cold War to the War on Terror*, examines how physical torture methods were augmented by the work of American and Canadian psychologists in the 1950s and 1960s. Their research, with covert government financing, led to the discovery that sensory deprivation, disorientation, and self-inflicted pain could more effectively (and more rapidly) break down the human psyche than could physical assaults[9] (McCoy 2006, 50; Price 2007, 18; González 2007a). Later, cultural assault would be added to the torture tool kit.[10]

During the Vietnam era, the defence community recognized that familiarity with indigenous, non-Western cultures was vital for counterinsurgency operations. The Director of the Defense Department's Advanced Research Projects Agency, R.L. Sproul, testified before Congress in 1965 that "Remote area warfare is controlled in a major way by the environment in which the warfare occurs, by the sociological and anthropological characteristics of the people involved in the war, and by the nature of the conflict itself" (McFate 2005b, 47). Thus, the US defence community determined that it must recruit cultural and social experts. Seymour Deitchman, DOD Special Assistant for Counterinsurgency, explained to a congressional subcommittee in 1965:

> The Defense Department has ... recognized that part of its research and development efforts to support counterinsurgency operations must be oriented toward the people ... involved in this type of war; and the DOD has called on the types of scientists—anthropologists, psychologists, sociologists, political scientists, economists—whose professional orientation to human behaviour would enable them to make useful contributions in this area. (McFate 2005b, 47)

An adviser to US troops in Vietnam in 1965, British expert Sir Robert Thompson suggested that anthropologists be used to recruit aboriginal tribesmen as partisans. This is reminiscent of when the British military used anthropologists, like Sir Edmund Leach, during World War II to arm and train native peoples for guerrilla warfare (Price 2008, 55-58). Special Forces in Vietnam, for example, were assisted by anthropologist Gerald Hickey in working with the Montagnards who were described as a group in opposition to the North Vietnamese. This process had begun under the French:

> The influential ethnographic publications by Ner, Jouin, Maurice and Guilleminet had explicit scientific pretensions and were all intended to provide the French administration with a framework for action in the Central Highlands, by representing Montagnard culture as valuable enough to protect against the Vietnamese, while simultaneously in need of development for economic, social, demographic or political reasons. (Salemink 1999, 304)

By the 1970s evidence had surfaced of anthropology's complicity in the establishment and maintenance of colonial empires (Asad 1973) and the involvement of American anthropologists in clandestine counterinsurgency work. For example there was the infamous Project Camelot,[11] a CIA counterinsurgency program in Latin America and the Thai Affair where ethnographic research in Northern Thailand was employed in counterinsurgency against communists in Indochina (Gusterson 2009; Horowitz 1968; Marcus and Fischer 1986, 34-35; McFate 2005a, 36-37). This led to a curious juxtaposition of a positive, emancipated academic anthropology with a negative past of colonial and imperial practice. According to Pels and Salemink "The 1970s generation of critics had a material interest—academic distinction—in presenting the work of the previous generation as politically suspect" (1999, 6).

As a result the AAA's Standing Committee on Ethics produced the 1971 "Principles of Professional Responsibility." The document tells us that the "anthropologist's paramount responsibility is to those he studies. When there is a conflict of interest, these individuals must come first" (González 2004, 46). The Principles of Professional Responsibility go on to say that "no secret research, no secret reports or debriefings of any kind should be agreed to or given" by members of the AAA (González 2004, 68).

By 1984 the Association's Principles of Professional Responsibility had been watered down to say that anthropologists had no "professional obligation" to provide reports or debriefings to government officials unless specified by the terms of employment. Price (2000, 68) cynically comments that this meant that no anthropologist had to be a spy unless he or she wanted to or had agreed to do so in a contract. By 1995, a commission to review the AAA code of ethics concluded that the AAA had neither the authority nor the resources to investigate or arbitrate complaints of ethical misconduct.

Culture and counterinsurgency

In a remarkably prescient article in *Military Review*, Congressman Ike Skelton, chairman of the House Armed Services Committee, examined the US Frontier Wars and the lessons they offer for future counterinsurgency: "For US military forces, it is almost certain that future conflicts will occur in regions where the enemy has a greater understanding of the physical environment and has better optimized his forces to fight" (2001, 3). It is of interest that he notes the importance of "human intelligence" even though he neglects to note the contribution of trained anthropologists in uniform to these Frontier Wars. Extrapolating from the US Indian Wars he remarks that, "crucial information will only be available through human interaction. The United States, even with its sophisticated intelligence, surveillance and reconnaissance systems, will have difficulty in complex settings unless it builds a more effective human intelligence capability in strategically important areas" (2001, 3-4).

Yet the Americans seem to have been caught off guard in Iraq. Marsellis tells us that when he first arrived in Iraq in 2003, he knew nothing about the general cultural milieu. Moreover, "the prevailing attitude at the time seemed to be that we didn't really *have* to understand" (2009, 1-2). He goes on to say:

> Well, one of the gravest shortfalls in the early years of Iraq "stabilization" was the lack of such understanding. That the tribes and religious sheiks had, in the midst of the political vacuum that developed after the fall of Saddam's regime, assumed control and influence. The majority of military and civilian leadership in Iraq did not understand these religious and ethnic nuances, which heavily contributed to the sectarian violence and militias that developed in areas like Najaf and Karbala. (2009, 2)

By 2004 Major General Robert Scales was testifying before the US House Armed Services Committee that "during the present 'cultural' phase of the war, intimate knowledge of the enemy's motivation, intent, will, tactical method and cultural environment has proven to be far more important for success than the deployment of smart bombs, unmanned aircraft and expansive bandwidth" (2004, 2). He described the conflicts in Afghanistan and Iraq as the "social scientists' war" believing that the United States must harness the potential of the social sciences in a manner not dissimilar to the Manhattan Project when theoretical physics was used to create the atom bomb.

The United States had begun to realize that cultural intelligence was important to success in Iraq and Afghanistan. "The value of military intelligence is exceeded by that of social and cultural intelligence. We need the ability to look, understand, and operate deeply into the fault lines of societies where, increasingly, we find the frontiers of national security" (Arthur K. Cebrowski, Director of Force Transformation, Office of the Secretary of Defense, Statement before the Subcommittee on Terrorism, Unconventional Treats, and Capabilities, Armed Services Committee, United States House of Representatives, February 26, 2004 cited in McFate 2005b, 47). One of the operational applications of this has led to the establishment of the Human Terrain System (HTS).

In 2005, anthropologist Montgomery McFate, one of the principle architects of the Human Terrain System published two controversial articles defending the use of anthropology in counterinsurgency operations. She argued that new adversaries and operational environments "necessitate a sharper focus on cultural knowledge of the enemy" (2005b, 43). In order to achieve victory in Iraq and Afghanistan,[12] it is equally important to understand the people and their culture.

> The curious and conspicuous lack of anthropology in the national-security arena since the Vietnam War has had grave consequences for countering the

> insurgency in Iraq, particularly because political policy and military oper-
> ations based on partial and incomplete cultural knowledge are often worse
> than none at all. (McFate 2005a, 24)

This lack of cultural consideration is a result of the Powell-Weinberger doctrine[13] which, according to McFate, institutionalized a preference for major combat operations over counterinsurgency. And although this doctrine was eroded during the Clinton years, during peace operations in Haiti, Somalia, and Bosnia and during the second Gulf War, no alterna-tive doctrine emerged to take its place until the Combined Arms Center at Fort Leavenworth under the command of General Petraeus issued the influential *Counterinsurgency Field Manual*[14] in 2006 (and published by the University of Chicago Press a year later). The manual cites the word "culture" more than 80 times (US Army 2007). On cultural awareness the manual tells us:

> Cultural awareness has become an increasingly important competency for
> small-unit leaders. Perceptive junior leaders learn how cultures affect military
> operations. They study major world cultures and put a priority on learning
> the details of the new operational environment when deployed. Different
> solutions are required in different cultural contexts. Effective small-unit
> leaders adapt to new situations, realizing their words and actions may be
> interpreted differently in different cultures. Like all other competencies,
> cultural awareness requires self-awareness, self-directed learning, and
> adaptability. (Ibid., 242)

This is a far cry from former Secretary of Defense Robert McNamara's statement about Vietnam: "I had never visited Indochina, nor did I under-stand or appreciate its history, language, culture, or values. When it came to Vietnam, we found ourselves setting policy for a region that was terra incognita" (McNamara 1995 quoted in McFate 2005b, 42).

McFate (2005a, 28) criticizes anthropology for being cloistered in the ivory tower of academia, prone to self-flagellation and postmodern in-coherence. She describes a long list of anthropologists who have worked hand-in-hand with government whether they were working for colonial administrators, offices of war information or the CIA. For McFate, ap-plied military anthropology is not anthropology of the military (such as Winslow 1997, Ben-Ari 1998 and Simons 1998 have done), rather it is anthropology in the service of the military in order to better influence the thinking of people. McFate is opposed to what she calls a "disengaged" anthropology.

> Regardless of whether anthropologists decide to enter the national-security
> arena, cultural information will inevitably be used as the basis of military
> operations and public policy. And, if anthropologists refuse to contribute,

how reliable will that information be? The result of using incomplete "bad" anthropology is, invariably, failed operations and failed policy. ... Despite the fact that military applications of cultural knowledge might be distasteful to ethically inclined anthropologists, their assistance is necessary. (McFate 2005a, 37)

And one has to admit it is frightening to think that the military might base an action or policy on research such as that commissioned by the US Air Force on "The Arab Mind" which identifies "key differences between Arab and Western thinking." In addition to information gleaned from sources, including business and travel guides, the researchers carried out "in-depth interviews with 16 Arabs from Egypt, Israel's West Bank, Jordan, Kuwait, Lebanon, Saudi Arabia and Syria and six westerners with extensive experience in dealing with Arabs from Bahrain, Egypt, Iraq, Israel, Jordan Kuwait, Lebanon, Saudi Arabia and the United Arab Emirates. Based on their research the study group identified "differences that can fuel misunderstanding and hostility during Arab-Western interaction" (Klein and Kuperman 2008, 100).

In addition to helping soldiers deal with the locals, McFate believes that cultural knowledge will help distinguish between friend and foe and is essential to winning the battle for hearts and minds. Culture can therefore be leveraged to a US advantage in order to improve the performance of US forces both in Iraq and Afghanistan where "Cultural ignorance can kill" (McFate 2005b, 44).

Fellow social scientist David Kilcullen[15] has also called for a deeper cultural and linguistic understanding of the conflict environment, an approach he calls "conflict ethnography" which is "deep, situation-specific understanding of the human, social and cultural dimensions of a conflict, understood not by analogy with some other conflict, but in its own terms" (2007). In his latest book Kilcullen (2009) points to the folly of mistaking what he calls accidental (local) guerrillas with violent Islamic militants whom he calls "Takfiris." The militants (often foreigners to the region themselves) capitalize on local grievances and social networks to promote their cause. The majority of fighters are locals who simply object to Western encroachment on their land. Casting local inhabitants and even the local insurgents in the wrong light can lead to disastrous policies and actions on the ground which only fuel resentment of foreign military forces. Kilcullen feels the local population and even accidental guerrillas can be won over if Western authorities can persuade them that they are better positioned to help the locals get what they want. There is, thus, a two pronged battle to be won—an anti-terrorist campaign against the Takfiris and a battle for the hearts and minds of the locals. And here is precisely where an engaged anthropology or conflict ethnology can make a difference: in distinguishing potential friend from real foe and in identifying and remedying local grievances.

Both McFate and Kilcullen, who has referred to counterinsurgency as "armed social work" (2006, item 23), have come under vicious attack by academics. He is criticised for his support of anthropology in the battlefield (Gusterson 2007a; González 2007a), his involvement in counter-insurgency strategy and policy in Iraq and is accused of plagiarizing his contribution to the *Counterinsurgency Field Manual* from T.E. Lawrence's *Seven Pillars of Wisdom* (González 2007b). McFate is also accused of pla-giarizing her contributions to *The Counterinsurgency Field Manual*[16] (ibid.). In the preface to *The Counter-Counterinsurgency Field Manual* (Network of Concerned Anthropologists 2009, i), the distinguished anthropologist Marshall Sahlins calls the field manual devious and dubious: "a pastiche of platitudes taken without acknowledgement from social science sources." McFate has also committed the unpardonable sin of being the principle spokesperson and architect of the Human Terrain System.

GETTING YOUR HANDS DIRTY: THE HUMAN TERRAIN SYSTEM

In this section we examine the US Army's early attempts to introduce cultural awareness into the counterinsurgency efforts in Iraq and Afghanistan. This entailed the creation of the Human Terrain System (HTS) where civilian social scientists find themselves in the field advis-ing military commanders amongst other things. This participation by civilians in counterinsurgency has been highly contested and criticized by the academic community, particularly by anthropologists. We then go on to describe the latest US Army efforts to introduce cultural awareness into military education.

HTS described

According to the official Human Terrain System website:

> HTS is a new proof-of-concept program, run by the US Army Training and Doctrine Command (TRADOC), and serving the joint community. The near-term focus of the HTS program is to improve the military's ability to understand the highly complex, local, socio-cultural environment in the areas where they are deployed; however, in the long-term, HTS hopes to assist the US government in understanding foreign countries and regions prior to an engagement within that region.

- HTS was developed in response to identified gaps in commanders' and staffs' understanding of the local population and culture, and its impact on operational decisions; and poor transfer of specific socio-cultural knowledge to follow-on units.

- The HTS approach is to place the expertise and experience of social scientists and regional experts, coupled with reach-back, open-source research, directly in support of deployed units engaging in full-spectrum operations.
- HTS informs decision-making at the tactical, operational and strategic levels.
- The HTS program is the first time that social science research and advising has been done systematically, on a large scale, and at the brigade level.

The HTS program has several components. In Afghanistan and Iraq it began deploying Human Terrain Teams (HTTs) in 2006. HTTs are composed of military personnel, linguists, area studies specialists, and civilian social scientists. According to the *Human Terrain Handbook* (given to HTT members when they arrive at Fort Leavenworth for their four month pre-deployment training):

> Human Terrain Teams (HTTs) are five- to nine-person teams deployed by the Human Terrain System (HTS) to support field commanders by filling their cultural knowledge gap in the current operating environment and providing cultural interpretations of events occurring within their area of operations. The team is composed of individuals with social science and operational backgrounds that are deployed with tactical and operational military units to assist in bringing knowledge about the local population into a coherent analytic framework and build relationships with the local power-brokers in order to provide advice and opportunities to Commanders and staffs in the field. (Finney 2008, 4)

The HTTs are assigned staff to the Brigade Combat Team and support the commander with open-source, unclassified socio-cultural analysis, performing a non-combat support role. The HTT's mission is to increase the ability of brigades, battalions, companies, platoons, and squads to understand the local populace that they live with and must operate among. The HTT works with the brigade staff to help ensure that the brigade operates with an understanding of the local population and environment. The HTT assists commanders in understanding the operational relevance, or the "so what?" of socio-cultural information as it applies to the military decision-making process (HTS website 2009).

It is the HTTs which have been at the centre of the controversy surrounding the HTS. Supporters say that they are indispensable: "[In Iraq] we saw some great work the [human terrain] teams are doing and got to sit down with many of the supported units—[the] best quote [was] from a BCT [Brigade Combat Team] commander—"if somebody told me they were going to take away my HTT, I would have a platoon of infantry ready to stop them."[17] Marseillis (2009) believes that Human Terrain

Teams and Provincial Reconstruction Teams have become vital in both Iraq and Afghanistan.

HTTs produce reports which vary widely in content and sourcing: some cite academic studies, others rely heavily on newspaper articles and information culled from the Web. They cover such topics as historical averages for school attendance, strategic marriage, soil and crops, graffiti, and governors' bios. Other reports examine bribery and corruption, the origin of local conflicts, resource issues, boundary maps and ethnicity or whatever else the military commander is interested in.

Another source of controversy is the database HTTs develop to help the military understand and deal with "human terrain." According to Kipp et al. the HTS is oriented at creating a

> Constantly updated, user-friendly ethnographic and socio-cultural database of the area of operations that can provide the commander [with] data maps showing specific ethnographic or cultural features. The HTT's tool kit is mapping software, an automated database and presentation tool that allows teams to gather, store, manipulate, and provide cultural data from hundreds of categories. Data will cover such subjects as key regional personalities, social structures, links between clans and families, economic issues, public communications, agricultural production, and the like. The data compiled and archived will be transferred to follow-on units. (Kipp et al. 2006, 13)

The HTS program also has its own contracted reach-back capability in the form of a cell at Fort Leavenworth, Kansas. This cell provides feedback to HTTs in Iraq and Afghanistan. In addition, the HTS Research Reach Back Center, staffed by military and civilian analysts, provides more in-depth research products culled from open-source materials. In addition, the HTS is building a large network of subject matter specialists. Scholars and practitioners with expertise in Afghanistan and Iraq are desired, in addition to experts with thematic expertise (such as political economy of developing societies, social organization of insurgent groups, etc.).

In September 2007 Secretary of Defense Gates authorized a dramatic expansion of the HTS and 25 additional teams were deployed in 2008. In addition to the strong support from US Secretary of Defense Gates, President Barack Obama has also expressed cultural needs for the 21st century military. During his presidential campaign, he addressed the importance regarding the future of the US military and the need for cultural awareness. In a campaign publication titled, *A 21st Century Military for America* he states, "As we rebuild our armed forces, we must meet the full-spectrum needs of the new century… We should invest in foreign language training, *cultural awareness*, and human intelligence and other needed counterinsurgency and stabilization skill sets…" [emphasis added]. (Obama quoted in Marsellis 2009, 6)

Controversy—ethnographic intelligence

There is an extensive debate on HTS and we can examine it only briefly.[18] However it is important to note that the debate echoes earlier protests by academics against anthropologists who worked for the security sector during the First, Second and Cold wars. They can be grouped roughly in four themes: do no harm to the people you study; get their informed consent before you study them; don't put other anthropologists at risk; and, be mindful of how your work is used by others.

There is another important thing to keep in mind. Groups like the Network of Concerned Anthropologists, which will be discussed below, are primarily made up of US academics who are theoretically driven and have more prestige than those involved in applied anthropology. Thus the current controversy among US anthropologists is marked by more highly ranked scholars who represent "pure" academic pursuits critiquing lower placed scholars (Ben-Ari 2009).

Members of the Network of Concerned Social Anthropologists[19] and others, contend that the civilians on HTTs are violating academic ethical standards. The website for the Network of Concerned Anthropologists tells us it is an "independent ad hoc network of anthropologists seeking to promote an ethical anthropology." Their primary activity seems to be to encourage anthropologists to sign a pledge condemning HTTs.

> The creators of the Human Terrain Team concept have spoken about integrating cultural and tactical intelligence on the battlefield, and Assistant Deputy Under Secretary of Defense John Wilcox has said that Human Terrain Mapping "enables the entire kill chain." Human Terrain Mapping will inevitably be used not just to avert fighting in some instances, but also to select people for death and injury in other cases.[20] We do not believe this is an appropriate use of anthropological knowledge … Human Terrain Mapping is undertaken to benefit the U.S. military, not the populations who often find themselves trapped between violent forces. (2009)

Academic critics of HTS see social scientists wearing military uniforms, carrying small arms and providing direct input to combat staffs that may use the information to apply deadly force. In addition, few are experts on the region they are supposed to culturally interpret. "There are not enough Afghan experts in the entire United States to staff more than one or two human terrain teams, which have been the Achilles' heel of the program from the start" (Chris Mason, a former State Department specialist on Afghanistan, quoted in Shachtman 2009).

Roberto J. González,[21] an associate professor of anthropology at San Jose State University, one of the leaders of the campaign against HTS argues that Human Terrain Teams should not deceive themselves that their work is actually progressive. Instead he sees them as scholarly imperialists seeking particular forms of cultural knowledge that might facilitate the American occupation of foreign lands.

At times González's accusations seem farfetched, but then so do the attitudes of some HTT members. In the following quote from an HTT member's blog one can easily see that "going native" has absolutely nothing to do with Iraqis or Afghanis. How then can this person advise commanders on the local human terrain?

> Going "native" in anthropology is a fairly common strategy to gain a better understanding of the people with whom one is working. I am about a month away from deploying to Bagdad as part of the US Army's new Human [T]errain System and have almost gone completely native. How am I doing this? First I am working out regularly … Second, I cut my hair in a high and tight style and look like a drill sergeant … third, I shot very well … at the range … Shooting well is important if you are a soldier regardless of whether or not your job requires you to carry a weapon. Fourth, I am trying to learn military language with all the acronyms and idioms otherwise alien to university professor such as myself … Today, among soldiers, I am looking and more often acting like them … That is what going native is all about. (Marcus Griffin[22] cited in González 2009b, 108-109)

Critics believe that if HTT members do in fact seem to be military, then people might feel coerced into answering their questions. The AAA 2007 Commission on the Engagement of Anthropology with the US Security and Intelligence Communities tells us "HTS anthropologists work in a war zone under conditions that make it difficult for those they communicate with to give 'informed consent' or, for this consent to be taken at face value or freely refused. As a result, 'voluntary informed consent' (as stipulated by the AAA Code of Ethics, section III, A, 4) is compromised." The Network of Concerned Anthropologists has also questioned whether informed consent is possible and whether the safety of research informants can be ensured in the context of armed conflict. In such contexts, these scholars suggest, local people may feel that researchers embedded with US military units can exert power over them and may therefore feel forced to participate in research.

The AAA has also expressed a clear concern that the HTS might repeat what happened in Vietnam during the CORDS (Civil Operations and Revolutionary Development Support) project. CORDS was formed to coordinate US civil and military pacification programs in Vietnam. It was used to map human terrain and identify individuals and groups that the military believed were sympathizers of the Vietcong; they were then targeted for assassination. Anthropological research was used and it resulted in the death of thousands (González 2009a, 6-7, 59-63, 71-77). And HTS was not helped when an article in *Military Review* (Kipp et al. 2006) appeared calling it "A CORDS for the 21st Century." The AAA thus stated

As members of HTS teams, anthropologists provide information and counsel to U.S. military field commanders. This poses a risk that information provided by HTS anthropologists could be used to make decisions about identifying and selecting specific populations as targets of U.S. military operations either in the short or long term. Any such use of fieldwork-derived information would violate the stipulations in the AAA Code of Ethics that those studied not be harmed. (AAA 2007)

Thus anthropologists working for HTS may have responsibilities to their US military units in war zones that conflict with their obligations to the persons they study or consult. The AAA Commission on Engagement with the US Security and Intelligence Communities concluded that:

The Commission recognizes both opportunities and risks to those anthropologists choosing to engage with the work of the military, security and intelligence arenas. We do not recommend non-engagement, but instead emphasize differences in kinds of engagement and accompanying ethical considerations. We advise careful analysis of specific roles, activities, and institutional contexts of engagement in order to ascertain ethical consequences. These ethical considerations begin with the admonition to do no harm to those one studies (or with whom one works, in an applied setting) and to be honest and transparent in communicating what one is doing. (Ibid.)

The AAA also says: "Because HTS identifies anthropology and anthropologists with US military operations, this identification—given the existing range of globally dispersed understandings of US militarism—may create serious difficulties for, including grave risks to the personal safety of, many non-HTS anthropologists and the people they study" (ibid.). Much like Boas' fears in World War I, there is a belief that anthropologists working for the military would endanger other anthropologists who are not working with the military but who might be suspected of doing just that or worse, be suspected of espionage.

The AAA concluded "The Executive Board sees the HTS project as a problematic application of anthropological expertise, most specifically on ethical grounds. We have grave concerns about the involvement of anthropological knowledge and skill in the HTS project. The Executive Board views the HTS project as an unacceptable application of anthropological expertise."

And even if HTTs' work is accurate, it is aimed at supporting the combat brigade commander's intent. "The HTS Mission is to provide commanders in the field with relevant socio-cultural understanding necessary to meet their operational requirements" (HTS 2009). How then will their advice be used? They certainly have no control over this. It was the anthropologist Alexander Leighton who said that administrators use the findings of social scientists as a drunk uses a lamp post—for support rather than illumination. It is not important what social scientists say so much as *how* what they say is used. Academics also fear that the HTS database can be accessed by those outside the US military such as the CIA, and then who knows how that information will be used.

Building cultural awareness as a capability

In 2008 *Nature*, one of the world's leading scientific journals, gave its endorsement to the Human Terrain System. By December of that same year, in an editorial that can only be described as scathing, *Nature* said the $130 million program is "failing on every level" and "needs to be closed down." The editorial went on to say

> the larger question is whether the Human Terrain System is viable at all. *Nature* is not opposed in principle to academics working with the military; we have said before that social science can and should inform military policy (*Nature* 454, 2008, 138). We continue to believe that the insights of science have much to offer strategies in a war zone—not least through training combat troops to understand the local cultures within which they operate. (*Nature* 2008)

And it is this point that is addressed by the US Army's Culture and Foreign Language Strategy (ACFLS) which sets out a program to train army personnel in cultural awareness and foreign languages. US Army schools and universities are asked to blend cultural awareness into on-going education, training and experiential learning.[23] The ultimate goal is to build and sustain an army with the right blend of language and cultural skills to facilitate Full-Spectrum Operations in the 21st Century (US Army TRADOC 2009). This means not only an expeditionary mindset but someone who is able to work in a joint and multinational coalition environment. Part of the strategy calls for the appointment of ACFL advisers such as myself, social scientists who help implement the strategy at army Centers of Excellence such as the Sustainment Center of Excellence in Virginia and the Fires Center of Excellence in Oklahoma.

As someone progresses in their career they move from *cultural awareness*—a minimal level of regional competence necessary to perform assigned tasks in a specific geographic area; being able to describe key culture terms, factors and concepts and having a basic understanding of how foreign culture might affect the planning and conduct of operations; through to *cultural understanding*—a well developed cross-cultural competence in a specific region; being able to anticipate the implications of culture and apply relevant terms, factors, concepts, and regional information to tasks and missions; being familiar with a specific region's economic, religious, legal, governmental, political and infrastructural features, and aware of regional sensitivities regarding gender, race, ethnicity, local observances and local perception of the United States and its allies. Finally one arrives at *cultural expertise*, which is an advanced level of cross-cultural competence in a specific geographic area. This generally entails some degree of proficiency in a language; skills that enable effective cross-cultural persuasion, negotiation, conflict resolution, influence, or leadership; and an understanding of the most salient historic and present-day regional structural and cultural factors of a specific geographic area (Ibrahimov 2010). A military member moves from learning to applying and finally, at a senior level, advising.

CONCLUSIONS

In an article on organizational amnesia Otham and Hashim (2004) argue that organizational learning is not merely the process of acquiring knowledge. The learning that takes place at the individual level has to be diffused to other parts of the organization. In writing down counter-insurgency doctrine (U.S. Army 2007) the United States has attempted to meet that challenge.[24] Lessons learned from Iraq are being applied in Afghanistan and the senior American commander in Afghanistan, General Stanley McChrystal, has called for a complete revamping of military strategy, insisting the International Security Assistance Force had been behaving like a bull charging at a matador and it was time to focus on winning the approval of the population (Judd 2009). This requires cultural awareness at even the most junior levels.

However, one wonders how long the interest with counterinsurgency will last and how long the military will be able to retain important cultural lessons learned in the process. Otham and Hashim mention two forms of organizational amnesia, i.e., losing organizational memory, one that occurs over time as individuals leave the organization and records lack details on trial-and-errors made to learn important lessons. Knowing what was tried and did not work can be as important as knowing what did. The second type occurs through distance when one part of the organization does not transmit its lessons learned to other parts of the organization. Learning may have happened at the individual level but that learning did not move to the organizational level (2004, 276).

Even with debriefings and the development of doctrine there is still the possibility that important "intuitive" or personal knowledge is lost. It is harder to articulate this personal tacit knowledge and often it is the explicit knowledge which is written down for posterity. Learning is also a social process and it is important for militaries to create environments where social networking can occur and where knowledge and experience can be shared between generations. In this sense communications net-works such as Facebook and Twitter are now being used by US military personnel to discuss their experiences in Iraq and Afghanistan.

This leads us to the debate described above about using civilian social scientists, particularly anthropologists, to supply the military with the cultural information necessary for counterinsurgency operations. The crux of the debate hinges on how organizations learn. Otham and Hashim (2004, 279) make an important observation: the cognitive map of the individual affects the retention process. The higher the degree of expertise a person has, the more complex is his/her cognitive map and the higher his/her ability to perceive patterns that others cannot. This is critical to observing cultural patterns. Is it possible to replace the intuitive/personal skills of decades of field work and ethnographic training that seasoned (civilian) anthropologists have? In terms of the HTS the danger of hiring civilian contractors who will return to the civilian sector at contract's end does not address the problem and recruitment becomes an issue. Do civilian contractors have decades of experience in the culture area? It would seem they do not. Moreover, the ACFLS is now attempting to build up just that type of cultural expertise over a person's military career.

HTS advocates indicate that without their help the military would be unable to understand and engage local leaders and the host population. Just as Malinowski argued in the 1920s, practical men need cultural information to govern and improve the condition of the natives. Then the question arises as to what type of cultural knowledge they really need. Do they need to understand all aspects of anthropology? I would argue that they do not. And out of practical necessity soldiers are able to gather cultural knowledge when it is useful to their endeavour.

> When it deployed to Iraq in mid-2007, TF [task force] Dragon inherited a heavily populated (400,000 people) area southeast of Baghdad … The requirement for new ethnographic information on its AO [area of operations] weighed heavily on the task force. Thus, the entire unit began focusing on systematically collecting and collating ethnographic information …
>
> Mapping this political, economic, and sociological information created a common human-terrain picture that enabled more proactive initiatives and faster, much more effective responses to events. For example, as incidents occurred in specific areas, the common map enabled all companies to plot the location of the incident, then identify the proper sheiks to contact for intelligence or answers to critical questions…
>
> Human-terrain mapping thereby allowed TF Dragon to understand the population and demonstrate its commitment to improving local communities. By addressing what the people felt were their priority needs, the task force was better able to cultivate relationships of significant trust with neighborhood leaders. In turn, these relationships led to the construction of an effective biometric database of military-age males. This information resulted in improved actionable intelligence on insurgent activities, greatly improving security. (Marr et al. 2008, 19-20, 24)[25]

What I like about this use of culture for military purposes is that there is no confusion. When someone gives up information to a military person they know what it means. With some training and insight I believe that the military can in fact be culturally aware and recognize cultural intelligence for what it is—Intel.

McFate (2005b, 46) and Kusiak (2008, 74) would argue that civilians must continue to be part of the solution to the military's socio-cultural deficit problem. However, a deficit is supposed to be a temporary situation where HTTs are a stopgap measure, waiting for the arrival of trained military personnel to take over the job. The new ACFL Strategy aims at building up cultural competency over time and along a career path. Developing cultural awareness has now been prioritized as a requirement to be woven into all courses and training.

As part of this strategy the US Army is hiring civilian anthropologists such as myself to advise, but not at the tactical end. Our goal is to build tailored cultural awareness into teaching programs for soldiers, NCOs and officers. At the Sustainment Center of Excellence I participate in classes, engage students in discussion and participate in gaming scenarios, writing in cultural challenges and scenarios. The program is in its infancy, but as a model for small nations it is a big bang for the buck since I also train the trainers. In this way, the US Army is institutionalizing an ethno-anthropological approach.

This said, the HTT model does offer an interesting approach which could be adapted to smaller armies and the British are already standing up a Defence Cultural Specialist (military) Unit in Afghanistan.[26] This unit is preparing a pool of deployable military cultural specialists[27] and provides cultural awareness training to the British military. As well as running trainings, the unit will define training requirements tailored to military needs. For example, military cultural specialists are currently mapping tribal dispositions and their allegiances and as a consequence are shaping battle plans. I do not believe this is a job for civilian social scientists for all the ethical reasons described above. And military officers are questioning the utility of contractors in culture matters. For example, in a recent article in *Military Review* a Marine Corps major noted that,

> American military staffs have proven capable of using cultural terrain to their advantage in the small wars of the early 20th century, in Viet Nam, and contrary to common wisdom, in Afghanistan and Iraq. Whatever weaknesses in cultural capability existed had always proven most evident at the onset of low intensity conflicts but were later rectified as war fighters adapted to the environment. (Connable 2009, 57-58)

Connable also believes that in the US military there is now sufficient momentum for a sustained focus on culture. "Given the proper institutional support, these training centers and cultural intelligence programs can be used to leverage the experience of both troops and staffs to create a long-term, organic approach to cultural competence." He is opposed to the HTS which takes cultural competence out of the hands of the military (ibid., 59-60).

As an academic, I believe ethnographic knowledge is not something to be collected like sea shells and placed in a classificatory grid; it emerges in the ethnographic occasion, which is the encounter between the ethnographer and the persons with whom the ethnographer produces the knowledge. This occasion is conditioned by the historical context, conflict and pacification, ongoing violence, power relations, role of mediators such as translators, the presence of the coalition forces, etc. In this case the ethnographer is the military person seeking knowledge for a very specific purpose.

As someone who has deployed to do research on military operations in Bosnia, the Golan and Afghanistan, I also value the combat experience that is necessary to the military operation. This is what trained military professionals bring to the table. I believe trained military officers and NCOs can do the job of collecting relevant cultural matters—something they did in the past, and are now having to re-learn as a skill.

> Commanders across Anbar Province continued to devise *intuitive* [author's emphasis] tactics designed to take advantage of tribal relationships, meet local economic needs, and avoid cultural friction. As early as February 2004, even those Marines poorly trained in cultural awareness were actively engaging with tribal, religious, and business leaders, targeting contracting monies based on PSYOP [psychological operations] and CA [cultural affairs] cultural and economic data, and conducting census polling. They built local information operations messages derived from cultural input pulled from patrol reports and human intelligence sources. Applied with relative consistency over a matter of years, these local programs—often devised by commanders down to the platoon level—directly contributed to the growth and success of the Awakening movement in Al-Anbar. By early September 2008, violence in Al-Anbar had plummeted to negligible levels and the province was returned to Iraqi control. (Connable 2009, 61-62)

Intelligence staffs should also be trained to collect and analyze cultural data and to include this data in all-source intelligence products. US doctrine clearly encourages the services to build and maintain this capability. In this way there will be no confusion about the purpose of culture research in operations since the military will be carrying it out for counterinsurgency purposes. It is also important that those officers who choose to develop ethnographic skills not be sidelined and end up in a career backwater. Only through an award and incentive program can cultural knowledge be valued.

In 1969 Dell Hymes edited a volume called *Reinventing Anthropology* which called for an anthropology relevant to the times, an awareness of its colonial past and the study of powerful institutions. This of course brings to mind the question of who should determine what is relevant. Is it the anthropologist? Those who fund research? The people being studied? Although every undergraduate student is made aware of anthropology's history, one wonders if they are prepared for the complex ethical issues of the job market in a globalized world. In an increasingly tight job market, young anthropologists are applying en masse to the HTS.[28] Yet again one must ask exactly how long the HTS will last.

The current surge in Afghanistan is finite and the United States is pulling out of Iraq. What, then, are HTS civilians going to do? Learn Chinese? Or Korean? Perhaps Russian. In addition to the US Army's Culture and Foreign Language Strategy that intends to develop linguistic capability in several strategic languages such as Dari/Pashto, Arabic, Korean and Japanese, the US Army is actively recruiting native speakers. In 2008, the US Secretary of the Army approved a pilot program to hire certain legal, non-immigrant aliens to provide medical and language/cultural skills vital to operations.[29]

Immigrants to the United States, who are permanent residents with documents commonly known as green cards, have long been eligible to enlist. But the new effort, for the first time since the Vietnam War, will open the armed forces to temporary immigrants if they have lived in the United States for a minimum of two years (Preston 2009). This is another model which could be adopted by smaller forces.

The pilot program, which was launched in New York in February 2009, seeks to enlist 1,000 military recruits, most of whom will join the army. Response to the program has exceeded expectations, drawing applications from more than 7,000 people around the country, many of them highly educated, defence officials said. Those who are accepted will get an expedited path to citizenship in return for their service (Zavis and Becker 2009). Language experts will serve four years of active duty while health care professionals (approximately 300–1,000) will serve three years of active duty or six in the reserves. As one sergeant commented on the value of having soldiers who are native speakers in the theatre of operations, "Now that we have soldiers as translators, we are able to trust more; we are able to accomplish the mission with more accuracy" (Preston 2009).

Civilian social scientists, meanwhile, should embrace the opportunities that the AAA and the editors of *Nature* advocate. These include studying military and intelligence organizations from the inside and educating the military about its own organizational culture and about other cultures and societies so that the military can carry out its own cultural intelligence operations. This is what I am attempting to do as a culture and foreign language adviser.

NOTES

1. See Hinsley (1999) for details on Bourke's work.
2. The French had a similar ethnographic tradition and maintained a distinction between academic ethnologists producing synthesizing works in the metropolis and "amateur" ethnographers. The latter would provide the former with research data which would then be used for scientific abstraction (Salemink 1999, 283-284).
3. See Price (2000; 2008, 7-8) for details on anthropologists' espionage work during WWI.
4. Bateson's research was later used in psychological warfare operations and "culture cracking" strategies by the CIA in Vietnam (González 2004, 10).
5. The Human Relations Area Files, is an international membership organization with over 300 member institutions in the US and more than 20 other countries. A financially autonomous research agency based at Yale University since 1949, its mission is to encourage and facilitate worldwide comparative studies of human behaviour, society, and culture. It mainly pursues this mission by producing and distributing two full-text databases on the Web, HRAF Collection of Ethnography and HRAF Collection of Archaeology. HRAF also sponsors and edits the quarterly journal, *Cross-Cultural Research: The Journal of Comparative Social Science*, and organizes and edits encyclopedias. The entire HRAF Collection of Ethnography, in paper, microfiche, and on the Web, covers nearly 400 cultures (accessed 15 June 2010 at http://www.yale.edu/hraf/).
6. See Price (2002, 17-19) for details.
7. Payson Sheets, an archaeologist working in Panama and Costa Rica in 1976, recalls how his U.S. AID funding was nothing more than a front for the CIA during a time when the Americans were interested in the Panama Canal (Price 2002, 16).
8. The *Kubark* manual became "less a guide to resisting interrogation than an interrogation manual to be used against enemies—with some forms of coercion that violated the Geneva Convention … The 'coercive interrogation' techniques *Kubark* described shade into torture by the application of intense stress or isolation in order to induce confessions" (Price 2007, 18-19). This manual is available at http://www.gwu.edu/~nsarchiv/NSAEBB/NSAEBB27/01-01.htm (accessed 15 June 2010).
9. The techniques were codified in the 1963 counterintelligence manual. Since 2002, US interrogators have used Behavioural Science Consultation Teams (so-called Biscuit teams) of psychologists and other social scientists.
10. According to McCoy, US agents at Guantanamo Bay have created a "de facto behavioural-research laboratory" that goes beyond using psychological stressors by attacking "cultural sensitivity, particularly Arab male sensitivity to issues of gender and sexual identity" (McCoy 2006; González 2007a).
11. According to Gusterson, Project Camelot was a "lavishly funded initiative to mobilize anthropologists and other social scientists to investigate the origins of peasant radicalism and insurgency and devise strategies to pre-empt, contain, and repress revolutionary movements" (2009, 48).
12. While some authors find the cause for military blunders in the social psychology or culture of the military organization (Dixon 1976; Winslow 1997, 2000), McFate (2005a, 2005b) cites a failure to understand foreign cultures as a major contributing factor in multiple national-security and intelligence failures.

13. Because the Powell-Weinberger doctrine meant conventional, large-scale war was the only acceptable type of conflict, no discernable present or future need existed to develop doctrine and expertise in unconventional war, including counterinsurgency. Thus, there was no need to incorporate cultural knowledge into doctrine, training, or war fighting (McFate 2005a, 27).

14. For a history of the manual's drafting see Nagel (2007).

15. Kilcullen is a senior fellow at the Center for a New American Security and a partner at the Crumpton Group, a Washington, DC strategic advisory firm. In 2007 he was senior counterinsurgency adviser to General David Petraeus and was part of the small team that designed the "Iraq surge." In 2005–06 Kilcullen was chief counterterrorism strategist at the US State Department, working in the Middle East, South Asia, Europe, Africa and Southeast Asia, including several operational activities in Afghanistan, Iraq, and Pakistan's Federally Administered Tribal Agencies.

16. For a detailed critique of *The Counterinsurgency Field Manual* see Price (2009, 59-76).

17. Montgomery McFate personal correspondence to author (7 June 2009).

18. A bibliography of relevant articles on the controversy is available at http://culturematters.wordpress.com/2008/08/21/annotated-bibliography-on-hts-minerva-and-prisp (accessed 15 June 2010).

19. See Network of Concerned Anthropologists 2009 and their website available at http://concerned.anthropologists.googlepages.com/ (accessed 15 June 2010).

20. I must call attention to the intellectual leap here. HTS will *inevitably* be used to select people for death. It is impossible to predict the future.

21. Roberto J. González is perhaps best known for his continued opposition to the involvement of anthropologists in the US military's Human Terrain System. In his 2009 book, he sums up his concerns with the delicate relationship between social science and the military. Who shapes the agenda? Is it ethical to "enable the kill chain"? Should social science be subordinated to the aims of the Department of Defense and the Central Intelligence Agency? These are all valid issues, of course, but González's work often seems tinged with a reactionary attitude as uncritical as those he claims to be challenging. For example, in his preface he refers to HTS working with the military as a "malignant collaboration" and goes on to say that "HTS represents a subversion of social science" (González 2009a, iii, 3).

22. Marcus Griffin had never been to the Middle East before he arrived in Iraq. Yet he was hired to help the US military decipher the country's intricate social nuances. An anthropologist from Christopher Newport University in Virginia, Griffin knew much more about the Philippines, having accompanied his social-scientist father on a two-year research project there as a teen. In Virginia he'd been studying Freegans, those super environmentalists who forage for food in restaurant and supermarket Dumpsters.

23. Education entails critical thinking about culture whereas training addresses skill development such as language training in tactical Dari and Pashto, the main languages of Afghanistan. Experiential learning is where education and training is translated into action, such as role playing in scenarios and actual field experience.

24. The *Counterinsurgency Field Manual* has led to several subsequent works such as *Field Manual 3-24.2, Tactics in Counterinsurgency* (2008a) and two *Counterinsurgency Readers* (2006, 2008b) and an *Interagency Reader* (2008c) continue this trend and emphasize the importance of cultural knowledge or cultural intelligence to the success of the operation.

    The US Marine Corps has made improvements in its pre-deployment culture training (see Salomi 2006 for details) and also set up the Center for Advanced Operational Culture Learning in Quantico, Virginia. According to its mission statement, the Center provides "regional, operational culture and language knowledge through training and education, in order to plan and operate in the joint expeditionary environment" (Connable 2009; http://www.tecom. usmc.mil/caocl/).

    The US Naval Postgraduate School has a Program for Culture and Conflict Studies and there is The Training and Doctrine (TRADOC) Command Culture Center (Hajjar 2006). In addition the US Army and Marine Corps Counterinsurgency Center was established in 2006 at Fort Leavenworth, Kansas. The Center's goal is to facilitate the implementation of the *Counterinsurgency Field Manual* (Connable 2009; http://usacac.army. mil/cac2/coin/index.asp). One of the chief objectives and purposes of the Counterinsurgency Center is to work towards establishing and institutionalizing an interagency planning framework that promotes intellectual collaboration across a range of agencies both within as well as outside of government.

25. See Marr et al. (2008) for very detailed description of how soldiers and officers carried out their ethnographic/human intelligence information gathering in support of their military objectives.

26. See http://www.mod.uk/DefenceInternet/DefenceNews/DefencePolicyAnd Business/MilitaryDevelopsItsCulturalUnderstandingOfAfghanistan.htm (accessed 5 March 2010).

27. These specialists train for ten weeks before being deployed.

28. I was told on a recent visit to Washington, DC in May 2009 that there were over 400 applicants for the HTTs. This said, many HTT members resigned when their positions were changed from generously-paid contractors to less-well-compensated government employees. As of February 2009, there were between 135 and 243 HTT members. Military officials won't give an exact number—"for reasons of operational security," according to Army spokesman Gregory Mueller (Shachtman 2009).

29. The languages and cultures considered strategically important are Albanian, Amharic, Arabic, Azerbaijani, Bengali, Burmese, Cambodian-Khmer, Chinese, Czech, Hausa, Hindi, Hungarian, Igbo, Indonesian, Korean, Kurdish, Lao, Malay, Malayalam, Moro, Nepalese, Persian (Dari and Farsi), Polish, Punjabi, Pushtu/Pashto, Russian, Sindhi, Sinhalese, Somali, Swahili, Tamil, Turkish, Turkmen, Urdu and Yoruba (US Secretary of Defense Robert Gates, 25 November 2008, Memorandum entitled "Military Accessions Vital to the National Interest [MAVNI]." See http://www.durrani.com/docs/ MilitaryRecruitingProgram.pdf).

REFERENCES

American Anthropological Association (AAA), Commission on the Engagement of Anthropology with the US Security and Intelligence Communities. 2007. *Final Report.* At http://www.aaanet.org/cmtes/commissions/CEAUSSIC/ (accessed 5 March 2010).

Asad, T., ed. 1973. *Anthropology and the Colonial Encounter.* New York: Humanities Press.

Ben-Ari, E. 1998. *Mastering Soldiers: Conflict, Emotions and the Enemy in an Israeli Military Unit.* Oxford: Berghahn Books.

— 2009. Anthropology, Research and State Violence: Some Observations from an Israeli Anthropologist. Unpublished paper, Hebrew University, Israel.

Boas, F. 1919 (2004). Scientists as Spies. (*The Nation*, 1919). Reprinted in *Anthropologists in the Public Sphere. Speaking Out on War, Peace and American Power,* ed. R.J. González, 23-25. Austin: University of Texas Press.

Connable, B. 2009. All our Eggs in a Broken Basket. How the Human Terrain System is Undermining Sustainable Military Cultural Competence. *Military Review* (March–April):57-64.

Dixon, N. 1976. *The Psychology of Military Incompetence.* London: PIMLICO.

Finney, N. 2008. *Human Terrain Team Handbook.* Fort Leavenworth, Kansas: US Government, Military.

González, R.J., ed. 2004. *Anthropologists in the Public Sphere. Speaking Out on War, Peace and American Power.* Austin: University of Texas Press.

González, R.J. 2007a. We Must Fight the Militarization of Anthropology. *Chronicles of Higher Education,* 2 February. At http://chronicle.com/weekly/v53/i22/22b02001.htm (accessed 12 October 2009).

— 2007b. Towards Mercenary Anthropology. The New US Army Counterinsurgency Manual FM 3-24 and the Military-Anthropology Complex. *Anthropology Today* 23 (3):14-19.

— 2009a. *American Counterinsurgency: Human Science and the Human Terrain.* Chicago: Prickly Paradigm Press.

— 2009b. Embedded: Information Warfare and the "Human Terrain." In *The Counter-Counterinsurgency Manual: Or, Notes on Demilitarizing American Society,* ed. Network of Concerned Anthropologists, 97-113. Chicago: Prickly Paradigm Press.

González, R.J., H. Gusterson, and D. Price. 2009. Introduction. War Culture and Counterinsurgency. In *The Counter-Counterinsurgency Manual: Or, Notes on Demilitarizing American Society,* ed. Network of Concerned Anthropologists, 1-20. Chicago: Prickly Paradigm Press.

Gusterson, H. 2007a. Anthropologists and War: A Response to David Kilcullen. *Anthropology Today* 23 (4):23.

— 2007b. Anthropology and Militarism. *Annual Review of Anthropology* 36:155-175.

— 2009. Militarizing Knowledge. In *The Counter-Counterinsurgency Manual: Or, Notes on Demilitarizing American Society,* ed. Network of Concerned Anthropologists, 39-55. Chicago: Prickly Paradigm Press.

Hajjar, Major R. 2006. The Army's New TRADOC Culture Center. *Military Review* (November/December):89-92.

Hinsley, C. 1999. Hopi Snakes, Zuni Corn. Early Ethnography in the American Southwest. In *Colonial Subjects. Essays on the Practical History of Anthropology,* ed. P. Pels and O. Salemink, 180-195. Ann Arbor: University of Michigan Press.

Horowitz, I., ed. 1968. *The Rise and Fall of Project Camelot.* Cambridge, MA: MIT Press.

Human Terrain System (HTS). At http://humanterrainsystem.army.mil/ (accessed 19 June 2009).

Hymes, D., ed. 1969. *Reinventing Anthropology.* New York: Pantheon Books.

Ibrahimov, M. 2010. Army Culture and Foreign Language Strategy, PowerPoint presentation, 5 March. Oklahoma: Fires Center of Excellence.

Judd, T. 2009. Armed Social Work: The Marines New Brief. *The Independent,* 9 September.

Kilcullen, D. 2006. Twenty-Eight Articles. Fundamentals of Company-Level Counterinsurgency. At http://www.d-n-i.net/fcs/pdf/kilcullen_28_articles.pdf (accessed 12 October 2009).

— 2007 *Religion and Insurgency Small Wars Journal Blog 12 May 2007*. At http://smallwarsjournal.com/blog/2007/05/religion-and-insurgency/ (accessed 10 March 2010).

— 2009. *The Accidental Guerrilla. Fighting Small Wars in the Midst of a Big One*. Great Britain: Oxford University Press.

Kipp, J., L. Grau, K. Prinslo, and D. Smith. 2006. The Human Terrain System: A CORDS for the 21st Century. *Military Review* (September–October):8-15.

Klein, H.A., and G. Kuperman. 2008. Through an Arab Cultural Lens. *Military Review* (May–June):100-105.

Kusiak, P. 2008. Socio-Cultural Expertise and the Military. Beyond the Controversy. *Military Review* (November–December):65-76.

Malinowski, B. 1922. *Argonauts of the South Pacific*. London: Routledge and Kegan Paul.

Marcus, G.E., and M.M. Fischer. 1986. *Anthropology as Cultural Critique*. Chicago: University of Chicago Press.

Marr, Lieutenant Colonel J., Major J. Cushing, Major B. Garner, and Captain R. Thompson. 2008. Human Terrain Mapping: A Critical First Step to Winning the COIN [counterinsurgency] Fight. *Military Review* (March–April):18-24.

Marsellis, N. 2009. Human Terrain: A Strategic Imperative on the 21st Century Battlefield. *Small Wars Journal*. At http://smallwarsjournal.com/mag/docs-temp/250-marsellis.pdf (accessed 15 October 2009).

McCoy, A.W. 2006. *A Question of Torture: CIA Interrogation, From the Cold War to the War on Terror*. New York: Henry Holt & Co., Metropolitan Books.

McFate, M. 2005a. Anthropology and Counterinsurgency: The Strange Story of their Curious Relationship. *Military Review* (March–April):24-38.

— 2005b. The Military Utility of Understanding Adversary Culture. *Joint Force Quarterly* 38:42-48.

Nagel, J.A. 2007. Foreword to the University of Chicago Press Edition. *Counterinsurgency Field Manual*, xiii-xx. Chicago: University of Chicago Press.

Nature. 2008. Editorial. Failure in the Field. The US Military's Human-Terrain Programme Needs to be Brought to a Swift Close. No. 456, 676 (11 December).

Network of Concerned Anthropologists. 2009.*The Counter-Counterinsurgency Field Manual: Or, Notes on Demilitarizing American Society*. Chicago: Prickly Paradigm Press.

Network of Concerned Anthropologists. At http://concerned.anthopologists.googlepages.com/ (accessed 2 June 2009).

Otham, R., and N.A. Hashim. 2004. Typologizing Organizational Amnesia. *The Learning Organization* 11 (3):273-284.

Pels, P., and O. Salemink, eds. 1999. *Colonial Subjects. Essays on the Practical History of Anthropology*. Ann Arbor: University of Michigan Press.

Preston, J. 2009. U.S. Military Will Offer Path to Citizenship. *New York Times*, 15 February.

Price, D. 2000 (2004). Anthropologists as Spies. (*The Nation*, 20 November 2000). Reprinted in *Anthropologists in the Public Sphere. Speaking out on War, Peace and American Power*, ed. R.J. González, 62-70. Austin: University of Texas Press.

— 2002. Interlopers and Invited Guests. Anthropology's Witting and Unwitting Links to Intelligence Agencies. *Anthropology Today* 8 (6):16-21.

— 2004. *Threatening Anthropology. McCarthyism and the FBI's Surveillance of Activist Anthropologists*. Durham, NC: Duke University Press.

— 2007. Buying a Piece of Anthropology. Part Two: The CIA and our Tortured Past. *Anthropology Today* 23 (5):17-22.

— 2008. *Anthropological Intelligence. The Deployment and Neglect of American Anthropology in the Second World War*. Durham: Duke University Press.

— 2009. Faking Scholarship: Domestic Propaganda and the Publication of the Counterinsurgency Field Manual. In *The Counter-Counterinsurgency Manual: Or, Notes on Demilitarizing American Society*, ed. Network of Concerned Anthropologists, 59-76. Chicago: Prickly Paradigm Press.

Salemink, O. 1999. Ethnography as a Martial Art. Ethnicizing Vietnam's Montagnards, 1930–1954. In *Colonial Subjects. Essays on the Practical History of Anthropology*, ed. P. Pels and O. Salemink, 282-325. Ann Arbor: University of Michigan Press.

Salomi, B.A. 2006. Advances in Pre-deployment Culture Training: The US Marine Corps Approach. *Military Review* (November–December):29-88.

Schaff, G. 2004. *From Racism to Genocide: Anthropology in the Third Reich*. Urbana: University of Illinois Press.

Scales, Major General R. 2004. Army Transformation: Implications for the Future. *Testimony before the US House Armed Services Committee*, 15 July.

Shachtman, N. 2009. Mass Exodus from "Human Terrain" Program: At Least One-Third Quits (Updated 6 April). At http://www.wired.com/danger-room/2009/04/htts-quit/ (accessed 9 June 2009).

Simons, A. 1998. *The Company They Keep. Life Inside the U.S. Army Special Forces*. USA: Mass Market Paperback.

Skelton, I. 2001. America's Frontier Wars: Lessons for Asymmetric Conflicts. *Military Review* (September–October):2-7.

US Army. 2006. *Counterinsurgency Reader*. Combined Arms Center Special Edition of Military Review. October.

— 2007. *Counterinsurgency Field Manual*. (US Army Field Manual No. 3-24, Marine Corps War Fighting Publication No. 3-33.5). Chicago: University of Chicago Press.

— 2008a. *Tactics in Counterinsurgency*. US Army Field Manual No. 3-24.2.

— 2008b. *Counterinsurgency Reader II*. Combined Arms Center Special Edition of Military Review. August.

— 2008c. *Interagency Reader*. Combined Arms Center Special Edition of Military Review. June.

US Army TRADOC (Training and Doctrine Command). 2009. Army Culture and Foreign Language Strategy. December.

US Secretary of Defense Robert Gates, 25 November 2008, Memorandum entitled "Military Accessions Vital to the National Interest [MAVNI]." See http://www.durrani.com/docs/MilitaryRecruitingProgram.pdf)

Winslow, D. 1997. *The Canadian Airborne Regiment in Somalia. A Socio-Cultural Inquiry*, 330. Ottawa: Minister of Public Works and Government Services Canada.

— 2000. Misplaced Loyalties: The Role of Military in Culture in the Breakdown of Discipline in Two Peace Operations. In *The Human in Command. Exploring the Modern Military Experience*, ed. C. McCann and R. Pigeau, 293-310. New York: Kluwer Academic/Plenum Publishers.

Zavis, A., and A. Becker. 2009. Army Extends Immigrant Recruiting. *The Los Angeles Times*, 4 May.

RESPECTFUL COLLABORATIVE STABILIZATION OPERATIONS AND RULE OF LAW

DAVID LAST[1]

Four examples of transitional missions under the United Nations are compared for the extent of involvement by small powers. The comparison suggests anecdotally that collaborative and consensual stabilization involving many small and supportive democracies is more likely to be associated with stable outcomes. This suggests a strategy of community building in which state policies are sensitive to the imposition of rules on others, including secession and incorporation of territory. Rule of law at home and democratic oversight of security services is linked to respect for internal debates abroad, including debates about social mores and market reforms.

My starting point for this paper was the question, what do European Union states and Canada have in common when it comes to the aims of their contemporary military operations? The answer in the title suggests a concern for popular sovereignty in weaker states, a rules-based international order that constrains powerful states, and cooperation by middle powers—themselves constrained by domestic law and democratic oversight—to achieve both. The comparative advantage of smaller powers lies in building cooperative international regimes, and concentrating development and security efforts where they are welcomed. We have neither the hubris to reshape the world in our image, nor the capacity to attempt the expeditionary wars of major powers.

Mission Critical: Smaller Democracies' Role in Global Stability Operations, ed. C. Leuprecht, J. Troy, and D. Last. Montreal and Kingston: Queen's Policy Studies Series, McGill-Queen's University Press. © 2010 Queen's Centre for International Relations, Queen's University at Kingston. All rights reserved.

We need to get stabilization right because a lot more of it looms on the horizon and it can only be done collaboratively. There is talk amongst planning staffs about stabilizing central Asia and inaugurating a Palestinian state. Concurrently we might confront the geopolitical fall-out of a looming energy and environmental crisis, exacerbated by the cultural clashes and domestic fragmentation brought about by global pressures. The odds are that we may also have to deal with domestic and transnational challenges like pandemics, earthquakes, and political crises, which will present opportunities for enemies abroad and evil opportunists at home. Mutual respect and collaborative norms are essential because we are all living in glass houses, which may soon be the targets of rocks we haven't even thought of yet.

Respectful, collaborative operations stand in sharp contrast with the American Quadrennial Defence Review of 2004, which prescribed unilateral and pre-emptive action by an unconstrained superpower in its Global War on Terror. The Obama administration has abandoned the label Global War on Terror, and at least some in the Pentagon would like to replace it with the concept of Rule of Law, as a way of regaining the moral high ground and preserving America's leadership in global security. Good intentions, however, can't change the reality of American size and power, or the imperative for it to be responsive to American interests. Writing in *Foreign Policy*, Peter Feaver makes the point that changes to the National Security Council's Interagency Management System continue long-standing practice under previous administrations.[2] Priorities are set in Washington, and resources are solicited from allies to contribute to these priorities and plans, as Oscar DeSoto, Director of Planning for the Office of the Coordinator for Reconstruction and Stabilization (S/CRS) explained to Japanese Allies.[3]

Like some Europeans, I think there were Canadians who were embarrassed by the strident tones of the War on Terror, and would welcome a return to Rule of Law—which I place in capitals to imply a general approach to strategy and operations, which accepts that even the most powerful are usefully constrained by rules that reflect the norms of international society.[4] But Canada also consistently supports, and benefits enormously from, the liberal international order of the Empire of the day—first *pax Brittannica* then *pax Americana*. This liberal international order sustains what some perceive to be the inequities of market forces and the iniquities of mercenary forces, justifying resistance to empire, from the Mahdi in Sudan to the Jihadis of the twin towers. Thus we are forced to ask hard questions like, "Rule of whose laws?" and "With whom can we collaborate?" Making sure that Rule of Law suits the interests of smaller powers may mean strategic cooperation not only between liberal democracies, but also with other states outside the ambit of superpowers, whose cooperation is necessary for stability.

This chapter is in three parts. First, I compare four cases of intervention, selecting for transitional mandates. This shows, somewhat anecdotally, that missions with more small power contributors tend to have more stable outcomes. Second, I deduce rules for a strategy of community building—what can small powers do together, based on what has worked in our collective experience? Finally, I consider the connection between rule of law at home in a liberal democracy and collaborative intervention abroad. This suggests, anecdotally again, that the correlation I find in the first part is not coincidental. It might be a corollary to democratic peace theory; democracies don't go to war with one another, and small democracies may be less likely to impose themselves on others.

COMPARATIVE CASES OF PEACE SUPPORT AND STABILIZATION

Stabilization missions are transitory, and seek to move from an unstable status quo to a more stable and sustainable situation. The transition can be quite short, or it can be lengthy, but it is not intended to be a permanent occupation, nor does it seek to preserve a status quo (as is the task eternal of UNFICYP in Cyprus or UNDOF in the Golan Heights). From all the examples of peacekeeping, peace support, and stabilization, I have focused here on a small group of UN transition missions to illustrate the nature of transition under rule of law. UNTEA/UNSF in West Irian (1962–1963), UNTAG in Namibia in (1989–1990), UNTAES in Eastern Slavonia (1996–1998) and UNMISET in East Timor (2002–2005) are four historical examples of modest successes, characterized by respect for the wishes of (at least some of) the parties, the consent (of most or all) of the parties, and legitimacy within an acceptable framework of law. However, they were also marked by *realpolitik*, pragmatism, and compromise. This is the balance we need to get right, because if we get it wrong, the mission can easily become interminable policing of a flawed status quo. Even when a mission looks like a success, as UNTEA/UNSF did, it may amount in hindsight to abandoning principle and acquiescing to a long-running civil war. To acknowledge that stabilization missions are transitory is to admit that the parties are ultimately responsible not to achieve an "end state" but to continue the work of political and social evolution as *they* see fit, not as outside parties dictate.

The UN Transitional Executive Authority and UN Security force (UNTEA/UNSF) in West Irian was an early example of post-colonial transition with UN assistance. The Netherlands had colonized West New Guinea (West Irian) in 1828 and the status of the territory was unresolved at the time of Indonesia's independence in 1949. While Indonesia claimed the territory, with US support, the Netherlands argued for self-determination of the ethnically distinct Papuan people. The issue was debated in regular sessions of the General Assembly from 1954 to 1961 without resolution. Following Secretary General Dag Hammarskjöld's death, U Thant appointed former US Ambassador Ellsworth Bunker as Special Envoy, and informal talks between the Netherlands and Indonesia took place in an atmosphere of rising recriminations and Indonesian acts of aggression alleged by the Netherlands. The Security Council became involved in May 1962, but agreement was achieved outside the Security Council with Ambassador Bunker acting as intermediary. U Thant announced an agreement in July, which would see a Transitional Executive Authority and Security Force under UN Authority. In an unprecedented step, the first elements—and observer force—were dispatched without prior authorization of either Security Council or General Assembly. The Secretary General acted on his own initiative, citing the urgency of the situation, as reported by his Special Envoy (United Nations 1996, 641).

The military observers, under the direction of the Secretary General's Military Advisor, Brigadier General Indar Jit Rikhye, established a cease-fire, and the Security Force deployed to ensure internal law and order, acting effectively as a police force responsive initially to Dutch colonial authorities, then to the Transitional Executive Authority. The Papuan Volunteer Corps ceased to be part of the Netherlands armed forces upon transfer of authority and played no role in the maintenance of order. As Dutch officers and ranks left, they were replaced with Indonesian officers, until the transition was complete in January 1963. Full administrative control was transferred to the Indonesian government on 1 May 1963. Rather than conducting a plebiscite, Indonesia created enlarged representative councils to address the question of self-determination. In July and August 1969 these assemblies chose to remain with Indonesia, without dissent (United Nations 1996, 461).

UNTEA/UNSF paid lip service to self-determination, but was actually a pragmatic sell-out, orchestrated by the US, in the face of Cold War pressures (Saltford 2002; Chesterman 2004). The Netherlands was removed as a colonial power, but Indonesia was given the authority to conduct a plebiscite on the future of the territory, without international supervision. For most of the citizens of West Irian, one colonial master was exchanged for another, and the liberation struggle continues intermittently to this day (Chavel 2004, 180-192).

UNTAG in Namibia, on the other hand, appears to have been a genuine success. It is one of the few transition missions that has clearly and unequivocally acted as "midwife to a nation," which remains a relatively free and stable member of the international community to this day.

Germany had annexed South West Africa in 1884 and retained control of it until the First World War. In 1915, South African forces defeated the German garrison and occupied the territory. The Permanent Mandates Commission of the League of Nations conferred the mandate for South West Africa on the British Crown, to be administered by South Africa as a

Class C Mandate—"…[administered] as an integral portion of the Union of South Africa." The validity of this mandate became contentious after the Second World War, when the United Nations assumed the responsibilities of the League. In advisory rulings, the International Court of Justice ruled that South Africa could not unilaterally change the status of the territory to incorporate it into South Africa.

The General Assembly recognized the South West African People's Organization as the sole legitimate representative of the people of South West Africa in Resolution 31/146 (1966), supporting all necessary means to achieve liberation. Resolution 2145 the same year revoked South Africa's mandate. The General Assembly established a Council for Namibia to replace South Africa in 1968, and the Security Council endorsed these actions in 1969. South Africa, in the meantime, continued to divide Namibia into black homelands and enforce white rule and ownership. A settlement proposal was developed in the Security Council under the leadership of non-permanent members, and with the assistance of the Commonwealth Secretariat, and approved in Resolution 435 (1978) (United Nations 1996, 205-207). From the adoption of this resolution in 1978 to its implementation in 1989 was a long slow process, during which the diplomatic resources of the Western Contact Group were essential. While three members of the Contact Group (US, UK, and France) were permanent members of the Security Council, considerable credit goes to Canada and West Germany for garnering diplomatic support from African states and the Commonwealth (Hearn 1999, 225). The imminent end of the Cold War, the withdrawal of Cuban support in Angola, and the alignment of permanent members of the Security Council contributed to the outcome, but the whole trajectory of self-determination in Namibia, including the involvement of a large cast of minor states in supporting roles, stands in sharp contrast to the quick and unilateral settlement of West Irian's claims.

The other two cases probably fall between these extremes of success and failure, and illustrate the difficulty of categorizing stabilization missions. The mandate of UNTAES was to secure the transition of Eastern Slavonia, with its majority Serb population, from the rump Yugoslavia (Serbia, Montenegro, and Vojvodina) to the new state of Croatia. This was accomplished, with modest costs in the form of population displacement and human rights violations. On the positive side, UNTAES negotiated the turnover of the Djelatovci oil fields from the Serbian Scorpion paramilitary and used the accrued revenues for the mission's budget and for reconstruction (Bhatia 2005, 213). On the negative side, UNTAES reflected an international mandate that took little account of the wishes of the majority of citizens most affected by the mission in Eastern Slavonia—national and international security trumped human security. The evidence for this is that the majority Serb population was uncomfortable as a minority in Eastern Slavonia, but the states of the international community were uncomfortable with changing state boundaries by force, and the Croatian successor state prevailed when the boundaries were re-established. The reintegration is still a qualified success because the framework of European human rights law ensures some oversight of minority rights for Serbs in Eastern Slavonia, as reports of the OECD Commissioner for National Minorities attest (Packer 1999, 168-183).

Timor was colonized by the Portuguese for sandalwood in the sixteen hundreds, and Portuguese control was reduced to the east half of the island after a fight with the Dutch in 1749. It was first on the UN agenda in 1960, about the same time as the West Irian. After India's annexation of Portuguese Goa and the collapse of colonial Angola, Portugal sought to establish a provisional government, and was faced with a civil war between pro-Indonesian forces with Jakarta's backing, and independence forces. The Portuguese withdrew in 1975 and Indonesia integrated East Timor as the 26th Province in 1976. At the request of members, the UN Secretary General has been routinely involved since 1982. Indonesia proposed limited autonomy in 1998, and an agreement was signed by Portugal and Indonesia on popular consultation about independence under UN auspices in 1999. The consultation was carried out under UNAMET, resulting in majority support for independence. This was followed by pro-integration violence supported by Indonesian militias. The UN authorized an Australian-led military force, INTERFET, to stabilize the situation, and this force handed over to a Transitional Administration (UNTAET) in 1999. UNMISET was then the follow-on mission to assist with developing the instruments of governance from May 2002 to May 2005 (UN Department of Peacekeeping Operations 2009).

The East Timorese joy at independence is unequivocal, but the lingering suspicion that intervention might have been contingent upon, or facilitated by, oil deals in the East Timorese gap leaves a sense of unease that there may be more self-interest than altruism underlying this mission.

The four examples above might be arranged on a scale from coercive *realpolitik* to respectful collaboration according to agreed rules. Although this is impressionistic, I think it tells us something about the sort of interventions that are supportable by democracies within a framework of national and international law. We understand that more states, especially small ones, are comfortable with the rule sets involved in collaborative intervention, but can be persuaded to abrogate those rules in self-interest. They did so repeatedly in the face of prospective communist takeovers during the Cold War, self-interest drove the abrogation of liberal-democratic principles in the earlier era of imperial expansion, and can also be counted on to influence choices today. The theory of democratic peace argues that liberal democracies constrain the aggressive behaviour of states. Institutions like separation of powers, pluralism, official opposition, judicial review, and free media can restrain foreign adventures. Civilian oversight of military and police, and complaints procedures like Canada's Military Police Complaints Commission, and America's Senate hearings can help to constrain coercive *realpolitik* and inhumane practice. This should correspond to greater acceptance and support for stabilization in target countries.

Table 1 is an impressionistic comparison of the four interventions considered, arranged with the most coercive on the left and the most collaborative on the right.

TABLE 1
Comparison of Interventions

	← *Coercive Realpolitik Intervention/Respectful Collaborative Intervention* →			
	UNTEA/UNSF *West Irian*	*UNMISET* *East Timor*	*UNTAES* *Eastern Slavonia*	*UNTAG* *South West Africa/* *Namibia*
Contributors	US, Pakistan and Canada (Canada and Pakistan both beholden to US)	55 contributing states, 9 non-colonial small Western democracies (16 percent)	31 contributing states, 10 non-colonial small Western democracies (32 percent)	50 contributing states, 17 non-colonial small Western democracies (34 percent)
Duration	1962 to 1963 Referendum 1969 Violence continues 1964–1986*	2002–2005	1996–1998	1989–1990
Stability	Six years, followed by sporadic insurgency	Four years, continuing	11 years, continuing	19 years, continuing
Finance	Indonesia and NL paid full costs in equal amounts	General assessments plus regional mission with Australian funding	General assessments	General assessments
Stakes (in *realpolitik* terms)	Cold War alignment	Offshore oil and gas?	Violent ethnic boundary change in European neighbourhood	National self-determination; post-Cold War credibility of West in Africa
Western public identification with elites	Yes (anti-communism, Sukarno)	Yes (charismatic nationalist "Xanana" Gusmão)	No	No
Accompanied by economic and legislative intervention?	Yes, by Indonesia	Yes, by UN Administration	Yes, by UN Administration	No

* Gurr 1993, 297. Note that Gurr similarly identifies the East Timorese independence struggle as "1974–late 1980s…. conflict suppressed," illustrating that this is a mere snapshot.

The first observation concerns the chronology and nature of the interventions. Chronologically, we begin on the left with coercive *realpolitik* against the background of Cold War concerns about falling dominoes, bounce to the right with the end of the Cold War, and then appear to inch back towards increasing coercion in an era of assertiveness under American leadership. But over the same four decades (1963–2005) there has been evolution in the formal rule sets governing intervention. This has included new regimes such as the UN Convention on Law of the Sea (UNCLOS), the experiment with International Criminal Tribunals for Rwanda and the Former Yugoslavia, the Land Mine Ban, the International Criminal Court, and the Report of the International Commission on Intervention and State Sovereignty (ICISS), *Responsibility to Protect.* Collectively, but particularly the last mentioned, these innovations provide a new framework for thinking about intervention.

The second observation concerns the contexts of the interventions. In every case, the missions have been mandated by the Security Council and justified under the UN Charter, representing a balancing act between the sovereign rights of states (Article 2) and the right of peoples to self-determination (Article 1). Drawing on impressions of public discourse in newspapers, government press releases of the day and academic accounts of the justifications, I think some patterns are discernible. The most coercive mission has the smallest base of contributors, and the most collaborative has the highest proportion of non-colonial small Western democratic contributors. The most collaborative was also the shortest intervention and subsequently the most stable (if we include the long gestation of the Indonesian-supervised referendum in West Irian). Public or government identification with elites might be a warning sign that the common good is not being served by an intervention.

Finally, all these interventions are, to some extent, zero-sum; there are identifiable winners and losers, but these are only identifiable at a snapshot in time. Ted Gurr's *Minorities at Risk* project, published in 1993, identifies both the Papuan and East Timorese ethno-national liberation struggles as having been suppressed (Gurr 1993, 297)[5] Another way to think of the continuum in Table 1 is therefore in terms of degrees of completion. Namibia (relatively complete) is unlikely to unravel; West Irian (relatively incomplete) is unlikely to settle down to stability. Eastern Slavonia is fairly secure within a framework of European minority rights protection, but East Timor is likely to continue to be problematic if the energy stakes rise. It might follow Kuwait or Biafra. This arrangement of transitional missions does not help to distinguish the relative merits of stabilizing a conflict along existing boundaries (as UNTEA, UNTAG and UNTAES did) and supporting secession (as UNMISET and UNMIK in Kosovo have). Evolving international law does, however, particularly the thinking developed by ICISS. If *Responsibility to Protect* had been an accepted yardstick in 1963, it is an open question whether Indonesia would have been as readily accepted as the successor to the Dutch colonial regime. If repressive activities had been as visible in 1963 as they were in 2000, then it is unlikely that a smooth transition to Indonesian rule would have been accepted.

My impressionistic review of these four transitional stabilization missions supports the contention that collaborative and consensual efforts involving a high proportion of small and supportive democracies are more likely to be associated with stable outcomes. Just as peacekeeping was widely identified as a mid-power occupation during the Cold War, respectful stabilization operations should be the focus of European-Canadian cooperation in the contemporary period. This is not a startling or original conclusion; indeed, the old label of "peacekeeping" is still quite serviceable, although peace support and stabilization may be more fashionable. There is a consistent emphasis on the role of middle powers in preserving international order. A Brookings study published in the year the US pushed the Netherlands and Indonesia into UNTEA begins with the assumptions of Adlai Stevenson and U Thant: even a superpower cannot assume sole responsibility for policing the planet (Cox 1963). The International Peace Academy's seminal *Peacekeeper's Handbook* was developed by contributors from Austria, Australia, Ireland, Norway, Sweden, Ghana, and Canada during the ten-year long diplomatic gestation of UNTAG (International Peace Academy 1978).

The prominent role of middle powers is showcased in every history of peacekeeping.[6] The UN's Brahimi Report (2000) spurred a collaborative study supported by some 50 countries, but with "crucial resources and support" from Argentina, Australia, India, Jordan, Norway, South Africa, and Sweden (Swedish National Defence College 2002). A recent comprehensive review of peacekeeping rejects privatization, and stresses the importance of sharing the burden internationally and engaging military and non-military assets to preserve legitimacy (Durch and Berkman 2006). The burden of preserving a rules-based order on a crowded planet, as in a crowded city, rests on the middle class!

The relative success of missions with lots of democratic contributors extends beyond this narrow sample, if we believe the historical reviews of success in peacekeeping by Alan James and William Durch and colleagues. James emphasises the utility of "impartial and non-threatening third powers" (James 1990, 362). Durch and colleagues articulate three basic hypotheses of peacekeeping, supported by focused comparative analysis of peacekeeping cases: peacekeeping requires local consent, and consent derives from local perception of impartiality and moral authority; it requires the support of great powers, and the US in particular; and it requires a change in belligerents' objectives, often associated with combat exhaustion (Durch 1993, 12-13, 474). Democracies may bring a better suite of resources—combining diplomatic, development and security instruments; they may pick their missions better because of domestic constraints; or they may form a more coherent support network for fragile stability. Certainly, collective efforts by middle powers seem to function better than minimalist coalitions assembled by major powers.

IMPLICATIONS FOR PRACTICE: A STRATEGY OF COMMUNITY BUILDING

What sort of problems do like-minded nations face? Mixing the high politics of energy conflict and the altruistic idealism of peace support, which serves all our interests, stabilizing Central Asia and the Middle East are high priority tasks. In the future, we might expect to find policies impeded by declining energy reserves and production (the peak oil problem) and by increasingly severe climate disruptions, both of which will have geopolitical fall-out. In our increasingly urban and diverse democracies, we may face escalating ethnic tensions, the response to which risks eroding democratic protections. We have already seen in the excesses of the post 9/11 Global War on Terror the potential for foreign operations and domestic politics to combine in counter-productive ways, so we urgently need to think through the principles that our experience suggests.

The first rule might be "do-as-you-would-be-done-by."[7] This principle would ask that Canadians consider the secession of Biafra, or perhaps the independence of East Timor, in the same light as the internationally supported secession of a newly oil-rich Newfoundland. We should be cautious about interventions that impose change on host countries when they are not in a position to negotiate that change as equal partners, even if these changes play well at home (like letting girls go to school). When there is a gap between rhetoric and operational reality, it should be the subject of public discourse, rather than perception management, and this requires new approaches to public affairs at home and information operations abroad.

There is another danger associated with intervention—the old story of rights and freedoms being hijacked by the powerful. Corporations receive the rights guaranteed to individuals; international capital claims economic freedoms supported by international forces, and buys up assets at a discount. Thugs like Foday Sankoh and Jonas Savimbi masquerade as democrats. We should be concerned when our own mechanisms for holding power to account are bypassed or minimized in their application to foreign operations. They are our defence against being "done-by-as-we-did." This rule suggests that the most useful partners for stabilization operations are those with a genuine appreciation for the utility of binding domestic and international rule sets. States with functioning liberal democracies and minimal imperial or colonial baggage form a sort of international middle class, and are natural allies.

It would be wrong to ascribe innate moral superiority to this group of natural allies. Modest powers have been atrocious colonial masters, and Canada's record of banking in the Caribbean and its mining and extractive industries all over the world are seen by some as egregious. But our rapacious instincts are constrained by limited abilities, and self-interest reins in our excesses, as it did when Talisman Oil was forced to withdraw from the Sudan (Kobrin 2004, 425-456).

We therefore make good partners for operations with collaborative rule sets. This suggests, of course, that there are other possible partnerships for different collaborative rule sets. These might be in opposition, as capitalism and communism were during the Cold War, yet find common cause in specific purposes like peacekeeping. NATO and Warsaw Pact members cooperated on the majority of UN Peace Observation and Peacekeeping missions between 1956 and 1989, with countries like Poland and Canada frequently being consciously paired. This suggests an approach to consciously building communities of practice in support of common endeavours. Since 2001 and the disastrous War on Terror, building a partnership with the Islamic world is a logical endeavour, requiring good will and super-ordinate goals. Fortuitously, stability in Afghanistan and a viable Palestinian state are urgent projects, which present both the opportunity and the requirement to reconcile Islamic values with secular democratic values within a framework of agreed rule sets.

How should we pursue the parallel projects of building communities of international practice and stable communities after conflict? We might think about the phases of intervention from the point of view of the country being subjected to it, applying the "do-as-you-would-be-done-by" rule. How can we assist a return to indigenous sovereign control? Intervention begins with the disruption of existing structures and the rupture of communities—with or without external involvement. As the conflict continues, the state usually loses its instruments of power: diplomats become refugees, security forces fracture, governance becomes impossible, and the tax base withers away into the informal sector, with opposition often funded by black markets and looting of resources. The intervention is often imposed or agreed by parties outside the target state. UNTEA was set up by the Netherlands and Indonesia without consulting Papuans; UNTAES required the consent of Zagreb and Belgrade, not Vukovar. The instrument of intervention includes clauses about status, putting the interveners beyond the law of the receiving state or territory, and with that the state loses control of its borders.

The Balkans saw an influx of thousands of non-governmental organizations from well-meaning mom-and-pop groups to well-funded religious groups that exacerbated sectarian conflict. The period from 1992 to 1995 was a period of confusion and lack of regulation. As the ethnic entities strengthened their grip, each of them manipulated the intervention, but a critical turning point was achieved with the establishment in Bosnia Herzegovina of a legitimate ministry for the regulation of international organizations operating in the country. Thinking this through, a collaborative way of approaching the management of permeable boundaries might have been to facilitate the early establishment of such a ministry, along with rule sets for the regulation and conduct of foreign nationals.

It is not easy to assess whether new thinking in the US is moving towards or away from this collaborative and community-building ideal. The US Army and Marine Corps *Counter Insurgency Manual*, sold publicly through the University of Chicago Press, pushes in the right direction in most places, but is still fundamentally a manual of occupation and coercive tactics, weak on the theory and practice of development, and comparatively oblivious of the social context of violence despite its effort to assert the primacy of the social and political context (Last 2009a).[8] More promising is the collaboration between the US Army's PKSOI and the US Institute of Peace to produce a capstone strategic framework for stabilization and reconstruction. Drawing on much of the thinking from the mid-nineteen nineties to the present, it posits five pillars: rule of law, safe and secure environment, social wellbeing, stable governance, and sustainable economy. Its most promising feature, however, is that first amongst the crosscutting principles at the centre of the Framework is: "host nation ownership and capacity." The proof will be in the application.

RULE OF LAW AT HOME AND COLLABORATIVE INTERVENTION ABROAD

If Rule of Law (capitalized) is a general principle that governs both the rich and powerful states engaged in stabilizing the world for their own benefit, and the poor and benighted countries being stabilized, then we should understand how these pieces fit together. Since I am not a lawyer and this is not a legal brief, I will recount some vignettes that illustrate the interconnectedness of Rule of Law for "us" and for "them," beginning with Canada and the US.

In August of 2006 the five senior legal officers of the American armed services—the Judge Advocates General—testified before the Senate Judicial Committee. The implication of their testimony was that their Commander in Chief, the President of the United States, had jeopardized American lives and undermined operational principles by supporting violations of the international law of armed conflict, including abrogation of the Geneva Conventions (MacDonald 2006). Against a background of cabinet pressure to sideline or remove the JAGs, the 2008 Defense Authorization Act increased their rank from two-star to three-star general officers, making the 40th Judge Advocate General, Bruce MacDonald, the first Vice Admiral JAG of the US Navy.

Admiral MacDonald, one of the five JAGs, has expounded his views on rule of law as the new moral high ground that would help regain the initiative for the incoming Obama Administration. Coincidentally, the

Canadian military legal establishment has been embroiled in a dispute with Canada's Military Police Complaints Commission. The MPCC is the watchdog over the conduct of Canada's Military Police. In September 2008, Mr. Peter Tinsley, the Military Police Complaints Commissioner, agreed to conduct an enquiry into the conduct of Canadian Military Police in surrendering detainees to Afghan authorities whom they knew (or should have known) would torture them.[9] The inquiry was to extend to the responsibilities of officers for the legal conduct of operations, and Canadian Forces JAG, on instructions from the Minister of National Defence, sought an injunction to prevent the inquiry from proceeding. Subsequently, parliament was suspended for three months, and the serving Military Police Complaints Commissioner's term was not renewed (Chase and Ibbitson 2009).

Parliamentary and presidential traditions have different means of achieving accountability. The division of powers in the American presidential system allows more scope for legal recourse, while Canada's parliamentary system allows more room for a Minister to exercise responsibility, accountable to Parliament. In this case it could be by adjudicating between the MPCC and the Chief of Defence, both of which report to him.[10] That the government chose to leave the dispute about the conduct of operations in the realm of a public enquiry while simultaneously obstructing that enquiry probably says more about post-Somalia Canadian politics than it does about the rule of law, which is equally robust (or threatened) north and south of the border. The unfolding of the JAG demarche to the US Senate and the MPCC exposé of detainee handling illustrates that relying on rule of law as a common ground for the conduct of operations can work only at the most general level; every state will deal with the devil of its own details when transgressions occur. But the similarity of the debates also suggests that basic values are not at issue. Combatants should be treated humanely; civilians should be protected; force should be proportional, and so on.

There are also debates, however, about fundamental values in the conduct of operations, and these can fall along cultural or national lines. When this happens, it raises the stakes for participants, and can call alliances into question. Israel and Afghanistan provide examples.

Israel's Prime Minister explicitly warned of a "disproportionate response" to the incessant, but not very damaging, rocket attacks from Gaza (Kershner 2009). The attacks were used to justify massive retaliation, even though it was understood at the outset that the outcome would be damaging to Israel.[11] Both Israeli and Palestinian leaders have been ambivalent about settlement, and an "eye for an eyelash" mentality seems to underlie the escalating death toll from the occupation (Cohen 2009).[12] Discussions about intervention and assistance to disengagement often stall on these differences of perception. At the same time there is room for optimism as Palestinian groups use litigation rather than violence to pursue land claims and restrictions on the encroachment of settlements (Banerjee 2009). A framework of transnational law, supported by international intervention, may yet provide a basis for regulating the asymmetrical violence operating between Israelis and Palestinians. This is a project to which Canada and European states are both contributing, for example through the European Union Police Co-ordinating Office for Palestinian Police Support (EUPOL COPPS).[13]

Less amenable to common adjudication is Afghanistan's flirtation with sharia law. A sovereign government passes its own laws, and expects its allies to respect them. But a commitment to assist that government seems to bring a proportional right to express concern about the nature of the laws it passes. Stories in the *London Times* and *New York Times* both interwove paragraphs about the commitment of troops with condemnation of the law:

> Stephen Harper, the Canadian Prime Minister, said he was troubled by the law and would lobby other leaders to support him in seeking to have it repealed. "This is antithetical to our mission in Afghanistan," he said. Stockwell Day, the Canadian Trade Minister, who is chairman of the Cabinet committee on Afghanistan, warned that if Kabul did not back down Canadian support for the Government could be imperiled. "If there is any wavering on this point, this will create serious difficulties, serious problems for the Government of Canada," he told reporters in Ottawa. Canada has 2,800 troops fighting in southern Afghanistan and has suffered the highest relative number of casualties of any contingent with 116 of its soldiers dead. (Coughlan 2009)

The Afghan case is interesting because abuse of women almost has the status of folk devil in western culture, inducing moral panic (leading to policy changes). Both these terms need to be defined. Folk devils are persons or groups portrayed by folklore and media as deviant outsiders, blamed for transgressions and often targeted for social retribution (Young and Arrigo 1999). Moral panic is a social reaction consisting of concern, hostility, and consensus about a threat to society, often culminating in a disproportionate reaction, which may appear and disappear capriciously.[14] Western societies are still making slow progress on their own misogyny; women have barely had the vote for three generations, and Canadian women still earn 27 percent less than men, on average. Yet fighting so that Afghan girls can go to school seems to have even more salience in socially conservative Alberta than elsewhere in Canada.[15] Recognizing the risk of folk devils and moral panics helps us put Afghanistan's laws in perspective. This is a developing country with internal divisions, and it is attempting to undergo social, economic and cultural change; passing laws that reflect the values of (some or many) citizens, and debating those laws without undue external influence is an important step in managing the cultural war, which underlies the insurgency. Imposing western standards on Afghan lawmakers, on the strength of our military presence, is likely to strengthen the forces that are resisting rights and democracy as alien impositions. This opinion is based on asking a few Afghan friends and colleagues in Canada, what do you think? But it also rests on the question, what would we think in their place? As an opinion, it bears closer examination.

The opinion above suggests that respect for the internal debate in Afghanistan is more likely to result in Afghans seeing western involvement as positive. It is an important pillar of the argument for respectful and collaborative intervention. It is difficult, however, to support with empirical evidence, because survey data from countries without a tradition of survey response are notoriously unreliable.[16] There is a long tradition of sociometric polling in war zones, beginning with American efforts in occupied territory as early as 1944, when the unreliability of individual responses was demonstrated (Dodd 1944, 265-282) so we can't put much stock in the 2009 ABC News Poll which found that Afghan support for Western forces declined from 67 percent in 2006 to 37 percent in 2009 (ABC News/BBC/ARD Poll 2009). More reliable is the broad base of the Pew Global Attitudes Project. Based on extensive polling in 47 countries, it reported "global unease with major world powers" since 2002. Declining opinion of the US led this trend. Opinion in Middle Eastern states had moderated since reaching a nadir with the invasion of Iraq in 2003, but remained overwhelmingly unfavourable, and had declined overall in 23 of 33 countries were trends were available, with negative views held by 86 percent of Palestinians, 78 percent of Egyptians and Jordanians, 69 percent of Malaysians, 68 percent of Pakistanis, and 56 percent of Moroccans, for example (Wike et al. 2007, 20-21). These views represent an important drag to American-led strategy, and have operational implications for everything from American embassy security to force protection and local contract costs (Americans pay more, because it is riskier to do business with them).[17] Again, the conclusion is that low-key, respectful interventions by minor powers with capacity but without ulterior motives are less likely to generate negative responses.

Rule of Law as a principle transcending state boundaries has historical roots in the liberal democratic ideologies of Europe. But in the 20th century, under the umbrella of the UN system, it has taken on a broader and more inclusive meaning exemplified by the UN Charter and human rights instruments. In this modern form, Rule of Law does not provide a coherent explanatory narrative like liberalism, communism, or fundamental religious views of the world. However, it does offer a coherent framework for social and political prescriptions as diverse as communism, Islam, and free-market capitalism. Each requires rules, and while we disagree on the explanation and prescription, we can argue rationally about the application of rule sets, and procedures for establishing the rules democratically.

But the enlightenment was a European phenomenon and there are competing views of law—traditional, tribal, religious, and ideologically framed laws. There is a tension in "liberal democracy" between liberal primacy of individual rights and equality before the law, and democratic primacy of majorities (however constituted) in framing laws. The 1955 Bandung Conference famously held up racial segregation and continued colonialism against the standards of the Universal Declaration of Human Rights, but also made a case for collective Asian and African values, in opposition to the primacy of the individual. The Organization of the Islamic Conference regularly insists on Islamic values and projects a view of the world that is often in stark contrast to that of the secular West.[18]

Consent of the governed is fundamental to sustaining rule of law, and we lost sight of this as European laws expanded with empire. We should expect rule sets to change as the governed assert themselves over time. Our own enlightenment on women's rights and sexual orientation is very recent. If we expect western secular humanist law to be the basis for international rule of law, we must be prepared to adapt or accommodate local variations, keeping in mind that "we" have the right to be wrong about fundamental value-orientations that affect us, and so do "they" when it comes to value orientations that affect them. That calls for means to adjudicate between rule sets that affect us mutually, but that is just another body of rules that must be collectively agreed.[19]

This is not moral relativism; Canada and European democracies have a stake in expanding the Western conception of law and human rights, and that means upholding it without expedient hypocrisy. Expedient hypocrisy might include citing individual freedoms and democracy as a justification for economic liberalization that destroys social networks. Destroying social networks is not part of US doctrine, but economic liberalization is. The US Office of the Coordinator for Reconstruction and Stabilization explicitly links stabilization to a market economy:

> The Core Mission of S/CRS is to lead, coordinate and institutionalize U.S. Government civilian capacity to prevent or prepare for post-conflict situations, and to help stabilize and reconstruct societies in transition from conflict or civil strife, so they can reach a sustainable path toward peace, democracy and a market economy.[20]

The essential task matrix for reconstruction includes private-public investment partnerships, strengthening relations with international financial institutions, early resumption of debt repayment, licensing of new banks, creation of conditions conducive to stock and commodity markets, increasing export diversification, ensuring legal and regulatory frameworks to support privatization, protection of intellectual property rights, and establishing a framework for the privatization of public assets (Office of the Coordinator for Reconstruction and Stabilization 2005, IV-1 to IV-17) Development economist William Easterly argues that this constitutes a "new imperialism" which is a good recipe for increasing the wealth of developed states, but not poor or fragile ones (2006, 271).[21]

So while there are a lot of powerful interests pushing for streamlining of contract law and protection of investors' rights, this might not be where post-conflict legislative drafting should start; states like Cambodia, Bosnia, Iraq and Afghanistan can lose control of their economies and damage the fabric of their societies before they gain control of their own legislation. Stabilization missions are fundamentally about changing the circumstances that we think lead to instability. What we in the West want to change, or think needs changing, may not be agreed by our partners in conflict-affected countries. We may argue that we fight to send girls to school, while our allies *and opponents equally* argue that they fight for the preservation of their culture and way of life in the face of western onslaught.

CONCLUSION

Where might such respectful and collaborative operations be undertaken in the future? In the Balkans, there is a serious question about whether the states of the region can police themselves, wrapping up almost two decades of escalating and de-escalating international involvement. Multilateral ventures in security sector reform in Bosnia Herzegovina, Croatia and Serbia compete with bilateral arm-and-train missions in Croatia, Albania and Kosovo, for which there is little consultation with neighbours, yet "re-entry" of NATO forces has been mooted recently. In Afghanistan, there has been a consistent tension between patient institution building and security-oriented ground operations, and confidence-damaging operations by coalition air forces. We fought Bader-Meinhof, ETA, Red Brigade, and IRA terrorists for decades without using artillery or air strikes. Nor have we employed drones against our own citizens, although they have begun to range over wider areas of Pakistan even as the government scrabbles to retain legitimacy. How would that play at home? Pakistan is a desperately poor nuclear-armed regional power with border disputes and domestic strife, which has nevertheless been a major contributor to international stabilization operations. It deserves understanding and support, but also has a lot to teach. Moving back to Europe's expanding borders, Israel is a part of the Euro-Mediterranean community, and establishing a stable Palestinian state is a matter of some urgency. Kurdestan, Iran, and the Caucasus loom as potential future conflicts that defy coercive intervention. These are all areas where indigenous solutions must accommodate regional interests to be sustainable, because the common challenge is cultural transformation and regeneration.

If we think about the domestic struggles of our own culture wars, including integration of minorities, gender equity, and flaws in the accountability of government, we have cause to be circumspect about our ability to support cultural transformation in foreign countries. It surprises me, for example, to hear officers or officials speaking confidently about reconstruction or democratization in Afghanistan when their knowledge of Canadian politics is limited despite growing up with the language and reading a newspaper now and then. We should understand our very limited capacity to intervene usefully in the political and social processes that really matter to stabilization.

When democracies get involved in imperial policing or coercive counter-insurgency operations overseas, they often run into problems with the rule of law at home. If they do not, it may be a reflection on the weakness of their own safeguards for human rights. We have already begun to experience this in Canada. When we come up against value differences in international operations, like sharia law in Afghanistan, we have to be careful to avoid treating these as differences as folk devils that spur us to the actions of rash outsiders. International polling data suggests that coercion stimulates rejection and resistance, and we have reason to expect that respect for indigenous frameworks of law will help us to be useful in the processes of political and social transformation that stabilization demands. The expedient hypocrisy of imposing free markets and economic liberalization for our benefit is not likely to be useful. These are issues on which Canada and European democracies might find common cause. They have a history of doing so, and generally greater willingness to engage in the most justifiable missions, partly because of the domestic constraints they must face.

Small powers are more aware of the limits to their capacity, and should be more sensitive about impinging on the sovereignty of weak and fragile states. Knowing our limits and respecting the targets of intervention, no less than we respect our allies, will help us build a robust international rule of law. This is an urgent task, because today's conflicts are probably just the beginning.

NOTES

1. The author would like to thank the organizers and participants of the conference New Missions, New Challenges, and is grateful for comments and assistance from Christian Leuprecht, Lew Diggs, and anonymous reviewers.
2. For the general structure, see Adams and Glaudemans (2009). The follow-on announcement linking domestic and international security priorities, see The White House (2009), for comment on continuity, see Feaver (2009).
3. "A Whole-of-Government Approach to Preparing for and Responding to Conflict," *Seminar on Training and Dispatching Civilian Peacebuilders*, Tokyo, Japan, 31 October 2007.

4. Without capitals, rule of law simply implies that laws are enforced. Economist R.T. Naylor observes that powerful actors will always bend the rules until they are forced to pay to rewrite them, but still end up with laws in their favour (2002). But having been written, law is blind to litigants, or there is not rule of law.

5. Note that Gurr similarly identifies the East Timorese independence struggle as "1974-late 1980s.... conflict suppressed," illustrating that this is a mere snapshot.

6. United Nations (1997); Durch (1993) as just two examples. Ramesh Thakur and Albrecht Schnabel (2001) describe the increasing importance of major power engagement as peacekeeping moved out of the Cold War in six "cascading generations" of peacekeeping, "Cascading generations of peacekeeping: Across the Mogadishu line to Kosovo and Timor."

7. Mrs. Do-as-you-would-be-done-by, and Mrs. Be-done-by-as-you-did were two characters in a popular morality tale for Victorian children, who turn out to be the same spirit—the "golden rule" personified (Kingsley 1863).

8. For more pointed criticism, see The network of concerned anthropologists (2009; especially David Price, "Faking Scholarship").

9. See the website of the Military Police Complaints Commission, http://www.mpcc-cppm.gc.ca (accessed 16 July 2010).

10. The extent to which the MPCC is independent is one of the issues in dispute. The step of proroguing parliament and allowing the position of Commissioner to lapse is unusual, and not related solely to the investigation of the Afghan detainee question.

11. Discussions with Israeli security officials at a Chatham House workshop, March 2009. It surprised me that the planned operations went ahead despite being understood as a lose-lose proposition. This illustrates cultural gaps in operational thinking. Israelis of the right and left were equally convinced that, although it would make matters worse, they had no option but to respond, while international observers felt that the war was discretionary and ill-advised.

12. On the escalating death toll, see Gordon (2008, xv ii).

13. Briefing by José Vericat, Press and Public Information Officer, EUPOL COPPS, Ramallah, 28 May 2009.

14. MacKay ([1841] 1985) was probably the pioneer in describing this, though without the current vocabulary (Cohen 1972; Ben-Yehuda and Goode 1994).

15. The conservative *Calgary Herald* trumpets, "Afghan Women Worth the Fight," Lauryn Oates, 25 April 2009; and Licia Corbella, "Here's Why the Fight in Afghanistan is Worth It," 4 April 2009.

16. Conrad Winn, founder and president of COMPAS and an experienced pollster, interview, June 2008.

17. This is quite aside from accusations of corruption (Jones 2009).

18. For example, the speech by the Secretary General of the Organization of the Islamic Conference, His Excellency Professor Ekmeleddin Ihsanoglu, at the 11th Session, Dakar 13 March 2008 is an enumeration of transgressions against the Ummah, in which Islamic states' consciences are offended by conflicts that are affronts by the non-Islamic world: "Palestine, Iraq, Lebanon, Jammu and Kashmir, Afghanistan, Azerbaijan, Darfour, Cyprus, Cote d'Ivoire, Somalia, and Comoros and elsewhere."

19. Parts of this argument are previously published in Last (2009b, 21).

20. US Department of State, Office of the Coordinator for Reconstruction and Stabilization website, www.state.gov/s/crs/ (accessed October 2009).
21. I have addressed this subject (Last 2006) in the context of peace operations.

REFERENCES

ABC News/BBC/ARD Poll. 2009. Support for U.S. Efforts Plummets Amid Afghanistan's Ongoing Strife, 9 February. At http://abcnews.go.com/images/PollingUnit/1083a1Afghanistan2009.pdf (accessed 14 June 2010).

Adams G., and D. Glaudemans. 2009. Obama's NSC: Org Chart and Implications. *Budget Insight: A Stimson Center Blog on National Security Spending*, 15 March. At http://www.stimson.org/budgeting/pdf/NSC_Organization_Chart_2-09.pdf (accessed 15 June 2010).

Banerjee, S. 2009. Montreal Firms Building Settlements in West Bank Want Civil Suit Dismissed. *Canadian Press*, 4 June. At http://www.bilin-village.org/english/articles/press-and-independent-media/Montreal-firms-building-settlements-in-West-Bank-want-civil-suit-dismissed (accessed 15 June 2010).

Ben-Yehuda, N., and E. Goode. 1994. *Moral Panics: The Social Construction of Deviance*. Oxford: Blackwell.

Bhatia, M. 2005. Postconflict Profit: The Political Economy of Intervention. *Global Governance* 11 (2):205-224.

Chase, S., and J. Ibbitson. 2009. MPs Join Forces to Order Release of Afghan Records. *Globe and Mail*, 11 December.

Chavel, R. 2004. Violence and Governance in West Papua. In *Violent Conflicts in Indonesia: Analysis, Representation, Resolution,* ed. C. Coppel, 180-192. New York: Routledge.

Chesterman, S. 2004. *You, The People: The United Nations and Transitional Administrations and State Building*. New York: International Peace Academy.

Cohen, R. 2009. Eyeless in Gaza. *New York Review of Books* 56:2, 12 February.

Cohen, S. 1972. *Folk Devils and Moral Panics: The Creation of the Mods and Rockers*. London: MacGibbon and Kee.

Coughlan, T. 2009. President Karzai's Taleban-Style Laws for Women Put Troop Surge at Risk. *London Times*, 2 April.

Cox, A.M. 1963. Prospects for Peacekeeping. Washington, DC: Brookings.

Dodd, S.C. 1944. On Reliability in Polling: A Sociometric Study of Errors of Polling in War Zones. *Sociometry* 7 (3):265-282.

Durch, W.J., ed. 1993. *The Evolution of UN Peacekeeping: Case Studies and Comparative Analysis*. New York: St Martin's.

Durch, W.J., and T.C. Berkman. 2006. *Who Should Keep the Peace? Providing Security for Twenty-First-Century Peace Operations*. Washington, DC: Henry L. Stimson Centre.

Easterly, W. 2006. *The White Man's Burden: Why the West's Efforts to Aid the Rest Have Done So Much Ill and So Little Good*. New York: Penguin.

Feaver, P. 2009. Has Change Come to the National Security Council? *Foreign Policy,* 27 May.

Gordon, N. 2008. *Israel's Occupation*. Berkeley, CA: University of California Press.

Gurr, T.R. 1993. *Minorities at Risk: A Global View of Ethnopolitical Conflicts*. Washington, DC: USIP.

Hearn, R. 1999. *UN Peacekeeping in Action: The Namibian Experience*. Hauppaughe, NY: Nova Science Publishing.

International Peace Academy. 1978. *Peacekeeper's Handbook*. New York: Pergamon.

James, A. 1990. *Peacekeeping in International Politics*. Houndmills, UK: Macmillan.

Jones, A. 2009. The Afghan Scam. *Third World Traveller*, 13 January. At www.third-worldtraveler.com/Afghanistan/Afghan_Scam.html (accessed 15 June 2010).

Kershner, I. 2009. Israel Threatens "Disproportionate" Response to Rockets. *New York Times*, 1 February. At http://www.nytimes.com/2009/02/01/world/africa/01iht-mideast.4.19846138.html (accessed 15 June 2010).

Kingsley, C. 1863. *The Water Babies*. London: Macmillan.

Kobrin, S.J. 2004. Oil and Politics: Talisman Energy and Sudan. *International Law and Politics* 36 (2-3):425-456.

Last, D. 2006. Private Sector Collaboration in Operations: Promise and Pitfall. Paper presented at the Seventh Canadian Conference on Ethical Leadership, RMC, Kingston, Ontario, 28-29 November.

— 2009a. Transformation or Back to Basics: Counter-Insurgency Pugilism and Peacebuilding Judo. In *The Transformation of the World of Warfare and Peace Support Operations*, ed. K. Michael, E. Ben-Ari, and D. Kellen. West Port, CT: Praeger Security International.

— 2009b. Rule of Law. *Peace Magazine* 25 (4):20-23.

MacDonald, Rear Admiral B., Judge Advocate General United States Navy. 2006. Testimony before the Senate Judiciary Committee, 2 August. At http://judiciary.senate.gov/hearings/testimony.cfm?id=757&wit_id=5647 (accessed 15 June 2009).

MacKay, C. [1841] 1985. *Extraordinary Popular Delusions and the Madness of Crowds*. New York: Farrar Strauss Giroux.

Naylor, R.T. 2002. *Wages of Crime: Black Markets, Illegal Finance, and the Underworld Economy*. Montreal: McGill-Queen's University Press.

Office of the Coordinator for Reconstruction and Stabilization. 2005. *Essential Task Matrix.* Washington, DC: S/CRS.

Packer, J. 1999. The Role of the OSCE High Commissioner on National Minorities in the Former Yugoslavia. *Cambridge Review of International Affairs* 12 (2):168-183.

Price, D. 2009. Faking Scholarship. In *The Counter-Counterinsurgency Manual, or Notes on Demilitarizing American Society,* The network of concerned anthropologists, 59-76. Chicago, IL: Prickly Paradigm Press.

Saltford, J. 2002. *The United Nations and the Indonesian Takeover of West Papua, 1962–1969: The Anatomy of Betrayal*. London: Routledge.

Swedish National Defence College. 2002. *The Challenges of Peace Operations: Into the 21st Century*. Stockholm: Swedish National Defence College.

Thakur, R., and A. Schnabel. 2001. Cascading Generations of Peacekeeping: Across the Mogadishu Line to Kosovo and Timor. In *United Nations Peacekeeping Operations: Ad Hoc Missions, Permanent Engagement*, ed. R. Thakur and A. Schnabel, 3-25. Tokyo: United Nations University Press.

The network of concerned anthropologists. 2009. *The Counter-Counterinsurgency Manual, or Notes on Demilitarizing American Society.* Chicago, IL: Prickly Paradigm Press.

UN Department of Peacekeeping Operations. 2009. *East Timor*.

United Nations. 1996. *The Blue Helmets: A Review of United Nations Peacekeeping,* third edition. New York: UN Department of Public Information.

— 1997. *The Blue Helmets: A Review of United Nations Peacekeeping.* New York: United Nations.

— 2000. Report of the Panel on United Nations Peace Operations (Brahimi Report). At http://www.un.org/peace/reports/peace_operations/docs/a_55_305.pdf (accessed 21 July 2010).

White House, Office of the Press Secretary. 2009. Statement by the President on the White House Organization for Homeland Security and Counterterrorism, 26 May. At http://www.whitehouse.gov/the_press_office/Statement-by-the-President-on-the-White-House-Organization-for-Homeland-Security-and-Counterterrorism/ (accessed 15 June 2010).

Wike, R. et al. 2007. *Rising Environmental Concern in 47-Nation Survey, Global Unease with Major World Powers.* Washington, DC: Pew Global Attitudes Project, 27 June.

Young, T.R., and B.A. Arrigo. 1999. *Dictionary of the Critical Social Sciences.* Boulder: Westview.

CONTRIBUTORS

FRANCO ALGIERI: Research Director of the Austria Institute of Europe and Security Policy, Maria Enzersdorf.

RITU GILL: Defence Scientist at Defence Research and Development, Toronto, Canada.

ARNOLD H. KAMMEL: Secretary General of the Austria Institute Europe and Security Policy, Maria Enzersdorf.

KAI MICHAEL KENKEL: Assistant Professor of International Relations, Catholic University of Rio de Janeiro, Brazil.

GERHARD KÜMMEL: Senior Researcher at the Bundeswehr Institute of Social Research in Strausberg, Germany and Lecturer for Military Sociology at the University of Potsdam.

DAVID LAST: Lecturer at the Department of Political Science at the Royal Military College of Canada, Kingston.

CHRISTIAN LEUPRECHT: Assistant Professor at the Royal Military College of Canada, Kingston and adjunct chair of Defence Management Studies, Queen's University.

SARAH JANE MEHARG: Senior Research Associate with the Pearson Peacekeeping Centre in Ottawa, Canada.

JOSEPH SOETERS: Professor of organization studies at the Netherlands Defence Academy and Tilburg University.

KRISTINE ST-PIERRE: Research Analyst with the Pearson Peacekeeping Centre in Ottawa, Canada.

Bo Talerud: Associate Professor in Educational Science at the Swedish National Defence College.

Megan M. Thompson: Defence Scientist at Defence Research and Development Canada in Toronto.

Jodok Troy: Lecturer at the Department of Political Science, University of Innsbruck, Austria and Affiliated Scholar, National Defense College, Stockholm, Sweden.

Ingrid van Osch: Researcher at the Netherlands Defence Academy and trainee of the Dutch Department of Defence.

Donna Winslow: Special Advisor to the Commandant, Army Logistics Management College, Army Logistics University, Fort Lee, USA.

About the Pearson Peacekeeping Centre

Peace operations have evolved significantly since the first deployment of peace-keepers over 50 years ago. Today's global environment requires states to mobilize whole of government resources to secure peace and to reconstruct failed states. This effort demands effective and unprecedented levels of synchronization among civilians, military and police.

The Pearson Peacekeeping Centre (PPC) integrates civilians, military and police in an open and collegial learning environment. This focus, coupled with years of experience in activity-based education and training, has earned it an international reputation for excellence in peace operations research-led training, education and capacity development.

The Pearson Papers

The Pearson Papers provide a forum where researchers and practitioners can openly explore the complexities of evolving peace operations. The journal is peer reviewed and brings together theorists and practitioners in an interdisciplinary venue.

The topics covered in each issue are developed based upon emerging trends within the international peace operations community.

Occasional Papers

From time to time the PPC publishes *Occasional Papers* on topics of interest that fall outside a given theme or scope of the current volume of *The Pearson Papers*. *Occasional Papers* include contributions from the field, research articles and/or topical reviews examining emerging trends in peace operations.

Books and Reports

The PPC has a robust research department that undertakes primary research in the field. Since 2007, the department has undertaken research in Africa, Asia, Europe, Latin America, and North America. Results have been published in books, articles and reports, and inform PPC training and education curricula. Visit the 'publications' link at www.peaceoperations.org

Our Courses

The PPC has a wide array of foundational, operational and strategic courses that can be delivered anywhere in the world. Our courses are for civilian police, military, humanitarians, government employees, and most importantly, stake-holders involved in peace operations.

Governments and institutions around the world can request to have the PPC deliver a custom-tailored course that meets specific objectives and requirements. Our learning products reflect an integrated, multi-dimensional approach to ac-commodate adult learning styles and cultural requirements.

Core Competencies for Police in Peace Operations

This course is a United Nations police pre-deployment training program designed to increase the operational effectiveness of international police officers participating in the African Union (AU) and United Nations (UN) Hybrid Mission in Darfur. Participants are provided with mission-specific information and competencies to fulfill their mandate while deployed on mission.

Sexual and Gender-Based Violence (SGBV)

This course aims to strengthen the capacity of United Nations police officers who work with Government of Sudan police on sexual and gender-based violence in Darfur by further developing effective mentoring and reporting competencies.

Planning for Integrated Missions (PIM)

This course supports the development of a strong understanding of the various dimensions of complex peace operations, and the way in which each contributes to the overall functioning of a multi-disciplinary / multi-dimensional integrated peace operations mission. Targeted participants are mid-level career officers in the police or military (senior captain to lieutenant colonel or equivalent) or humanitarian or development workers in middle-leadership positions.

Advanced Planning for Integrated Missions (APIM)

This course reinforces and enhances the understanding of the critical issues in planning and leading complex peace operations. The focus is on exploring key questions pertaining to security, humanitarian operations, legal and ethical issues, and mission credibility and success. Targeted participants are upper-level career officers in the police or military (lieutenant colonel to colonel or equivalent) or humanitarian or development workers in middle-leadership positions.

United Nations Integrated Mission Staff Officers Course (UNIMSOC)

This six-week course is a major defence-diplomacy initiative of the Canadian Department of National Defence's Military Training and Cooperation Program (MTCP). It shares Canadian culture, values and approaches with selected intermediate and senior military officers from MTCP member countries, while preparing them to fill key staff positions in a UN-integrated mission headquarters.

Senior Management Course on Integrated Peace Missions (SMC)

This course is a major defence-diplomacy initiative of the Canadian Department of National Defence's Military Training and Cooperation Program (MTCP) in which it shares Canadian culture, values and approaches with selected senior military officers from MTCP member countries while preparing them to fill key staff *advisory* positions within peace operations or within their home governments.

For more information on the Pearson Peacekeeping Centre, our courses and publications, please contact info@peaceoperations.org, or visit www.peaceoperations.org.

Queen's Policy Studies
Recent Publications

The Queen's Policy Studies Series is dedicated to the exploration of major public policy issues that confront governments and society in Canada and other nations.

Manuscript submission. We are pleased to consider new book proposals and manuscripts. Preliminary enquiries are welcome. A subvention is normally required for the publication of an academic book. Please direct questions or proposals to the Publications Unit by email at spspress@queensu.ca, or visit our website at: www.queensu.ca/sps/books, or contact us by phone at (613) 533-2192.

Our books are available from good bookstores everywhere, including the Queen's University bookstore (http://www.campusbookstore.com/). McGill-Queen's University Press is the exclusive world representative and distributor of books in the series. A full catalogue and ordering information may be found on their web site (http://mqup.mcgill.ca/).

School of Policy Studies

Canada's Isotope Crisis: What Next? Jatin Nathwani and Donald Wallace (eds.), 2010, Paper 978-1-55339-283-5 Cloth 978-1-55339-284-2

Pursuing Higher Education in Canada: Economic, Social, and Policy Dimensions, Ross Finnie, Marc Frenette, Richard E. Mueller, and Arthur Sweetman (eds.), 2010, Paper 978-1-55339-277-4 Cloth 978-1-55339-278-1

Canadian Immigration: Economic Evidence for a Dynamic Policy Environment, Ted McDonald, Elizabeth Ruddick, Arthur Sweetman, and Christopher Worswick (eds.), 2010, Paper 978-1-55339-281-1 Cloth 978-1-55339-282-8

Taking Stock: Research on Teaching and Learning in Higher Education, Julia Christensen Hughes and Joy Mighty (eds.), 2010, Paper 978-1-55339-271-2 Cloth 978-1-55339-272-9

Architects and Innovators: Building the Department of Foreign Affairs and International Trade, 1909–2009/Architectes et innovateurs : le développement du ministère des Affaires étrangères et du Commerce international,de 1909 à 2009, Greg Donaghy and Kim Richard Nossal (eds.), 2009, Paper 978-1-55339-269-9 Cloth 978-1-55339-270-5

Academic Transformation: The Forces Reshaping Higher Education in Ontario, Ian D. Clark, Greg Moran, Michael L. Skolnik, and David Trick, 2009, Paper 978-1-55339-238-5 Cloth 978-1-55339-265-1

The New Federal Policy Agenda and the Voluntary Sector: On the Cutting Edge, Rachel Laforest (ed.), 2009. Paper 978-1-55339-132-6

The Afghanistan Challenge: Hard Realities and Strategic Choices, Hans-Georg Ehrhart and Charles Pentland (eds.), 2009. Paper 978-1-55339-241-5

Measuring What Matters in Peace Operations and Crisis Management, Sarah Jane Meharg, 2009. Paper 978-1-55339-228-6 Cloth ISBN 978-1-55339-229-3

International Migration and the Governance of Religious Diversity, Paul Bramadat and Matthias Koenig (eds.), 2009. Paper 978-1-55339-266-8 Cloth ISBN 978-1-55339-267-5

Who Goes? Who Stays? What Matters? Accessing and Persisting in Post-Secondary Education in Canada, Ross Finnie, Richard E. Mueller, Arthur Sweetman, and Alex Usher (eds.), 2008. Paper 978-1-55339-221-7 Cloth ISBN 978-1-55339-222-4

Economic Transitions with Chinese Characteristics: Thirty Years of Reform and Opening Up, Arthur Sweetman and Jun Zhang (eds.), 2009. Paper 978-1-55339-225-5 Cloth ISBN 978-1-55339-226-2

Economic Transitions with Chinese Characteristics: Social Change During Thirty Years of Reform, Arthur Sweetman and Jun Zhang (eds.), 2009. Paper 978-1-55339-234-7 Cloth ISBN 978-1-55339-235-4

Dear Gladys: Letters from Over There, Gladys Osmond (Gilbert Penney ed.), 2009. Paper ISBN 978-1-55339-223-1

Immigration and Integration in Canada in the Twenty-first Century, John Biles, Meyer Burstein, and James Frideres (eds.), 2008. Paper ISBN 978-1-55339-216-3 Cloth ISBN 978-1-55339-217-0

Robert Stanfield's Canada, Richard Clippingdale, 2008. ISBN 978-1-55339-218-7

Exploring Social Insurance: Can a Dose of Europe Cure Canadian Health Care Finance? Colleen Flood, Mark Stabile, and Carolyn Tuohy (eds.), 2008. Paper ISBN 978-1-55339-136-4 Cloth ISBN 978-1-55339-213-2

Canada in NORAD, 1957–2007: A History, Joseph T. Jockel, 2007. Paper ISBN 978-1-55339-134-0 Cloth ISBN 978-1-55339-135-7

Canadian Public-Sector Financial Management, Andrew Graham, 2007. Paper ISBN 978-1-55339-120-3 Cloth ISBN 978-1-55339-121-0

Emerging Approaches to Chronic Disease Management in Primary Health Care, John Dorland and Mary Ann McColl (eds.), 2007. Paper ISBN 978-1-55339-130-2 Cloth ISBN 978-1-55339-131-9

Fulfilling Potential, Creating Success: Perspectives on Human Capital Development, Garnett Picot, Ron Saunders and Arthur Sweetman (eds.), 2007. Paper ISBN 978-1-55339-127-2 Cloth ISBN 978-1-55339-128-9

Reinventing Canadian Defence Procurement: A View from the Inside, Alan S. Williams, 2006. Paper ISBN 0-9781693-0-1 (Published in association with Breakout Educational Network)

SARS in Context: Memory, History, Policy, Jacalyn Duffin and Arthur Sweetman (eds.), 2006. Paper ISBN 978-0-7735-3194-9 Cloth ISBN 978-0-7735-3193-2 (Published in association with McGill-Queen's University Press)

Dreamland: How Canada's Pretend Foreign Policy has Undermined Sovereignty, Roy Rempel, 2006. Paper ISBN 1-55339-118-7 Cloth ISBN 1-55339-119-5 (Published in association with Breakout Educational Network)

Canadian and Mexican Security in the New North America: Challenges and Prospects, Jordi Díez (ed.), 2006. Paper ISBN 978-1-55339-123-4 Cloth ISBN 978-1-55339-122-7

Global Networks and Local Linkages: The Paradox of Cluster Development in an Open Economy, David A. Wolfe and Matthew Lucas (eds.), 2005. Paper ISBN 1-55339-047-4 Cloth ISBN 1-55339-048-2

Choice of Force: Special Operations for Canada, David Last and Bernd Horn (eds.), 2005. Paper ISBN 1-55339-044-X Cloth ISBN 1-55339-045-8

Force of Choice: Perspectives on Special Operations, Bernd Horn, J. Paul de B. Taillon, and David Last (eds.), 2004. Paper ISBN 1-55339-042-3 Cloth 1-55339-043-1

New Missions, Old Problems, Douglas L. Bland, David Last, Franklin Pinch, and Alan Okros (eds.), 2004. Paper ISBN 1-55339-034-2 Cloth 1-55339-035-0

The North American Democratic Peace: Absence of War and Security Institution-Building in Canada-US Relations, 1867-1958, Stéphane Roussel, 2004. Paper ISBN 0-88911-937-6 Cloth 0-88911-932-2

Implementing Primary Care Reform: Barriers and Facilitators, Ruth Wilson, S.E.D. Shortt, and John Dorland (eds.), 2004. Paper ISBN 1-55339-040-7 Cloth 1-55339-041-5

Social and Cultural Change, David Last, Franklin Pinch, Douglas L. Bland, and Alan Okros (eds.), 2004. Paper ISBN 1-55339-032-6 Cloth 1-55339-033-4

Clusters in a Cold Climate: Innovation Dynamics in a Diverse Economy, David A. Wolfe and Matthew Lucas (eds.), 2004. Paper ISBN 1-55339-038-5 Cloth 1-55339-039-3

Canada Without Armed Forces? Douglas L. Bland (ed.), 2004.
Paper ISBN 1-55339-036-9 Cloth 1-55339-037-7

Campaigns for International Security: Canada's Defence Policy at the Turn of the Century, Douglas L. Bland and Sean M. Maloney, 2004. Paper ISBN 0-88911-962-7
Cloth 0-88911-964-3

Centre for the Study of Democracy

The Authentic Voice of Canada: R.B. Bennett's Speeches in the House of Lords, 1941-1947, Christopher McCreery and Arthur Milnes (eds.), 2009. Paper 978-1-55339-275-0
Cloth ISBN 978-1-55339-276-7

Age of the Offered Hand: The Cross-Border Partnership Between President George H.W. Bush and Prime-Minister Brian Mulroney, A Documentary History, James McGrath and Arthur Milnes (eds.), 2009. Paper ISBN 978-1-55339-232-3
Cloth ISBN 978-1-55339-233-0

In Roosevelt's Bright Shadow: Presidential Addresses About Canada from Taft to Obama in Honour of FDR's 1938 Speech at Queen's University, Christopher McCreery and Arthur Milnes (eds.), 2009. Paper ISBN 978-1-55339-230-9 Cloth ISBN 978-1-55339-231-6

Politics of Purpose, 40th Anniversary Edition, The Right Honourable John N. Turner 17th Prime Minister of Canada, Elizabeth McIninch and Arthur Milnes (eds.), 2009.
Paper ISBN 978-1-55339-227-9 Cloth ISBN 978-1-55339-224-8

Bridging the Divide: Religious Dialogue and Universal Ethics, Papers for The InterAction Council, Thomas S. Axworthy (ed.), 2008. Paper ISBN 978-1-55339-219-4
Cloth ISBN 978-1-55339-220-0

Institute of Intergovernmental Relations

Canada: The State of the Federation 2009, vol. 22, *Carbon Pricing and Environmental Federalism*, Thomas J. Courchene and John R. Allan (eds.), 2010.
Paper ISBN 978-1-55339-196-8 Cloth ISBN 978-1-55339-197-5

Canada: The State of the Federation 2008, vol. 21, *Open Federalism and the Spending Power*, Thomas J. Courchene, John R. Allan, and Hoi Kong (eds.), forthcoming.
Paper ISBN 978-1-55339-194-4

The Democratic Dilemma: Reforming the Canadian Senate, Jennifer Smith (ed.), 2009.
Paper 978-1-55339-190-6

Canada: The State of the Federation 2006/07, vol. 20, *Transitions – Fiscal and Political Federalism in an Era of Change*, John R. Allan, Thomas J. Courchene, and Christian Leuprecht (eds.), 2009. Paper ISBN 978-1-55339-189-0 Cloth ISBN 978-1-55339-191-3

Comparing Federal Systems, Third Edition, Ronald L. Watts, 2008.
Paper ISBN 978-1-55339-188-3

Canada: The State of the Federation 2005, vol. 19, *Quebec and Canada in the New Century – New Dynamics, New Opportunities*, Michael Murphy (ed.), 2007.
Paper ISBN 978-1-55339-018-3 Cloth ISBN 978-1-55339-017-6

Spheres of Governance: Comparative Studies of Cities in Multilevel Governance Systems, Harvey Lazar and Christian Leuprecht (eds.), 2007. Paper ISBN 978-1-55339-019-0
Cloth ISBN 978-1-55339-129-6

Canada: The State of the Federation 2004, vol. 18, *Municipal-Federal-Provincial Relations in Canada*, Robert Young and Christian Leuprecht (eds.), 2006.
Paper ISBN 1-55339-015-6 Cloth ISBN 1-55339-016-4

Canadian Fiscal Arrangements: What Works, What Might Work Better, Harvey Lazar (ed.), 2005. Paper ISBN 1-55339-012-1 Cloth ISBN 1-55339-013-X

Canada: The State of the Federation 2003, vol. 17, *Reconfiguring Aboriginal-State Relations*, Michael Murphy (ed.), 2005. Paper ISBN 1-55339-010-5 Cloth ISBN 1-55339-011-3

Canada: The State of the Federation 2002, vol. 16, *Reconsidering the Institutions of Canadian Federalism*, J. Peter Meekison, Hamish Telford, and Harvey Lazar (eds.), 2004.
Paper ISBN 1-55339-009-1 Cloth ISBN 1-55339-008-3

Federalism and Labour Market Policy: Comparing Different Governance and Employment Strategies, Alain Noël (ed.), 2004. Paper ISBN 1-55339-006-7 Cloth ISBN 1-55339-007-5

John Deutsch Institute for the Study of Economic Policy

Discount Rates for the Evaluation of Public Private Partnerships, David F. Burgess and Glenn P. Jenkins (eds.), 2010.
Paper ISBN 978-1-55339-163-0 Cloth ISBN 978-1-55339-164-7

Retirement Policy Issues in Canada, Michael G. Abbott, Charles M. Beach, Robin W. Boadway, and James G. MacKinnon (eds.), 2009.
Paper ISBN 978-1-55339-161-6 Cloth ISBN 978-1-55339-162-3

The 2006 Federal Budget: Rethinking Fiscal Priorities, Charles M. Beach, Michael Smart, and Thomas A. Wilson (eds.), 2007. Paper ISBN 978-1-55339-125-8
Cloth ISBN 978-1-55339-126-6

Health Services Restructuring in Canada: New Evidence and New Directions, Charles M. Beach, Richard P. Chaykowksi, Sam Shortt, France St-Hilaire, and Arthur Sweetman (eds.), 2006. Paper ISBN 978-1-55339-076-3 Cloth ISBN 978-1-55339-075-6

A Challenge for Higher Education in Ontario, Charles M. Beach (ed.), 2005.
Paper ISBN 1-55339-074-1 Cloth ISBN 1-55339-073-3

Current Directions in Financial Regulation, Frank Milne and Edwin H. Neave (eds.), Policy Forum Series no. 40, 2005. Paper ISBN 1-55339-072-5 Cloth ISBN 1-55339-071-7

Higher Education in Canada, Charles M. Beach, Robin W. Boadway, and R. Marvin McInnis (eds.), 2005. Paper ISBN 1-55339-070-9 Cloth ISBN 1-55339-069-5

Financial Services and Public Policy, Christopher Waddell (ed.), 2004.
Paper ISBN 1-55339-068-7 Cloth ISBN 1-55339-067-9

The 2003 Federal Budget: Conflicting Tensions, Charles M. Beach and Thomas A. Wilson (eds.), Policy Forum Series no. 39, 2004. Paper ISBN 0-88911-958-9
Cloth ISBN 0-88911-956-2

Our publications may be purchased at leading bookstores, including the Queen's University Bookstore (http://www.campusbookstore.com/) or can be ordered online from: McGill-Queen's University Press, at **http://mqup.mcgill.ca/ordering.php**

For more information about new and backlist titles from Queen's Policy Studies, visit http://www.queensu.ca/sps/books or visit the McGill-Queen's University Press web site at: **http://mqup.mcgill.ca/**